MW00390202

For Boo and Ken Weldon
With best wishes
Nick Zeyher

Sept. 20, 2008

When Conscience and Power Meet

Eugene N. Zeigler Jr., 1966. Collection of the author

When Conscience and Power Meet

A Memoir

Eugene N. Zeigler Jr.
Foreword by Dan T. Carter

The University of South Carolina Press
Published in Cooperation with the South Caroliniana Library with the Assistance of the
Caroline McKissick Dial Publication Fund and the University South Caroliniana Society

© 2008 University of South Carolina

Published by the University of South Carolina Press
Columbia, South Carolina 29208

www.sc.edu/uscpress

Manufactured in the United States of America

17 16 15 14 13 12 11 10 09 08   10 9 8 7 6 5 4 3 2 1

Library of Congress Cataloging-in-Publication Data

Zeigler, Eugene N.
    When conscience and power meet : a memoir / Eugene N. Zeigler Jr. ; foreword by
Dan T. Carter.
        p. cm.
    "Published in cooperation with the South Caroliniana Library with the assistance of the
Caroline McKissick Dial Publication Fund and the University South Caroliniana Society."
    Includes index.
    ISBN 978-1-57003-744-3 (cloth : alk. paper)
        1. Zeigler, Eugene N. 2. Legislators—South Carolina—Biography. 3. South Carolina.
    General Assembly—Biography. 4. Lawyers—South Carolina—Florence—Biography.
    5. Florence (S.C.)—Biography. 6. World War, 1939–1945—Personal narratives, American.
    7. Civic leaders—South Carolina—Biography. 8. Episcopal Church. Diocese of South
    Carolina— Biography. 9. Art patrons—South Carolina—Biography. 10. South Carolina.
    Board of Corrections—Biography. I. Title.
    F275.42.Z45A3 2008
    328.757092—dc22
    [B]
                                                                        2008013978

This book was printed on Glatfelter Natures, a recycled paper with 30 percent postconsumer
waste content.

Dedicated to my wife,
ANNE,
whose affection and encouragement
sustain me in good times and bad

Contents

Illustrations

Foreword

I met Nick Zeigler in the spring of 1960 when I was a nineteen-year-old reporter for the *Florence Morning News* and living proof that callow youth, inexperience, and ignorance are no bar to being a budding journalist. A group of us often gathered at a local coffee shop for nonstop discussion informally chaired by Peter Hyman, a Florence lawyer and city magistrate who never met a political yarn he couldn't top or a conversation he couldn't dominate. Nick seemed to take his law practice too seriously to be a regular, but he did stop by one morning. I was both impressed and a bit taken aback by his sarcastic reference to our "southern way of life" and his enthusiastic recommendation for a book he had just read on American politics. Neither skepticism about the racial status quo (by whites) nor a passion for books was all that common in Florence in the late 1950s, but Pete had an explanation: "You have to remember," he said with a mocking smile, "Nick went to Harvard." I had also never known anyone who went to Harvard.

My brief foray into journalism ended that year as I went on to finish my undergraduate and graduate degrees before becoming a historian, but through conversations with my parents who lived out in the county and journeys back to visit them, I kept up with Nick Zeigler's career. I followed with particular interest his 1972 race against the state's living right-wing institution, Senator Strom Thurmond. When the national Democratic Party nominated George McGovern as the party's presidential candidate, I had no illusions that Nick would win, but I was disappointed by Thurmond's overwhelming margin of support among South Carolina's white voters. One of my old high school classmates later told me that he thought he was one of only a handful of whites in his rural precinct who had voted for Zeigler. A friend corrected him: "As far as I know you were the only white person."

But reading *When Conscience and Power Meet,* I discovered how little I really knew of Nick's life. He has always been a bit of a maverick. In 1936, having read and been impressed by John Strachey's *Theory and Practice of Socialism,* Nick announced to startled fellow summer campers that he had become a dedicated socialist. While this commitment would prove to be temporary, it's difficult to imagine many fifteen-year-old South Carolina teenagers proclaiming their hope for a peaceful socialist revolution.

If his political views became more traditional, his passion for books would continue for the rest of his life. At his Florence home several years ago, I expressed my admiration for the outstanding library of historical and literary works he had collected over his lifetime. Nick's wife, Anne, looking around at the bookshelves lining wall after wall and the scattered open volumes, seemed a bit less enthusiastic. "If I marry again," she said with a tight smile, "I think I'll choose someone who is illiterate."

In his memoir Nick Zeigler describes himself as a young provincial when he went away in the fall of 1938 to Sewanee, the University of South. He was barely seventeen, and the small, isolated college with its mixture of traditional Anglicanism, a deep reverence for the Confederate cause, and a classical nineteenth-century education would seem to have been the kind of institution that simply reinforced parochial attitudes. But books and ideas have a way of slipping their bounds. At Sewanee he learned the pleasures of encountering ideas, even heretical ones. He was elected to Phi Beta Kappa, won the campus prize in English, and developed a life-long passion for theater. His senior year he wrote and performed in his own satirical (and updated) version of the comic opera *Mikado,* substituting campus figures for the classic Gilbert and Sullivan characters. The vice chancellor, who took the place of Ko-Ko as the Lord High Executioner in Zeigler's version, was not amused.

Nick may have seen himself as an unsophisticated Florence County boy when he went off to Sewanee, but the next six years as a naval officer and as a student at Harvard Law School transformed him even as events changed the nation and challenged the traditions of his southern roots. My old professor and mentor, George Tindall, would often refer to himself with mock solemnity as part of that "heroic band of World War II veterans—the 'Greatest Generation.'" This would be followed by a gleeful listing of a rogue's gallery of thieves, con men, crooks, and cunningly amoral politicians who, along with George, served in uniform. But Nick Zeigler gives credence to that claim.

"Join the Navy and See the World," proclaimed the pre–World War II posters. Like many fellow southerners of his generation, wartime service introduced him in practical ways to a world stretching far beyond the Florence of his childhood, a process he describes vividly in his memoir. Serving aboard the light carrier USS *Cabot*, Zeigler took part in combat operations through 1944 and aboard the USS *Cape Gloucester* and the USS *Siboney* until the war's end in August 1945. The GI Bill made it possible for him to attend law school at Harvard a year later, an experience that he came to regard with mixed feelings. While he recognized the quality of the education he received, the three years in Cambridge were far from the pleasant interlude he had experienced at Sewanee. He is at his most self-deprecating in his insistence that—during examination time—he looked around the room in vain to see "who was dumber than me" (77).

If *When Conscience and Power Meet* is an engaging, insightful, and often amusing account of a personal life, it is also a valuable historical document. We have a number of memoirs and autobiographies by journalists and well-known southern political figures describing their experiences in the postwar period. But we have very few accounts of the day-to-day gritty politics of small-town life as it revolves around courthouse cliques and loosely allied coalitions in the one-party South of the era, and certainly none so engagingly written.

Nor do we often learn much about the day-to-day pleasures of small-town life in the postwar era. Although I am a few years younger than Nick, I think we both shared the aspirations of a new generation of middle-class southerners as the region emerged from generations of poverty and isolation. In an era before television and prepackaged mass popular culture, we unconsciously accepted the notion that education was designed to encourage "elevated" forms of cultural expression: the fine arts, music (classical or perhaps jazz), and serious theater. We see this in Zeigler's support for the creation of a local museum and particularly in his commitment to the Florence Little Theatre in the late 1940s and 1950s. More than a reflection of his personal love for the theater, his account is a revealing window into a moment when local drama groups routinely performed works like *The Winslow Boy*, *The Importance of Being Earnest*, and *The Caine Mutiny Court-Martial*. He believed that serious dramatic works (like great literature) could make "people think beyond the local problems and prejudices" that dominated their daily lives; that it could incite a "feeling for a larger view, a clearer perspective of the human condition" (110). While there are certainly exceptions, one would be hard pressed today to find contemporary local theaters in the region that present anything other than endless reruns of musicals, slapstick plays, and shallow regional dramas that play on safe and comfortable dramatic clichés.

But of course it is race that serves as a leitmotif running through *When Conscience and Power Meet.* The growing challenges to racial segregation, particularly after the Supreme Court's 1954 *Brown v. Board of Education* decision posed the gravest moral challenge to white southerners of Nick Zeigler's generation. It was clear at the time (and clearer in these memoirs) that Nick was never "safe" on the subject. He vividly recalls the moment when he learned that the Supreme Court had outlawed segregation in the *Brown* case, a decision that he saw as right and just. His own feelings were strengthened by what he called the "blatant racism" of his home state and the martyrdom of his close friend Jack O'Dowd. (O'Dowd, editor of the *Florence Morning News,* was forced to resign and leave the state after he wrote an editorial telling his readers that the *Brown* decision was the law of the land and had to be obeyed.) Scattered through his memoirs are telling and sometimes painful recollections of his encounters with racism.

Many other white southerners with Zeigler's background reacted quite differently, passionately defending the racial status quo and railing against "outside agitators." I don't think it is ever possible to explain fully why some white southerners accepted and even rationalized that system while others recognized and fought against the cruelties of racial discrimination. In Nick Zeigler's case it's clear from his earliest childhood that he had an independent streak, an insatiable curiosity for new ideas that his family encouraged rather than repressed, and an instinctive sympathy for the weak and the oppressed that was deeply founded in his religious faith. Like many other white southerners of his generation, the war also pulled him away from the world that most whites accepted as "normal" and distanced him from that culture. In describing his experience as a Harvard law student, he makes a particularly insightful comment about himself. "It has been my observation that the farther north I went the more southern I became and, conversely, the farther south I went the more northern I became" (84).

Under normal circumstances Nick Zeigler might have lived out his career quietly confiding his misgivings to friends and working quietly behind the scenes to ameliorate the worst aspects of the Jim Crow system. But he is frank to acknowledge his political ambitions; he wanted to serve, and he believed politics was the arena where he could make the greatest contribution. In an environment in which blacks had almost no voice and whites were emotionally committed to maintaining the "southern way of life," the easy choice for any rising politician was to ride the wave of resistance to victory. Strom Thurmond and later George Wallace were the archetypical beneficiaries of that white anger.

But individuals like Nick with a conscience (and a genuine repugnance for racial discrimination) had to walk a tightrope. At a time when the political risks were great, he worked quietly and often openly to end the discrimination that had so deeply marred the history of his community and the state, serving on the Human Affairs Commission and on the Board of Corrections where he continued his long-term campaign for more humane and compassionate treatment of the state's juvenile and adult prison population. During his run for the legislature in 1960 at the height of the angry white political backlash that had swept the region, Nick told a group of voters that he thought segregation was best for both races. It was not a statement he repeated when he ran again in 1962 (or ever), and ten years later when a reporter reminded him of that remark, he bluntly responded that he had "been a hypocrite in making the statement" (160). What is remarkable is Zeigler's willingness to acknowledge his mistake. Most political figures of his era blithely embraced segregation and—when it was no longer advantageous—cheerfully donned the cloak of amnesia.

Ultimately statewide office eluded Nick Zeigler; his campaigns against Senator Thurmond in 1972 and for the governorship in 1974 failed. Despite those disappointments, he continued to serve in public life. And he continued to push against the grain. In the mid-1990s, when the great majority of middle-class whites and upper middle-class whites in his community had joined the Republican Party, he spoke to the Florence Rotary Club, explaining why he remained a Democrat. He told a largely unsympathetic audience of his loyalty to the legacy of Franklin Roosevelt, a Democrat whose policies and programs had helped transform the impoverished South of his childhood for the better. He bluntly condemned the racial polarization made worse by the Republican "southern strategy" and defended the role of the national government in alleviating the hardships of the poor and the disadvantaged.

To this day, Nick Zeigler proudly embraces the description of himself as a liberal, a word that has become the scarlet letter of American politics in general and southern politics in particular. "My definition of liberalism in politics," he says, "is that it is the willingness to try new solutions to solve old problems," particularly taking risks "to help solve social problems and help the needy" (301).

In the terminology of today's politics, Nick Zeigler is correct in describing himself as a liberal. But, as he himself has recognized, at heart he combines those passions with the balanced temperament of the American theologian Reinhold Niebuhr, who constantly struggled to reconcile the uncompromising ideals of his Christian faith with the practical realities of American democratic politics. As Zeigler notes, when he served in the South Carolina Senate, he kept in his top desk drawer, a quotation from Niebuhr's *Moral Man and Immoral Society*: "Politics will, to the end of history, be an area where conscience and power meet, where the ethical and coercive factors in human life will interpenetrate and work out their tentative and uneasy compromises" (301).

And though it may seem far fetched, I also like to think of him as a twentieth-century survivor of the Enlightenment generation of the Founding Fathers. In January 2005 when I spoke at the dedication of the South Carolina History Room of the Florence Public Library named in his honor, I described the passion of these eighteenth-century men for books and ideas that would help guide them through the difficult choices of the practical world. Some, like Thomas Jefferson and James Madison, came from privileged gentry. But others, like John Adams and Ben Franklin, sprang from what would have been called common stock. Franklin was self-educated; Adams was a farmer's son who obtained a scholarship to Harvard and, as he pointed out, "discovered books and read forever."

What bound them together was their belief that ideas have consequences; to live a full and rewarding life, we have to look into and beyond ourselves. When Jefferson, speaking for them, talked about the "pursuit of happiness" in the Declaration of Independence, he was not referring to the acquisition of wealth or even the pleasures of good times. At their best, what he and his fellow revolutionaries sought was the enlargement of the human spirit through the arts and the attainment of the good society through that life of the mind.

With typical modesty, Nick Zeigler quotes his wife Anne's observation that he had "never done any one outstanding thing, but just a lot of 'little things.'" I cannot help but think of the words of Dorothy Day, the Catholic writer and lifelong activist for human rights. "People say, 'What is the sense of our small effort?'" she wrote to a friend. "They cannot see that we must lay one brick at a time, take one step at a time."

Brick by brick, step by step, Nick Zeigler has built a remarkable life of service: as a youthful naval officer in World War II, as a decent and conscientious young attorney in his hometown, as a public servant who struggled to follow his conscience, and as an individual of religious conviction who tried to translate those beliefs into practice. To be sure, there are "lots of little things" to be found in this memoir. But there is much more: a gracefully written account of a life of service and generosity well lived.

DAN T. CARTER

Preface

Justice Oliver Wendell Holmes wisely observed, "Life is action in passion. It is required of a man that he should share the passion and action of his time at peril of being judged not to have lived."

Being involved in the action in passion of one's time involves risks. One must be prepared for the pain of failure. It has often been my experience that no matter how favorable the circumstances or how auspicious the beginnings, there is never any assurance that one's efforts will be crowned with success. My life has been filled with a number of adventures, some successful and some failed. It has never been my good fortune to be the prime mover of some great reform or the hero of some outstanding political movement. When the University of the South, my alma mater, awarded me an honorary degree in 1992, my friend and former roommate asked, "For what?" My wife sagely observed that I had never done any one outstanding thing but a just a lot of "little things."

I recall an essay on Edmund Burke in which the author said that Burke always seemed to be on the verge of something important that never took place. I have often had the sense of being on the verge of some important office or effort, but I have had to be satisfied with failure or simply being a part of an event in which I was only a minor player.

This assessment should not convey the impression that I have not counted my blessings, even if I've counted them one by one. I could have died of malaria as a teenager or gone down with a ship in the Pacific or Atlantic Oceans. I could have married unhappily or had children who were a disappointment. None of these events occurred, and I have lived beyond the biblical three score and ten years. Granted the last years have been plagued by the ills of old age, but I have been blessed with so many of the good things of life that are denied others that I should be ashamed to curse fate for not having given me more.

The "little things" that have preoccupied me include state offices that gave me the opportunity to participate in legislation that began to reform state and county government. For the city of Florence I have endeavored to accelerate its transition from a railroad town into a cultural and commercial municipality in the center of the Pee Dee region. Above all, my life has given me the opportunity to be a part of the action and passion of my time.

Acknowledgments

I am indebted to many people who helped and encouraged me in writing this memoir. My wife, Anne, has been indefatigable in encouraging me to complete the work and aiding me in doing so in every way. Herbert Hartsook, Nicholas Meriwether, and Helen Zeigler Ellerbe aided in getting the manuscript considered for publication by the University of South Carolina. George Hobeika, Bill McRee, and Margaret Collar of the Florence County Library have assisted with research. Belton T. Zeigler, my son, helped with editorial advice. Alexander Moore, my editor at the University of South Carolina Press, has helped guide me though the process of preparing and submitting the book for publication. Mitchell Pritchett of CompuForce and Benjamin McInville gave me invaluable advice regarding the technical aspects of preparing the manuscript. Maureen Chapman's stenographic assistance and advice in preparing the manuscript were invaluable.

Part I *The Inward Journey*

Jesus of Nazareth, in summarizing the Decalogue, said, "Thou shalt love the Lord thy God with all thy heart, with all thy soul, and with all thy mind. This is the first and great commandment." We are creatures made by God in his image, and I am confident that part of fulfilling that first and great commandment is to live our lives using fully the personality, abilities, interests, gifts, relationships, and opportunities given us. As the parable of the talents teaches us, God rewards those who put their abilities to practical use in the world and chastens those who do not.

My understanding of the first and greatest commandment is, in part, that everyone has a paramount duty to become what he or she is capable of becoming. It is imperative to live fully as a whole human being. I would like to think that I strove for the first thirty-seven years of my life to do this and to comply with the Greek injunction "Know thyself."

Part 1 of this book covers the years from my birth until I first sought public office in 1958. My work with the theater, the Florence Museum, Big Brothers, and the Carney case was public service, but to me it was chiefly part of my striving to know myself.

I

More Nationality Than Most

I was born in the early hours of July 20, 1921, in Saunders Memorial Hospital, Florence, South Carolina. On that day an elderly black man, Moloch Smalls, appeared in the hospital room where my mother was recuperating. Moloch had been a slave before the Civil War, later he was an itinerant Methodist preacher, and by the time I was born, years of working with the Townsend family had made him a devoted family friend. The hospital where I was born was segregated, as all hospitals were in the South at that time. That Moloch had gained entrance to the room where my mother was recuperating was startling enough and testament to his eloquence, his determination, and the sheer force of his presence. Moloch burst into my mother's room wearing a Prince Albert coat and a black tie and carrying a top hat. "Stand aside ladies," he said in an authoritative tone to the startled nurses who stepped between him and my mother as she held me in her arms. "This is Belton O'Neall Townsend's grandson, and he gets here with more nationality than most babies generally gets here with."

Whatever Moloch meant by these words, they were literally correct. My ancestors were German, English, Welsh, Scots-Irish, and Irish. Most of them came to America before the American Revolution and settled on the fertile coastal plain of eastern and central South Carolina, and most made their living before the Civil War as farmers of modest but respectable holdings.

I was named for my father, who was born on Christmas Day 1887. He was given the first name "Eugene," meaning "well born," and the middle name "Noel," meaning "Christmas." His family were mostly German emigrants, "poor Protestants" who were transplanted from the Palatine provinces in the mid–eighteenth century to Orangeburg, South Carolina.

My grandfather Frank A. Zeigler, who rode with Gen. Joseph Wheeler in the Civil War, surrendered after the Battle of Bentonville in North Carolina and walked to Orangeburg, South Carolina, his birthplace, having given his horse to Wheeler, who had lost his. He married Elizabeth Miller, had a

*Belton O'Neall Townsend,
grandfather of the author,
1876. Collection of the author*

Eugene N. Zeigler Sr., father of the author, 1950. Collection of the author

large family, and died when his thirteenth child, my father, was only two years old. Eugene Zeigler, or Gene, was raised by his brother Edward, who was twenty-one at the time of Gene's birth. What land there was in the family had gone to other sons by the time my father came of age, so he moved from Orangeburg County to Florence, South Carolina, to work for the Atlantic Coast Line Railroad. He made the move about 1910, while he was still quite young, and remained a conductor for the rest of his life.

He married my mother, Helen Livingston Townsend, in 1913. They had one other child, a daughter named Leah Townsend Zeigler born in 1914.

My mother was an extraordinary woman. She was born October 13, 1887. A graduate of Winthrop College, she taught several generations of first graders in the public schools in Florence. She loved small children and they loved her. But she was a strict instructor. She pinned a note on the jacket of every child, when he or she left school for home, that described the bearer's conduct and progress as "good," "fair," or "poor." In one instance my mother sent a "poor" note home with a Syrian boy whose father ran a grocery store in Florence. The next morning when the boy reported to class he brought my mother a bag containing a present with a note from the boy's father that read, "I beat the boy and send you bananas."

My sister, Leah, was born in 1914. I came seven years later. When I was born, my mother and father were living with my grandmother on the south end of Dargan Street. It was a handsome brick house, with a bedroom and bath downstairs and four big bedrooms and two baths upstairs. My earliest recollections center around that house. It was located on a large city lot. Even though the house was in town, it had a flower garden, vegetable garden, chicken yard, barn, and livestock lot for cows and a horse.

My grandmother was an indefatigable gardener. I can recall her vegetable garden and the framed structure in which she raised prize chrysanthemums. A flower shop and nursery near my grandmother's house had what I regarded as extensive greenhouses. I recall going into those greenhouses and being overcome by the smell of carnations. The flower shop had a small fountain with goldfish, and at one time a baby alligator was housed in a separate tank. In my child's mind it was a place of pure enchantment, the next thing to the Garden of Eden.

I must have been accident prone. While my parents were constructing a house on Laurel Street in 1925, my mother took me there to inspect construction. I fell off the front porch and impaled my legs on several large nails. This required a trip to the hospital.

But my worst accident happened while we were living on Laurel Street. I was always eager to witness the execution of chickens by the cook. In 1926, when I was five years old, I went out into the backyard to watch the cook wring the neck off a chicken. The headless body flopped about but seemed to come straight for me. I fled from it and, seeking a place of refuge, ran up on a large pile of cow manure that was waiting to be spread in our garden. Unfortunately there was a pitchfork on top of the manure pile, and I fell on it. My mother came out of the house and pulled the pitchfork from my leg.

Helen Livingston Townsend (Zeigler), mother of the author, 1913. Collection of the author

There was no car available, so she put me in a small child's wagon and pulled me up Dargan Street to Saunders Memorial Hospital. A tetanus shot was administered.

Even in my earliest days the turmoil of the outside world intruded on my young life. In 1922 railroad employees went on strike, and my father felt compelled to carry a pistol in his traveling case. Although only one year old at the time, I went in my father's case and found the pistol, carried it into the bedroom where my mother and father were sleeping, and waved it around saying, "Shoot Daddy." I do not recall the response, but I have been uncomfortable with handguns ever since.

My mother tried valiantly to have me called "Noel." My stepgrandfather had a different idea. He thought I was a bad little boy and said, "This is Young Nick with Old Nick in him." ("Old Nick" was slang for the devil.) From then on everyone called me Nick.

Like the other small children in the neighborhood, I had a series of African American nurses who took care of me. I was so devoted to these nurses that when time came for them to go home I would endeavor to follow them, but they never let me get very far. The nurses were allowed to take us to the movies. These were silent movies, of course, and since blacks were required to sit in the balcony, we sat there with them. I could not read the subtitles, so I constantly asked my nurse, "What does it say? What does it say?"

In 1926 my family moved into the house at 606 South Dargan Street owned by my great-aunt, Mary Ann McClenaghan. Aunt Mary was a maiden

McEachin and Zeigler families posed on the steps of the Dargan Street residence, 1923. Left to right: Peter Hector McEachin (uncle of author and later senator), Daniel Malloy McEachin Sr. (stepgrandfather of author), Leah McClenaghan Townsend McEachin (grandmother of author), Leah Townsend Zeigler (sister of uthor), Eugene N. Zeigler Jr., and Eugene N. Zeigler Sr. Collection of the author

lady who had run a successful millinery store in Florence. I remember Aunt Mary as a somewhat straightlaced Victorian woman. She died the year after we moved into her house, and she willed the house to my mother, my sister, and me. It would be my home until 1937, when my parents bought a house on the Darlington Highway.

My mother thought I should go to kindergarten, an idea that became a virtual necessity when she began teaching in the city schools. Mrs. Spears's kindergarten, where I was enrolled, was located on the south side of West Evans Street adjoining Florence's business district. The kindergarten was conducted in a large two-story frame house. The house had a large front porch, and the classroom had an entrance from the porch. During recess the children were allowed the freedom of a backyard, which had a henhouse for chickens. Once, my fellow pupils decided it would be great fun to entice a handicapped fellow pupil into the henhouse and lock him inside. He was almost blind and had great difficulty extricating himself from confinement, screaming and crying while doing so. The prank upset me because I thought I too might be a victim.

My fears escalated a few days later. We were told to do some sort of homework and bring it in the next morning. I forgot to do it, and as I went through the classroom, Mrs. Spears asked in a somewhat threatening manner, "Did you do your homework?" I confessed I had not. Confinement in the henhouse seemed likely. I went to the hall, and instead of hanging up my coat, I walked out the front door and headed for home.

On the way home I stopped and sat on a coping just above St. John's Church and contemplated what I should tell my mother I had done at kindergarten that day. Nature study seemed the best fabrication, and I screwed up my courage to walk on. I did not know that my mother had been called in that day as a substitute teacher at Central School (later Poynor), which I would have to pass it on my way home. As I strolled leisurely past the school, I looked in its direction and to my horror saw my mother coming like an avenging fury toward me. An inattentive pupil had been looking out of a classroom window and spied me. He said, "Mrs. Zeigler, isn't that your son walking down the street?" I knew that a good switching was to be my fate, but when I told the story of the lockup in the henhouse, mother withdrew me from kindergarten. I was a free man until 1927, when I began first grade.

Miss Lillian Gentry, my mother's friend, was my first grade teacher. They had gone to Winthrop College together, and she had been a bridesmaid in my mother's wedding. At midterm in my first year, construction of Circle School (later McKenzie) was completed and all of the students at

Central were marched down Cheves Street to the new building. During the yearly spring exhibit a controversy arose between Miss Gentry and the art teacher. It was the custom to select some of the students' best work to display on the walls of the first floor of the building. Miss Gentry, being a true southerner, had her pupils draw a Confederate flag and print below it some tribute to the glorious Lost Cause. When the art teacher, a Yankee lady, spied these examples of southern patriotism, she insisted they be withdrawn from the exhibit. Miss Gentry refused. Charges of insubordination were brought against her, and the United Daughters of the Confederacy fiercely defended her. The result was an unpleasant environment, as the result of which Miss Gentry took a position with the schools in Scarsdale, New York, where she became a noted educator. Not the typical southern lady going north.

My mother, too, was an unreconstructed Rebel. Gen. Robert E. Lee was as close as we good Episcopalians had to a patron saint in our household. Various icons—mostly lithographic—of the great general were set up in places of honor in the house. Memorial Day in the South, or, more properly, memorial days, made for an interesting set of contrasts. Florence was home to a national cemetery where Union soldiers, most of whom died as prisoners at the Florence Stockade, were buried in the last year of the Civil War. The cemetery was less than a mile from our house on Dargan Street, but we were never allowed to go there on "Yankee Memorial Day." Our house was close enough that I could hear bugles blown, salutes fired, and occasionally band music on that day. I had no idea what strange rituals were being performed by the Yankees.

Confederate Memorial Day, May 10 in South Carolina, was a different matter altogether. The schoolchildren were marched to Mount Hope Cemetery at the end of Dargan Street, where the remains of some sixty Confederate soldiers were buried. They had died in Florence at the Wayside Hospital across the street from Gamble's Hotel and were buried at the Presbyterian church. A monument was placed there in the 1880s, and when the church relocated, the remains and monument were moved to Mount Hope Cemetery. Each child was equipped with a basket of spring flowers, and as the ladies sang "The Ode"—"Cover them over with beautiful flowers / Crown in your hearts these dead heroes of ours"—the children circled the monument, throwing flowers on the graves.

The memory of defeat in the Civil War cast a shadow over the lives of southern children in my generation. Before World War II when someone made reference to "the war," we all understood it was a reference to the Civil War. "Damned Yankees" were so demonized that as a child I thought it unlikely I would ever venture north of the Mason-Dixon line. My mother insisted on standing any time Dixie was played and uttering a feminine version of the Rebel yell. This tendency on her part resulted in deep embarrassment to my children when *Gone with the Wind* was released in the 1960s in wide-screen format. Mother took my three oldest children to an early screening, taking seats near the front of the cinema. Whenever a recognizable strain of "Dixie" came from the soundtrack, she rose to her feet with her hand over her heart and stood until the music moved to another theme.

As I grew older, I began to question the unassailable virtue of the southern cause and the institution of slavery. My mother's defense of slavery was that the Yankees sold wooden nutmegs to unsuspecting southerners. Even in my childish mind the two did not seem to offset each other, but one didn't argue with my mother about the virtue of the southern cause.

The pain of defeat in the Civil War was evident in our lack of celebration on the Fourth of July. For us that was the day the battle of Gettysburg was lost and Vicksburg fell to the Yankees. No fireworks were ignited to celebrate that memory. Fireworks were reserved to celebrate Christmas. It was illegal to start the firecrackers before midnight, but on Christmas Day the sound of exploding firecrackers was everywhere. Boxes of fireworks were considered absolutely necessary for celebrating Christmas, "Silent Night" notwithstanding.

My family kept Christmas well. It was a happy family time with all sorts of great-uncles, aunts, and cousins going from house to house and having Christmas dinner together. The chief argument was whether "white fruit cake" was better than "dark fruit cake." To add to the excitement and mystery of Christmas, I never saw a Christmas tree in my early youth until Christmas morning. My mother, father, and Aunt Deda (Leah Townsend) would bring the large tree into the house after I had gone to bed. When I awoke, there it would be, as though some miracle had taken place.

But at other times the house was haunted by a sense of tragedy: my grandfather Belton O'Neall Townsend died in 1891, at the age of thirty-five. He was alone in the house when it was consumed in a fire. No one was sure whether he had been murdered, committed suicide, or died accidentally. But whatever the cause, his death changed my mother's and aunt's lives dramatically. He died at a time when the South was desperately poor. My mother and Aunt Deda remembered their relationship with their stepfather as being very difficult. I recall waking up in the night and hearing discussions between my mother and Aunt Deda about the wretched lives they had lived at that time. They believed their stepfather had been indifferent to their education and welfare and quick to use corporal punishment for minor infractions.

Leah Townsend (known as Aunt Deda), historian, attorney, and aunt of the author, 1925. Collection of the author

Perhaps for this reason my mother impressed on me the subliminal imperative that I had to succeed where her father had failed. Belton O'Neall Townsend was a lawyer, a brilliant writer and thinker who published a series of articles in the *Atlantic Monthly*. But he drank too much, he was unhappily married, and he wasted his energies on public improvement at the expense of making a living. He left his widow and two daughters with very little. My mother's personal sense of her father's failure, against the backdrop of the multiple failures and degradations of the South, combined to create in me a sense that I was called to succeed and put some part of these things right. Though I was unfamiliar with Shakespeare at the time, I later felt that my early life contained echoes of the youthful Hamlet: "The time is out of joint. O cursed spite, / That ever I was born to set it right!"

Despite these early shadows I had a happy childhood. Dargan Street with my friends was a wonderful place. The ice truck came around almost every day in the summer. Large blocks of ice had to be trimmed to fit into family iceboxes. We eagerly sought the chips of ice created by this trimming. Vegetable sellers came by with wagons of fresh produce. I remember one seller my mother was particularly fond of, and she was concerned when he did not come for almost a month. When he finally appeared, my mother told him that she had missed him. He replied, "Mrs. Ziggle, I been cut, en shoot, en stob."

There was little traffic on that end of Dargan Street, so we organized teams to play hockey on roller skates. We also made lanterns out of shoe boxes, illuminating them with a candle, and dragged them down the sidewalks. We did not want for an audience for these and other projects. All of the houses on Dargan Street had large front porches, and in the absence of air conditioning most residents sat on their porches in rocking chairs, talking and telling stories. Perhaps they reminisced about "old, unhappy far-off things / And battles long ago." I sometimes dreaded the thought of coming back to Florence and ending my days in a rocking chair.

As children we were fascinated by the funeral processions that came down Dargan Street to Mount Hope Cemetery. Very early in my youth the Episcopal bishop came to St. John's, and I declared thereafter—to the delight of mother's friends—that I wanted to be an Episcopal bishop when I grew up. My chief reason, which I did not disclose, was that I thought I would look good in a bishop's vestments. That changed, however, when a prominent member of the Ku Klux Klan died and the funeral procession with Klansmen in full regalia, their faces hidden behind masks and a drummer beating a solemn cadence, came down Dargan Street. My friend Lloyd "Bubber" Weeks and I joined in the procession. We were about six or seven years old. My mother was told later by an acquaintance that Bubber and I were everywhere during the funeral and nearly fell in the grave and were buried with the dead Klansman. After that I announced that I had changed my mind about being a bishop. Now I wanted to be a Klansman. I thought their robes were more impressive than a bishop's vestments.

I had no idea, of course, what evil the KKK stood for. The men in my family had nothing to do with the Klan. In fact, several years before I was born my father and grandparents saved a young black man from being lynched. The man was a chauffeur for J. W. Ivey, who ran a restaurant at the railroad passenger station. A small white boy ran out into the street and was struck and killed by the automobile the black man was driving. A crowd gathered and grew increasingly hostile toward the driver, who then ran down Gaillard Street and crawled under my grandmother's house. As a group of white men surrounded my grandmother's house and dragged the terrified black man from under it, the crowd prepared to hang him from an oak tree in front of the house.

My grandmother, who had survived Yankee occupation and Reconstruction, was fearless. When she heard what was taking place in front of her house, she was outraged. She armed herself with a large butcher knife, went out of the house into the crowd, and confronted the leaders. Wielding the butcher knife in a menacing fashion, she shouted, "You shall not do this thing!" My father and stepgrandfather grabbed the young man, forced him into my father's car, and, with the mob running at their heels, drove him to the city jail for safekeeping.

George McClenaghan, my cousin, became a textile executive. When I was fourteen, I was invited to visit him and his wife, Betty, in Montgomery, Alabama. As the son of a conductor I could get free passes on the railroad, so getting there was no problem. It was the first trip of any great distance I had taken by myself. I had a wait in Savannah, Georgia, and I ventured forth from the station and went down Main Street, fearful that any minute I might be robbed or kidnapped.

The visit was a wonderful experience. Betty McClenaghan treated me almost as an adult. We went to the state capitol, and I stood where Jefferson Davis had stood when he took the oath as president of the Confederacy. I had heard talk about the *Scottsboro* case and asked to see the Alabama penitentiary. That was arranged, and I was permitted to view the electric chair and even sit in it. I could hear loud shouts in the background and was told it was the Scottsboro boys.

When I arrived in Montgomery, I wore knickers, a white shirt, a necktie, and a large cap. I must have resembled a mushroom with a long thin stem. My cousin George told me that he would give me a quarter if I would not wear that cap when sightseeing in Montgomery.

There was labor unrest in the city, and either a strike was in progress or about to take place. One night George went out to the driveway and conferred with someone who looked slightly sinister. I believed it was an informer who was there to give information on labor organizers. It was my first experience with labor unrest.

My next trip was in early June 1936 to visit my childhood friend George Green Lynch. George and his younger brother Dolph had been part of the Dargan Street gang, but they had moved to Macon, Georgia. They invited me to spend a couple of weeks with them, and I accepted. It was far more adventurous to get to Macon using railroad passes than it had been to get to Montgomery. I had to travel the Atlantic Coast Line Railroad to Camack, Georgia, and change to a train to Macon. This line was known as the Central of Georgia, and the coaches looked as though they might have been used in a western movie. They still had potbellied stoves in the corner for heat. This was not a necessity in June, of course, when windows were opened for ventilation, allowing soot and cinders to blow into the coach.

As we approached Macon, I realized that the railroad tracks went directly through several Indian mounds at the famous Ocmulgee site, which is now a national monument. I had read that it was being excavated and made up my mind to return as soon as possible.

George and Dolph were taking a summer school course as a result of their move from South Carolina to Georgia. That left me with the mornings to myself. I figured out that I could reach the Ocmulgee site by following the railroad track and walking across the trestle, which was high, long, and without any means of escape should a train appear.

I crossed the river and found myself in the middle of a real archaeological excavation. The council chamber at the site had been fully excavated, and a temporary roof had been constructed over it. I had a camera and took many pictures, but I never got up the courage to talk to any of the archaeologists working on the site. I have returned to the Ocmulgee site several times. The Ocmulgee National Monument now has a fine interpretative museum, and the restored council chamber beneath a small mound is among the most numinous places I have visited.

When time came to leave Macon, I boarded the antique coach of the Central of Georgia Railroad. This time the only other occupants of the coach were a soldier and a woman with a baby. The soldier came and sat on the seat beside me, and the woman and baby were three or four seats behind

us. I had never engaged in conversation with a soldier, and after the prelim-
inaries he proceeded to tell me how in one of these same coaches he and a
woman were the only passengers so they decided to have sexual intercourse
to while away the time. My embarrassment at hearing in vivid detail the difficulties of having intercourse in a railroad coach and the pleasures he experienced were obvious to the soldier and incited further tales of his sexual
exploits. In the meantime the woman behind us started nursing her baby, an
activity I had not previously witnessed. The intermittent slurping sounds
added to the sensuousness of the journey from Macon to Camack.

In the summers during my early youth my family vacationed on the
coast for a couple of weeks. The first trip I remember was when I was
five years old. We had rented a cottage at Ocean Drive (now North Myrtle
Beach), and we stopped in Conway to buy a large block of ice. To get to the
cottage it was necessary to cross the Waccamaw River on a primitive and
perilous one-car ferry.

The journey from the Waccamaw River to the coast stretched through
an endless desert of sandy roads where getting stuck was a constant problem. There were few buildings at Ocean Drive, the most prominent being a
pavilion where a small band played in the evenings.

Myrtle Beach, the first time I remember it, had about fifty cottages, a
pavilion, and a boardwalk that extended out from the pavilion to the cottages. There were several shops and eating places, but the tone of the place
was very low key.

Billy Royall, my childhood friend, and his family invited me to visit
them at Myrtle Beach a few years later. The Royalls had a cottage there and,
sometime later, one at Ingram Beach that was developed as part of Ocean
Drive. I was fortunate to visit the Royalls many summers at both places.

Billy and I were almost the same age. We were both baptized at St. John's
Church and both classmates from the first grade through high school, and
he was my closest friend. Sam Royall, Billy's father, was a successful lawyer
in Florence and had expressed a wish that we might become lawyers and
practice together.

Automobiles, although not entirely new creations, were still rather
primitive in the 1920s. The first car I remember was a Franklin. One of
the family's entertainments on Sunday afternoons was to take a ride in the
Franklin. There were no windows to roll up and down but isinglass curtains
that had to be attached manually if it began to rain. There were no heaters,
so in winter we kept warm in blankets with the nostalgic name "buggy
robes."

George Lynch and I founded a neighborhood newspaper called *Hot News*. It was printed by hand and sold for one cent. The discovery of an empty whiskey bottle in the neighborhood was deemed good investigative reporting. The boys in our gang had a club named the Cobra Club. We met in the upstairs of the garage behind the Weeks's house on Dargan Street.

My family was involved in politics. In the 1928 presidential election one of our fellow students in the second grade was identified as a Republican. He was "Peaches" House, whose family owned the flower shop and nursery on Dargan Street. I had obtained a miniature derby hat symbolizing Al Smith, the Democrats' candidate, and my fellow Democrats and I tormented Peaches unmercifully during recess.

The joy of going to the "moving pictures" on Saturday afternoons is hard to describe. I insistently demanded ten cents for admission to the theater and an extra nickel for candy to eat while watching the movie. My favorite actors were Hoot Gibson and Tom Mix. There was no soupy romantic stuff in their movies, just straight-out fighting—good guys against outlaws or Indians. I never got into the singing cowboy fad. Real men didn't sing, they just fought mean people. Frequently the Saturday afternoon juvenile crowd would shout to the actors on the screen warning them of danger or trouble.

In the summer we generally walked barefoot up Dargan Street to the movies. That presented certain hazards, not the least of which were cigarettes that had been thrown on the sidewalk without being completely extinguished. Pieces of glass and sandspurs also inflicted injury on unshod feet, but nothing diminished the pleasure of walking barefoot. Due to illnesses the first ten or twelve years of my life were not carefree, but the most enduring image of my youth is walking barefoot up Dargan Street to the moving picture show with ten cents for admission and an extra nickel for candy.

2

Summer Camps and CMTC

"Nick is not a good mixer." That was the judgment of Bill Covington, director of Camp Nixon, which was sponsored by the Florence YMCA. He was probably right, but in 1930, when I read it on the written report from my first experience with summer camps, I wanted to say, "You're right. There are some people I don't care to mix with." The Depression had begun early in the South, and all families were feeling the pinch, so summer camps of any sort provided a great service.

Covington organized a camp for boys on land donated by the Nixon family at Cherry Grove Beach, immediately north of Ocean Drive. The campsite was about a fourth of a mile back from the beach in what were known as pine flats. There were cabins, a meeting hall, a dining hall, and a latrine we called "little Egypt."

I was nine years old and had never been away from home and family before. But since most of my friends were going to Camp Nixon, I begged to be allowed to go. The counselors were high school students, and I thought they were demigods. There was a counselor for each cabin, and the camp was generally well organized.

Our transportation to the camp was in the back of a large truck in which about fifteen of us, with our baggage, rode in the open air the seventy miles to the coast. It was a hot, perilous, and exhausting trip, but we enjoyed it to the fullest, shouting and singing most of the time.

Each day we were transported across the hot, sandy roads to the beach to swim in the ocean. The most exciting trips in the truck were to the beach at night, where we would, in the light of a flashlight, form a circle around the nocturnal sand crabs. When the light was extinguished, the crabs would escape over our bare feet.

It was possible in those days to drive on the sand at low tide to Myrtle Beach. I recall seeing the metal framework of the unfinished Ocean Forest Hotel on which work had been abandoned because of the Depression. We referred to it as the million dollar hotel. There was a treasure hunt on Tilgh-man Beach and trips to Little River to buy candy and postcards and to go deep-sea fishing. On all of these excursions we rode in the open bed of a truck.

The next summer I went again to Camp Nixon, but the bloom of fresh-ness was gone. I had begun to read and was content to read rather than play softball or any other sports. The campfire songs were not as funny, and I felt uneasy when we sang religious hymns. Covington's stories about World War I became shopworn by constant retelling. That probably influenced his assessment of me as a nonmixer.

The following year I did not go to camp, but by then I had joined the Boy Scouts. Troop Eight, in which most of my friends, including Billy Roy-all, were members, met on the third floor of a building that had been used as a Masonic hall. One of the joys of going to Scout meetings was we had permission to buy a hot dog from a vendor who had a small concession behind the old building. We seldom had hot dogs in my mother's house, and Aunt Deda, who came to live with us in 1931, said they would burn a hole in my stomach. How they would do this was never explained.

I made it as far as first class in the Scouts. My mother never put much faith in scouting. She said that she had only known two Eagle Scouts and both of them had had shotgun weddings. However, in 1933 I was per-suaded to go to the Boy Scouts' Camp Coker in Darlington County. It was a miserable experience.

As in the Camp Nixon experience we were transported to Camp Coker in an open truck. Camp Coker was in the desolate pine and turkey oak sand hills north of Hartsville. When we arrived, we were told to grab our baggage and run to the cabin of our choice. I had no idea of the arrangement of the cabins, so I took my suitcase, went to the first cabin I encountered, and put my bags on a bunk. No sooner had I done so than an older Scout came in and said that was his bunk but he was looking for another; if he was unsuccess-ful, he said, he would return to claim that bunk. About ten minutes later he returned and said that I would have to look elsewhere for accommodations. Wearily I dragged my belongings with me, seeking a place. Finally I found an empty bunk in a cabin with seven boys who were strangers. Bunking with them turned out to be a disastrous experience. There were not enough coun-selors to house one in each of the cabins, and we were expected, as good Boy Scouts, to discipline ourselves. Each cabin was to be cleaned for inspection every morning and the ground around it put in neat order. My cabin mates routinely ignored this duty, and I found myself sweeping the cabin and polic-ing the grounds while they lolled about making fun of me. Frequently, while I was sweeping around the cabin, they would lock me outside.

The real crisis came when they went into my suitcase, in my absence, and appropriated candy my mother had sent me. Worse than that, they found several letters my mother had written and read them aloud. It was painfully embarrassing. My mother would begin her letters with the salutation "Dearest Darling Boy." This caused endless derisive laughter, and I was taunted by my cabin mates as "Dearest Darling Boy."

I stood this humiliating treatment for several days, but I felt keenly that my privacy had been invaded and my personal belongings taken without my consent. I was not a particularly courageous boy, but I made up my mind that, unless I was moved from that cabin, I would telephone my parents to come and get me.

The head of the Boy Scouts was Charles Lea. I am sure he was a good man and sincerely wished the scouting experience to be helpful to the campers. The financial charges for participating as a camper for two weeks were nominal. The mess hall was arranged so that Lea and the counselors ate at one table and the Scouts dined helter-skelter at the other tables. Because we were in the depths of the Depression the fare was simple and wholesome, but each table had a container of blackstrap molasses. This poured over bread or biscuits would finish off any meal and stave off future pangs of hunger.

I decided to confront Lea after a midday meal. He usually remained seated until all of the boys had left the mess hall. I went over to his table and said, "Mr. Lea, I have a problem that I need your help in solving."

He replied in an agreeable manner, "Well, tell me what it is."

I began my catalog of grievances against my cabin mates and concluded by stating that I could not get along with them and wished to be moved to another cabin. Lea's tone became authoritative and severe. "A good Scout should be able to get along with anyone," he said. I replied, "Well, I am sorry but I can't get along with these Scouts." There was several minutes of silence, and then I issued my ultimatum: "Mr. Lea, if you do not move me out of that cabin, I will call my parents to come and get me." Mr. Lea got up and left the mess hall without saying another word.

I went back to my unhappy situation not knowing whether I had succeeded or failed. In about an hour one of the counselors came and told me I was being moved to another cabin. I hastily got my possessions together and was taken to a cabin where one of the occupants was being moved out to take my place in the original cabin.

It was almost as though retributive justice had prevailed. The boy who was moved to take my place had a terrible case of eczema. He was referred to in the usual callous way of youth as "Scaley." My new cabin mates proved more civilized, and although I was reproached by my former associates, I told them that it served them right for having used me so outrageously. I begged my mother in the future not to address letters to me as "My Darling Boy."

Despite my bad experience I returned to Camp Coker the following year. This time I got together with Billy Royall and some of my fellow Florence Scouts, and we descended on a cabin en masse to take it over. Camping proved a more agreeable experience that year.

Lea gave me a wide berth the second year, but I began to harbor another grievance against him. On campfire night we assembled in a circle, and one of the counselors, wearing an Indian headdress, invoked the power of the Great Spirit and a flame mysteriously came down and lighted the campfire in the middle of the circle. Of course it was done by a wire, but it was effective.

On one of these occasions Lea made a speech that was really a sermon. He stated that there was only one book that anyone needed to read, the Holy Bible. He went so far as to say that if all of the books that had been written could be destroyed, all would be well if only the Bible survived. I felt my intelligence had been insulted, but I said nothing.

I did not go to camp the following year. Malaria still existed in South Carolina in 1935, and that year I nearly died from it. There were times when I had fevers of 104 degrees for several days. I took so much quinine that I nearly developed hepatitis. My mother then tried "666," one of the bitterest tonics I ever had the misfortune to take. I later learned that this was the numerical designation of the beast in the Book of Revelation. I think it was appropriately named. I managed in the fall to keep going to classes between periodic bouts of chills and fever.

The next camping trip, in 1936, was one of the most redeeming experiences of my youth. Col. John W. Moore, superintendent of the Florence City Schools, owned and operated a camp near Brevard, North Carolina. It was named Camp Transylvania and attracted counselors and campers from all over the South. It cost more to go there than either of the other camps I had attended, but my mother wisely agreed to send me there for six weeks.

The camp was in an idyllic setting in a valley with a lake, nine-hole golf course, central administrative building, dining hall, and gymnasium. Each camper was assigned to a cabin, with two campers and a counselor on each side of the cabin. The cabin to which I was assigned was on the side of a hill and was reached by a series of steps. I had two bags to carry and was trying to decide how I would get both up to the cabin. To my surprise, another camper, Givens Young, came up and asked if he could help me by carrying one of the bags. I have never ceased to be grateful to Givens for an act of friendship that contrasted so sharply with my previous camping experiences.

After reveille all campers and counselors went down the hill for calisthenics in pajamas. When that was completed, the whole crowd took off their pajamas and skinny dipped in the cold waters of the lake. Next we cleaned the cabins and prepared for inspection. The schedule of activities included golf lessons, tennis lessons, horseback-riding lessons, track, basketball, hiking, nature study, and crafts. The experience opened avenues for me that until then I had never had the opportunity to explore.

The greatest of all benefits was the opportunity to be associated with the counselors. They were college students of substance and more mature than the counselors I had previously known. I formed an abiding friendship that lasted the rest of my life with one counselor, Lucas Dargan. Lucas taught nature studies. He had just finished three years at North Carolina State College and would eventually make forestry his career. I hung on his every word and volunteered to help him collect specimens. Lucas liked snakes. Although I found it difficult to put my hands on them, I forced myself to do so in order not to lose face in Lucas's eyes.

I was embarrassed twice. One incident was self-inflicted, and the other I had no control over. During the year I was sick, I did a lot of reading. Among the books that Aunt Deda had was John Strachey's *Theory and Practice of Socialism.* It made such an impression on me that I became an ardent advocate of socialism. My fellow campers were sons of doctors, lawyers, and business executives and generally from conservative upper-middle-class families. My strange advocacy of socialism must have made them think that I was either a nerd or freak of some sort. I had not yet become familiar with the saying that a person has no heart if he is not a socialist before the age of twenty-one and no brain if he is a socialist after twenty-one.

The other incident involved a visit from my sister, Leah, and her boy friend, J. K. Thomas. They arrived at camp on a motorcycle. My sister was unconventional according to the standards of the time. She learned to pilot an airplane when she was sixteen; she majored in physics at the University of South Carolina; she got a license as a civil engineer when she graduated from college and was working toward a master's degree in aeronautics at the University of Michigan. Her appearance in helmet and goggles, riding on a motorcycle behind her boyfriend, reinforced the opinion that my family background and ideas were strange.

Campers at Camp Coker were divided into two groups that competed with each other in sports. We were expected to earn points for our team in all activities. Having become accustomed to being regarded as being a pariah in sports activities, I was determined to earn my share of points for my team. I surprised everyone by making third place in the final track meet.

Fortunately my mother decided the following year that I should go a second time to Camp Transylvania. When I arrived at camp, Colonel Moore asked me to come to his office. He stated that he wanted me to be captain of one of the two teams in which the campers were divided for the whole six weeks of camp. I was overwhelmed by the confidence Moore showed in me. He was the first person to say that he thought I had leadership ability. I resolved not to disappoint him.

The counselor in my cabin was named Joseph Alfred "Fred" Miller. Fred had just graduated from West Point and was a star athlete. He was genuinely kind, considerate, and caring in a manly way. My admiration for him was unbounded, especially when he organized an overnight camping trip for our cabin to climb Mount LeConte in the Great Smoky Mountain National Park.

For several years after I left camp, I exchanged letters occasionally with Miller. He was killed in the Battle of Anzio in Italy, and his brother, a naval officer, died on a submarine during World War II.

One incident caused me to be firm in my commitment to Colonel Moore. The leader of the other camp team was Dickie Fuller from Savannah, Georgia. He was Moore's nephew and was considerably more sophisticated than I was. We were only allowed to go to the movies in Brevard on Saturday afternoons and only then under supervision. Dickie found out that a war movie was being shown at the theater. He took me aside and said that since the two of us were the leaders in the camp, Moore should allow us as a special privilege to attend a movie during the week. He asked if I would go with him to ask Moore to grant us that privilege. I reluctantly agreed.

We waited until lunch was finished and approached Colonel Moore at his table. Dickie, as spokesman, went through an explanation of the virtues of this war movie and our desire to see it. He then made what I instantly recognized as a tactical mistake. Dickie said, "We thought you would make an exception for us in this case." There was a minute or two of silence. Then Moore rose from his chair and faced us with folded arms and said in his most authoritative tone, "I make no exceptions!" We stumbled, humiliated, out of the mess hall.

Dickie fumed as we went back to our cabins. He decided to defy Colonel Moore and go to see the movie. He asked me to join him. I told him I could not. Moore had shown so much trust in me by making me a captain that I felt I could not disobey him. Dickie scoffed at this attitude and said he was going despite Moore's refusal to grant permission. I watched from the administration building as Dickie made his way across the golf course to the edge of the camp's property. He hesitated at the fence that marked the camp's property line. He was beginning to have second thoughts. He stood at the fence a few minutes then turned and came back to the administrative building. He would not speak to me for several days thereafter.

My last camping experience had a more serious aspect. In the spring of 1940 the war in Europe was going badly for the Allies. I was convinced that sooner or later I would have to serve in the military, so I began to look about for some way to get some experience before I was inducted. I discovered the Civilian Military Training Corps (CMTC). Under this program a college student could go annually for three summers to camp for six weeks and get a commission as a second lieutenant in the U.S. Army. The timing would be right for me if the United States did not get into the war before I graduated from college in 1942. I then discovered that two other men from Florence, Herndon Williams and Everett Thomas, were scheduled to go to Fort Bragg in North Carolina.

One difficulty arose unexpectedly. Colonel Moore wrote me asking that I consider being a counselor at Camp Transylvania that summer. I made up my mind that I should decline the invitation. On spring break I went to Moore's office and discussed the matter with him. I said I was convinced that this country would inevitably get involved in a war and I needed to discover the branch of service that would suit me best.

Moore listened patiently and finally said he agreed with me. He was disappointed that I would not be at Camp Transylvania, but he, like me, felt that inevitably the United States would be drawn into the war. He said that the country was building an army and in every case when this country had built an army, it used that army. I was pleased that he understood my problem.

I left for six weeks duty at Fort Bragg in the middle of June 1940. Anyone familiar with the intense summer heat in the midlands of North and South Carolina can understand what a painful baking lay ahead of me. Herndon, Everett, and I got off the train in Fayetteville and were taken to Fort Bragg. There was a tent city on the right side of the old main complex of buildings. During the 1930s a Civilian Conservation Corps (CCC) camp had operated at Fort Bragg. Knowing how tight the budget for the military was in 1940, I believe the tents we occupied were left over from this camp.

There were about six hundred young men from North and South Carolina in the camp that summer. The large tents in which we were billeted had eight bunks each. A big fan supplied ventilation, and the latrine was a short walk away. Our uniforms were World War I vintage. We wore boots that laced up to the knee, jodhpurs (because the field artillery for which we were being trained had been horse drawn), long-sleeved shirts, field scarves (neckties), and Smokey Bear–type campaign hats.

When I went through the mess line my first morning there, I was appalled at the French toast: the slices of bread had been soaked in egg and then given only a few seconds on the grill. When syrup was generously poured over it, the result was that I was, in effect, eating raw egg floating in syrup. I thought that surely I would not survive six weeks of this kind of food.

Most of the training was done with nearly obsolete French 75-mm cannons. The war was raging in Europe, but there was no money for live ammunition. There was approximately four hours of close-order drill in the morning, except when we were drilling on the 75-mm cannons, and two hours in the afternoon. The heat was overpowering, and every day I was sure I would faint, be disqualified, and be sent home in disgrace. It never happened. Some of my fellow trainees who seemed stalwart in physical vigor fainted on the days when we had a full review by some colonel or general. We were required to dress in freshly pressed uniforms, including field scarves and boots. We stood endlessly at attention in the blazing summer heat and men fainted or fell out regularly, but I never did.

I had never known what it meant to be dying of thirst, but I discovered those pangs painfully that summer. Water drunk in great gulps from a spigot did not seem to quench the craving for water. In the mess hall I began to eat everything in sight. Several weeks into my tour I discovered that the collard greens on my plate included a large grasshopper. Prior to that time it would have turned my stomach, and I would have stopped eating immediately. I was so ravenously hungry, however, that I merely pushed the grasshopper aside and cleaned my tin tray.

I did all of the things recruits have to do in boot camp. I stood sentry duty and took my turn at KP. A bakery at Fort Bragg made morning deliveries of freshly baked bread. The smell of warm bread was so delicious that I was almost tempted to snitch a slice or two when it was being unloaded, but fear of a firing squad restrained me.

Our instructors explained to us the reason for our somewhat quaint uniforms. This year, for the first time, horses would not be used to drag the cannons into position for firing. Instead of a day's march on foot with horse-drawn artillery, we would be transported in trucks. I was relieved to learn that but soon found that riding in a truck over dusty roads in July heat was not a pleasant experience.

While I was in CMTC training, the Allies were taking a beating in Europe. Paris fell to the Germans, and the British Isles were in peril of being invaded. As I became more emboldened, I began to ask the regular army enlisted men instructing us about our nation's woefully obvious lack of preparedness. We were not given rifles or sidearms because they were in short supply. Instead of firing the 75-mm cannons when we drilled, we were told that only four shells had been allotted for our training; at the end of six weeks we would be taken to a site to see these four shells fired and hear the noise they made. It seemed the height of folly to have six hundred young men for six weeks and not give them any real training for war. As a result of my experience I made one important decision: if I had to join the military, I would choose any branch other than the army.

3

Public Schooling

The public schools in Florence were good. They were probably not first rate, but the instruction at the time was adequate, so I was not unprepared or unmotivated when I went to college. Because my mother taught in the public schools, I felt under a burden to do well. In fact my mother was like a mother in Sparta—come back with or on your shield. If I made a B or a C grade, I kept my report card concealed until Aunt Deda came home from the law office. My mother's scorn and reproach was so heavy that I needed a sympathetic aunt nearby to sustain me.

An incident in my lower school experience stands out in my mind clearly when I listen to debates about school prayer and teaching religion in public schools. One of my grammar-school teachers decided we should learn the Ten Commandments and be prepared to recite them in class when called upon. That seems to be a praiseworthy project, but it caused me great embarrassment. I was raised in the Episcopal Church, so when I was told to learn the commandments, I went to the Book of Common Prayer to find them and dutifully learned from that text. The next day I was called upon to recite the fourth commandment in front of the class. I rose, went to the front of the class, and began, "Remember that thou keep holy the Sabbath-day. Six days shalt thou labor, and do all that thou hast to do—" when I was interrupted by laughter from my classmates. The teacher, after calling them to order, turned to me and said, "Where did you learn that?" I replied from the Book of Common Prayer on the assumption that anyone of intelligence would know what that was. The teacher professed that she did not know what kind of book that was and that the proper wording was "and do all of your work." Being humiliated about my religion in front of the class was devastating because I began to think there was something wrong with my church, perhaps even that it was subversive.

Periodic chapel programs conducted by the various temperance organizations in the city reinforced the feeling that there was something wrong with the church I attended every Sunday. At one of these programs we were instructed to sing, "Beer and whiskey both a curse / I drink water safety first." We were exhorted to sign pledges that we would never drink any alcoholic beverages. My parents told me not to sign any pledges. In the first · place I was too young to know what I was doing, and in the second place neither my parents nor my church disapproved of drinking socially. I knew that my parents drank what they called a "toddy" from time to time, and I again was made to feel uncomfortable about my church. I might add that most of my classmates in grammar school who signed these pledges clearly did not regard them as binding in adulthood.

My experiences in junior high school were not stressful. Although I escaped punishment, one boy in junior high study hall was struck over the head with a ruler by the geography teacher with so many blows the ruler splintered in the process.

High school was uneventful my first year, but in the fall of 1935 I suffered from a severe case of malaria. I struggled to keep up with my courses, but the sickness so drained my physical stamina that I could not engage in any athletics. My teachers were concerned about my physical condition and called my mother in for a conference. They suggested some sort of special help. My mother took umbrage at being called in and finally told them, "It is not possible for you to be more ambitious for my son than I am." That ended the conference.

My junior and senior years in high school saw a gradual comeback. Summer camp in the mountains brought an end to my bouts of malaria, and I was feeling more and more comfortable with my schoolwork. I took chemistry in my junior year and did well enough to get a nonpaying student job as the student instructor in the laboratory.

In my senior year I seemed to come out of my retirement. I took American history under one of the best teachers I had experienced, Hazel Osteen Gee, whose husband had drowned in front of her eyes at Ocean Drive Beach. She was determined to make a career for herself and became a first-rate teacher. All the students were afraid of her because she enforced discipline in her classroom and would tolerate no foolishness. We were required to take the newspaper published for students, which carried summaries of national and international news, and once a week we had to be prepared to stand in front of the class when called upon in random fashion and give a summary of one of these news reports. There was a near panic of apprehension before Gee selected one of the students to perform. She would tolerate no shoddy speech making. She drew a circle on the floor, and the chosen orator had to stand in that circle while speaking while she graded each performance.

Hazel Gee had a profound influence on me. She represented tough love, and though her students dreaded her discipline, she genuinely cared about their intellectual development. Posted on the right side of the entrance into her classroom was a quotation from Étienne de Grellet: "I shall pass through this world but once, if, therefore, there be any kindness that I can show, or good thing I can do, let me do it now; let me not defer or neglect it, for I shall not pass this way again."

I like history. Aunt Deda had received a doctoral degree in history before she read law and came to practice with her brother in Florence. Her friend Anne King Gregorie insisted that she have her doctoral thesis published. It was not an easy task during the worst part of the Depression. Arrangements were made with the Florence Printing Company, the publisher of the *Florence Morning News*, to publish the book. It was the era of Linotype printing, and I was fascinated by the molten lead that had to be prepared in the machines for setting the print. The proofs came to our house in rolls that looked like Greek or Roman scrolls. Published in 1935, her *South Carolina Baptists before 1800* was regarded as one of the best local histories to come out during the Depression in South Carolina.

My interest in history goes back to that period, when I studied hard because I wanted to know more. In fact when I graduated, I was awarded the medal given to the student showing the greatest interest and proficiency in the history of the American Civil War. I also did well in English and wrote short stories for the school newspaper. I took part in the senior class play and made a great hit in the senior class amateur night by doing an impersonation of Col. John Moore. And my winning a statewide playwriting contest boosted my status as a writer.

I was selected to give one of the three addresses at commencement. This was in lieu of a valedictory address. The subject assigned to me was new frontiers in biology and chemistry. I had to submit my manuscript to my English teacher, Mrs. Wilmer Poynor, for her approval, and she made me take out one word. I had written that at Oxford University the students referred to chemistry as a course in "stinks." Poynor said that it was not proper to use the word "stinks" in a public address, and I was forced to substitute the words "unpleasant odors." I am sure the substitution would have made the Oxford students laugh.

Socially, the first third of the twentieth century was entirely different from the first years of the twenty-first. High school boys were required to enter on one side of the building and girls on another. And teachers were stricter. My gym teacher, for example, had an unpleasant way of correcting us when taking calisthenics. He kept his belt in his hand, and if we made a mistake, he gave us a whack on the behind as a reminder to do better.

One incident has remained in my mind throughout the years. One day Colonel Moore called all of the senior boys into a meeting in the hallway on the second floor. We had no idea why. After we had gathered there, Moore said the janitor had reported to him that one of the senior boys had made a nasty racial remark to him. Moore did not say what the remark was, but we gathered that it reflected on the legitimacy of the janitor's birth and involved the word "nigger." Moore said, "You do not treat the janitor like a gentleman because he's a gentleman but because you are a gentleman. I don't want to hear of this sort of remark from any of you again."

I regard Colonel Moore as the person outside my family who had the most positive effect on my development. During the desegregation crisis in 1957 he wrote one of the articles published in a pamphlet titled *South Carolinians Speak* urging moderation in dealing with the integration of the public schools. He was the first outsider of any importance who believed that I had leadership ability even though I was a sickly, reticent, gangling teenager.

There were two German brothers in Florence High School when I was a student. Their surname was Eitner. They made an effort to be friendly with me, probably because I had a name of Germanic origin. We would have discussions during our recesses. It was when the Spanish Civil War was taking place, and we engaged in heated debates about the conflict. I was firmly on the side of the Republicans opposing General Franco, while the Eitners supported Franco's rebellion.

The Eitner brothers told me stories of how things were in Germany before they came to stay with a relative in Florence. They were supporters of Hitler and enthusiastic members of the Hitler Youth, which they described as being like our Boy Scouts. They urged me to come with them when they went back to Germany for a visit. I did not have the means or the inclination to do so, but I have often wondered what my life would have been like if I had gone with them and seen firsthand what Nazi Germany was like. I do not know what became of the Eitners. They were intelligent, and I believe their friendship with me was genuine. They left Florence before 1938, and I have always assumed they returned to Germany.

My senior year I entered a nationwide essay contest sponsored by the *American Magazine.* The title of my essay was "The America Which I Would Like to See." I won an honorable mention prize. I also was active in one of the two literary societies in the high school. Each year there were contests between the two societies, the Criterion and the Utopian, for a loving cup that was kept in a display case in the front lobby of the high school. I entered the contest to represent the Criterion Society in the oratorical contest. I chose as my subject General Lee's being offered command of the Union army at the beginning of the Civil War. The title of the oration was "An High Mountain." I put it in the context of the temptation of Jesus, who was taken up on "an high mountain" and shown the kingdoms of the world. I chose the subject because during a visit to Washington in 1935, I had stood in front of the Custis-Lee Mansion at Arlington Cemetery and looked down on Washington, much as Lee must have done when he returned from the Blair Mansion after refusing President Lincoln's offer to command the Union army. It is, incidentally, the same place where President Kennedy stood and, looking down on Washington, said he could stay up there forever.

I did not win the contest, but the final line of my oration has stuck with me: "But if it is ever ours to refuse the kingdoms of the world for what we believe to be right, let our spirit, like Lee's, be ennobled, let us be great in defeat." This youthful espousal of Stoicism became a reference point for me in later life.

I graduated from high school a month before my seventeenth birthday, and I now believe I was the very image of the naive, unsophisticated provincial. I thought I was destined to go to the Citadel, a military college, because my friends were going there. I was invited to spend a week in Charleston with the Kirk family, whose grandparents lived in Florence and were friends of my family's. It was an enchanting experience. The Kirks lived in a house at the lower end of Church Street. I recall the first night I spent in their house. There was no air conditioning, and I could hear St. Michael's chimes and the street vendors selling their produce on the street in the morning. Tourists had not yet discovered Charleston, so it was possible to ride a bicycle through town and visit the historic buildings I had read about. Most notable among these was the Old Exchange Building, which had been converted into a post office. It was the site of the drama I had written about Col. Isaac Hayne, *As an American Should,* for which I won the high school playwriting contest. I returned to Florence in July 1938, still believing I would go to the Citadel.

4

Sewanee

The University of the South

I regard myself fortunate for having received a "Gothic and monkish" college education. Gothic because the architecture of the buildings and the curriculum of the college I attended were more medieval and English than modern, and monkish because of the all-male faculty and student body, the communal living arrangements of the students, and the isolation of the campus from any metropolitan area. It was the kind of education that would be difficult to reproduce today.

The University of the South in Sewanee, Tennessee, was founded in 1857 by southern bishops of the Episcopal Church led by the Right Reverend Leonidas Polk, bishop of Louisiana. Bishop Polk was a graduate of West Point. When the Civil War came in 1861, he put a general's uniform on over his vestments. He died in a battle outside Atlanta in 1864. His fellow bishops in the North saw his sponsorship of a southern university as an indication of his encouragement of secession. They were scandalized when he became a fighting bishop and would probably have not recognized him as a bishop had he survived the war. The cornerstone for the first building on the campus, laid before the Civil War began, was blown up by Federal troops in 1863 and the fragments taken as souvenirs. It was seventy-five years later that I became a student there. The blend of Anglican and Confederate traditions gave Sewanee a special mystique.

I matriculated at Sewanee in September 1938. I had reached the age of seventeen only a month and half before that time and was an unsophisticated provincial. I did not choose Sewanee; my parents chose it for me. I was scheduled to go to the Citadel, but my mother went to Charleston two weeks before the Citadel opened and talked with Maj. Alexander Lucas, who told her that if her son really did not want to go to the Citadel, he should not be sent there. She announced on her return from Charleston that I was going to Sewanee.

I had never seen the University of the South, nor had I been in the state of Tennessee. I knew one student from Florence who was a rising senior at Sewanee, but I knew no other students. The professor of French there, David E. Frierson, was married to a former Florence resident and promised my parents to take a paternal interest in my welfare. The rector of St. John's Episcopal Church in Florence, the Reverend Wilmer Poynor, was an alumnus, and he and his wife were enthusiastic advocates of my going there. They foresaw a career for me as a priest.

The Reverend Poynor had warm feelings about his education at Sewanee but lamented the fact that it had, in his words, "become a rich man's school." The ignorance of my family about Sewanee prompted my mother to warn me that I would be attending a rich man's school and that I would not be able to afford or indulge in the luxuries available to my fellow students. I was cautioned to remember that although we had a proud family tradition, my father was a railroad conductor and my mother taught school. Above all it was impressed on me that my family was making a great sacrifice to send me to Sewanee and I should not disappoint them by being a failure academically or personally.

The journey to Sewanee was an adventure in itself. I rode the night train from Florence in a Pullman car and arrived in Atlanta early the next morning. There was a two-hour layover in Atlanta. I then took the Louisville and Nashville train to Chattanooga and from there the train went through a small crossroads town, Cowan, Tennessee, where I disembarked at about three in the afternoon. The university was seven miles away on top of the Cumberland Plateau. The arriving students engaged a taxi to take us up the mountain to Sewanee. The school's ten-thousand-acre domain would be my home away from home for the next four years.

I was assigned to Cannon Hall. My roommate was an upperclassman with whom I had little in common, so a classmate of mine, Frederick R. Morton, who was assigned to the same dormitory, and I worked out a plan to have Fred transferred to my room and my first roommate to his. The scheme worked. Fred and I were roommates for our freshman year and remained friends for life.

At Sewanee in the 1930s, and still to some degree today, there was an intimate relationship between faculty and students. The number of students in the college in 1938 was approximately 230, and there were 16 students in the theological seminary. The faculty consisted of 29 members, so the ratio of faculty members to students was approximately one to eight. In class the ratio of faculty to students grew higher for the upper classes, and in my senior year there were several classes in which the ratio was one faculty member for two or three students.

The isolation was remarkable. Chattanooga was fifty miles away and Nashville eighty miles away—long distances given the poor roads and scarcity of automobiles in the 1930s. None of the students had cars. Monteagle, the nearest village, was seven miles from Sewanee. Far from being snobbish, the students were on a relatively equal footing because of the college's isolation and common mess hall where we all took seated meals. Even membership in the fraternities was only halfheartedly based on social position or money or one's family. The fact that fraternity houses were only for social events and not for housing members made this possible. Practically any student could become a member.

The closest outside recreation was Clara's restaurant in Monteagle. Clara's was a somewhat rowdy roadside café frequented by travelers and soldiers stationed nearby. It was the only place students could find a meal off campus and a beer. I frequently walked or rode a bicycle the seven miles there and back just to get a steak dinner that cost one dollar and a bottle of beer for ten cents. Clara's was almost regarded as an adjunct to Sewanee because it was such a popular place for students to congregate.

All students were required to wear coats and ties to classes and while on the main campus. Membership in the Order of Gownsmen made this part of the dress code relatively unimportant during the junior and senior years. Students who made above a C average in their first two years became members of the Order of Gownsmen and were required to wear academic gowns when attending classes or on the main campus. Gowns covered a multitude of sartorial incorrectnesses, but failure to wear a gown to class was counted as an absence.

The chapel occupied a central position on the campus. Chapel attendance was required, which meant attendance four weekdays per week and three Sundays a month for full credit. Proctors recorded chapel attendance, and if the requirements were not met, there would be no diploma from Sewanee. I enrolled in the choir, which sang at all of the services held in the chapel, so attendance was no problem. Paul McConnell, the organist and choir director, became my friend and mentor, and music was an important part of my college experience. Chapel was held every weekday except Saturday and consisted of morning prayer without a sermon; on special occasions there was a guest speaker. Once the guest speaker was Dean Roscoe Pound of Harvard Law School. Notices were posted that the title of Dean Pound's remarks would be "The Recrudescence of Absolutism." Most students did not know what he would be talking about. Curiosity, not desire for enlightenment, swelled the attendance at chapel to hear him.

The presence of the Sewanee Military Academy on the edge of the college campus added color to Sunday morning services. The cadets, who were high school students, came marching up the street in dress uniform with a color guard and a band playing "Onward, Christian Soldiers." Many of the professors who attended Sunday service wore colorful academic hoods, and some students wore gowns. Services almost had a Gilbert and Sullivan atmosphere, which pleased my taste as a Savoyard.

The students, except for about fifteen who lived in a dormitory named Tuckaway with its own dining room, ate all three meals together in Magnolia Hall. When the diners assembled, a blessing was said. Students served as waiters in Magnolia and brought food to their assigned tables on large oval trays. In my first year I took a job as a waiter in order to earn money to help pay for my tuition. I was not a good waiter and disliked the job because it required a considerable amount of physical stamina that I lacked. If I had any serious notion about becoming a priest, waiting on the "theologs" (theological seminary students), cured me. I found them to be both rude and loutish.

The course that made the biggest impression on me as a freshman was taught by Sedley Ware, a bachelor of arts graduate of Oxford with an LL.B. from Columbia University and a Ph.D. from Johns Hopkins. Ware taught English history, a required course for all freshmen. His teaching method was very much like what I believed was found in English schools, and his obvious pleasure in teaching medieval history was complemented by the Gothic architecture of the campus. Ware was flamboyant and colorful, and his classes frequently became theatrical performances. He had monthly oral quiz sessions in which small groups of freshmen were brought before him, and their ignorance, revealed publicly, brought down on their heads vociferous, unmerciful scorn. He bought red ink by the gallon, and when written test papers were returned, they were generally peppered with caustic comments. "Goosie! Goosie! Goosie!" might be Ware's scribbled comment on some inaccuracy or display of ignorance on a test page. Certain things irritated him profoundly, and he was given to saying, "Every damned school marm in the country has got it wrong!" Woe to any student who addressed him as "Professor Ware." He would shout, "A professor is a magician's assistant! I am Dr. Ware." His lecture on World War I was famous because, although he was a man in his sixties, he would charge the enemy's position by leaping on his desk, shouting, and waving his arms to encourage unseen battalions to follow him.

The first year I was at Sewanee I was sickly and hospitalized with influenza. Physical exercise was required, but I did not really become proficient in any sport until my junior and senior years, when I played handball regularly. Fred Morton and I took long hikes through the endless trails on the university's domain, which had breathtaking views of the valleys below. The most glorious time was in the spring, when nature burst forth in foliage and wildflowers.

I struggled with French, did well in freshman English and history, and took to botany like a duck to water. To avoid waiting on tables my second year, I got a job as student assistant in the botany laboratory.

Music had the next greatest influence on me my freshman year. Singing in the choir, doing simple oratorios, and learning weekly anthems required a concentration that was new to me, and McConnell pushed the choir to its limits. I was also fortunate my freshman year to take a course in music appreciation. It opened horizons of pleasure that have remained with me throughout my life.

Sewanee had been a pioneer in collegiate football in the late nineteenth century and was a founding member of the Southeastern Conference (SEC). The yearly game against Vanderbilt University was the occasion for a trip to Nashville on the train since none of the students had automobiles. "Don't send my boy to Georgia Tech, the dying mother said / and rather than to Vanderbilt, I'd rather see him dead," was sung with gusto during the football season.

It was on my first trip to Nashville for the Sewanee versus Vanderbilt game, which incidentally we never won, that I met Ashby Sutherland, who would become my roommate my sophomore and junior years. I arrived at the train station just as the train for Sewanee was pulling out and missed it, as did two other freshmen, Frank Carter and Ashby Sutherland, both Texans. We commiserated and got rooms in a hotel and returned to Sewanee together the next morning. It was the beginning of a friendship with Ashby that lasted the rest of our lives.

There was a bond between students and faculty at Sewanee that could only exist in a small college. Students were urged to visit the faculty in their homes on Sunday evenings, and most of us did. It gave a human dimension to the process of learning. There was a sense of camaraderie among the students. During spring breaks it would have been unusual if one of my classmates did not spend vacations with me.

My sophomore year at Sewanee, 1939–40, began under a cloud. Lying in bed at home in September 1939 I listened to a radio broadcast in which Neville Chamberlain declared that a state of war existed between Great

Britain and Nazi Germany. The United States was not immediately involved, but the handwriting was on the wall; we would enter that war.

Ashby Sutherland and I roomed together in Johnson Hall that and the following year. We got along well because our temperaments and interests were different. He provided the sharpness of intellect and critical judgment that I needed to help me shed my provincialism. My original intent was to major in history, but Ware was the only history teacher and I did not feel I would have a well-rounded major under his tutelage. However, I took a course in American history after 1865, which was taught by a new professor, Thomas Govan. The course was influential in the development of my thinking but not sufficient to keep me from changing my major to English.

There are some events that change a person's whole life. There is a line from William Wordsworth's *Prelude* that asks, "Who knows the individual hour in which / His habits first were sown, even as a seed?" I know. This happened with me in my sophomore English class. The course was called "Nineteenth Century English Criticism" and was taught by Tudor Seymour Long, who had a profound influence on my life. We were required to read six books—John Henry Newman's *On the Scope and Nature of University Education,* Matthew Arnold's *Culture and Anarchy,* Walter Pater's *The Renaissance,* John Ruskin's *Seven Lamps of Architecture,* Thomas Carlyle's *Past and Present,* and John Morley's *On Compromise.* Reading these books was my first encounter with tough, analytical thinking on a vast scale, and I felt as though I had emerged from the comfortable softness of provincialism into another world in which mind was more important than matter. This intellectual epiphany was like the physical experience of standing on the Cumberland Plateau and looking down upon the valley below, which stretched miles to the horizon.

In my freshman year I joined a fraternity, Delta Tau Delta. It was the fraternity most of my friends, including Ashby Sutherland and Fred Morton, joined. The Delts had a reputation for being more subdued and academically inclined than other fraternity men. I was not a good member, although my roommate Ashby Sutherland was president and I was vice president in our senior year. Hazing pledges was particularly repugnant to me. I threatened to resign from the fraternity in my sophomore year if certain physical ordeals and indignities that pledges suffered were not discontinued.

I also began to take a more active part in extracurricular activities. One of these was the Sopherim Literary Society. Membership in Sopherim inspired me to write a one-act play in the summer of 1940. I read it at one meeting of the Sopherim, but it was not well received.

The following year I wrote a one-act play titled *And It Came to Pass.* Being an overdramatized essay on the plight of the South, it was not suitable for stage production. The play was set in the bedroom of John C. Calhoun when he was dying, his last words being, "The South, the poor South." It was published in the Sopherim yearbook, and I believe that Allen Tate on reading it stated that he was impressed by the intense pessimism it displayed.

In fall 1939 Sewanee got permission from the Civil Aeronautics Authority to enroll twenty students in a project called the Civilian Pilot Training Program. Sewanee had inherited two Packard automobiles that were used to transport students to the airport at Manchester, Tennessee, approximately twenty-five miles from the campus, for the flight course taught by two young men of unquestioned skill but questionable manners.

Ground training at Sewanee consisted of instruction in meteorology, navigation, mechanics, and civil air regulations taught by Sewanee professors on campus in addition to flight school. I found learning to fly the small Piper Cub aircraft difficult. We had to become proficient in taking off and landing, both of which I mastered fairly quickly, but I struggled hard to master the skill of putting the airplane into a stall and then counting the number of revolutions it turned as it plunged downward.

I had to make a solo flight to Nashville and return at the end of the course. The flight up was uneventful. I tried to figure out the positions of the Confederate and Federal armies at the Battle of Murfreesboro when I flew over the site. I made a proper landing in Nashville and went to the Noel Hotel, feeling good about myself, to spend the night. The next morning I got up early and arrived at the airport in Nashville as my plane was being rolled out of the hangar by airport personnel. First they inadvertently damaged the fabric covering on the wing, then the plane's wing struck me on my head and knocked me sprawling to the pavement. Nothing but my self-esteem was damaged. The damage to the plane however necessitated delaying my takeoff until the afternoon while the wing was repaired. I called the airport in Manchester and told them of the accident and flew the plane back without mishap that afternoon.

I got my private pilot's license but made a covenant with the Good Lord that if he would allow me to get a license, I would not disturb the heavens by piloting a plane up there. I violated the covenant only one time and narrowly escaped having an accident. I never again violated my covenant.

The vice chancellor thought it would be a good idea to give the students their pilot licenses in the chapel on Ascension Day. This caused me to write one of the few poems I submitted to the Sopherim Literary Society, and it smacked of the sophomoric spirit of lèse-majesté that was still lingering in my mind. It pointed out the absurdity, if not blasphemy, of equating secular flying with spiritual ascension.

My junior year at Sewanee was relatively uneventful. In the summer of 1941 I went to Colorado with my former roommate, Fred Morton. He was going to take some courses at the University of Colorado at Boulder, and his parents had given him an automobile, an unknown luxury in our college days. My sister was then living in San Diego. I decided to go with him to Colorado, take several courses, including my mathematics requirements and a course in oil painting, and then go on by bus to San Diego.

While at Boulder I began to explore the possibility of writing a Sewanee version of Gilbert and Sullivan's opera *The Mikado.* It all began when I changed the words of the song from "Our great Mikado, virtuous man, when he began to rule our land began" to "Our great vice chancellor, virtuous man, when he to rule our school began." Things started clicking in my mind, and I thought there was a possibility of adapting the entire *Mikado* as a satire on life at Sewanee.

The effort to adapt *The Mikado* did not resume until I left Colorado and visited with my sister and her husband, Frank Johnson, in Mission Beach, California. I went into San Diego and found a record shop that sold scores along with musical instruments. I bought the score of *The Mikado* and then asked permission to listen to the D'Oyly Carte recordings. I listened so long that the proprietor told me that unless I was going to buy the records, I should cease and desist. But I had listened sufficiently that the idea to rewrite *The Mikado* as a satire of Sewanee was fixed in my mind.

I returned to Florence and went to Sewanee, only to discover that due to a polio scare, Sewanee's opening had been postponed for a week. Getting to Sewanee a week ahead of time gave me the leisure time to write the first draft of what became the *Sewanee Mikado.* I gave it the title *The Vice-Chancellor or the Town of Se-wa-nee.* While the satire of the university and Alexander Guerry is biting, there was no intention to disparage Guerry's task of pulling the college through the Depression and saving it during World War II. The difference between satire and burlesque is that in satire there is a basic acceptance of the legitimacy of the idea or person satirized. Burlesque, on the other hand, denies the worth or value of what is being laughed at. I never questioned the essential worth of Guerry or his noble effort to save and improve Sewanee; however, I was never sure that he understood the difference between satire and burlesque. For all his gifts, he lacked a sense of humor.

My friendship with Paul McConnell made the difference between having the play produced or having it ignored. Paul thought it brilliant and persuaded the faculty member who directed *The Purple Mask*, Tony Griswold, to hear it auditioned at the home of Miss Charlotte Elliot and Miss Marie Truslow, two grande dames of Sewanee whose sponsorship could not be criticized. Paul played the accompaniment, and I sang through the score and read the dialogue. Tony liked it and agreed to its production. Paul McConnell agreed to direct the choir in the musical portions of a production scheduled for May 1942.

Meanwhile there was a great celebration when Lord and Lady Halifax visited the campus in the spring of 1942. He was the British ambassador to the United States and only recently passed over for the prime minister's position in favor of Churchill. Sewanee was already pro-British, but the conferring of an honorary degree on Lord Halifax was the occasion for even more anglophilia. As a member of the choir I had a front-row seat at the hooding, and I thought that to receive an honorary degree would be the crowning achievement of my life.

In the fall of 1941 and spring of 1942 my friend Bayly Turington and I persuaded Long to teach a course in Dante (in translation) and Edmund Burke. With only two of us meeting once a week, it was the ideal situation. Our final examination was given on a bench outside of the library. Mr. Long sat in the middle, and Bayly and I sat on either side of him.

My main course in English my senior year was under Professor Abbot Cotton Martin, generally known by students as "Abbo." He taught a course in the English romantic poets, principally Wordsworth. Sewanee's natural beauty made it an ideal place for reading Wordsworth, so I took to his *Prelude* with enthusiasm.

As the time for the production of the *Sewanee Mikado* approached, a real problem arose when Vice Chancellor Guerry learned that he was the central figure being satirized. In my version the vice chancellor is depicted as Ko-Ko. The chancellor, who was also a bishop, was only a minor role, which was reinterpreted as the Mikado, and his "daughter-in-law elect" became "the benefactor elect," the first of a never-failing series of *wealthy* benefactors. We prayed regularly in the chapel for benefactors, but I inserted the word "wealthy." As portions of the script began to leak to the community, the vice chancellor called Paul McConnell into his office and expressed his concern that the production might seriously damage the university. He made it clear that he would hold McConnell personally responsible if the play exceeded what he deemed good taste or was a breach of academic propriety.

The members of the choir acted and sang well. Paul McConnell and Fred Morton played the accompaniment. The play was produced two nights, May 4 and 5, 1942, and was an overwhelming success. Andrew Lytle, who lived at Monteagle, was called in to help direct. After the final performance the cast had a party at Clara's restaurant, where I was crowned "King Ziggy" and Morton and McConnell were given the titles of princes. I saw Tony Griswold and Abbo Martin at Clara's that night, and Martin reminded me of the ridiculous figure I had cut when I was a freshman showing little grace and no promise. Griswold came to my defense and said, "All freshmen are ridiculous." Abbo's final remark was, "This is a great occasion for you. Enjoy it. There will never be any in the future like it."

There was a movement to have a repeat performance during commencement week, but Guerry refused permission. The *Sewanee Mikado* was my valedictory to college life and to the University of the South I had known, for it would never be the same after World War II. The days of the ideal known as the "Sewanee gentleman" were waning.

Although the previous year I been inducted into Phi Beta Kappa, I had never had much of a reputation on campus as a person of any promise. After the play's success I was lionized. Within the month I was elected to Blue Key and Omicron Delta Kappa. To cap it all, I was awarded the Guerry Medal for excellence in English given in memory of Bishop Alexander Guerry, the vice chancellor's father. I recall at commencement a conversation with Bishop Guerry's widow. She and her husband were residents of Florence

At the University of the South, Sewanee, 1942: Tony Griswold, the author, and Paul McConnell on set of the Sewanee Mikado. *Collection of the author*

Graduation from the University of the South, Sewanee: Benjamin Zeigler (1992) and the author (1942 and honorary degree, 1992). Collection of the author

when he was rector of St. John's Church in the 1880s. Mrs. Guerry sought me out and told me after the commencement ceremony that she was delighted that a boy from Florence won the Guerry Medal. I don't think Vice Chancellor Guerry shared her enthusiasm.

Commencement was a glorious affair. The commencement speaker was Gerald Johnson of the *Baltimore Sun.* I later bought several of his books, including *American Heroes and Hero-Worship.* There were forty-two in my graduating class, and the commencement service, said in Latin, was held in the chapel with several bishops in attendance. The Sewanee graduation ends with a Latin charge by the vice chancellor in which the graduates are addressed as "chosen and now honored youths" who have had the benefit of a college education. The charge sounds better in Latin than it does in English, for it asks the graduates to bear themselves with uprightness and integrity *ad gloriam Dei, in honorem republicae, et in splendorem huis Universitatis* (to the glory of God, to the honor of the nation, and in the good name of this University). It ends with the simple command *Valete* (Go forth)! I left believing that I had a mission to go forth and accomplish great things for God, the nation, and college.

John Henry Newman in his book *On the Scope and Nature of University Education,* wrote, "A University is, according to the usual designation, an Alma Mater, knowing her children one by one, not a foundry, or a mint or a treadmill." Although much has changed since 1942, I still get emotional when I think about Sewanee. It is no longer Gothic and monkish, but it retains many of the traits that make it unique and evokes the warmest feelings about the four years I spent there. Sewanee will always be my dear mother.

5

A Ninety-Day Wonder on the USS *Ranger*

In December 1941 I was a senior at the University of the South in Sewanee, Tennessee. After Sunday dinner it was an established custom for the members of the Delta Tau Delta fraternity to walk to Señor Lewis's house for after dinner coffee. Lewis, a bachelor living with his mother, was the faculty sponsor of the Delta Tau Delta fraternity and head of the Spanish department.

I was there on Sunday, December 7, 1941. Some of us took our coffee into the adjoining living room, where the radio was turned on. Suddenly there was a news flash that the Japanese had bombed Pearl Harbor. All of us in the room sat in stunned silence. We sensed that our lives would be changed forever.

In the following days Congress held a special session, and I listened to President Roosevelt make his famous speech about the "day of infamy" on a radio in the student union. Congress declared war on the Japanese Empire, and Germany declared war on the United States. What I had for years considered inevitable was now a reality. I would have to decide what branch of the military service to enter.

From my early youth the navy fascinated me. Aunt Deda had encouraged me to believe that a career in the navy should be my ambition. She worked hard to get me an appointment to the United States Naval Academy. The war had started and I would go from Sewanee into the U.S. Navy, but not via Annapolis.

Midterm examinations at Sewanee came at the end of January. I had made inquiries the previous summer about the various programs the navy offered for college students. I had learned of the *Prairie State,* an old battleship moored in the Hudson River where college students were trained to become Naval Reserve officers. I also learned that the navy had developed a V-7 program for college students that required graduation as a prerequisite to enlisting. When I was at home on Christmas holiday, I investigated how to enlist in this program.

Two weeks following my midterm exams, I hitchhiked to Nashville, Tennessee, to join the navy. I got a ride to Monteagle and began to thumb passing cars. I had only been there about ten minutes when a pickup truck stopped. I told the driver where I was going and for what purpose. I was in luck. He was going to Nashville and would take me to the navy recruiting office. I was sworn into the navy on February 14, 1942. Under the V-7 program my active duty date was deferred until my graduation in June.

It is hard to describe the letdown of returning to Florence after the euphoria of my graduation and theatrical triumph to face the grim reality of military service in a war. The navy notified me that I would not be admitted to the Naval Academy because I lacked a credit in solid geometry in my high school record. Aunt Deda was furious. She called the academy, and I heard her say, "No wonder we had a Pearl Harbor. I shall expect some more."

I was uneasy because I had not taken physics, so I decided I would go to summer school and take a course while I waited to be called into active service. The University of Virginia appealed to me, so I took a bus trip to Charlottesville and got in a line to register. The line was so long and the contrast between Sewanee and the university so great that I dropped out of the line, got on a bus, and went to Lexington, Virginia, and enrolled at Washington and Lee. I found a room in a large Victorian house on the street that ran between the Virginia Military Institute and Washington and Lee.

I fell into a deep feeling of depression. The contrast between my triumphant exit from Sewanee to living in a rooming house, in a strange place where I knew nobody and nobody knew me, was overwhelming. Fortunately the other student at Miss Duval's, Frank Johnson, turned out to be one of the finest young men with whom I have had the good fortune to be associated. He eventually became an Episcopal minister, and we kept up with each other for many years after that summer.

It was difficult for me to concentrate on the physics class, so I sought refuge in the college library, which had a good collection of Gilbert and Sullivan records. But my real salvation came through my friendship with Frank. He was well schooled in the classics and was a good conversationalist and an enthusiastic hiker. He persuaded me to join him on long walks in the country. On one occasion we walked several miles to Goshen Pass, where there was a lake in which we swam. On these walks the natural beauty of that part of Virginia intrigued me. We walked to Natural Bridge, seven miles from Lexington, had lunch on the way at a plantation house, visited Natural Bridge, and returned by bus to Lexington.

I received my orders to report to midshipman school at Columbia University in New York City on July 20, my twenty-first birthday. I returned to Florence by bus and took the train to New York. On the same train I met Henry Richardson from Jacksonville, Florida, who was en route to enter midshipman school. We got along well, and he guided me though the intricacies of the New York subway system to the exit at 116th Street and Columbia University.

I was sworn in as an apprentice seaman on August 14, 1942. By chance Henry Richardson was assigned as my roommate in Furnald Hall. We were issued khaki pants and shirts and caps without insignia. Because apprentice seaman is an enlisted rating, for two weeks we went through a basic course as navy enlisted men.

At the end of the two-week period those who were not "bilged," in other words had not failed, were sworn in as midshipmen. Midshipman is a rank between warrant officer and ensign, and if I had attended Annapolis, it would have been my designation as a student there.

Our meals were eaten in John Jay Hall, and we drilled on the main mall or yard in front of the library of Columbia University. Most of our drilling, however, was done up and down 116th Street and its cross streets. The only time I got a demerit was during one of the marches down a street near the university. We were given strict orders to look straight ahead when we were marching. The Columbia University fraternities had put out banners across the street and the temptation was too great. I glanced up at one of them and the platoon officer saw me and put me on report. This meant that instead of having one Saturday off I had to stay and do guard duty under the watchful, critical eye of a duty officer.

We were required to take courses in navigation, seamanship, ordnance, communication, damage control, and first aid. I made passing grades in all and was never put on a "tree," a list of those who had failed in the week's work. Being put on a tree meant deprivation of liberty on the weekend and the danger of being bilged. In the final standing I was safely in the middle of the graduating class.

I sang in the school's choir. It intrigued me that on Sunday evening after the battalion mustered, the Roman Catholics were directed to fall out and regroup on one side and the Jews and Protestants on the other. The two groups went to separate services. The Jews and Protestants marched to Riverside Church, where evening services were conducted from the Episcopal Book of Common Prayer by Lt. Joshua Goldberg, a Jewish rabbi, and Lt. Cdr. C. Leslie Glenn, an Episcopal minister. There were about forty of us in the choir, and we rehearsed in a room in the tower of Riverside

Church. One of the high points of the choir's performances was the singing of an anthem composed by T. Tertius Noble, "Fierce Was the Wild Billow." Noble wrote several hymns in the Episcopal hymnal, and he personally trained the choir to sing his anthem. It was Noble's opinion that one line of the anthem that described the storm, "Oars labored heavily, foam glistened white," to be heard correctly should be sung as "Whores labored heavily, foam glistened white." We dutifully and gleefully sang it that way. We also sang for the Jewish baccalaureate service in Temple Emanu-El.

While we were there, several other Sewanee boys and I were invited to have dinner with Señor Lewis's nephew, who lived in New York. His name was Crandell, and he had a staff position with the commandant of that naval district. He was friendly with Cdr. John D. Buckeley, about whom I had read in W. L. White's book *They Were Expendable.* He arranged for Buckeley to take us on a tour around Manhattan Island in his PT boat and indicated that if I liked PT boat service he would ask that I be assigned to one. I made the decision to ask for duty on an aircraft carrier instead, and the request was granted.

There were eleven hundred in the class that graduated on December 2, 1942, the largest Naval Reserve class to be sworn in as ensigns in the history of the navy. The ceremony, held in Riverside Church, was impressive. After we took the oath as ensigns, the carillon pealed out "Anchors Aweigh" as we made our way back to Furnald Hall. We were called "Ninety-Day Wonders" because our training lasted ninety days and most of us had never set foot on a naval vessel.

Getting fitted with uniforms was a pleasant task. As officers we had the choice of which department store in New York to patronize. We were not required to buy swords, but gray gloves, a white scarf, a bridge coat, and dress blues and whites were mandatory. We learned that etiquette dictated when first reporting on board ship we must present a calling card, as soon as possible, to the commanding officer. We had to have the cards engraved before leaving New York.

I was ordered to report to the USS *Ranger* (CV 4) in Norfolk, Virginia, on December 10, 1942. That meant I would have a little less than a week at home to strut about in my new ensign's uniform. It was the first time I remember my father giving signs of approving of my accomplishments. All good things must come to an end, and I left Florence by train for Norfolk and arrived at approximately 3:30 A.M. on December 10.

I was so revved up at the prospect of reporting to the *Ranger* that I hardly slept before getting up for breakfast at 7:00 A.M. While I was eating breakfast, I engaged in conversation with other officers seated at the same table with me. When I told them I would be reporting to the *Ranger* for duty, one officer said, "Well, you'd better hurry because she's scheduled to get under way this morning."

I bolted from the table and ran back to the Bachelor Officers' Quarters (BOQ), where I asked for transportation as quickly as possible. I had a valpack (a small zip-up travel bag) and a large suitcase, and since the weather was cold, I put on my bridge coat, silk scarf, and gray gloves. A pickup truck with an enlisted driver carried me to Pier 7, where the *Ranger* was docked. When we arrived at the pier the *Ranger* was being "walked" down it, which meant the mooring lines were free and being hand carried as the ship backed slowly into the harbor. Pier 7 was very long, and although the *Ranger* was just getting under way, it was in motion. I asked the driver of the pickup truck if he could drive out on the pier, and he said he could. When we got abreast of the bridge, some fifty feet above the pier, I got out of the truck and shouted, "Is there any way I can get on board?" A number of men on the hangar deck thirty feet above the pier motioned for me to go farther down the pier. I ran.

When I reached the midpoint of the ship some men threw a Jacob's ladder—a rope ladder with wooden rungs—over the side from the hangar deck. The ladder was of ancient vintage, with short and narrow wooden rungs and ovate sides. It seemed more adapted for use on a sailing vessel than a modern man-of-war. The men on the hangar deck swung the Jacob's ladder back and forth outward from the ship's hull because there were camels (floating wooden fenders) between the ship and the pier. That motion gave me the ability to grab the ladder when it swung outward toward the pier. I did this and swung back into the side of the moving ship.

I hung there suspended over the camels, endeavoring to climb the Jacob's ladder. Then I realized that my bridge coat, which reached below my knees, was buttoned so tight that I could not raise my knees to climb. It crossed my mind that when the ship reached the end of the pier I would be suspended over deep water. With great effort I unbuttoned the lower buttons of the coat so that I was finally able to raise my knees and climb toward the hangar deck. Up until this point I had given no thought to my luggage. I looked back over my shoulder toward the pier and saw that the men on the hangar deck had swung a boom out and lowered a line with a large hook on it. My valpack and suitcase were in midair being lifted onto the hangar deck.

When I reached the hangar deck, two enlisted men grabbed me by the shoulders and pulled me on board. My first thought was that I should behave in a manner befitting an officer reporting for duty. I told an experienced warrant officer, who apparently had supervised my unceremonious arrival, that I would like to be shown to the captain's cabin. He responded that the captain was busy at the moment and I should postpone my visit. It would be New Year's Eve before I got to meet Capt. C. T. Durgin.

The *Ranger* was an old ship. It was launched in 1933 and was the first aircraft carrier built "keel up" as a carrier. It displaced 14,500 tons and could handle up to seventy-two aircraft. The *Ranger* had all of the vestiges of a luxurious peacetime ship. There was a band on board, which played concerts regularly in the hangar deck. The officers ate in the wardroom, and the executive officer, the second in command, presided over meals there. In the evening three musicians went through the passageways in officers' country playing "Beef for Old England" to give notice that dinner would be served in approximately ten minutes. Officers were seated in accordance with their rank and commissioning date. No one was allowed to sit before the executive officer entered the wardroom and was seated, and no one was suppose to leave the wardroom, without permission, until the executive officer left. Except when the ship was under way, officers were required to wear coat and tie at meals.

Ten of my classmates from midshipman school had been ordered to report to the *Ranger*, but I was the only one who had managed to get on board that day. The ship was not leaving for a wartime mission but going for training exercises on Chesapeake Bay.

During the *Ranger*'s training cruise I wandered at will about the ship but spent a good deal of time on the forecastle, where I met Lt. Cdr. J. R. Hume. There was an air of sadness about him that I interpreted as coming from the fact that he had survived the sinking of the carrier USS *Wasp* in the Coral Sea. Hume seemed to take a kindly interest in me and asked if I would like to be assigned to the first lieutenant's office. I had only a vague idea what the duties of a first lieutenant were, but I said I would like that. It turned out that Lieutenant Commander Hume was the first lieutenant.

The shipboard office of first lieutenant went back to the days of sailing ships. The first lieutenant was the next in command of a sailing man-of-war. In the modern navy the second in command of ship is the executive officer. The first lieutenant was still in charge of all of the ground tackle (lines, fittings, and chains) and in charge of the boatswain's locker, where equipment for mooring and anchoring tackle were stowed. Therefore he was responsible for the anchoring and mooring of the ship. His duties included supervision of all repairs to the ship and the "R" Division, which included shipfitters ratings (welders and carpenters). He was in charge of damage control and responsible for the cleanliness of the ship.

When the exercises were completed, we returned to Norfolk but were sent to a mooring at Portsmouth for some repairs that lasted beyond January 1, 1943. I spent both Christmas and New Year's Day in the Norfolk area, but the New Year's Eve celebration proved the most memorable. On December 30 Lieutenant Commander Hume asked me to come to his office. He wanted to know if I had any plans for New Year's Eve. I said I did not. He said that Captain Durgin had invited his former secretary to a party at the officers' club and he needed a date for her. Would I agree to escort her to the party? I said I would be honored to do so. Hume said that I would be invited to the captain's cabin before we went to the officers' club and to be there at 1800 sharp.

I presented myself at Captain Durgin's cabin. It was the first time I met the captain. He told me that he had witnessed my arrival from the bridge and thought I was some ensign who had delayed too long parting from a girlfriend or wife. The young lady arrived along with other guests. She was an attractive young woman who appeared to be in her late twenties. We were driven in style to the officers' club, where the captain had a table reserved. My presence with the captain's party excited all sorts of curiosity. Several of the *Ranger's* officers wanted to know what my relationship to the captain was and found it difficult to believe that I was only a casual guest.

It was a delightful evening with dancing, drinking, and merrymaking. I left with the young lady to escort her to the ferry and take her to her lodgings in Norfolk. It came as a surprise to find that Captain Durgin was at the ferry, and he told me that he wished the honor of taking the young lady over to Norfolk. I bowed out, of course. I knew my place and asked no questions. I never saw Durgin again except at a distance in the Pacific, when he came on board the USS *Cape Gloucester*, and by then he had been promoted to the rank of admiral.

The *Ranger* was kept in the Atlantic Ocean because its watertight integrity was compromised. It was presumed that it would be less vulnerable to submarine and air attacks in the Atlantic than it would in the Pacific.

The first time the *Ranger* put to sea, I was terribly seasick. Dinner that night in the wardroom had consisted of curry with chutney and other condiments. The sea was rough when we entered the Atlantic. I began to feel sick, but general quarters was sounded and my station was in a damage-control center in the bowels of the third deck. All watertight doors were closed, and all ventilation was shut down. I was given a bucket in which to vomit. I vomited until I had the dry heaves, and the seasoned sailors and officers stationed with me offered little comfort.

When secure from general quarters was announced, I struggled back to the bunkroom and fell, or rather climbed, into my upper bunk. After a day in which I could hardly move about, the seasickness passed, and I was relieved to discover that it was not a permanent malady. After a couple of days I got my "sea legs" and was not affected by seasickness afterward. It was reassuring to learn that the sea had had a similar effect on Lord Nelson.

The *Ranger* voyaged up the coast to Boston, and I made contact with my former college roommate, Ashby Sutherland, who was at Harvard. We got together, and it was the first time I saw the Harvard Yard. I was able to reciprocate by giving him a tour of the *Ranger* before we departed.

The wartime mission of the *Ranger* at that time consisted of ferrying airplanes for the army across the Atlantic to Morocco. The hangar deck was filled with fighter planes (P-40s), and when the carrier was approximately sixteen miles off the African coast, the fighters were launched and the *Ranger* returned to Norfolk. Crossing the Atlantic through the Sargasso Sea with its remarkable patches of seaweed and flying fishes was a memorable experience.

I got along well with the first lieutenant, and he made me, as a collateral duty, the "berthing officer," responsible for assigning all personnel to certain berths on the *Ranger*. I also was required to supervise the mess attendants, who were mostly black and who, when not cooking or serving in the wardroom, cleaned the officers' cabins. I had an elaborate chart made, and each mess attendant was assigned to clean certain cabins. It would take about an hour to do this, but there was constant difficulty in getting it done.

One mess attendant who could not have been much older than eighteen consistently failed to clean the rooms assigned to him. After two or three times I warned him that I would have to put him on report if he failed again to do his assigned work. Despite my warning he again failed to do his assigned task. I had no choice but to put him on report. That meant he would have to appear at captain's mast.

Captain's mast, for lesser offenses, was conducted by the executive officer. He was a commanding figure when he presided, flanked by two armed marines with an American flag behind them. I told the executive officer of my difficulty in getting the young mess attendant to perform his duties. When I had finished, the executive officer turned to the mess attendant and asked, "What have you got to say for yourself?"

He paused for a moment, then simply said, "I'se tired." I don't recall his punishment, but I had no further trouble with him.

By the time the *Ranger* had finished its second crossing of the Atlantic, a new threat had emerged to the north. I understood that a German battleship was preparing to make a sortie into the North Sea. The *Ranger* was dispatched with a task force to Argentia Bay, Newfoundland. Although it was April, Newfoundland was still covered in snow. We took a trip to St. John's, the capital, and another officer and I took several walking trips around Argentia Bay.

The most pleasant activity centered around the officer's club at the shore base. The *Ranger* was anchored in the bay, so getting to the club involved a cold ride across Argentia Bay, but the food and drink made the trip worthwhile. On one occasion when I was in the officers' club, I went to the bar to get a drink. A high-ranking admiral in front of me was being urged by two junior officers to leave. "Come on, Admiral, let's go," they kept saying to him. I assumed that the admiral had drunk too much, and a smile must have crossed my face. I did not realize that there was a mirror across the back of the bar. Suddenly the admiral wheeled around and confronted me.

"What are you smirking at?" he shouted. The area around us fell silent.

"Nothing, sir," I managed to reply.

"Where are you from?" he demanded.

My first inclination was to say South Carolina, but luckily I said, "From the *Ranger*, sir."

"Oh, one of my boys! Step right up." And he staggered away, followed by his solicitous aides. I was vastly relieved to have escaped a possible court-martial. When I enquired who the admiral was, I was told he was in command of the whole task force.

While we were operating off Newfoundland, the Germans announced that the *Ranger* had been sunk. It was my understanding that the ship may have been fired on with torpedoes launched from a German submarine, but they had missed. The difficulty was that we were at sea and could not break radio silence. The newspaper headlines in the United States, including the *Florence Morning News,* published the German claim that the *Ranger* had been sunk, and the captain of the German submarine launching the torpedo attack was decorated.

The news devastated my family, who believed I had perished at sea. It was not until a week later, when the *Ranger* returned to Argentia Bay, that the officers and men were allowed to notify their families that they were still alive. The messages we sent were drafted by naval authorities and had wording that did not reveal the *Ranger*'s location. It was thought the Germans might have invented the story in order to find out where the *Ranger* was operating.

On June 11, 1943, orders came detaching me and two other officers: "HEREBY DETACHED PROCEED TO PHILA PENN REPORT COM 4 AND WHEN DIRECTED BY HIM PROCEED TO CAMDEN NJ REPORT TO SUPSHIP NEW YORK SHIPBLDG CORP DUTY CFO CABOT AND ON BOARD WHEN COMMISSIONED." We were flown in a navy plane to New York City. I took the train to Florence.

I was allowed to delay reporting to Philadelphia for approximately five days and decided to spend that time at home.

While I was in Florence, I learned that Peter McEachin, my uncle, had been stationed near Philadelphia during World War I and had become acquainted with a Mrs. Blanche Ostrander. She was still alive and lived in Philadelphia, but her second husband had died, and she was now Mrs. Kennedy. When I arrived in Philadelphia I called on her, and she invited me numerous times to dinner. Mrs. Kennedy, who must have been in her late seventies, was a perky, sharp-tongued Yankee lady. When I asked about her first husband, she replied, "There are two kinds of widows—bereaved and relieved. I was bereaved the first time and relieved the second."

Several officers who were on precommissioning details had rented rooms at a house on Locust Street very close to Rittenhouse Square. I was able to get a room there until the *Cabot* was commissioned on July 24, 1943. I had the equivalent of shore duty for approximately a month.

6

Baptism of Fire on the USS *Cabot*

To fill the need for more air power in the Pacific theater as quickly as possible, cruiser hulls already under construction in the early months of the war were converted into small, fast aircraft carriers. Nine of these cruiser hulls were converted in 1942 into *Independence*-class light carriers, or CVLs. What made them valuable to the Pacific Fleet was their ability to make 31.6 knots, sufficient speed to be part of the fast carrier strike forces. The USS *Cabot* (CVL 28) was one of these small, fast aircraft carriers. It displaced eleven thousand tons, had a crew of 1,569 officers and men, and could carry thirty-seven planes, which included TBM torpedo bombers and F6F fighters.

A member of the precommission detail of a ship was a "plank owner" in the parlance of the navy. The term was particularly appropriate for aircraft carriers because the flight deck was made of wooden planks to absorb the impact of landing planes. When I reported for duty, the crew assembling for the *Cabot* met at the New York Shipbuilding Company in Camden, New Jersey. There was a morning muster at the shipyard and classes for those of us who were to serve on the ship when it was commissioned.

Because my experience on the *Ranger* was in the first lieutenant's office, it was logical that I would be assigned to that office on the *Cabot*. I met Lt. Cdr. C. J. Heath, the first lieutenant, and became quite friendly with him. He was a slight, wiry man, an Annapolis graduate, and much interested in trying to modernize the navy. Heath immediately made me the R Division officer. That meant I was in charge of the welders, machinists, and carpenters, in addition to standing junior officer of the watch once we were under way.

At one of the ship officers' meetings, I introduced myself to the officer sitting next to me. He said his name was Marshall Field. I asked if he was from Virginia. He said he was not, that he was from Chicago, but he had attended the University of Virginia and that had probably affected his accent. I thought no more of his origins until the executive officer made a speech in which he stated that he did not care about the civilian background of his officers. "Some of you may have parents who are capable of buying one of the these ships, but that carries no weight with me," he declared. Later, when I expressed my inability to understand why the executive officer had made such a strange remark, I was told, "He's probably referring to Marshall Field. His family is one of the richest in America." Field had been severely wounded in the sinking of the USS *Wasp,* and this was his first shipboard duty since his recovery. We became good friends and played chess frequently.

I was not so lucky in making other friends. This was the first time I met and tried to get along with men who, in navy parlance, were "mustangs," or former enlisted men who had been promoted to officer rank. Their value to the navy was obvious since they were experienced and knowledgeable in the details of running a ship, but they were notoriously clannish. One mustang assigned to the R Division office had been a warrant officer before Pearl Harbor. He had been promised a promotion to lieutenant, but when his commission came through he was only given the rank of ensign. I sensed that he held a grudge against the navy for that reason and had an abiding contempt for Ninety-Day Wonders or, as he called us, "feather merchants." When he was detached from the *Cabot* about a year later, he fired a final salvo at us. His last entry in the damage-control log was "Feather merchants, take over."

The last phases of the *Cabot's* commissioning were accomplished in the Philadelphia Navy Yard. When the ship was commissioned on July 24, Capt. Malcolm F. Schoeffel took command. The executive officer was Cdr. G. A. T. Washburn, who ruled the wardroom with an iron hand. I saw him put officers under hack (temporary punishment of an officer by a superior officer by confining him to quarters pending investigation into the misconduct) for talking while an announcement was being made in the wardroom or for presuming to leave the wardroom before he left.

I was billeted in the forwardmost cabin on the port side with three other officers. Ens. D. R. McNeal from Pennsylvania was in the Supply Corps, Ens. E. C. "Red Dog" Duggins from Tennessee was in the Gunnery Department, and Lt. (j.g.) Reinald "Werry" Werrenrath from Illinois was the squadron fighter director stationed in Combat Intelligence Central (CIC). We were together, without any serious disagreements, from July 1943 until I was detached in November 1944.

For the first month and a half the *Cabot* underwent trials in Chesapeake Bay, and on September 14 it began its shakedown cruise to the island of Trinidad. Shore leave in Trinidad was my first experience in a foreign country. When we went ashore for the first time, we were besieged—not by West

Indians but by East Indians. They were the most persistent and intense street vendors I have ever encountered. "Effendi," they cried as they pushed their trinkets at us blocking our way. I was unaware of the history of the West Indies and did not know that at one time the British had brought in workers, chiefly from India, to work on the sugar plantations.

Trinidad was still a British colony, and there was a British officers' club, called the Macaripe Club, on the side of a mountain. To get there and back it was necessary to ride in a bus provided by the U.S. Navy. Naturally liquor was consumed freely, and fights among the officers were not uncommon. It had been the policy to allow the aviators stationed on board to carry on their belts a hunting knife. Under the influence of liquor, unfortunately, these became dangerous weapons. One of the aviators' favorite sports when we were in Trinidad was to go up to a fellow officer grab his necktie and cut it off below the knot. If the victim took umbrage, a dangerous encounter involving hunting knives could ensue.

Being a junior ship's company officer, I thought I was immune from these high-spirited encounters, but I was wrong. Returning by bus after one of my visits to the club, I sat next to a former football player who was an officer attached to one of the air squadrons. He was quite drunk. Suddenly he seized me by my necktie, just below the knot, and called me a "baby-faced bastard." He tightened his grip so that I could not breath, and I feared his next move would be to cut either my throat or my necktie. Fortunately some other officers on the bus intervened and pulled him off of me, and I escaped strangulation with my necktie intact. Shortly after that the captain issued an order that prohibited officers from carrying hunting knives on shore leave.

The *Cabot* returned to Philadelphia and underwent several more trials along the Atlantic coast. The first week in November the *Cabot* sailed to the Panama Canal, and by November 14 it had transited the canal to the Pacific side and proceeded to San Diego, California.

By November 27, 1943, the *Cabot* was moored at Ford Island, Hawaii, in Pearl Harbor. The main fleet was not there when we arrived, having sortied to attack the Japanese in the Gilbert Islands. While the ship was at Pearl Harbor, most of the vessels of the Pacific Fleet returned. I walked out on the pier to watch as they came into the harbor. If anyone suffered from a lack of patriotism, this experience would have cured him. The huge battleships, the sleek cruisers, the great aircraft carriers, and the nimble destroyers, all following each other in a line, manned by thousands of men, and passing by me made my eyes fill with tears. I could hardly repress my desire to sing the "Star Spangled Banner." I knew I was fortunate to be a citizen of the United States.

The task force, of which the *Cabot* was a part, began using advanced bases in the captured islands, so I had only one shore leave after the *Cabot* joined the fleet, when we returned once to Hawaii. Ensign McNeal and I were anxious to get off the ship, but the difficulty was that the entire task force came back together. Approximately twenty-five to thirty thousand men were turned loose at one time on Honolulu. We went on shore leave only to find that the numbers of sailors and officers overwhelmed public transportation. We went to Trader Vic's to have a drink. The Scotch whiskey they served was made with fermented pineapples and some sort of flavoring that tasted a great deal like iodine. The restaurant was crowded, so we went out on the street to catch a bus. They were overloaded and did not stop. While we were standing on the curb looking desolate, a car pulled up and a woman who looked as though she might be Polynesian asked if she could give us a ride. We said we would be grateful and got in the car. She asked what our plans were, and we replied that we were looking for a place to eat. She introduced herself as Mrs. Lucas and told us that she must go to her house on the way to Waikiki. Would we like to go on a picnic with her family? We said we would.

It turned out that her family, many years ago, had been granted a tract of land that ran from the mountain ridge to the ocean. McNeal and I could not believe our good luck. We had a wonderful meal and were driven back to the ship.

The *Cabot* joined Task Group 58.2 and crossed the equator on January 22, 1944, causing the riotous initiation of Pollywogs, those like me who had never crossed the equator, into the noble order of Shellbacks, those who had. King Neptune was welcomed on board, and the uninitiated were made to endure humiliations of various sorts until the celebration came to an end.

From January 29, 1944, until I was detached in November 1944, the *Cabot* was part of the following battles and engagements:

Marshall Islands occupation (January 28–February 1944)
Asiatic and Pacific raids (February 16–May 1, 1944)
Hollandia operation (April 21–June 1, 1944)
Marianas operations (June 19–August 1944)
Western Caroline Islands operations (September 6–October 14, 1944)
Leyte operation (October–November 1944)

Junior officers rotated through the various watches. As junior officer of the deck, I was required to stand watch when the ship was under way. That meant standing on the ship's bridge with the officer of the deck and helping him with the steering of the ship. The ship's wheel was in the pilothouse a deck below the open bridge, and orders were issued to the quartermaster, who manned the wheel in the pilothouse through a voice tube from the bridge. Standing watch under way and in port was done in addition to the regular ships duties assigned to each officer. Although I was promoted from the rank of ensign to lieutenant junior grade while serving on the *Cabot*, I only stood junior officer of the watch under way. The officer of the deck had the responsibility for the operation of the ship while he had "the con" (responsibility for steering the ship).

The command "general quarters" ordered the crew to prepare the ship for battle or to repel attack. My battle station was on the second deck as officer in charge of a damage-control repair party. There were about ten enlisted men in my repair party, and we had sound-powered telephone communications with the damage-control center on the third deck. It had been the experience of men on other ships hit by bombs or torpedoes that their legs could be broken if they were standing when the ship was hit. As a consequence all of us had to lie on our backs when attack was imminent. Many casualties were caused by flash burns after an explosion, so we were required to use flashproof headgear and tuck our pants in our socks. In the tropics, especially with no ventilation, this could be very uncomfortable. As the officer in charge of the group, I was required to wear sidearms during general quarters.

I had a longing to win a Purple Heart so that when I was discharged, I could say I shed my blood for my country. During the many attacks upon the *Cabot* by suicide planes and submarines, I lay on my back trying to decide in what part of my anatomy I would prefer to be wounded. The fleshy part of the arm or the thigh took precedence over wounds to more vital parts.

In serious air attacks I could generally tell when the Japanese planes were close to the *Cabot*. There were 5-inch guns on the fantail, and there were 40-mm guns, 20-mm guns, and clusters of .50-caliber machine guns, all designed to shoot the Japanese planes down before they could dive into the ship. Lying on my back wrapped in flashproof clothing, looking up at the overhead, I could tell how close the Japanese planes were by the steady boom, boom of the 5-inch guns, which meant they were about a mile away; the rack, rack, rack of the 40-mm guns meant they were half a mile away; and the ratty-tack, ratty-tack, ratty-tack of the 20-mms meant they were close to the *Cabot*. And finally, when the banks of .50-caliber machine guns sounded—tack, tack, tack—they were right on top of the *Cabot*. By the time the 50-caliber guns started firing, I was saying a silent prayer: "Not this time, Lord. I don't want the Purple Heart that bad. I'll wait until next time."

The danger was not only from enemy fire but also from accidents at sea. In April 1944 the *Cabot* had a near collision with the heavy cruiser USS *Wichita*. To understand the hazard of collision, it is necessary to understand that the task force units operated in a circular formation. The carriers were centered in the middle of the circle, the battleships and cruisers were in the next ring of the formation, and the destroyers were on the perimeter. In all wartime operations the ships were in blackout condition, which made visual contact very difficult, and the distance between ships was something like one thousand yards. To keep track of the position of neighboring ships, there was a radar scope on the bridge.

To add to the danger of the operations, it was generally necessary when operating in a war zone to zigzag. There were plans for zigzagging, usually keyed to the odd and even hours. If a signal came to commence zigzagging at a certain time, the officer of the deck automatically went to the course shown on the plan for that hour. If a ship did not commence zigzagging or went to the wrong course, it posed an immediate hazard to the other ships in the formation. That is apparently what happened to the *Wichita*.

At 0135 hours the forward lookout reported to the officer of the deck on the *Cabot* that one of the vessels in the formation was off course and coming straight toward the *Cabot*. The officer of the deck immediately gave the order for all engines to back full and ordered the rudder to hard right full. The *Wichita* cut across the *Cabot's* bow with only six feet of clearance. I was asleep in my bunk, which was right off the forecastle. If the *Wichita* had hit the forecastle, I would probably have been crushed in the collision. If the *Wichita* had hit the *Cabot* midships—the worst case scenario—it would probably have sliced the *Cabot* in two.

Once, when I was standing junior officer of the watch with Lt. John Wheeler, we made a similar mistake. It was the midwatch under blackout conditions when the order came to commence zigzagging. Although it was the odd hour, we both looked at the plan for the even hour. Fortunately we realized our mistake and quickly corrected the error. I recall looking through the binoculars and seeing the battleship *Iowa* dead ahead. It seemed to fill the entire horizon; we were headed straight for it. I said to Lieutenant Wheeler in as calm a voice as I could muster, "You'd better look out for the *Iowa*." We did.

Once when I was on the forecastle, one of our major battleships was anchored next to us in the harbor. It had suffered a collision with another ship, and its bow was pushed back a considerable distance. An old mustang on the *Cabot* looked at the damaged battleship and observed, "We're spreading the regulars too thin."

Another hazard was during flight quarters. The bridge on the *Cabot* (and on the two escort carriers, or CVEs, on which I subsequently served) was a rather vulnerable-looking structure that gave the impression of being an afterthought in the design of the ship. The pilots who served on the aircraft carriers on which I served were well trained and skilled. Occasionally, however, there would be accidents because the returning plane's landing hook did not catch the restraining wires on the flight deck. That generally resulted in the plane crashing into a barrier that kept the aircraft from plowing into any planes on the forward flight deck. On several occasions when I was on watch standing on the open bridge, a plane would crash, and on one occasion it seemed to somersault into the barrier, passing very close to where I was standing watch.

I never had any personal contact with Captain Schoeffel, except when he was on the bridge and I was standing junior officer of the watch. He was a good captain, and I had great confidence in his skill. When the *Cabot* was first assigned to a task force, our code name was "Mohawk." It became customary for Captain Schoeffel to end his announcements to the crew with, "Mohawks, up and at 'em!" This inspired an artist on board to paint a picture on a steel plate showing an Indian, tomahawk in hand, stomping on a tattered Japanese flag. This emblem was attached to the bridge of the ship, and when Japanese airplanes and ships were reported destroyed, the appropriate symbols were painted beneath and beside it.

Of all of the engagements in which the *Cabot* took part, four stand out most vividly. The first of these was the First Battle of the Philippine Sea. This became known as the "turkey shoot" because in the course of the engagement 395 Japanese planes were lost in combat, while the United States lost only 20. The invasion of Guam by the United States was a success. The Japanese fleet endeavored to send in its aircraft from a distance beyond the round-trip potential of our carriers' aircraft, attack our ships, refuel on Guam, and return to the Japanese fleet. Their operation ended in failure.

The Japanese fleet was contacted, but at such a great distance that sending our planes after it was hazardous. It meant the risk of having the planes run out of fuel and having to land after dark. Although our aircraft were able to damage the Japanese fleet, their return to the task force at night ended in confusion. In spite of the danger of submarines the carriers were ordered to turn on their running lights, and aircraft were ordered to land on any of our carriers they might find. Numerous aircraft from other carriers landed on our deck. Since space on the *Cabot* was limited, it became impossible to put them in the hangar deck. The pilot and crew got out, and the plane was pushed overboard to make room for others to land.

One of the *Cabot* squadron's pilots was shot down and survived by remaining in a rubber raft for three days. He said he saw a whale boat approaching and, not knowing whether it was one of ours or Japanese, as it got within hailing distance, he shouted, "Friend or foe?" A voice came back, "What the hell do you care!"

The second most memorable experience on the *Cabot* was the raid on the island of Formosa, which took place October 11–14, 1944. The task force had carried out air strikes on Okinawa and, after completing these, attacked Formosa. The task force was operating within forty miles of Formosa. On the afternoon of October 13 the cruiser USS *Canberra* was hit by a Japanese torpedo and could only make four knots. The *Cabot* was ordered to detach itself from the task force and fly cover over the *Canberra*. Later the same day a torpedo hit the cruiser USS *Houston*, and the USS *Cowpens* was ordered to join the *Cabot* in giving air protection to the two crippled cruisers. As I stood on the flight deck and watched our powerful task force disappear over the horizon, I had a sinking feeling that the *Cabot* was a babe in the woods with Japanese wolves trying to eat us alive.

To minimize attack from Japanese submarines, it was necessary for the two carriers to run in circles around the two cruisers that were towed by two seagoing tugboats making only about four knots. On the *Cabot* we stayed at general quarters almost twenty-four hours a day. On October 16, fighters from the *Cabot* shot down thirty-three Japanese planes, but the Japanese were able to get through and torpedo the *Houston* a second time.

We learned later that Admiral William Halsey had deliberately put the *Cabot* and *Cowpens* in harm's way, hoping to lure the Japanese fleet to attack. The code name for our task group was "Slippery Bait." The Japanese did not take the "bait," but it was primarily on the basis of the performance of the ship and squadrons in this encounter that the *Cabot* earned a Presidential Unit Citation.

The third memorable battle experience was in the Second Battle of the Philippine Sea, also called the Battle of Leyte Gulf. The main objective in this encounter was to stop the Japanese navy's effort to destroy the ships supporting Gen. Douglas MacArthur's amphibious landing on Leyte. This was probably one of the greatest sea battles in history. It involved aircraft carriers, battleships, submarines, cruisers, destroyers, and PT boats. The *Cabot* was part of the Third Fleet, which was guarding the passage through the San Bernardino Straits. The ship was assigned to Task Group 38.2, which included the battleship USS *New Jersey*, Admiral Halsey's flagship. Planes from the *Cabot* were in the group that attacked the Japanese ships as they were making their way through San Bernardino Straits. I had the night watch on the *Cabot* with Lt. John T. Wheeler, officer of the deck. Our position in the task force was next to the *New Jersey*. After the successful attack on the Japanese during the daylight, "night fighters" were sent to report the position of the damaged Japanese ships. The reports of the night fighters were transmitted by TBS (talk between ships) from the USS *Independence* to the *New Jersey*.

Lieutenant Wheeler and I were able to plot the position of the advancing Japanese ships because we could hear the report transmitted by TBS. It was clear to us that the Japanese ships, although damaged, were still advancing toward entrance of the San Bernardino Straits and would be able to enter the Philippine Sea. Before our watch ended, an order came for the task force to turn north and leave the area. Admiral Halsey had discovered that there was a Japanese task force to the north that had aircraft carriers. He mistakenly thought it was the main striking force and determined to meet and destroy it. When he turned the task force and proceeded in a northerly direction, he left the entrance to San Bernardino Straits open. It was what the Japanese hoped he would do. The error on the part of Admiral "Bull" Halsey was referred to afterward as "Bull's run."

The Japanese battleships, cruisers, and destroyers were able to get though San Bernardino Straits into the Philippine Sea and attack the escort carriers in Leyte Gulf. The Japanese played havoc with the small, slow aircraft carriers and their destroyer escorts, several of which were sunk by gunfire from the battleships. Fortunately the Japanese admiral thought the escort carriers were part of a large task force and broke off the engagement and retreated though the San Bernardino Straits before our task force could return to oppose them.

The fourth memorable engagement was almost my last. It took place on November 25, 1944, off the Island of Luzon. Enemy planes were detected approaching the task force, and the ship went to general quarters. This was in the early stage of the use of kamikaze attacks. Kamikaze planes attacked and hit both the *Intrepid* and the *Cabot*.

The first kamikaze hit the *Cabot's* flight deck forward on the portside, causing a fire and extensive damage. The second Japanese plane exploded close on the port quarter only five minutes behind the first hit. It exploded before actually hitting the ship, but it was so close to the ship that the catwalks and gun mounts near the explosion were sheared off the ship and fell into the sea. All the men stationed there were blown overboard and lost. If the plane had hit the ship, I probably would have been a casualty.

I knew the ship was in trouble, but it was difficult to know the extent of the damage. An aircraft carrier was filled with tanks of gasoline and fuel oil as well as magazines stacked with explosives. The fire from a bomb hit could turn the ship into a blazing inferno and a pyrotechnic nightmare. The *Cabot*'s sister ship, the USS *Princeton*, was lost in the Second Battle of the Philippine Sea after being hit by one bomb. The sense of relief I felt at not having been blown up in the two attacks quickly turned to apprehension about what might follow.

My damage-control station was immediately below the hangar deck. I detected the strong smell of gasoline, which seemed to come from the hatch opening to the hangar deck. If planes in the hangar deck had been damaged and gasoline was spreading over the deck above us, we would be in great danger. I ordered the damage-control party under my command to move to another compartment, and we took the two or three fire extinguishers that were handy, opened their valves, and filled our station with as much carbon dioxide as possible.

It was not long before the captain announced over the speaker system that the ship was damaged but that the damage and fires were under control. The hatch above us eventually opened, and wounded crewmen were brought down the ladder to the sick bay. I remember that there was a lot of blood,

Kamikaze airplane hitting the USS Cabot, *November 1944. From J. Ed Hudson,* A History of the USS Cabot (CVL-28): A Fast Carrier in World War II *(n.p.: privately printed, 1986). Reprinted by permission of J. Ed Hudson*

and my damage-control party began to mop it up. Thirty-five men died or were lost by being blown overboard, and seventeen were seriously wounded. My friend Lt. John Wheeler was blown overboard, and an enlisted man, Gerald G. Bennett, QM2C, who frequently stood watch with me, was fatally wounded.

It was ironic that before the ship got under way for this mission, orders had come for me to be detached and sent back to the States to be assigned to other duty. It was normal procedure to rotate officers as they gained experience to newer ships where they would be assigned greater responsibility. It crossed my mind that it would be just my bad luck to be killed before I could be reassigned. When the damaged ship returned to our advanced base, I was detached and transferred to the USS *Intrepid*. Damage to the *Intrepid* was so extensive and serious that it was ordered to the West Coast for repairs.

The trip to San Francisco on the *Intrepid* took approximately thirty days. It was essentially a dreary passage, for I knew no one on the *Intrepid* and there was a generally depressed feeling in the ship's company because so many lives had been lost in the attack. Numerous bullet and shrapnel holes in the bulkheads were a constant reminder of the tragedy.

In San Francisco I was billeted in the St. Francis Hotel until my new orders for a new duty assignment came through. Soon I received orders to report to the precommissioning detail of the USS *Cape Gloucester* (CVE 109) in Tacoma, Washington. I was allowed fourteen days' leave, which I used to return to Florence.

The most memorable years of my wartime experience were spent on the *Cabot*. After I was detached, the *Cabot* was engaged in the later battles in the Pacific and earned the nickname the "Iron Woman" because it was engaged in every big sea air battle in 1944 and 1945 and its airplanes shot down approximately 250 Japanese planes and sank 30 ships. The ship was loaned to Spain in 1967 and subsequently bought by the Spanish government and renamed *Dedalo*. In 1991 it was returned to the U.S. government. The Cabot Association made a noble, unsuccessful effort to preserve the *Cabot*, and the ship was eventually sold to scrap-metal dealers.

7

Peril at War's End on the
USS *Cape Gloucester* and USS *Siboney*

Gloom, impenetrable gloom, settled over me when the time came to leave Florence in January 1945. Billy Royall, my childhood friend and companion, had been killed in Holland in November 1943, and other friends in the army were reported missing in combat. I had a brush with death that convinced me that this was probably my last visit with my family.

My parents drove me to Columbia, which had better rail connections, to catch the train to Chicago and, from there, Seattle, Washington. I got on the Pullman car and took my seat, but as the train pulled out, I walked back to the men's restroom where several men were smoking. I must have appeared to be on the verge of tears because one man in the washroom said, "You look like you need a drink." He pulled out a flask and poured some whiskey into a paper cup and handed it to me. I said, "Thank you" and slugged it down. It helped. The trip took three days and four nights. It seemed that the train went through endless space filled with snow and mountains before finally reaching Seattle. I had plenty of time to brood over the prospects of never coming back home.

When I arrived in Seattle in the middle of the night, January 13, 1945, it was cold. I found my way to the BOQ at the CVE precommissioning school in Bremerton. It was probably the bleakest, most spartan accommodation I occupied during the war and added further to my generally depressed state.

The USS *Cape Gloucester* was named for an action in the South Pacific during World War II. In December 1943 the U.S. Marines landed and took over a corner of the Bismarck Archipelago, thereby effectively cutting the Japanese supply line to its southernmost fortifications in the South Pacific. The area taken by the marines was named Cape Gloucester, hence the name of the new carrier. It was appropriately named because the air squadrons assigned to the ship were all Marine Corps units and most of the air personnel on board were marines.

Of the ship's officers serving on the *Cape Gloucester* (the *Cape*), only two were Annapolis graduates, the captain and the executive officer. The rest of us were reservists. It was a new ship almost completely manned by "feather merchants." The CVEs were tanker hulls converted into aircraft carriers. They could only make sixteen knots and therefore could not operate with the fast carrier task forces that were in the forefront of the offensive against the Japanese. It became obvious to us that the *Cape*, because of the U.S. Marine air squadrons and personnel attached to it, was designed for close air support for the invasion of Japan. This was not a cheering thought.

The *Cape*'s captain, John W. Harris, was a 1921 graduate of the U.S. Naval Academy. He was competent, but even for a ship's captain he seemed distant from the officers he commanded. At times he appeared unnecessarily cautious and protective of the ship. His junior officers, in their callous manner, nicknamed him "Shaky Harris."

The executive officer, Cdr. J. W. Gannon, was a 1931 graduate of Annapolis. Amiable, friendly, and approachable, he was, by way of contrast with the captain, universally liked by the officers of the ship.

My berth on the *Cape* was on the main deck almost immediately off a passageway that opened onto the hangar deck. I was the assistant first lieutenant. My boss, Lt. Cdr. R. C. Weymouth, the first lieutenant, had fifteen years in the merchant marines and a master's license. I found him easy to get along with and a highly competent naval officer with a superb knowledge of seamanship and shiphandling.

Two of the officers assigned to the *Cape* with whom I formed lasting friendships were Lt. Cdr. Francis "Frank" Shackelford and Lt. Charles "Charlie" Dodsley Walker. Frank was in the communications division, and Charlie was, I believe, attached to the chaplain's office. In civilian life Frank was an attorney and a graduate of Harvard Law School. It was primarily my talks with him that persuaded me to apply to Harvard Law School when I was put on inactive duty. President Truman appointed him undersecretary of the army after the war.

Charlie Walker was a musician. He played the organ, directed the orchestra he organized on board the ship, and was a generally delightful companion. Most important of all, Charlie had an automobile while the *Cape* was in the Tacoma-Seattle area and could provide transportation when we wanted to go out for dinner or engage in other recreational activities.

When the ship was in San Diego, we went to La Jolla, and Charlie volunteered to play the piano for the crowd in the bar. He was so popular that I thought we would never get back to the ship.

The *Cape* left for Pearl Harbor and arrived there on May 30. There was time for training and for shore leave before we joined the main fleet. The *Cape* left Pearl Harbor on June 14 and covered approximately five thousand miles of ocean to get to the combat area. The ship anchored in San Pedro Bay on the island of Leyte in the Philippines on June 29. On July 1, 1945, we left for the East China Sea, where the *Cape* was ordered to provide air cover for minesweeping operations. The war was still going on, and our position put us between the island of Formosa and the Japanese mainland, so there was good reason to believe that the *Cape* would be a target for the kamikazes.

Our air group shot down five or six Japanese planes and we were constantly at general quarters, but no serious attacks occurred in the East China Sea. The ship anchored in Buckner Bay, Okinawa, just at the end of that campaign, and there was a constant threat of attack. The USS *Pennsylvania*, anchored a couple of thousand yards from the *Cape,* was hit by an aerial torpedo. It suffered some damage, and ten or twelve men were killed.

Lieutenant Zeigler (right) *and officers on flight deck of the USS* Cape Gloucester, *1945. Collection of the author*

While we were anchored in Buckner Bay, a group of us took a jeep and toured one of the battle sites. It was a horrifying spectacle. There were unburied bodies decaying over the battle-scarred fields, and two recently killed Japanese soldiers lay beside the road.

I received a promotion to the rank of lieutenant on August 1, 1945. On August 15, 1945, the message came over the loudspeaker that the Japanese had surrendered. All hands assembled on the flight deck for the formal announcement, and there was general jubilation. Other tasks and dangers lay ahead however.

As a precautionary measure the *Cape* was ordered to fly air cover over the mine craft that were sweeping the East China Sea. Violent storms riled up the sea and produced waves sometimes reaching thirty feet high. This constituted an extra hazard for the *Cape* because when launching aircraft, the ship had to turn into the wind and plow through the large waves. An added danger was the fact that much of the forward ventilation system had openings on the forecastle. In heavy seas it was necessary to cover these openings with steel plates. The damage-control watch was required to send a working party to the forecastle to accomplish this before the ship turned into the wind.

I was in my room between officer of the deck watches reading *The Education of Henry Adams.* It was just before lunch. Since I was standing officer of the deck watches, I was not part of the damage-control watch routine, but I knew the duty of the damage-control watch to secure the forward ventilation intakes. My roommates asked if I would join them in going to the aft wardroom. I was preparing to do so when I felt the ship begin its turn into the wind to launch aircraft.

Our cabin was on the forward ventilation system, and I realized from the air still flowing from the system that the covers had not been placed over the openings on the forecastle. I told my roommates to go ahead, but I would go to the forecastle to see why the ventilation covers were not in place.

When I got to the forecastle, I found a damage-control working party of five men who were leisurely preparing to secure the covers over the openings to the ventilation system. The ship was well into its turn into the wind, and I urged the men to "bear a hand" (make haste) in getting the covers in place.

I felt the ship's bow drop as it entered the trough in front of a large wave. I had just bought a new pair of shoes, and it occurred to me that some water would inevitably come over the forecastle as the ship entered the oncoming wave, so I stepped up on a coil of hose to preserve my new shoes.

Suddenly I found myself in water up to my waist. When I recovered from the shock, I realized that the next pitch downward of the bow would probably submerge me completely and I would be in danger of being swept overboard in a rough sea with little chance of being rescued. There was a round ventilation duct over my head, so I reached up and locked my arms around it just as I felt the ship sink deep into a trough before the next wave.

This time I was completely submerged, and I did not know how long it would be before the ship would rise out of the wave. Fortunately there was a pocket of air immediately over my head in the space between the ventilation duct and the deck above. I pulled up and gasped the air trapped in that space. As the ship rose from the wave, a new hazard presented itself.

When we were in port the last time, crates of Irish potatoes had been bought, and because space was limited, the extra ones had been lashed to the deck on the forecastle. The lines securing them were not strong enough to resist the pressure of the water that came over the forecastle, and they broke. As the bow rose clear of the wave, the crates of potatoes came crashing down the forecastle deck on top of me. I battled the crates and discovered that mixed with them were several men who were members of the working party that had been on the forecastle. They helped me open a watertight door leading to a ladder down to the main deck. Together, standing in waist-deep water, we managed to get the watertight door open and, with several crates of Irish potatoes and a flood of water, threw ourselves down the ladder and to safety.

Although we had been saved, a considerable amount of flooding occurred because the ventilation system had not been secured and because the watertight door we had opened to escape from the forecastle had allowed a great amount of water to flood into the main deck. We were thankful to have escaped, and when we began counting heads, we realized that one member of the working party was missing. He had been washed up to the flight deck by the wave and had been able to clutch the catwalk and save himself.

I was in my room, still dripping wet, when a messenger sent by Captain Harris arrived. He stated that the captain had ordered me to be put "under hack." This meant that I was to be disciplined in some way and was confined to my cabin, even for meals, which would be brought to me. I knew that I had done nothing wrong since I was not part of the damage-control watch and had no responsibility for what had happened on the forecastle. I was tempted to say, "Good, I need a rest and I have plenty of books to read," but of course I simply said, "Thank you," and the messenger left.

The first lieutenant came to my room, and I told him why I had been on the forecastle. He said that he would go and talk with the captain on my behalf. In a couple of hours he returned to my room and said the captain apologized and that I was no longer under hack. Although I saw the captain many times after that, he never apologized to me personally.

Later, when we were moored to a buoy in the harbor of Nagasaki, Japan, another incident took place. The *Cape* was the first U.S. ship to go into Nagasaki after the Japanese had surrendered about two weeks earlier. Our orders were to take into American custody Allied prisoners of war who had been imprisoned in Japan. Of course we were very curious to see what damage the atomic bomb had done, but the area was so contaminated that we were allowed to go only to a restricted area on shore. It was obvious from the parts of the city visible from the ship that terrible devastation had occurred. It is estimated that over forty thousand people died in the explosion.

Because a typhoon loomed on the horizon, it was decided that the *Cape* would be moored to a buoy, stern first, so that if it became necessary to get under way, it would not be necessary to turn the ship around. The typhoon hit us with winds in excess of 110 miles per hour. I had the watch from 1600 to 2000 hours, the time that it seemed the worst of the winds would occur. Three steel cables led from the *Cape's* stern to the buoy and were believed strong enough to withstand the wind's force. The difficulty was that the wind was coming from the direction of the stern of the ship, putting tremendous stress on the three cables.

It was determined in a conference with the first lieutenant that if the stern cables broke, the ship would be allowed to swing around, the engine room would be ready to steam ahead, and when the ship completed its swing and was headed toward the buoy, the ship would move up to the buoy and the anchor would be dropped. It sounded like a simple maneuver, but it had to be performed in the howling wind and rain, which hit everyone's face with such force that it felt as though faces were being punctured by pins.

I had been on duty with the captain for a short time that afternoon when the fantail watch reported that the first stern cable had broken. Anxiety increased, and Captain Harris constantly asked me if I had contact with the forecastle through sound-powered phones manned by the enlisted man on watch with us. At about 1730 hours the fantail watch reported that the second stern cable had parted. It seemed inevitable that the last cable would break at any moment.

Under our system of standing watch, I was due to be relieved by another officer so that I could go to the wardroom and eat supper before returning to the bridge to complete the watch. The last cable had not parted when I was relieved to go to supper. Relieved was a good word to describe my state of mind, for I did not relish being the officer of the deck when the last line broke. I confess that I ate a leisurely supper, had a cup of coffee, and returned to the bridge confident that the last line had parted and the crisis was over. Fate was not so kind.

When I returned to the bridge, nothing had changed. I went though the usual procedure for relieving the officer of the deck, and I had "the con." Captain Harris was on the bridge and was in a highly agitated frame of mind, constantly going from one side of the bridge to the other. I had not assumed the con for more than thirty minutes when the fantail lookout reported that the last cable had parted. The ship began to swing around in the harbor.

The enlisted man with the sound-powered phone was fully clothed with a pullover weatherproof top. This meant that the line leading to the headset was run under the top part of his rain gear. The captain was running back and forth on the open bridge to see what was happening as the ship's swing accelerated. He shouted orders to me, and I had to repeat them to the demoralized enlisted man. I followed Captain Harris back and forth so that I could hear his orders and transmit them to the forecastle. It was not easy to hear, and as the critical moment drew near, the enlisted man seemed unable to react fast enough to suit the captain, who shouted at me, "Take those phones yourself!" I grabbed the headset and put it on my head, but there was no time to free the line from beneath his pullover top. The two of us were like Siamese twins joined face to face. When the captain rushed from one side of the bridge to the other, the two of us raced, like dancing partners doing sidesteps, after him. The maneuver was completed with precision; the ship steamed up to the buoy, the anchor was dropped, and the

Cartoon of the typhoon that hit the USS Cape Gloucester, *1945. Left to right: Capt. John W. Harris, Lieutenant Zeigler, and an unknown enlisted man. Collection of the author*

ship weathered the typhoon. A British destroyer moored below the *Cape* sent us a message: "Well done!"

The war was over, but getting out of active duty was a different problem. I knew I would probably be among the last servicemen to receive consideration for an early discharge. I was only twenty-four, unmarried, and had not left any job to join the navy.

Then there was good news. The *Cape* was ordered back to San Diego. On the journey back to the States I was startled one morning when a messenger came to my room and said Captain Harris would like to see me on the bridge. I was still smarting from his unjustified action in putting me under hack following the forecastle incident, and I was apprehensive about what new grievance he might have against me. I dutifully went to the bridge, where Harris was seated in the captain's chair on the port side of the bridge. I saluted and said I understood that he wanted to see me. He said that there was a directive from the navy ordering all commanding officers to try to get experienced officers to agree to remain on active duty. He would recommend me for such duty, he said, if I agreed to serve three more years. As an incentive, Harris stated that I would get a "spot" promotion to the rank of lieutenant commander.

I thanked the captain for his consideration, but I had now completed over three and half years in the navy, most of it on shipboard, and I was anxious to get on with my life as a civilian. He expressed disappointment. I saluted, left the bridge, and never conversed with him after that. It gave me satisfaction to refuse his offer.

On the return voyage Charlie Walker, Frank Shackelford, and I decided to promote the publication of the story of the *Cape*. We were fortunate in having many photographs, and one of the enlisted men in the R Division, Charles W. Sisler, was a gifted cartoonist. He had drawn many hilarious sketches of happenings on the ship. We were able to get enough subscriptions for the publication. I wrote most of the text, and Charlie, when the *Cape* reached San Diego, arranged for its publication.

Bad news awaited me. I learned I was to be detached and ordered to further duty. The *Cape* reached San Diego on November 10, 1945, and I was ordered to report to the commandant of the Twelfth Naval District in San Francisco for my new assignment. The men in the R Division made me an old-fashioned sea chest; in the bottom of it Sisler drew a cartoon of my profile, and all the men in the division signed their names, wishing me good luck in my new ship. A gift of gold could not have pleased me more.

On reaching San Diego, I made my way to San Francisco. My orders designated me first lieutenant on the USS *Siboney* (CVE 112), a sister ship of the *Cape*. The *Siboney* was named for an amphibious landing made by the

U.S. Marines in Cuba during the Spanish-American War. I did not reach the *Siboney* until November 26 because it was in Saipan and I had to be flown from San Francisco to Hawaii and from there to Saipan. When I boarded the *Siboney*, I was in charge of the entire department administered by the first lieutenant. In every physical detail the *Siboney* was identical to the *Cape*. It seemed that I was in a bad dream. I knew all of the surroundings, but every human face was different. I did have different accommodations on the *Siboney*, however. I shared a stateroom with the gunnery officer, Bernard Cline, a likable young man from Virginia.

The *Siboney's* commanding officer, Capt. S. C. Ring, was one of the most approachable and amiable of the commanding officers I had served under. Captain Ring, however, insisted that all of the punctilios and protocols of naval conduct be observed. One of my fellow officers who stood officer of the deck under way was standing watch while Ring was seated in the captain's chair on the bridge. The officer issued an order to the enlisted helmsman and addressed him by his first name. Ring wheeled around and asked what he had just said. The officer of the deck replied that he had issued an order to the helmsman. "Oh," the captain said, "I thought I heard you call him by his first name." The officer of the deck replied, "I did, sir." Captain Ring exploded: "I'll have none of that hoop-de-doop on my bridge! You call enlisted men by their last names." The chastened officer replied, "Yes, sir."

The excitement and danger of wartime cruising were gone. We still conducted flight operations, but there were no reports of enemy planes shot down or ships sunk and the chilling excitement of being under attack was gone. I stood officer of the deck under way and ran the first lieutenant's office. The ship was terribly untidy since there had been no first lieutenant for several months, so I undertook to put things in better order. I got along well with the executive officer, who gave me free rein in doing so.

The most memorable event of the duty on the *Siboney* was a visit to Hong Kong, China. The *Siboney* was the first U.S. ship to visit Hong Kong since the Japanese surrender. We entered the Pearl River and moored to a buoy in the harbor opposite the city. I was in my office when a messenger came and said the officer of the deck would like me to come up to the quarterdeck, the area where the port watch was stood, because there was a group of women who wanted to see me.

When I arrived at the quarterdeck, there were about twenty Chinese women vying with one another for the right to receive and remove the ship's garbage. Arrangements for garbage disposal in port and at sea came under the jurisdiction of the first lieutenant. Some of the women had pre–World War II letters from U.S. ships verifying that Mrs. Wong or Tong or whoever, had performed the duty of removing garbage from the ship in an exemplary fashion. I could hardly read the testimonials because the women raised such a competitive clamor.

It took me some time to realize that our garbage was like gold to these poor women and their families, so I made a decision. Every afternoon at 1530 hours the ship's garbage would be lowered in buckets from the hangar deck. Anyone interested could come and get a share.

On the first day the garbage was lowered in large metal trash cans. After it had been lowered, I went to the hangar deck to see why it was causing so much commotion. When I got there, I saw approximately fifty sampans beside our ship. (A sampan is a small boat.) They were armed with boat hooks to grab the line attached to the garbage cans to divert one to their sampan. It was a horrifying spectacle for a spoiled American to watch, realizing the poverty that drove these poor people to fight over our garbage. One day a particularly distressing incident occurred. Since many of these families lived on their sampans, there were small children on board participating in the struggle. I saw one toddler fall overboard while his parents were flailing at the line to get the garbage can. The child's parents simply used the boat hook to retrieve the child from the water and continued to struggle along with the assembled fleet of sampans.

On my first shore leave I went with a group of officers to visit Hong Kong. When our liberty boat reached a dock in the city, we walked to the street and were confronted with a multitude of Chinese trying to get us to employ them and their rickshaws. They were so insistent and aggressive that we found it difficult to get past them. Suddenly the police appeared to make them give way. The policemen were Sikhs, magnificent men, six feet tall, wearing turbans. They wielded their wooden billies indiscriminately and with ferocity to make the rickshaw drivers stop. Heads were being wounded and blood splattered among those unfortunate enough to be within arms' reach of the Sikhs. I begged the one closest to me to stop, quickly engaged a rickshaw, and was driven off by a man who spoke no English and went in a direction of his choosing. Fortunately he took me to an English hotel.

I enjoyed shopping in Hong Kong and found a shop where I could barter American cigarettes for beautiful china and ivory carvings. I was turned off by the markets where dried beetles were sold like jelly beans, dogs and snakes were sold for eating, and sanitation seemed to be an unknown virtue. Particularly disturbing were the night scenes in Hong Kong. We would come upon as many as fifty children huddled together on the streets at night covering themselves with croaker sacks or some other remnants of cloth. These children were orphans with no place to go at night and were, therefore, forced to sleep on the streets. I longed to do something for them but felt helpless.

The *Siboney* made a leisurely voyage back to the States. Along the way it stopped in Manila in the Philippines, and I had an opportunity to go into the city and view the extensive damage it had suffered when the Americans recaptured it. We finally arrived in San Diego on February 10, 1946.

My sister, Leah, and her family had moved to Los Angeles, California, and upon reaching San Diego, I made contact with her. She had two small children, I discovered, and her husband, Frank Johnson, was working for Lockheed at a plant near Burbank. They had just bought a house and were moving in. I spent a weekend with them before returning to the ship.

I had only been back several days when the executive officer came to my room and told me that my brother-in-law had been in an airplane accident and was seriously injured. I immediately applied for emergency leave to be with my sister.

Frank had been flying in an airplane he had designed when it crashed. Both he and the pilot escaped but were seriously injured. My mother persuaded her African American servant, Rosa McCoy, to go to California to help my sister. Rosa was a kind, dear person and a wonderful help to my sister.

On February 23, 1946, I was ordered to report to the officer separation center in Charleston, South Carolina. I took the train from San Diego to Charleston with a brief stopover in New Orleans. En route I caught influenza, and when I arrived in Charleston at 0600 on February 28, 1946, I knew I was sick. I got a taxi and went to the Charleston Naval Base. I inquired at the main gate if I could be taken to the hospital, but the guard at the gate directed me to a first-aid station.

At that early hour there was no one but a pharmacist mate on duty. He said that the duty doctor would not be in until 0800 but allowed me to lie down on one of the beds in the first-aid station. When the duty officer arrived at approximately 0900, he examined me and said I had influenza and that he was sending me to the base hospital. I was placed in a room with one other officer who was waiting to have a hernia operation. I felt very ill for the first three days and slept most of the time. There was a daily check in the morning to see if all the patients were in their hospital beds. My roommate would wait until the morning check was completed, then dress and spend the day in Charleston.

Several days after I was hospitalized, following the morning check and my roommate's departure for the city, a medical officer in a captain's uniform awakened me. Several other officers in the medical corps accompanied him. The captain asked that I sit on the side of the bed and drop my pajama pants. I thought this unusual, but a mere lieutenant doesn't argue with a captain. He then began to probe my groin with his finger, and it suddenly dawned on me that he thought that I was the officer who needed a hernia operation. "Sir," I said, "I think you are making a terrible mistake." The captain removed his hand, gave me a startled look, and said, "What do you mean?" I told him I was hospitalized with influenza and that the patient in the unoccupied bed was the one he was looking for. He said, "Damn!" then turned abruptly and left the room followed by the other officers.

I was placed on inactive duty with the Naval Reserve and discharged from the naval hospital on March 5, 1946. I took the train from Charleston to Florence, where I was met by my mother, father, and aunt. The war was over. I had survived. I had not shed blood for my country, but I had shed a lot of sweat from work and anxiety.

8

Harvard Law School

I had been home only a short time when I applied for admission to the Harvard Law School. I was entitled to GI bill benefits so financing my law school education was no problem. I was put on a waiting list, but in May 1946 I received a telegram stating that I would be admitted in June. I was given temporary quarters in one of the old dormitories on Harvard Yard when I arrived. The law school had only one medium-sized dormitory for law students, and we were told that when Roscoe Pound was dean he opposed the building of dormitories on the grounds that students would work harder if they were dispersed to private rooming houses and garrets, away from the social distractions that dormitory life encouraged.

In his remarks to the entering class of students at Harvard Law School in June 1946, Dean Erwin N. Griswold said that if it were not for the small percentage of students who made As and Bs, it would not be worth the time and expense necessary to operate the law school. In effect the vast number of students who made Cs (70 to 80 percent) were merely tolerated. The dean also stated that he was proud of the fact that the students at the law school did not have time to organize a glee club. This caused me, out of sheer perversity, to join the choir at Christ Episcopal Church almost immediately.

I attended Sunday services at Christ Episcopal Church on Cambridge Commons, and after one service I asked the Reverend Gardiner Day if he knew where I might find a room. A parishioner had told him that her family would be willing to take in a student who needed a room, and he gave me the name of the Misses Emery on Concord Avenue. It was a fortunate suggestion. The following day I went to 17 Concord Avenue, and an elderly lady opened the door. She said that her daughters were not at home but invited me in. I sat and talked with her for about ten minutes. She was a lively conversationalist and expressed sympathy for John L. Lewis, president of the United Mine Workers of America, and the plight of the poor coal miners who were on strike. She told me to come back the next day when her daughters would be at home. When I returned, I met Nan, Margaret, and Violet Emery, all charming middle-aged ladies. They told me that the family moved up to Hopkinton, New Hampshire, for the summer and would be happy to rent me a room while they were gone. In fact they turned the entire house over to me while they were out of town. I formed a close friendship with the Emery family while I was at Harvard and was particularly close to Miss Nan Emery, who had been a secretary to the housemaster of Lowell House at Harvard.

The Emery house was a compact, colonial-style building. I set up my typewriter in the living room and fixed my own spartan breakfast. When I was preparing to leave at the end of the summer, Miss Violet Emery said she was so glad that I had used "the Cornwallis chair" in the living room when I was sitting at my typewriter. I asked why it was so called, and she said that one of her ancestors had received it after the British surrendered at Yorktown.

I knew that the arrangement with the Emerys would have to terminate in the fall, so I applied for a room in the Episcopal Theological Seminary. There was a tradition that some law students took rooms in the seminary's Winthrop Hall. William Alexander Percy, who graduated from Sewanee in the early 1900s, had rooms there when he attended Harvard Law School. I was successful in getting a room, and one of my classmates with whom I had become friendly, William "Bill" Conant Brewer, asked if he could become my roommate at the seminary. We had a room together there for the following year.

I was fortunate in discovering that a former Florentine, Covington Hardee, was living in Cambridge. He had married the daughter of a former professor at the law school, and I feel sure he was instrumental in my being proposed for membership in the Lincoln's Inn Society. The society was incorporated in 1908 and is the oldest eating club at Harvard Law School. In 1946 it had approximately three hundred members. In 1942 the society sold its building and was in the process of locating a new one. In the first months of the summer, society members had their meals in the Hasty Pudding Club before we moved into the society's new building at 44 Follen Street. Lunch and dinner were served at the club.

Harvard Law School is notorious for placing an enormous amount of pressure on its students. I was constantly amazed by my fellow students, who had what I called "steel-trap minds." When examination time drew near, I found myself looking around the classroom trying to figure out who was dumber than me. Usually I came to the unhappy conclusion that I was at the bottom of the class.

It seemed a calculated policy of the law school to inculcate a sense of humility in most of us. My recollection is that almost 90 percent of the students in my class had been Phi Beta Kappa in college, and it was a given that most of them would have to be satisfied with C grades. The school stated that after our first examination only 10.7 percent had failed and conceded that ours was a superior class of students. On the train going home for a vacation immediately following one of the examination periods, I was in a coach with a fellow law student who was suffering from postexamination shock. He confided in me how disconcerted he was by the idea of not doing well in law school. He said, "I got out my college annual just to convince myself that I really wasn't as dumb as they are convincing me I am."

One of the advantages of going to Harvard Law School was its faculty. The faculty gave a student the opportunity to come in contact with masters in their chosen disciplines and to experience, firsthand, how such minds worked. I recently received a survey questionnaire from the law school in which I was supposed to name the three professors who had made the greatest impression on me. I had no difficulty in stating that Thomas Reed Powell, who taught Constitutional Law, Austin Wakeman Scott, who taught Trusts, and Karl Nickerson Llewellyn, who taught Jurisprudence were my favorites.

Thomas Reed Powell came the closest to being like the scholarly curmudgeons who made Harvard Law School famous. I was fortunate to take his constitutional law course and recall on one occasion he stopped lecturing, picked up the seating chart that showed the assigned seats of students, and said, "Mr. Jones?" Jones was seated in the front row and raised his hand and replied, "Yes, sir." Powell looked at him severely and asked, "Are you chewing gum?" Jones replied that he was. Powell then said, "Would you please stop? That bovine rolling of the jaws offends me." Jones dutifully removed the gum.

I recall Powell telling us about a faculty meeting at the beginning of our country's entrance into World War II. The faculty was gathered in a meeting room that adjoined the principal reading room of the library in Langdell Hall. After Pearl Harbor, he said, the question was whether to give the law students in their senior year who were being called into the armed forces their diplomas without taking a final examination or to withhold granting a degree until the departing seniors returned, if they survived, to complete their courses after the war was over. Apparently Justice Felix Frankfurter was present, and Powell said, "You know how Felix is—everything becomes a serious moral question. 'Shall we compromise the high standards of the school by giving diplomas without requiring final examinations? Or, shall we be so hard hearted as to deny these brave young men who might be killed in battle the satisfaction of knowing they had completed their law school studies?'" Powell said that he got bored and walked out into the reading room and looked about the room where the students were reading. He said, "And there they were. Feet on the desks, chewing gum, no waistcoats on. I wouldn't be intimately associated with a one of them." He never told us how the question was decided, and he apparently had little interest in its resolution.

During one of his lectures Powell stated that he had taught constitutional law to five justices of the U.S. Supreme Court. He said that he then went back to see what grades he had given them. "I found that I had not given any of them a grade higher than a C." He paused and added, "I have seen nothing since then to change that opinion."

I nearly allowed myself to get into trouble with Powell. In the 1948 presidential election a classmate of mine, Jim Bell, suggested I go with him and ask Powell to be honorary chairman of a committee to draft Justice Douglas as the Democratic Party's nominee for the presidency. He argued that President Truman did not have a chance of being elected. I did not have any strong political opinions, but I agreed to approach Powell after one of his classes. Jim started off by telling Powell that he did not believe that President Truman had a chance of being elected and that the Democratic Party needed a strong candidate. He ended his speech by stating, "Since you taught constitutional law to Mr. Justice Douglas, we thought you would be an ideal person to serve as honorary chairman of the committee to draft him as the nominee." There was a profound silence for a minute. Then Powell turned on us and said, "You want me to vote for that unreliable son of a bitch?" Jim and I said, "No, sir!" several times as we stumbled backward out of the classroom. I made a C on constitutional law, but apparently I was in fairly good company.

Austin Wakeman Scott was not so much the scholarly curmudgeon as he was the scolding headmaster. When a student was asked to recite the facts of a case under discussion, Scott would often say, "I know your type. You like to wallow in the facts." He would frequently engage in a verbal sparring match with a student and showed little mercy when demonstrating how foolish the student's statements were. On one occasion a rattled student balked and said, "You can't run over me slipshod like this, sir." Scott never hesitated and replied, "Roughshod, yes; slipshod never!" He occasionally said that before he studied law he was engaged in intellectual activity.

I took a course in jurisprudence under Karl Nickerson Llewellyn, a visiting professor at Harvard. I liked him and his course because he had a more speculative mind than the other steel-trap professors. At any rate I enjoyed his lectures, and it was the only class in which I made an A. Llewellyn had a wonderful sense of humor. He referred to teachers of jurisprudence as "jurisprudes."

By the time I got to Harvard, Dean Roscoe Pound had retired, but he was still to be seen occasionally on the campus. All of the law students were divided into groups for moot court arguments that were held throughout the year. I was in the Powell Club, named after Thomas Reed Powell, and in my first year I argued a case before a three-judge panel that included Dean Pound. We won the case, and I thought of hearing his lecture at Sewanee, "The Recrudescence of Absolutism." I later enjoyed reading Justice Holmes's comment on Pound: "His vast learning has seemed to me perhaps to prevent any great poignancy of thought. He has not the sting of genius, but he seems to me big and has a great and impressive grasp. The number of things that chap knows drives me silly." Perhaps he just enjoyed being a jurisprude.

One of the courses in which I did poorest was Labor Law, taught by Archibald Cox. It is odd that I spent a great deal of time in later life dealing with labor law cases, but coming from a rural southern background, I was completely at sea with ideas and labor disputes I had never thought about. Cox was a very nervous lecturer. He would pace up and down the podium and occasionally step up on the desk and sit down cross-legged and weave back and forth like an overheated polar bear. I found his lectures very difficult and his performances strange.

I really felt better about him after the "Saturday night massacre," when he and Elliot Richardson defied President Richard Nixon. It was the type of courageous conduct that makes me proud to be a member of the legal profession. I had known Elliot Richardson through Covington Hardee, and he frequently came to Lincoln's Inn, where I had the pleasure of dining with him. I earned his scorn my last year at law school however. I had determined that the face of the building that the society had bought on Follen Street needed sprucing up. I enlisted some fellow members of the club, notably Billy Stewart and Frank Hamilton, to help me make a large version of the society's coat of arms to be fixed above the entrance of the building. Shortly after it had been installed, I had lunch with Elliot at the club and asked him what he thought of our efforts. He replied with cool disdain, "It might look very well over the door of some midwestern fraternity house, but it is not appropriate for Lincoln's Inn at Harvard." After our class graduated, it was removed.

I was disappointed when I took the course in evidence law that the class would be taught by a visiting professor from Texas, Charles Tilford McCormick. His name was unfamiliar to me, and I felt somehow cheated that I was not getting one of the law school's regular faculty but instead the dean of the University of Texas School of Law, a man I learned later had written the definitive treatise on the law of evidence. It was the first time I had heard directly about the problems of racial integration in a southern university. I was convinced from what Dean McCormick said that there was no other way for the country to go other than racial integration of schools and colleges.

' I was fortunate in having a class in equity under Zechariah Chafee Jr. He was not a professor with a steel-trap mind, but equity law is not supposed to develop that type of thinking. There is some room in equity law for the milk of human kindness. Chafee gave an avuncular impression when he discussed equity law, and there was always the chance of a literary reference in his discussions. The reading list that he helped author for first year students included Charles Dickens's *Bleak House* and Anthony Trollope's *Orley Farm*. And there was always also a chance of hearing him quote from Gilbert and Sullivan. A combination of a Trollopian and a Savoyard was bound to capture my attention and admiration.

Faculty members were not very kind to each another, particularly if they felt a faculty member was not intellectually on a high enough level. One faculty member said of a colleague that he was not able to think his way out of a paper bag. Another narrowly escaped serious injury when he inadvertently stepped into an open elevator shaft and fell from the second to the first floor. A colleague asked if what he had heard was true, that in such circumstances one's whole life flashed before one. "No," the injured professor replied, "I could think of nothing." His fellow professor condescendingly replied, "Oh, I see the old saying is true."

Bill Brewer tried to interest me in going on skiing trips, and I was tempted to try my luck at this sport. But I noticed that several of the people who went with him came back with broken legs, and this cooled my ardor. I found it difficult enough walking with two functioning legs though snowdrifts and across icy streets to risk having to do so on crutches with a leg in a cast.

I did engage in two sports that gave me the opportunity to break from studying law. In the winter I played squash, and in the summer I rowed on the Charles River. The transition from handball to squash was not too difficult. There was a squash court close to the law school and finding a partner was not difficult. Rowing was an entirely different discipline, and it took me some time to work my way up to handling a single scull.

I thoroughly enjoyed rowing on the Charles River. My routine, when I was able to manage a single scull, was to row approximately a mile upstream to Watertown, where there was an abandoned abattoir. If I decided to row downstream, I went as far as MIT. One incentive to becoming skillful in rowing a single scull was to avoid falling into the Charles River, which at the time was terribly polluted. The only time I accidentally tipped over and fell into the river, I practically "walked on water" to get to shore.

The Lincoln's Inn Society made my days in Cambridge much brighter. The ability to associate with other men of similar tastes and interests, most of whom were veterans, added a personal touch to the frigid impersonality of the law school. I got on well with my fellow members, and they responded by electing me treasurer of the society in 1948. Despite my unpromising beginnings, I felt I mixed well. It was the first office of importance to which I was elected. My chief duty as treasurer was to write checks to pay the expenses of running the organization, and being treasurer made me a member of the board.

Since the building on Follen Street, which had been bought during my first year, was formerly a residence, it was not arranged so that we could make room for a bar. There was a large basement but no access to it except through the kitchen. While I was treasurer, I proposed that we cut a stairwell in one of the front rooms and make a bar in the basement. The society's board of governors voted to allow me $750 to accomplish all of this. We engaged a local carpenter to do the work, and with the help of Billy Stewart, Frank Hamilton, and William A. Geoghegan, we converted the basement into a bar and decorated the walls with murals taken from Gilbert and Sullivan's *Trial by Jury* and Lewis Carroll's *Alice's Adventures in Wonderland*. Many members of Lincoln's Inn were Savoyards, and most had a sense of literary whimsicality, so the new bar and its decorative panels were appreciated. When I returned to Harvard forty-three years later, the panels had been removed. I suppose it was an indication that a more serious-minded generation of law students, whose interest in social and political issues was so intense it did not include whimsy, was now in attendance.

I took the fall term off and went to Chapel Hill in 1947. When I returned to law school in February 1948, I could not find a room in Winthrop Hall, but the Episcopal Theological Seminary eventually allowed a friend and me to move into one of its regular dormitory rooms. This was a building of three stories in which most of the theological students were housed. I was constantly disconcerted by the raucous behavior of the "theologs." On one occasion the theologs managed to get a motorcycle into the building and were riding it up and down the second-floor hall. I stood it as long as I could but finally went upstairs and told them I was just a hard-working law student who needed to concentrate on his studies and would they please be a little less noisy. I was relieved in the fall to be moved back into Winthrop Hall, where such capers were virtually impossible.

My trips into Boston brought great pleasure. Boston seemed more like an overgrown small town in contrast to New York. The latter's multicultural maturity seemed never to have included any time when it was a small town.

Boston's theater was not as exciting as New York's, but I did manage to see the D'Oyly Carte productions of Gilbert and Sullivan when they came to town. One play did impress me. It was called, at that time, *Charleston 1822* but was renamed *Set My People Free.* Written by DuBose Heyward's wife, Dorothy Kuhn Heyward, it involved the Denmark Vesey slave uprising in Charleston. I thought it unfortunate that it did not receive a more favorable reception because I found it to be a very honest portrayal of that tragic moment in South Carolina history.

My friend Ashby Sutherland entered the law school a term behind me. Since his grandmother died, he had no close family to visit in Texas on vacations, so he spent many vacations with us. My mother began to regard Ashby almost as another son. Ashby had a fine mind, and he could be a very entertaining companion when he wished to be.

It was a strange coincidence that my friend and former shipmate on the *Cape Gloucester,* Charles Walker, also appeared at Harvard in the summer of 1946. He was getting his master's degree under the famous organist E. Power Biggs and was also the director of the choir at Christ Church. I sang regularly in the choir while Charlie was directing it and found it a rewarding experience. The Christ Church choir and the choir of the Watertown Methodist Church did a joint concert of Handel's *Messiah,* and the choir did a Bach cantata, *Christ lag in Totesbanden.* The several times that I attended concerts of the Boston Symphony Orchestra was a great boost to my interest in serious music, especially when watching Serge Koussevitzky conduct. So vigorous were his gestures, I found myself sometimes getting apprehensive that he might hurl himself into the orchestra.

There were many other cultural activities in the Cambridge and Boston areas. What appealed to me most was the intellectual ferment that permeated Harvard. I attended a series of lectures by William Ernest Hocking, who taught philosophy at Harvard, which was a great consciousness-raising experience. One of the few times I went to services at Memorial Chapel on the main Harvard campus, I was privileged to hear Reinhold Niebuhr preach. His sermon contained allusions to Lot's wife's becoming a pillar of salt. This event should not be thought of as miraculous by modern Christians, he said, for if you went into the boardroom of most big corporations you would find portraits of former board members—modern versions of the biblical pillar of salt. The intellectual ferment extended even to graffiti writers. Evelyn Waugh's novel *Brideshead Revisited* was popular at the time, as was a restaurant in Harvard Square know as McBrides. In the men's room of McBrides some avid reader with a nautical background wrote over the urinal, "McBrides Head Revisited."

Perhaps the greatest honor I received my last year at the law school was membership in the Choate Club. The Choate Club was a group of about thirty law students who met periodically to have dinner and listen to some distinguished person speak. It kept no records of members or of meetings, and there was no formality when it met, although there was a president or presiding officer of the group. The members assembled, drinks and dinner were served, and after dinner the members sat around smoking cigars (which sometimes made me feel uncomfortable), talking with and listening to an invited speaker. I remember telling my friend Ashby how impressed I was with Massachusetts representative Christian Herter (later secretary of state), who spoke on one occasion. Ashby, who was not a member, rebuked me for being "taken in" by smart-talking Yankees. The whole atmosphere of the Choate Club, however, was one of sophisticated gentility.

Many years after I graduated from the law school, my wife's niece Margaret Stanback, who had just graduated from Radcliffe, came through Florence with a friend, a former Harvard undergraduate who had worked on the student newspaper, the *Harvard Crimson*. They had lunch with us, and during the conversation I enquired about the young man's experience as a reporter on the *Crimson*. He told me with enthusiasm that he had uncovered a secret organization at Harvard Law School—so secret and elitist that it kept no record of membership or minutes of meetings. He exhibited great pride in having exposed this obvious departure from American egalitarianism. I revealed to him that I had been a member of the Choate Club and that I found none of the evils he apparently felt he had exposed. That ended the discussion.

All of the historical places were not as moving, but one had the sense that Cambridge and Harvard were steeped in a reverence for what had happened in the past. In Christ Church a bullet fired by British troops was still lodged in the wall, and in old Memorial Hall the names of Harvard students who had died in the Union army during the Civil War covered the lobby walls. Harvard has steadfastly resisted having a memorial to the alumni who died fighting in the Confederate army.

I attended some dramatic productions in old Memorial Hall and during intermission was standing with some fellow law students in the lobby when one of them, to put me on, said, "Don't you feel uncomfortable looking at all the names of soldiers, some of whom your ancestors may have killed?" I would not take the bait and replied, "No. I think they must have done very well to kill so many. I wish they had killed a few more." It has been my observation that the farther north I went the more southern I became and, conversely, the farther south I went the more northern I became.

Bill Brewer, my former roommate, also took the fall term off in 1947 and traveled to France. There Bill met a young American lady, Ann Wicks, and they fell in love and became engaged. They were married on December 18, 1948, in St. James Episcopal Church in New York City. Bill asked me to be his best man, and I was honored to do so. The account in the *New York Times* of the wedding fancified my name; it appeared as "E. Nicholas Zeigler." It was a very fine wedding in a posh church, and the occasion marked the first time I had worn a morning suit. The reception was held in the Ritz-Carlton Hotel, and since Ann's father was a prominent lawyer in New York, many of his legal colleagues were at the reception. I was seated by one fine-looking, prosperous New York lawyer who asked me what I intended to do after I graduated. I told him I intended to return to a small southern town to practice with members of my family. He was silent for a moment, then said, "There are times when I wish that I had done the same thing."

I graduated from law school in February but did not go to the graduating ceremony that summer, even though the summer before, on the same occasion, Secretary of State George C. Marshall made a speech in which he announced the Marshall Plan.

One should have a warm place in one's heart for an alma mater, but I have never felt that way about Harvard Law School. Dean Griswold and the faculty probably did not intend that there be any emotional feeling about the school, at least among those who had to be satisfied with C averages. I am grateful for the education and intellectual discipline I received there, but I have no emotional ties to Harvard Law School. Gratitude is not a substitute for affection.

9

The Delta and the Law

For many people perhaps the only connection between the study of law and the study of anthropology is that they are both dry fields of endeavor. I was infected by the archaeological bug in my early youth, so it was inevitable that, sooner or later, I would find myself actively engaged in legal matters and archaeology simultaneously. This happened in 1947, when I visited the Peabody Museum while a law school student. The Peabody Museum was a place of endless fascination for me. After making a few preliminary inquiries, I met Philip Phillips, the chief archaeologist for southeastern Indian culture at the museum.

In order to get to Phillips's office, I had to enter the building through the back basement door used by employees. That required my walking through a long, darkened basement crowded with Aztec and Mayan artifacts as well as boxes of bones and preserved animals. It was like the set for a spooky movie. I was captivated by Phillips's charm and learning, so I volunteered to work one afternoon a week during the following year.

Phil Phillips was forty-nine years old in 1949, but he regularly gave me beatings on the squash court. It is not surprising when I reflect on his career as an athlete at Williams College, where he was captain of the track team and excelled at the high hurdles. In 1922 he married Ruth Schoellkopf and entered the Harvard School of Design, from which he graduated with a master's in architecture in 1927. He practiced architecture in Buffalo until 1932, when he returned to Harvard and began taking courses in anthropology. Phillips once told me that when the Depression came he realized that he would not be building the structures he wished to build and therefore turned to anthropology. He became assistant curator of southeastern archaeology for the Peabody Museum in 1937. He was attracted to the Macon Plateau, later the Ocmulgee National Monument, which I had visited in 1936, when it was being excavated by James A. Ford and James B. Griffin. Phillips was well rounded in many disciplines, including literature, art, and politics. He received a doctoral degree from Harvard in 1940.

When I graduated from the law school in January 1949, Phillips asked me to accompany him on a field trip to Mississippi. I hesitated because there was the small matter of taking the bar examination in South Carolina, and it was well known that graduates of Harvard Law School constituted the greatest percentage of South Carolina bar examination failures. But the influence of Phillips was irresistible. While I contemplated with misgivings the pending bar examination in May, I readily accepted his invitation. We agreed that he would pick me up in Florence in a pickup truck furnished by Peabody Museum, and we would drive to Yazoo City, Mississippi.

The expedition was a joint project of the University of Michigan, the American Museum of Natural History, and the Peabody Museum. Its purpose was to establish a chronology for the American Indian civilizations of the lower Yazoo basin. The focus of our expedition was an elaborate ceremonial site about eleven miles west of Yazoo City on an old meander of the Mississippi River known as Lake George. The routine was for us to employ farmhands, who in the late winter and early spring were not employed, to dig stratigraphic pits four feet by four feet. The excavation was done in four-inch layers that were sifted on a large screen installed near the pit, and all of the objects found in each level were put in cloth bags. At the end of every four inches of excavation I was required to sketch the four-foot area in a notebook so there was a record of the general features at that point. This done, another four inches was excavated until we reached the point at which there had been no human occupation. It was necessary for me to become generally familiar with an alidade and other surveying equipment in order to function as Phillips's assistant.

Generally I supervised four or five black men who did the digging and sifting of the excavated dirt. This seems harmless enough, but I was left on the Mississippi Delta with a truck on which was stenciled, on both sides in red paint, "PEABODY MUSEUM / HARVARD UNIVERSITY." My presence excited curiosity among passersby in pickup trucks equipped with rifle racks. Even more sinister was the knowledge that the rifle racks in these trucks carried rifles with telescopic sights. It was a time when Yankee visitors were not welcome in Mississippi. Some never made it back alive.

When these white natives would get out of their trucks and come over to inquire what was going on, I would vehemently tell them that I was a native South Carolinian descended from a multitude of Confederate veterans. My impression was that they did not understand my explanation of stratigraphy and thought we must be searching for buried treasure.

The Mississippians in Yazoo City invited Phil Phillips to speak to one or more service clubs. He charmed the locals so much that two of them volunteered to take us in one of their boats down the Sunflower River to the inaccessible remains of another large pre-Columbian Indian site.

The expedition stayed in Yazoo City for about a month and then moved to Greenville, Mississippi. Near Greenville is the Winterville site, which consists of a spectacular group of ceremonial mounds. The central mound, similar to the one at Lake George, is a truncated pyramid, the top of which provides an almost unbroken view of cotton fields. We stayed in Greenville for a little over a week and did one stratigraphic pit on the Winterville site.

The week preceding Palm Sunday I attended services at the Episcopal Church in Greenville, and after services I went to the cemetery to find the graves of William Alexander Percy and his father, LeRoy Percy. Both had gone to college at Sewanee, and I had read *Lanterns on the Levee* by William Alexander Percy. I found the graves and was emotionally moved by the statue of a knight in armor that William Alexander Percy had placed at the head of his father's grave. The inscription on the monument bears lines from Matthew Arnold's poem "The Last Word":

> They out-talked thee, hissed thee, tore thee?
> . . . .
> Charge once more then and be dumb!
> Let the victors, when they come,
> When the forts of folly fall,
> Find thy body by the wall!

I knew little about the great Mississippi flood of 1927 and the central roles both Percys played in it. The story has many of the elements of Greek tragedy. It is difficult to imagine the plight and suffering of black workers virtually impounded by National Guardsmen on the levee during the 1927 flood. William Alexander Percy wanted them removed, but he was thwarted by his father, LeRoy, who deliberately intervened, preventing their removal in order to keep them as laborers on the cotton plantations. It is equally difficult to imagine floodwaters covering the entire delta, including the area in which we had been working.

I came home by bus, going first through Memphis, Tennessee, to Sewanee. After a brief visit in Sewanee, I returned to Florence and applied myself to the task of studying for the bar examination. There were no cram courses offered in South Carolina then. And at that time those who attended the University of South Carolina Law School were admitted automatically upon graduation, without having to take a bar examination. One of the penalties imposed on those who went out of state to law school was the requirement to take the South Carolina examination.

I did some desultory reading in Uncle Peter's office before I took the examination and found it was a grueling experience that extended over three days. There were only twelve of us taking the examination, which was held in the old Supreme Court room on the ground floor of the state capitol building. Uncle Peter was still in the S.C. Senate, and I shared a hotel room with him throughout the ordeal. In the recesses from the examination I went to visit him in the Senate chamber, little realizing I would later spend six years of my life there.

I passed the examination and was admitted, with eight others, to the bar on June 4, 1949, in the same room in which the examination had been given. The antique oath required us to swear that we would not engage in a duel as either a principal or a second. I have not violated that oath.

When I was on the Mississippi expedition with Phil Phillips, we would frequently eat in cafés, at hot dog stands, and sometimes at restaurants. Most of the time there would be jukeboxes playing popular tunes. I recall one of these songs was "My Alice Blue Gown," but what seemed to be an all-time favorite had the opening lines, "Brush those tears from your eyes and try to realize that . . ." Ruth Phillips worried that I was not spending enough time studying. When I received the news that I passed the bar examination, I sent a telegram to Dr. and Mrs. Phillips: "Brush those tears from your eyes and try to realize that I passed the bar examination."

My one claim to fame as an archaeologist is one sentence in Phillips's report of his survey of Indian sites in the lower Mississippi Valley. The two-volume work, *Archaeological Survey in the Lower Yazoo Basin, Mississippi, 1949–1955*, was published by the Peabody Museum at Harvard in 1970. The third sentence in the preface of the first column states, "This second round of work began in the spring of 1949 when E. N. Zeigler of Florence, S.C., a student at Harvard Law School with unsatisfied yearnings toward archaeology, and I, established ourselves in Yazoo City, Miss., and worked up and down the Yazoo River."

I thoroughly enjoyed the two months of work in Mississippi, but it was my swan song as an archaeologist. Sometimes when my friend Ashby Sutherland was visiting Florence, I would take him to nearby sites where I had found arrowheads and sherds just to see what had happened to the sites. On one of these jaunts, Ashby, famous for his sardonic wit, said, "I don't see why you fool around with this Indian stuff. If they were alive today, you wouldn't have anything to do with them."

10

Young Lawyer

The First Years, 1949–1953

I approached the practice of law with something like missionary zeal. Since September 1938 I had been four years in virtual seclusion at Sewanee; three and a half years on active duty with the U.S. Navy, the greater part of it on shipboard at sea; and three years in the confinement and demanding rigors of Harvard Law School, with a three months' stint at Chapel Hill. I convinced myself that since I had survived the war, I was obligated not only to live life to the fullest but also to accomplish more than normally expected in order to justify my survival. Many of my friends had perished.

When I returned to Florence as a lawyer, Uncle Peter invited me to join the firm he and my aunt, Leah Townsend, had formed in the early 1930s. My first cousin, Daniel "Dan" M. McEachin Jr., Uncle Peter's son, also joined the firm at the same time. In 1951 the firm's name was changed from McEachin and Townsend to McEachin, Townsend, and Zeigler. The office was located in several rooms over the J&J Drug Store on West Evans Street. My uncle and aunt occupied the three rooms facing Evans Street, while Dan and I had space across a hall that divided the front offices from those in the back. I did most of my work in a library on the back side of the building, which had two windows overlooking the roof of the drugstore beneath. A staircase led from Evans Street to the hallway separating the spaces.

I felt myself fortunate to be able to associate with my uncle and aunt. Both had fine reputations—my uncle was one of the best trial lawyers in the state, and my aunt was a thorough and competent lawyer who specialized in title law and equity cases. Uncle Peter was serving his last year in the South Carolina Senate in 1949.

The arrangement I had with my uncle was that I would receive one-third of the fees I brought in, and if I brought in no fees, I would receive nothing. It put pressure on me to start building up a clientele. My aunt was on a salary basis, and I regarded the arrangement between my Uncle Peter and his son as a family matter between them.

I spent as much time as I could in the courtroom observing the trying of cases, particularly those in which my uncle was involved. The courthouse was immediately behind our offices and could be reached by a narrow alley. The county jail was behind the courthouse, and it was necessary, in order to get to the courthouse, to come within earshot of prisoners who called out from the second-story windows begging assistance of passersby.

The ground floor of the next building to the east of the J&J Drug Store was occupied by the Florence Fashion Center, a ladies dress shop. Claude Sexton practiced dentistry in offices above the Fashion Center. Since his office was reached by a staircase that opened onto the alley only about thirty feet from the one on Evans Street that led to our offices, people seeking Sexton mistakenly came up to the library door and asked, "Is this where the tooth dentist is?"

Uncle Peter combined intelligence with emotion in a very skillful way, and no one ever seriously questioned his honesty or intellectual integrity. In some ways he was like my friend Ashby Sutherland in that he could be engaging and charming or he could turn a person off with chilling coolness. It was amazing that he was successful in politics. His wife, Margaret Howard McEachin, Aunt Margaret, said that he was a synthetic politician. He liked hunting and kept bird dogs and read extensively about Civil War history.

There were only two secretaries when I joined the firm, and they divided the work between themselves, one being primarily responsible for Uncle Peter's and Dan's work and the other for Aunt Deda's and my work. There was no air conditioning, and in the summer my work place in the library became almost insufferably hot, chiefly because the two windows in the library opened onto a tar-covered roof that liquefied under the sun's heat. Putting my arms down on papers in those months was hazardous because the perspiration on my hands or arms would frequently cause the papers to stick to me. There was no photocopier, and if multiple copies of documents were needed, it was frequently necessary for them to be typed, retyped, and retyped again to avoid producing carbon copies of diminishing clarity.

The courthouse and the courtroom were not air conditioned either, and it was necessary to keep the large windows facing Irby Street in the courtroom open to get some cooling ventilation. This, of course, admitted the sound of traffic, which sometimes became so loud that proceedings in the courtroom would have to be suspended to allow trucks or buses with defective mufflers to pass. Since the courtroom couldn't be cooled, it was the practice to suspend all courts by the end of May, and no proceedings would be resumed until mid-September.

There were only about thirty lawyers practicing in Florence County, and of these about twenty were trial lawyers. Judge G. Badger Baker was the resident judge of the court of general sessions and of the court of common pleas in the Twelfth Judicial Circuit, which included Florence, Marion, Georgetown, and Horry counties. There was a "county court," the civil court of Florence, which had lesser jurisdictional authority than the court of common pleas. Judge R. W. Sharkey was the judge of that court when I returned to Florence.

The South to which I returned was still racially segregated. The law firm's offices had no separate waiting room for white clients. They were provided seating on several wooden chairs and a large sofa upholstered with some sort of synthetic leather in the room occupied by the secretaries. These constituted the "white waiting room." The black clients sat in the hall and were provided with a series of old theater seats that had been acquired by my uncle when one of the local movie houses was renovated.

Uncle Peter and Aunt Deda had a fairly large following among the black citizens of Florence, chiefly because they had the reputation for being as zealous in preserving and advancing the interests of their black clients as they were of their white clients. Aunt Deda was particularly respected and almost revered by black clients of the firm. On one occasion she represented some black clients in Georgetown County who wanted to show their appreciation by sending her a live turkey by railway express. The turkey was placed in a croaker sack, a hole was cut so that the head of the turkey extended from the sack, and the parcel was addressed to "Miss Tansy, Attorney, Florence, S.C." It was delivered to my aunt without difficulty.

Early in my practice I was retained to represent Cecilia C. Cox, whose husband, G. O. Cox, was a prosperous mulatto who had acquired a large number of rental houses that made him in the public's eyes a slum landlord. They had no children, and when he died without a will, his next of kin tried to keep Mrs. Cox from getting her fair share of his estate. Mrs. Cox was a Roman Catholic and had been educated in a convent in the Midwest. It was clear to me she was more American Indian than any other race, but she was a fine lady of good sensibilities and a devout member of St. Anthony's Roman Catholic Church in Florence, to which she contributed generously.

I represented Mrs. Cox for nearly fifteen years, and she was one of my early and important clients as a partition suit had to be filed to divide the property left by her husband. When it became known that I had undertaken to represent her, other attorneys warned me that I would be committing a terrible mistake if I publicly addressed her as "Mrs. Cox." My reply was that if I addressed her as "Cecilia," it would imply a greater familiarity. I consistently addressed her as Mrs. Cox, but at one hearing held in the probate court the lawyer who was representing her deceased husband's kin addressed her as Cecilia. She very quietly reproached him by responding, "Mrs. Cox, please." He never addressed her directly after that.

I knew from having lived in the North, and particularly from having been taught by Dean McCormick, that the race issue was becoming a crisis and that there was no way the old system of racial segregation could or should last. I did little criminal work, but on one occasion when I was new at the legal business, I accepted a retainer to represent a black man who was in the city jail. The city jail was located immediately behind the city hall and the Colonial Theater. At that time the jail was a disgrace, and it almost made me sick to go into it. When I was waiting for my client to be brought down, two police officers brought a black man who was not my client into the area where I was standing. Apparently they did not like his attitude, and they proceeded to hit him with their fists in the head and face with such violence that he was bleeding from his nose and mouth. There I was in my seersucker suit and bow tie witnessing the terrible things that I had heard about the South but had not previously observed. I went into the jail's office, where the officer who had charge of the jail was sitting at a desk, and protested the treatment I had just witnessed. I received no reaction from the officer, so I said, "I hope that if I am arrested you will not treat me that way." The officer looked up and said in a snarling tone, "You're not a nigger."

One of the first cases Uncle Peter turned over to me involved a tobacco farmer's grievance against the Agricultural Stabilization Cooperative Service (ASCS). Tobacco farming in Florence County was a big—if not the biggest—source of income at the time, and since the government's regulations limited the number of acres a tobacco farmer could plant, there were frequent issues between the farmers and the ASCS about acreage allotments.

I was allowed to do a good deal of appellate work and thoroughly enjoyed writing briefs and arguing before the South Carolina Supreme Court. The Supreme Court met in the courtroom that had been established on the first floor of the state capitol during Reconstruction. One of the first cases I tried, briefed, and argued, *Waller v. Waller*, 220 S.C. 212, 66 S.E. 2d 876 (1951), had to do with the difference between a possibility of reverter and a reversion in the construction of a will. It was almost a textbook case on the difference between the two.

Peter represented the Florence Printing Company, which published the *Florence Morning News.* I assisted him on several cases, and he allowed me to try some of the smaller cases on my own. John M. O'Dowd, who owned the *Florence Morning News,* was a good man. He was a devout member of St. John's Episcopal Church and gave generously to its support. He was married twice but had no children by either of his wives. His first wife persuaded him to adopt two children, a son and a daughter, who were related to her.

The son, John Howard O'Dowd, known as Jack, was seven years younger than I was, and when I returned to Florence I became friends with him through both St. John's Church and our firm's representation of the newspaper. Jack graduated from the Citadel after World War II and worked as a reporter for the *Charleston News and Courier* for two years before returning to Florence at about the same time I returned to practice law. For several years he was employed by his father as a reporter but eventually advanced to become editor of the *Florence Morning News.*

I regard myself as fortunate to have had Jack for a friend. He asked me to be godfather for his oldest son, Johnny; when I was married in 1953, he was one of my groomsmen; and he was a godfather for my son Belton. In the great turmoil that developed around racial integration in the 1950s, we shared similar views on the nature of the problem and the necessity for acceptance without violence of a racially integrated society. Since the newspaper's office on Irby Street was around the corner from our office, it became customary for Jack to meet me for coffee in the J&J Drug Store during our morning break, and in those meetings we discussed many of the issues we were facing in the nation and the South.

On my return my living arrangements were somewhat bizarre. My parents lived on the Darlington Highway in a two-story house that had only three bedrooms, but there was a garage behind the house that had a large living space on the second floor. This had been adapted as a living space for my grandmother, and I now occupied it. It was a rather idyllic life for the first year and a half following my return. I ate breakfast and supper with my parents and Aunt Deda, and I ate lunch in town, usually at the Sanborn Hotel on Evans Street. I took an active part in the Florence Little Theatre and became active in efforts to expand the Florence Museum. I also had become involved in founding a chapter of Big Brothers of America in the Florence area.

I met my future wife through a series of unusual events. When I took time off to go to Chapel Hill in the fall of 1947, Margaret Lide, a Florence native, was married to Tom Stanback, who was moving to Chapel Hill to become a professor of economics. I became friends with them at Chapel Hill, and during the Christmas holiday in 1947 I had a cocktail party at my mother's house and invited Margaret and Tom Stanback and her sister Florence, who was married to Bill Snider. I did not invite their younger sisters, Anne and Alice. I thought they were too young.

Anne's father, Lewis Maxwell Lide, had a hunting place on the Marion County side of the Pee Dee River across from Snow's Island. I was invited to go down for a day in December 1947, and since I did not hunt, Anne was detailed to keep me company while I explored the Indian remains on the banks of the Pee Dee River. There was a series of earthworks at Dunham's Bluff that had been part of some fortification during the Revolutionary War. While I was feverishly probing this feature, I looked up suddenly and saw Anne looking at me. It was one of those penetrating glances that goes to one's heart, and I fell in love with her at that moment. There was no love-making at that time because I regarded her as a mere child, but from that time forward I hoped our lives would be joined. We began dating even though she was still in college.

Tragedy struck in August 1950 when my father died. I was never very close to my father, but I had great respect for him. He was a man's man— fond of hunting, farming, tending livestock, and repairing machinery. The number of things he could do seemed endless. I never doubted that my mother loved my father, but they never had a social life as a couple outside the family circle. When Aunt Deda returned to Florence in 1930, she lived with my parents for the remainder of their lives. It was an unusual situation, but my father took it in good stride. On one occasion when Aunt Deda was suggesting that certain arrangements needed to be made to improve the garden, my father reluctantly did as she asked and commented, "If this doesn't suit you, then you and Helen will have to find yourselves another husband."

Besides working as a conductor on the railroad, my father began farm-ing extensively when they moved to the Darlington Highway house in 1937. The house was located on a ten-acre tract in the fork of the Darlington Highway and Mechanicsville Road. The surroundings were predominately rural, although the house was only a mile from the city limits of Florence. There was a large barn on the back of the property, and my father kept a cow and a horse that I rode in the afternoons when I was in high school. There was also a henhouse and chickens.

My father rented land in the neighborhood and maintained a large veg-etable garden, while Aunt Deda had an extensive flower garden. Aunt Deda was an early fancier of camellias; there were over fifty camellia bushes in the yard and an extensive pyracantha hedge along Mechanicsville Road. There were several pecan trees and many fig trees surrounding the house. One friend who visited the family during World War II commented on the boun-tiful products gathered from the family's "fertile acres."

My father's death brought to an end the carefree year and a half I had en-joyed. I now assumed the responsibility for comforting my mother and try-ing to bring in more income to sustain myself. The year following my father's death was a most unhappy year, for there seemed a black hole of emptiness that I could not fill.

Anne and I continued to see each other. She graduated from Chapel Hill in 1951 and went to work for the Naval Research Laboratory in Washington. She would come back and forth on the train, and my mother's servant, Rosa McCoy, and Mrs. Lide's servant, Caroline Jackson, were a communication link about planned visits until our courtship became firmly established. We were in love, and I wanted to get married, but I knew I did not have sufficient income to take that step. I visited Anne in Washington once, but our courtship depended on Anne's willingness to travel back and forth by train to Florence because she had a free pass on the Atlantic Coast Line. When Anne was in town, I would leave to visit her promptly after supper. When my father was still alive, he would ask where I was going. I would reply in a semi-impudent manner, "Out." Once he inquired whether "out" was in town.

The prospects for more income increased when I was detailed to take over a lawsuit that Aunt Deda had commenced in Dillon County involving the construction of a will. The case was first heard by a probate judge in Dillon County, who decided against my clients, and we appealed to the court of common pleas. Judge J. Woodrow Lewis, who later became chief justice of the South Carolina Supreme Court, heard the appeal and upheld the probate judge's finding.

I appealed, and the South Carolina Supreme Court reversed the case in our favor. The case is *A. McKeithan Rogers et al. v. Luther Rogers et al.*, 221 S.C. 360, 70 S.E. 2d 637 (1952). Chief counsel for the defendants was one of the keenest lawyers practicing in the Pee Dee area, Samuel Want. We had a sizable money recovery, and when I went with my clients to pick up the check, my client took it and said, "Better luck next time, Mr. Want." Mr. Want replied, "Careful, it may be at your expense."

With my share of the fee I felt that I had capital enough to take the plunge into matrimony, and in June 1953 Anne and I were engaged. Sallyann and Mandeville Rogers had a surprise engagement party at their house, and I gave Anne an engagement ring on the way to the party. I find it difficult to put into words the most important event of my life. I think it was George Bernard Shaw who said you can tell a lot about people by what they laugh at and who they marry. I am willing to be judged by the Shaw test.

The Reverend Edward Byrd and the Reverend Wilmer S. Poynor married us on June 13, 1953, in the First Baptist Church in Florence. When Anne and I went to talk with Reverend Byrd about the marriage ceremony, he greeted us with a cheerful smile and said to me, "Nick, I suppose you've come to talk to me about romance." I replied dourly, "No, sir, I've come to talk about matrimony." There were strained relations between us after that. To Anne's and my surprise, however, Byrd agreed to use the Book of Common Prayer and to allow Poynor to participate in the ceremony. Byrd said to me on the evening of our wedding that he was asked where the Lide-Zeigler wedding was to take place and responded, "At the Baptist Episcopal Church."

Our wedding took place under the most trying circumstances. Anne's father and mother had separated, and there was grave doubt as to whether Mrs. Lide would attend our wedding. Anne's grandmother, Mrs. R. W. Lide, who was in her nineties, was taken ill, and it was uncertain whether or not she would live. Anne's sister Flo Snider came from Greensboro to help put the wedding on.

My financial state was precarious, but I used some of my funds to remodel the garage apartment so that it would be livable when we returned from our honeymoon. My Indian collection had to be boxed and moved out, and proper heating and air conditioning installed. One wit remarked that I had moved the Indians out and moved Anne in.

To further complicate matters, Uncle Peter and Aunt Margaret had the rehearsal party at their house on Dargan Street and served both Baptist and Episcopal beverages. Knowing the Reverend Byrd's aversion to alcohol, a bar was arranged on the side porch of the house, and unspiked punch was served in the dining room—where Reverend Byrd was directed. He later told Anne's mother that he knew what segregation must be like since most of the guests preferred refreshments on the side porch.

The wedding day came. I was so excited and concerned about the wedding going off on schedule that I neglected to tell my brother-in-law, Frank Johnson, to see that my mother and Aunt Deda got to the church on time. When I met Poynor at the church, he did not have on vestments. I asked if he intended to vest. He replied, "I don't think I will. Brother Byrd asked me if I was going 'to wear that white thing.'"

The music was wonderful, but when it came time to begin the service, I could hear the organist repeating what had already been played. I asked one of the groomsmen what the trouble was, and he told me that my mother and Miss Leah had not arrived. They were, in fact, twenty minutes late. They had been left alone on the Darlington Highway, and when they were getting in the car to leave for the church, Margaret Meriwether, Aunt Deda's friend from Columbia, drove up and wanted to change into an evening dress. Mother and Aunt Deda dutifully reopened the house and waited for Margaret to change clothes and then came to the church, where approximately 750 people were awaiting their arrival.

When Anne and I were pronounced man and wife, Poynor grasped Anne warmly by the hand, but when she turned with hand extended toward Byrd, he declined to follow suit. The reception was held at the Lide's house on Coit Street, and just as Anne and I got there, a terrible thunderstorm broke and buckets of rain came down. This cut down on the number guests at the reception.

Anne and I got away around eleven-thirty and drove to Charleston, South Carolina, where we had reservations at the Fort Sumter Hotel. The hotel, now a residential apartment, is on the Battery, and we made it there at about 3:00 A.M. on June 14. After getting some rest, we drove to Jacksonville, Florida, and the following day we drove to Miami. From there we took a flight over to Nassau the next morning. Anne, who had gone through so much emotional trauma because of her family situation, said that it was an enormous relief to see the ocean separating us from the mainland.

Nassau was still a British colony, and it had a storybook appearance and appeal. The Duke of Windsor was still its governor. We stayed in the Royal Victoria Hotel, which was built during the American Civil War to accommodate blockade runners. There was in Nassau the feeling of antiquity and of a way of life that was vanishing. As we drove up to the main entrance of the hotel, "Blind Blake" Higgs was playing his marvelous calypso music in the bar.

There is so much that could be written about one's honeymoon and much that should be repressed. I called it our "SSS" experience—sun, sustenance, and sex. There was plenty of all three. Swimming and sun bathing, however, had to be accomplished by trips to Paradise Beach, which could only be reached by ferry. It was an expedition that took almost a day. Paradise Beach, the original name of which was Hog Island, was then practically uninhabited except for a small club that served food and drinks and afforded beach umbrellas. When the ferry deposited its passengers on the island, it was then necessary to walk a quarter mile to get to the club, but it was all worth the time and effort for we thoroughly enjoyed our outings there.

On our return trip, when we landed in Miami, paid the rental on our car parked at the airport, and bought gas, I discovered that, because we had bought some antique silver, we had only a few dollars left. The plan was to drive to Atlanta and spend the night with my sister, but we wondered if we could make it with only a dollar or two in cash. But we made it to Atlanta, where Leah and Frank Johnson invited friends to celebrate our return, and I was able to get enough cash from her to enable us to reach Florence.

When we returned to Florence, we took up residence in the remodeled garage apartment, but there were dark clouds on the horizon as Anne's parents became involved in a divorce. The Lide family house on Coit Street had to be closed down and sold, and Anne's mother moved to Coward, South Carolina, where she remodeled the home in which her mother was living.

To boost our income, Anne took a job teaching at Timmonsville High School. She taught five separate courses, everything from algebra to general science. As a collateral duty she was assigned sponsorship of the junior class, which entailed directing the junior class play. Since I had experience with the Florence Little Theatre, I agreed to help her, and it proved an entertaining and rewarding experience.

II

Continuing Involvement in the Naval Reserve

I will always treasure my time in the U.S. Navy and believe it was good for me. I went on active duty when I was twenty-one, and I had not yet reached my twenty-fifth birthday when the war ended. My time in the navy helped me mature. I was entirely on my own and had time to think about my future. Shipboard life may have been hard, but it appealed to my egalitarian side. Accomplishing the ship's mission took precedence over any personal interest or ambition, and there was a comradeship on board that resulted from our mutual work and the closeness of our living quarters.

The U.S. Navy did not discharge me but put me on inactive status in the Naval Reserve. In the rush of events following my release from active duty however, I did not have the time or the inclination to join a Naval Reserve unit. I endeavored, unsuccessfully, to organize a composite Naval Reserve drilling unit in Florence and wrote letters to all of the Naval Reservists I knew in the area. Nothing came of this effort.

In May 1951 I learned that there was a naval electronics unit that had been drilling at the old Florence Air Base. This was during the Korean War, and I felt some pangs of conscience that I was doing nothing to help the war effort. On May 12, 1951, I agreed to take command of the unit.

It was an odd situation. I was going to take command of a reserve unit at a place I had never visited and a with crew I had never met. The crew consisted of one chief petty officer, Frank Warr, and six enlisted men. I introduced myself to them and, with all of the savoir faire and authority I could muster, said, "I am your new commanding officer."

I told the crew that the first order of business would be to find new quarters and start recruiting new members. We did both. During the following year I made approximately ten speeches to various high schools in the area in an attempt to get new recruits, and by May 1952 I reported that the unit had two officers and eleven enlisted men and that two applications for enlistment were pending.

By September 1952 I had arranged to get six rooms on the ground floor in the Florence County Agricultural Building on Irby Street. On December 11, 1952, a ceremony was held in that building changing the status of the unit to Electronics Division 6-10. Again I was made commanding officer. At the time the unit was commissioned as an organized electronics company, there were eight officers and thirty-five enlisted men in the unit.

On December 2, 1952, I was required to sign an affidavit that my civilian occupation would not "prevent my immediate mobilization in case of war or national emergency." By the spring of 1953 the unit consisted of two companies and over fifty enlisted men and seven or eight officers. By July 1, 1960, the unit became Naval Reserve Electronics Battalion 6-8, with two companies and a total of approximately one hundred enlisted men and twelve officers.

During my activity with the reserve unit, I received steady promotions and reached the rank of captain on April 17, 1964. When my children asked why I didn't get promoted to admiral, I told them, tongue in cheek, that Strom Thurmond was a senior member of the Senate Military Affairs Committee and I could hardly expect him to approve my promotion even if I were qualified.

The biggest change for the Naval Reserve program in Florence came with the construction of a Naval Reserve building at the Florence Airport in 1957 and the assignment of a full-time station keeper to man the facility. The building was formally accepted by the navy and dedicated by the commandant of the Sixth Naval District, Adm. George C. Crawford, on September 26, 1957. At the time of the dedication of the new building there were 104 enlisted men and 14 officers drilling in the units.

In order to maintain my status in the active reserves, I was required not only to attend weekly drills but also to go on active duty yearly. To get credit for a satisfactory year of federal service, it was necessary to earn a certain number of points. Weekly attendance at drill and two weeks of active duty were not sufficient to earn the required number, so it was necessary to take courses from the Naval War College. I took numerous courses during my years in the Naval Reserve. Two I particularly remember: a course in counterinsurgency and a course in international relations. When I retired, I had been credited with over twenty-seven years of satisfactory federal service.

The most memorable trips with my family were the two tours of duty I did on the USS *Shangri-La* at Mayport, Florida, and two tours of duty at Key West, Florida. I did two weeks of active duty at the war college at Fort

McNair in Washington, D.C., in 1961. Classes there were taught by some of the top foreign-policy experts. I particularly remember Henry Kissinger, who lectured in such a heavy German accent that most of us could not understand what he said. Those attending the classes were led to believe that nuclear war with Russia was inevitable and that every citizen should make a bomb shelter. When I returned to Florence, I dutifully converted the ground floor of the garage apartment behind the house on the Darlington Highway into a bombproof shelter.

I retired from the Naval Reserve on July 1, 1973. While I was serving, two wars were fought—the Korean War and the Vietnam War. The aircraft carriers on which I served in World War II were largely irrelevant to modern warfare. My skills as a naval officer were equally obsolete. The draft was no longer a threat to young men, and the entire feeling about military service had changed. The Naval Reserve unit in Florence lost its relevance and was decommissioned. The Charleston Naval Base suffered the same fate.

The navy still holds a warm place in my heart. I think of those with whom I served who died during the war or who have died since then, and I try to live life to the fullest in order to justify my survival. I still feel a deep sense of comradeship with "those in peril on the sea."

12

Florence Little Theatre

I wonder what a philandering husband thinks of his mistress after they have parted. Some smoldering embers of passion must remain no matter how bitter and acrimonious the final breach. I have never had the pleasure, or the trauma, of having a mistress or even a casual affair with a flesh and blood "other woman," but I have had a long love affair with the theater, which persisted long after I had determined that my profession would be the law.

I don't know when my fascination for the theater began, but it became an important part of my life. Even though some parts may be repetitious, the retelling is essential to the understanding of my life. My mother delighted in recounting the story of the blossoming of my enthusiasm for acting when I was in the first grade. The reading primer in the public schools featured Baby Ray, who had a dog, a cat, and other pets. To dramatize the menagerie and their characteristics, the teacher decided to assign her students roles of the various animals and their vocal calls. I was chosen to be the dog. When I told my mother about my part in the drama, I added that the teacher "sure knew how to pick a good dog!"

After my canine triumph my mother and Aunt Deda persuaded me to enter the statewide declamation contest for the fifth grade. Aunt Deda decided that I should recite Lewis Carroll's poem "The Walrus and the Carpenter" because it was the hundredth anniversary of Carroll's birth. I won a gold medal, and the idea became embedded in my mind that stage performance was a way that I could secure approval and praise.

Getting approval and praise was not easy for me in my childhood. My sister, Leah, and I were entirely opposite in temperament and talents. Leah was a superb athlete, while I was thin, somewhat sickly, and awkward. She used to boss me whenever the opportunity presented itself. Years later one of my sons asked his aunt why she had given me so much grief when we were growing up. My sister replied, "Because he was such a cutie pie."

It was not easy to be a cutie pie, a "sissie" in other words, while making one's way through public schools. I was not good at sports. To aggravate the situation, my mother insisted that I take dancing lessons. I had little aptitude for dancing, and to make matters worse the vogue in the early 1930s was tap dancing, for which I had almost zero talent. My only dancing school success came during the bicentennial of the birth of George Washington in 1932. The Daughters of the American Revolution promoted a dancing routine that featured Martha Brunson and me doing a minuet and singing songs with an eighteenth-century flavor such as "An Old Fashioned Garden" and "An Old Spinning Wheel in the Parlor." Our skit became a popular entertainment for patriotic organizations, service clubs, and church circles, but it did not enhance my image as a typical eleven-year-old boy.

As I grew older, I dreaded the times when at recess or on Boy Scout camping events each team was asked to choose up sides and then given the right to pick one person in rotating order. I always knew that I would be chosen last and knew that no one really wanted me on the team.

My first breakthrough at playwriting came in the early 1930s. We had a gang of about five or six boys for whom making an extra nickel or two was a matter of serious concern. I suggested that to make money we produce a play on the side porch of our Dargan Street home. Admission would be one cent. I composed a melodrama that bore the title *Vinsflanx the Villain*.

There were no girls in the gang, so the youngest boy, George Weeks, had to be the heroine. George was only five or six years old and a more masculine type would be hard to imagine. The play was so bad and the acting so outrageous that it attracted an audience of fond parents and curious neighbors. The production made a profit and confirmed my feeling that I had a calling in the theater.

My malaria in the mid-1930s drove me even further away from the usual vigorous athletic activities of teenagers. The result was that I became more introverted and bookish. Denied success in the conventional world of teenage-boyish activity, I invented characters and plots to amuse myself.

When I reached my senior year in high school, I had recovered some spunk. I was chosen for a minor part in the senior class play; I entered the oratorical contest for my literary society; and I won the school essay-writing contest. My big opportunity came with a statewide playwriting contest for high school students sponsored by the drama department of the University of South Carolina. I wrote a one-act play and submitted it. The contest required that the play deal with South Carolina in some manner.

It was a time when I was feeling very patriotic. Although war had not yet broken out in Europe, my family believed that inevitably there would be another war and that the United States would become involved. I chose to write about the last day in the life of Col. Isaac Hayne. Hayne was captured, tried for breaking his parole, and hanged in Charleston in 1781. What attracted my attention to Hayne was that he had said, on being sentenced, that he would die as an American should; hence the play's title, *As an American Should.*

The play won first prize and was produced by university students in Drayton Hall at the University of South Carolina. It was an intoxicating experience to see one's play done in grand fashion. To cap it all off I was given a gold medal. I thought that playwriting surely was my way to win world recognition.

In the summer of 1939, while on vacation from Sewanee, I became aware of a movement to revive theatrical activity in Florence. Sanborn Chase invited me to participate in a dramatic production he was directing that would be staged in the backyard of his home. His home, now the Florence Museum, had been the talk of Florence since its construction the year before. Sanborn was one of the most talented people I have been privileged to call a friend.

The drama was really a spoof of the old Victorian melodrama called *The Drunkard; or, The Fallen Saved.* My part was relatively minor. I was the good brother who rescues his sister from a fate worse than death. My recollection is that the play ran for two nights, and at the end of the final production the "villain" was unceremoniously thrown into Sanborn's swimming pool. The production was a success, and Sanborn began a serious effort to revive an amateur theater group that had languished during the Depression. After *The Drunkard* a stage was constructed behind the old Sanborn Hotel on Evans Street, and several plays were produced there at the end of summer 1939.

My earliest experience with theater was going to Columbia in the early 1930s to see a Gilbert and Sullivan production, *H.M.S Pinafore*, produced at the Town Theatre. But until 1939 I had never been to New York City, nor had I seen a professionally produced play. On my New York trip to the World's Fair, the glories of a real Broadway production were revealed. In addition to daily visits to the fairgrounds, we saw two plays—Lillian Hellman's *Little Foxes* and an outrageous musical review called *Hellzapoppin'*. It was *The Little Foxes* with Tallulah Bankhead that made a profound impression on me. *Hellzapoppin'* left me with a distaste for Broadway musicals from which I have never recovered. I began to think of Broadway musicals as just another means for folks to "raise up their behind legs and holler Wahoo!" as Brer Rabbit says.

In September 1939, when I returned to Sewanee for my sophomore year, I became more involved in literary activity than before. The Sopherim Literary Society encouraged me to write a one-act play called *In Sheep's Clothing*. My theatrical "triumph" came in my senior year, when I successfully adapted the lyrics of Gilbert and Sullivan's opera *The Mikado* as a satire on Sewanee. That success convinced me that my real talent lay in writing plays. While in midshipman school in the summer and fall of 1942, I saw as many plays on Broadway as was possible. But it was on the damaged USS *Intrepid*, during its thirty-day journey from the war zone to the States, that I began writing again. It was a novel titled *The Songless Dance*. It was not well conceived, and in my depressed state I was hardly in the frame of mind to do any serious writing. The horror of the war had left its shadow over me.

Although getting through Harvard Law School was a demanding task, I did manage to see as many plays as possible while I was there. Notably, I saw John Gielgud's production of Oscar Wilde's *The Importance of Being Earnest* and John Webster's *Duchess of Malfi*.

To my delight the D'Oyly Carte Company came to Boston twice while I was at Harvard, and I saw as many productions as possible. Martyn Greene was still performing, and a group of fellow Savoyards in my eating club and I invited him to have lunch with us. He was almost as entertaining off stage as on. Also a group of Harvard undergraduates did a series of classical plays that I found highly entertaining.

The terms at law school were conducted on an accelerated basis with no breaks or long holidays. By September 1947 I had completed in two years the equivalent of three years of courses and needed a break. On my break I wanted to go to Chapel Hill in North Carolina to take a course in playwriting. I had also become interested in what seemed to be the seemingly endless problems, both economic and social, the South was experiencing. I knew that Howard W. Odum at Chapel Hill was reputed to be an expert in dealing with southern social history and problems, so I decided to combine the two areas of interest and apply for a continuation of GI bill support for a three month "holiday" at Chapel Hill.

Events broke in my favor. Morgan, who taught courses in evidence at Harvard, had during the previous term stated that the final examination would be based on Shakespeare's play *Othello*. I argued convincingly that a grasp of drama as well as a knowledge of southern problems fit neatly into the category of training for the legal profession. I was granted GI bill coverage for the adventure.

Chapel Hill was run on quarters, so that if I entered in the September quarter, I would have completed the term in December 1947. I enrolled in what I thought was Odum's class on southern regions, Samuel Selden's course on playwriting, and to fill the space between, a course in European drama before Ibsen taught by Kai Jurgensen. It turned out that Odum was on sabbatical, so Gordon Blackwell, who later became president of Furman University, taught the class. The courses were tremendously stimulating. Blackwell opened my mind to ideas that were articulated in W. J. Cash's *Mind of the South*, Ben Robertson's *Red Hills and Cotton*, and W. A. Percy's *Lanterns on the Levee*. The course in European drama made me read more plays than I had ever done.

The playwriting course required me to write a one-act play and submit it for possible production during the term. I wrote a play about Judas Iscariot called *Saint Judas*. In the play I tried to present a more sympathetic picture of Judas as a man caught in the dilemma of choosing to regard the gospel of Jesus as a message of social justice or to accept the mystery of Jesus as the Son of God. It was selected for experimental production and was voted the best of the three produced at the end of the term.

I passed the South Carolina bar examination and was admitted to practice in June 1949. Toward the end of that summer my friend Sanborn Chase asked me to consider taking a part in his production of *Arsenic and Old Lace*. The Florence Little Theatre had been reestablished following World War II. Productions had been presented in the auditorium of Florence High School (later McClenaghan High School), but when the theater that was part of the U.S. Army Air Force's installation outside of Florence was returned to the city, it was offered to the theater group. That building remained the Little Theatre's home during the 1950s until the organization was strong enough to build its own theater in 1958.

The part Sanborn offered me was the Boris Karloff–like character named Jonathan. It was a challenging job, and I flatter myself in believing that it is hard for me to play a villain. I was both actor and director for Lillian Hellman's play *The Little Foxes*. I played the part of Horace, Regina's ailing husband. This production was a landmark for the Florence Little Theatre. It was the first "serious" drama produced by the group and involved adult issues such as adultery, homicide, and fraud. It also had a few "bad words" that were considered inappropriate for Florence audiences. One problem in its production was that two of the parts, including a major supporting role, were for black servants. Although 41 percent of the population of Florence was black, it was still taboo to put whites and blacks together in a social context like a stage production. Two of the members of the group, whites, agreed to do the parts, appropriately made up.

Following the production of *The Little Foxes*, I began writing *The Cult*, which was intended to be a satire about a small southern town located near extensive middle Mississippi Indian remains. The central character is a mad archaeologist who has discovered in the ruins near the town a sacrificial knife similar to those used at Chichin Itza and Uxmel by the Aztecs. He wishes to have the satisfaction of using it on a real human victim, and the opportunity presents itself when the "Rooster Boosters" of the town promote a festival, with a reenactment of a human sacrifice, to highlight the town's middle Mississippi Indian connection. The "Young Man of the Year," an award given annually by the Rooster Boosters, was logically chosen to be the proposed victim of the sacrifice. One line that titillated the local audience came in the last act, in which the Rooster Boosters were all costumed as Aztec priests or nobles. One character asked a companion if his appearance was that of an Aztec. His companion replies, "You look more like a half Aztec."

The play ran for two performances and was received with only mild approval. It had a trick ending. After the mad archaeologist's plot is uncovered and while the ceremony is proceeding, it is discovered that the real sacrificial knife has been taken, and the characters left on stage make a dash to prevent the Young Man of the Year from literally being sacrificed. The curtain falls without resolving whether or not they succeed. I suspect that the Florence Jaycees had the last laugh. I, a nonmember, was given their award as Florence's Young Man of the Year in 1952.

In January 1951 I played in and directed *The Winslow Boy.* I am an admirer of Terence Rattigan and thoroughly enjoyed directing the production and playing the part of Sir Robert Morton. In one scene Miss Winslow says to Sir Robert that she understands he is slated to become a judge. Sir Robert, who knows more of the political intricacies of judicial appointments, replies, "The robes of that office would not suit me." In later years, when I was under consideration for appointment to the federal bench, those words came back to haunt me.

During the summer of 1951 I rewrote the lyrics of Gilbert and Sullivan's *Utopia Limited,* converting them into *Pressley's Crossroads,* a satire about rural southern life at the time. Getting the musical score for *Utopia Limited* was a problem. It was never a popular part of the D'Oyly Carte repertoire, and we finally secured a microfilm copy of it from the New York Public Library. Betty Ann Darby helped adapt the score and played the accompaniment during its production by the Florence Little Theatre in September 1951.

The central character is a young southern woman who is running for the state senate. She was educated in New England, and her Yankee friend comes south to help her get elected. In true Gilbertian style the two can only keep their liberal attitudes and views safe from the corrosive effects of southern politics by drinking pure New England spring water. The candidate is told by her friend, "The choice is either Yankee witchcraft or southern bitch craft." There is no resolution as to which prevails in the election.

In December 1952 the Little Theatre did a production of *The Importance of Being Earnest.* By that time the theater had become so well established that it hired a young Dillon man, Phil Bernanke, as a paid director. I played the part of John Worthing. Harry Coble, who had worked with the Playmakers at Chapel Hill, played John's brother.

During the production of *The Importance of Being Earnest,* I voiced concern that the Florence Little Theatre was falling into the habit of producing what was regarded as "standard little theater fare." The board of directors rejected *She Stoops to Conquer* for fear the public would not be interested in seeing a play written in 1773. I expressed my concern about the reluctance to produce classics in an op-ed piece in the *Florence Morning News* of November 27, 1955. The article ends with this pessimistic view: "Perhaps the day is far off when classics produced by the Florence Little Theatre Guild will be the biggest hits of the season. The theater organization will do its part—the community must also do its part by supporting the little theater and encouraging these productions."

It was Harry Coble's unique talents as an actor and dancer that spurred my idea of having the Little Theatre, the McClenaghan High School chorale, and the Florence Symphony produce *The Mikado.* It would have to be staged in the McClenaghan High School auditorium since the Little Theatre building at the air base was too small for such a large production. It was also fortunate that Al Johnson was the musical director of the McClenaghan chorale and the Florence Symphony. His talent was essential to the opera's success. Someone of Al's experience had to be in command of the orchestra and the choral music, especially when there were about twenty-five amateur musicians in the orchestra. Production was planned for the fall of 1953.

The Mikado opened on November 5, 1953, and played for two nights. It turned out remarkably well, chiefly due to Al Johnson's skills. I played the part of Pooh-Bah, the Lord High Everything Else, and Harry played the part of Ko-Ko. The *Florence Morning News* published an enthusiastic review that inspired us to do *The Pirates of Penzance* the next season.

A new full-time director, Gene Graves, directed the staging of *The Pirates of Penzance.* It was produced in October 1954, and I played the part of Major General Stanley. After that there was not as much enthusiasm for doing any more productions involving the Florence Symphony, the McClenaghan chorale, and acting members of the Little Theatre.

October 1956 saw my last effort as an actor-director with the Florence Little Theatre in the production of *The Caine Mutiny Court-Martial.* I felt a strange connection with the novel because the central character, Willie Keith, entered Columbia's midshipman school in December 1942, just as I was graduating, and he lived in Columbia's Furnald Hall, where I had been housed. The production also provided an opportunity for many to reminisce about World War II and the U.S. Navy. I played Barney Greenwald and recruited former naval officers and uniforms for the cast. I was well pleased with the production, and if there had to be a swan song for my connection with the theater, I am gratified that this was it.

I had another connection with *The Caine Mutiny Court-Martial* that preceded the Little Theatre's production. In May 1954 I had gone on two weeks of active duty as part of my commitment to the Naval Reserve. I served on board a destroyer escort that went from Charleston to New York. This gave me a weekend in New York, and I was fortunate enough to see *The Caine Mutiny Court-Martial* on Broadway with Lloyd Nolan and Henry Fonda. It was a moving experience for me, especially since I was in naval uniform and still essentially a part of the navy. During the intermission I met a law school classmate from whom I learned that the U.S. Supreme Court had reversed the "separate but equal" doctrine and ordered the integration of the public schools. That event had an indelible effect on my life and influenced my interests and activities thereafter. To paraphrase a line from Lillian Hellman's play *The Watch on the Rhine,* I was shook out of the magnolias. The blatant racism in my native state and the spiritual martyrdom of my friend Jack O'Dowd, editor of the *Florence Morning News,* made me realize that I must leave fantasy and acting behind and become a part of the real world.

I ran for the South Carolina House of Representatives in 1958 and during the campaign was told by a supporter, "You have got to give up this theater business." I asked why, and he responded, "In this last election it was rumored all over Lake City that you had played the part of a Jap." It took me a few minutes to realize that my connection with Gilbert and Sullivan's *Mikado* was seen as playing the part of "a Jap." I promised that I would devote myself to my new duties and forsake the theater. I have done so and, like a recovering alcoholic, fear taking even one sip lest it precipitate my former addiction.

I have great affection for the theater, but the spark of romance is gone. In the 1950s I saw the little theater movement as a humanizing influence in a small town like Florence. Serious plays and classics made people think beyond the local problems and prejudices that often preoccupied them. It incited a feeling for a larger view, a clearer perspective of the human condition. Unless one went to larger cities like New York, only local theater could supply that influence.

The situation changed dramatically with the advent of television. Superb productions such as PBS's *Masterpiece Theater* became available to the public via television, and television began bringing the humanizing influence and sophisticated materials to small towns and rural areas that previously theater had. South Carolina Educational Television, which was created when I was in the House of Representatives, accelerated the advance and availability of superior theater. Local theater now seems more of a social and recreational activity for those involved in the production than for the audiences, and the productions have become more and more like professional theater. The Florence Little Theatre has become a major cultural asset to the community.

13

Florence Museum

It could have been a scene from Coleridge's *Rime of the Ancient Mariner*. An aged figure in a heavy hooded cape grasped a startled young man and held him firmly by the arm. The lines "By thy long gray beard and glittering eye / Now wherefore stopp'st thou me?" were inappropriate because the elderly figure was a woman, Jane Beverly Evans, Miss Jane. She held me with her "skinny hand" and fixed me with her "glittering eye."

The encounter took place on a blustery January day in 1950 as Miss Jane was coming to our house for Sunday dinner. I had brought her in my car, and we were going into the house when she took me firmly by the arm. "Promise me that you will not allow the Florence Museum to fail!" she said. I quickly promised to do everything in my power to prevent its failure, and we went in to dinner. Miss Jane died several months later, but her spell was cast. "The Mariner hath his will."

My connection with the Florence Museum and Miss Jane went back to my teenage years, but my family's connection with the Evanses went back to the 1860s. One of the advantages, or disadvantages, of having a southern background is that southerners feel themselves caught in a continuum of time, place, and personalities, both living and dead. So it had been with my family and the Evans family for at least three generations.

After the Civil War Miss Jane's father, James Evans, settled in the Mars Bluff community east of Florence. Evans had been a surgeon in the Confederate army, but during Reconstruction it was hard to make a living by practicing medicine, so he lived on a farm adjoining that of my great-grandfather, Honorine Horatio McClenaghan. My great-grandfather, also a Confederate veteran, had numerous children, as did Evans. My grandmother, Leah McClenaghan, was born in 1865. Miss Jane, with whom she was lifelong friends, was born the following year. In the hard times of the 1870s the Evans children and the McClenaghan children walked about a mile to the Mars Bluff Academy to attend school. Miss Jane once told me that she and my grandmother were playing a game of jackstones when they were supposed to be studying and were caught by the teacher. As punishment they were reprimanded in front of the class and made to stand in a corner. Miss Jane began to cry, but my grandmother showed no signs of emotion. After school my grandmother, whose nature was truly stoic, chided Miss Jane for weeping, saying, "Why did you give them the satisfaction of showing you cared?"

Miss Jane was an artist and never married, but my grandmother married Belton O'Neall Townsend, who moved to the village of Florence at about the same time Evans moved his family to Florence. My grandfather, although much younger, became a friend of Dr. and Mrs. Evans. When my grandfather founded Florence's first library in 1878, Mrs. Evans agreed to be the secretary of the library association. When the movement to establish Florence County began in 1885, Dr. Evans was the chairman of the organizing committee and my grandfather was its secretary.

Although most of the Evans children moved from Florence as adults, they maintained contacts there. Miss Jane's brothers married wealthy women, and Miss Jane studied art in both Philadelphia and Italy. She returned to the United States before 1914, bringing with her seeds of Italian cypress trees that she had the local nursery in Florence plant and raise. In the 1930s she distributed the young seedlings throughout the city. They lived for years, but none of them have survived. This horticultural venture, however, was her attempt to join the cultural heritage of the Renaissance in Florence, Italy, to Florence, South Carolina.

After the United States entered World War I, Miss Jane made her deepest mark. She served as state chair of the League for Women's Service, and my grandmother was the local chair in Florence. Part of the local war effort was selling war bonds, but to support the troops who were constantly passing though Florence on the railroad, a restaurant named the Blue Bird Tea Room opened. Eight ladies in Florence, including my grandmother, took turns preparing lunch, which in those days was a heavy meal. The tea room operated from the old office of James Evans. Each of the ladies took their own cooks and supervised the preparation of food, and young women volunteered to act as waitresses. The Blue Bird Tea Room closed in 1919, having accumulated several thousand dollars.

Miss Jane became the chief promoter of a movement to erect a suitable memorial to the soldiers from Florence who had served in World War I. The idea of a memorial library was suggested to Miss Jane, and it appealed to her so strongly that she threw her whole soul into the project. The effort to raise the necessary funds through contributions proved to be unsuccessful. Legislation was proposed and passed that would create a library as part of the Florence School District and, subject to approval in a referendum, authorized a three-mill tax for its support. The women's clubs in Florence lobbied strongly for passage of the referendum, and the voters approved the tax millage. The library board was created in 1923, with Miss Jane as the only woman on the board. The Florence Library was opened in 1925.

In 1924–25 Miss Jane went to New Mexico for her health and there became fascinated by southwestern Indian art. She tried to persuade the curator of the museum in Santa Fe to allow her to purchase some of the pottery in the museum's collection. Only museums, however, could buy objects from the Santa Fe Museum. In order to make the purchases, Miss Jane sent a telegram to the Blue Bird Tea Room Committee asking them to constitute themselves as the Florence Museum Committee. The committee, obedient to Miss Jane's request, sent her the tea room money to purchase a collection that became the nucleus of the Florence Museum. The objects were stored in a large closet on the second floor of the new Florence Library and were not displayed until ten years later.

In the early 1930s I made a discovery that brought me into the world of archaeology. While hunting with my single-shot .22-caliber rifle one afternoon, I found an Indian arrowhead and the rim sherd of an Indian pot in a field. I quickly realized that looking for Indian arrowheads and potsherds was more interesting than trying to shoot birds.

It was a hobby my family encouraged. It required a good deal of walking out in the open air, and it was free of the danger of a hunting accident. I recall that Miss Jane learned of my collecting Indian relics and told me, on a visit with my family, that I should start a notebook of sketches of arrowheads and potsherds. Drawing was not supposed to be one of my accomplishments, but under Miss Jane's urging and tutelage, I did begin a sketchbook that I proudly exhibited to her. She further whetted my appetite for archaeology in 1935 when she invited Ralph Magoffin to lecture at the Florence Library to stir up interest in a museum. Magoffin was a classical archaeologist and spent much of his time excavating the Roman Forum. He expressed surprise that someone of my age had any interest in archaeology and sent me one of his publications on the forum. I was hooked.

Miss Jane was fond of saying, "There is something about a city that has a museum that sets it apart from a city that hasn't." A town with a museum, in her view, was generally regarded as more culturally advanced than one that had none. She ardently wanted Florence to be culturally advanced and devoted the last years of her life to the establishment of a museum. The Florence Museum was chartered in February 1936, chiefly as a result of Miss Jane's persistent efforts.

One of the most unusual projects Miss Jane undertook to raise money for the museum was the staging of tableaux vivants that she called "The Living Masters." I participated along with most of my friends in Della Robbia's "Singing Boys." To look like marble, we were greased with cold cream and covered with flour. I recall seeing ladies on the ground floor of the library making angel wings for the production.

My Indian collection continued to grow, and by the time I graduated from high school I had several hundred arrowheads and a large collection of potsherds. In the fall of 1938 I went to Sewanee, and Miss Jane launched a community drive to buy cases for the collection housed in the library's upstairs closet. In February 1939 I got an invitation to the opening of the Florence Museum, which was to be housed in the three basement rooms of the library. Miss Jane had written on the inner envelope, "For E. N. Zeigler, the first contributor to the Florence Museum." It was, of course, not true, but it flattered my ego, probably what Miss Jane had in mind.

Miss Jane continued to add to the museum's collection, but her efforts were largely directed toward Asian objects. Her family helped her acquire Chinese material in Philadelphia and New York, and when a notable collection of Chinese objects became available in the 1940s, she raised the funds to purchase it. Much of the collection came from missionaries who returned from China.

The difficulty the museum faced was that its exhibits were static. If one visited the collection in 1940, for example, and returned in 1950, the objects displayed would not have changed. The community was gradually being turned off by the idea of a museum filled chiefly with pottery from China and southwestern Indians. The collection seemed strangely out of place in a small southern town, and increasingly the museum was viewed as irrelevant to the progress of Florence. Not even the old canard that the Chinese and Carolinians were alike because they both drank tea, ate rice, and worshiped their ancestors helped bridge the gap. Even Miss Jane's friends did not help in promoting the image of a museum as a vital and essential part of the cultural growth of the city. I recall Walter Alexander writing a guest editorial for the *Florence Morning News* on behalf of the museum that bore the devastating title "A Plea for the Pansies."

In 1938 Miss Jane paid a visit to Sanborn Chase's mother in the new house Sanborn built on Spruce Street. The building was unique in Florence because of its art deco exterior and ultramodern interior. Miss Jane said when she stood inside, "This is the Florence Museum." It was a prophecy that was fulfilled fifteen years later.

After Miss Jane's death, true to my commitment, I wrote a series of articles for the *Florence Morning News* in which I outlined what I thought the Florence Museum should be. It was my hope that I could begin to change the perception that the museum was not essential. The result of the publication of these articles was that in May 1951 I was elected a trustee and the president of the Florence Museum all in one meeting.

The articles stressed the need for the collections displayed by the museum to interpret the natural, social, and political history of Florence and the Pee Dee area. Since the Florence Museum was chartered as a museum of art, science, and history, I argued, among other things, that traveling exhibits of artists would attract repeat visits to the museum. I naturally put in a plug for a first-rate exhibit of local Indian artifacts as part of the history of the area as well as exhibits interpreting the geological history of the area. After Miss Jane's death the board of trustees passed a resolution to change the name of the museum to the Jane B. Evans Memorial Museum. When I became president of the museum, I consulted the Evans family, who agreed with me that Miss Jane had chosen the name Florence Museum and that its potential for growth would be restricted if it was named as a memorial to one individual.

A window of opportunity opened in 1951. Thomas Evans, Miss Jane's brother, a bachelor who lived in Philadelphia, offered to give fifty thousand dollars to the museum if the group could raise ten thousand dollars and persuade the city of Florence to take over its operation. I appeared before the Florence City Council to make a plea that they accept the offer. With the usual adroitness of political leaders, council members said they would have a city-wide referendum to see whether the people wanted them to accept the offer.

The referendum was my real baptism into the treacherous world of politics. First we made arrangements with Sanborn Chase, who agreed to sell his house on Spruce Street and the remainder of the property he owned between the house and Park Avenue for seventy-five thousand dollars. With the aid of Sallyann Rogers, we invited William Burns, a curator with the American Museum of Natural History, to organize a campaign to persuade the public to accept the offer. Sallyann had charmed Burns with her lively letters and convinced him that his aid would be invaluable. Burns agreed to come and referred to Sallyann in his letters as "that flying saucy."

When Burns came to Florence to help, I met him at the train station in the early morning hours in February 1952. I had not met him before. When the train came in, it was easy to spot Burns, who was wearing a homburg hat and a black overcoat with a velvet collar.

I went up to him and said, "Dr. Burns?" He answered that he was indeed Dr. Burns. I said that I was Nick Zeigler, and I was here to greet him and take him to a motel. As we were walking to the car, Burns said, "You must be the son of the president of the museum." I replied that I was the president of the museum. Burns looked shocked and, with his accustomed bluntness, said, "I didn't know I was dealing with a bunch of cadets."

We drove to the motel. To break the silence, I told Burns I had purchased a fifth of bourbon whiskey and put it in his motel room. Burns said, "I never touch the stuff." That was followed by a more profound moment or two of silence. Burns then said, "With my left hand." We became good friends after that.

The campaign was hectic. For two weeks Burns and I made speeches to any group that would listen to us. Once, after speaking to a ladies' literary club, I asked if there were any questions. One of the ladies present said bluntly, "Well, I'm going to vote against it because I don't want to see Sanborn and Madge (his wife) get all that money."

To get some variety in the exhibits we began to move objects out of the cases and have special traveling exhibits. One of the best of these was an exhibit of ancient Greek vases on loan from the Metropolitan Museum in New York. These were displayed in August 1952.

The referendum was scheduled for September 23, 1952. We had raised seven thousand dollars and felt sure of getting the remaining three thousand dollars, but we were caught in a crossfire. At one Florence City Council meeting, someone asked if blacks would be admitted into the museum. I did not hesitate and said, "Yes, it will be a public building to which all people will be admitted." That raised the ire of the segregationists, who ran an ad in the *Florence Morning News* opposing the referendum on the grounds that blacks should be excluded from the building. This was followed by an ad paid for by the local NAACP opposing the plan. Their argument was that the money should be spent for other purposes. There was a general opposition to the use of city money for anything other than "essentials."

I was stunned by the NAACP opposition and made a point to seek out one of its leaders. I told him of my disappointment and stated that they were playing into the hands of the segregationists by opposing the museum. To my dismay he responded, "We'll take care of them later." The referendum failed by 71 votes—428 for and 499 against.

Lucille Hay, who worked hard for the referendum, called me, weeping. "Too many PB's, too many PB's," she said. "PB" is an acronym for the southern expression "po' buckra," a Gullah expression that literally means "poor white." It has a deeper meaning than mere poverty. It has come to mean someone who is spiritually barefoot regardless of his or her wealth.

It was fortunate that Evans was of an understanding nature. He agreed to give the fifty thousand dollars to the museum in increments of five thousand dollars over a ten-year period if the organization would acquire the Sanborn Chase residence and move in. The organization entered into an agreement with Sanborn Chase to purchase the house and one and a half acres surrounding it. The deal was consummated.

One of the first moves the board made was to employ a part-time director. I got a grant of $750 from the city of Florence, and Eugene Kauffman, an art teacher in the Florence public schools, agreed to be the first part-time director-curator of the museum.

Raising money in Florence for a museum was one of the most difficult tasks I have ever undertaken. In 1957 the museum decided to sponsor a beaux arts ball as a fund-raiser. To get publicity, we invited Bernard Baruch, who was at his plantation near Georgetown, South Carolina. He accepted, and a special park bench was added to the decor so that he could sit, as was his custom, and give advice to the revelers.

One civic leader, when approached for a contribution, stated flatly that he did not think a museum was a fitting objective for a city like Florence. He was not alone. Selling the idea of a museum as a vital institution for a growing city proved to be a formidable task. One businessman refused to become a museum trustee because, he said, "somebody might accuse me of it."

The Florence Museum moved to the Chase building and was opened to the public on October 7, 1953. As president I invited two men of different backgrounds to speak. Samuel G. Stoney of Charleston gave a speech titled "South Carolina, Appraising a Culture," and John R. Craft, a classical archaeologist and director of the Columbia Museum of Art, spoke on the need to encourage the arts in the state. The opening exhibit in the main gallery consisted of paintings by a group of South Carolina artists who called themselves the Carolina Five: William Halsey, Eugene Massin, Edmund Yaghjian, Gilmer Petroff, and Armando Del Cimmuto.

The museum now had a building and the opportunity to make itself an interesting, viable part of the community. The problem of lack of support, however, continued. The emphasis on art, chiefly painting, reached a point of diminishing returns. The task of getting more public support did not get easier after the school desegregation decision in May 1954. The old charge that the museum was open to blacks was raised again, and criticism persisted that it would be a waste of taxpayers' money.

The second director of the Florence Museum was a full-time employee, Jerome A. Donson. He and his wife, Naomi, were from New York and were given quarters in the downstairs apartment in the museum building. He remained director until the end of 1956. More financial support from the city and county of Florence was needed if the museum was to survive. The constitutionality of a direct appropriation to a private organization was raised; it was a problem I felt could be solved by creating a city-county historical commission. This commission would receive tax funds and decide how to use them. It was, in effect, a conduit to resolve the constitutional objection of grants to a private institution that performed a public function. I persuaded the county legislative delegation to enact a law creating the commission in March 1957.

The museum was making progress. In 1954 the Guild of South Carolina Artists had its statewide meeting at the Florence Museum. The gallery was presenting new exhibits of art, primarily paintings, regularly, but the science and history exhibitions were languishing because of lack of space. Donson was a tough-minded Yankee who pushed aggressively to create programs of interest to the public. In a newspaper article he summarized the activities of the museum from September 1955 to May 3, 1956: "The museum has had 35 temporary exhibitions; 14,631 attendance; 37 art class enrollments; 75 lectures and guided tours; 80 extension services; 72 receptions, events, etc.; 63 group meetings; 182 recent acquisitions; 30 'DISCOVERY' radio programs; [and] 341 members."

Donson was so brash that he challenged Congressman William Jennings Bryan Dorn to a debate in the Florence Museum. To my surprise Dorn accepted the invitation to debate his remark, made in the U.S. House of Representatives and printed in the *Congressional Record,* that modern art was a figment of communist imagination. The opposing view was to be argued by John R. Craft, of the Columbia Museum of Art, and Gilmer Petroff, an architect and former president of the Guild of South Carolina Artists. As president of the museum, I would moderate the debate, which was to be held on December 3, 1956.

Anne and I probably made a tactical mistake in inviting the congressman, Craft, and Petroff to dinner at our house prior to the debate. Congressman Dorn was an astute politician. It did not take him long to realize over our dinner conversation that he would be outgunned by Craft and Petroff.

When the time came to make his opening statement, Dorn did not repeat the outrageous assertion that all modern art was inspired by communism. Instead he said, with feigned meekness, that he had come to Florence to be instructed by the distinguished gentlemen opposing him. It was a wise decision because Craft and Petroff showed how patently absurd his view of modern art was.

Petroff produced a framed canvas that contained what appeared to be a rather abstract combination of various geometric shapes. The audience displayed some aversion to the painting. He then produced several yards of cloth and asked if anyone in the audience would consider buying it. There was generally more approval for the idea of this purchase. He then showed that the framed abstract painting was merely a portion of the strip of cloth. He said the cloth had been purchased at Belk Department Store, hardly an organization that was part of a communist conspiracy.

I continued to be president of the Florence Museum until 1960. In 1958 I ran unsuccessfully for the South Carolina House of Representatives; I was determined to succeed the second time I ran, so I relinquished the presidency of the museum.

During the ten years of my presidency, the museum acquired an outstanding collection of William Harrison Scarborough paintings and several paintings by William Henry Johnson, the noted African American artist who was a Florence native. I donated some of my Indian artifacts to the museum and gradually objects relating to the history of the area were acquired, but the goal of interpretive exhibits relating to the history of Florence and the Pee Dee area seemed as elusive as ever. More space and more financial support were required.

Thomas Evans died in 1966. In his will he left the Florence Museum the contents of his rooms in the Racquet Club in Philadelphia, the contents of his house on Jupiter Island, Florida, and a sculpture that was part of his swimming pool there. In order to settle his estate, I accompanied William S. "Jack" Dowis, who succeeded me as museum president, and our wives to Philadelphia to inventory the contents of the rooms there. We then went to Jupiter Island to meet a wealthy midwesterner, R. L. McGehan, who had a purchase contract from the Evans estate and was occupying the home on Hobe Sound. McGehan wanted to buy the fountain. When we arrived, Anne and Joyce Dowis found the temptation irresistible, and we all went to swim in the ocean.

After swimming we returned to the house, and the ladies went downstairs to shower and dress. Our host took Jack and me upstairs to a study. There was an adjoining bathroom and shower, and I deferred to Jack, who began to shower.

McGehan and I were left standing in the study. He was fully clothed while I was in my wet bathing trunks. He said casually, "If you will give me your bathing trunks, I will hang them to dry." I agreed to do so with some misgiving since I had no towel or robe to wear after I stripped. I took off my bathing suit and stood naked, feeling awkward and out of place in the study. My host returned and I, naked as a jaybird, attempted an air of nonchalance. He said in a very business like manner, "Now let us discuss the terms of sale."

I am familiar with the legal term *nudum pactum*—a "naked" contract that is not legally binding—so I assumed that this would be the result of my nude negotiations. At length Jack emerged fully clothed, and I escaped to the privacy that the shower afforded, leaving Jack to complete negotiations.

I have always winced at the criticism that the Florence Museum is only a good collection of odds and ends without any sense that its objects tell a coherent story. The sort of interpretative exhibits that I hope eventually will be seen in the Florence Museum require more money and space than have ever been available.

A failed attempt was made in 1972 to get the city and county to take over the museum's operation. On May 11, 1972, in the midst of my campaign for the U.S. Senate, I introduced a bill to create a Florence County museum commission and provide a one-mill tax to be effective upon conveyance to it of the museum's real and personal property. A referendum was held in the general election of 1972, and the voters of Florence County turned down the initiative. The vote in Florence County was 6,649 in favor and 11,457 against. Even the vote in the Florence city precincts failed by a narrow margin—3,011 in favor and 3,517 against. At times when the museum has been rebuffed by the electorate, my wife shrewdly observed, "Well, water will eventually wear stone away." My response has been the biblical lament, "How long, O Lord, how long?"

To solve the space question in 1986, I undertook to get the county to have the old Sears building opposite the Florence City-County Complex renovated to house the Florence Museum. I even got a grant to finance the engineering study, and Dave Sennema, former director of the South Carolina Arts Commission, and Jack Dowis made a proposal that would have been a turning point in the museum's history. Unfortunately the board of trustees of the museum was halfhearted, at best, in pushing the proposal, and the county lost interest.

The struggle to sustain a museum in Florence has not been easy. After the museum moved out of the library, the rooms it occupied were used for the classrooms by an extension of the University of South Carolina that eventually became Francis Marion University. Thus the library proved to be the incubator of cultural institutions. In the constellation of cultural activity the Florence County Library, the Little Theatre, the Florence Museum, the Center for the Performing Arts, and the Civic Center should be generously supported by the public and by the city and county. Miss Jane was right—a city with a museum is better than one that doesn't have one.

14
Big Brothers

When I returned to Florence in 1949, I had very little interest in criminal law or the reform of penal institutions. I knew the deplorable conditions in the county and city jails, but I felt it was the responsibility of elected officials to change them, and I did not intend to run for any public office. There was a juvenile reform school on the edge of the city for white boys called the Florence Industrial School for Boys. It was established in 1913 and was the first state correctional agency to deal with the problem of juvenile delinquency by treating youth offenders separately from adult offenders. It was customary to tell young people that if they didn't behave properly, they would probably end up in the industrial school. When I was a high school student, some of the industrial school boys were allowed to attend high school in Florence. I was impressed by the fact that they were well behaved and quite smart. I could not understand what they might have done to be punished.

Before my father died in August 1950, he required surgery and multiple blood transfusions. Hospital officials told me that they preferred to have the family replace the blood that had been given to patients. Family or friends could donate blood, or there were some boys at the school who frequently volunteered to give blood. My blood was not acceptable because I had contracted malaria in my youth, so I called the school and told the officials my problem. The following day I was told that several boys were willing to replace the blood supply.

I was moved by the kindness of these boys and asked the officials at the Industrial School if there was any way I could demonstrate my gratitude. I was told that there was a volunteer group that taught Sunday school and I might wish to join them. On further enquiry I discovered that the group came from Calvary Baptist Church in Florence. I was welcomed into the teachers' group and soon discovered that I was the only non-Baptist member.

I am a committed Christian, but I have never felt comfortable with Sunday schools and regarded attendance at St. John's Sunday School as a painful experience. I had tried to be a faithful member of my church's Young People's Service League, but the Sunday evening meetings always concluded with the singing of "Taps." Combined with the prospect of having to go to school the next day, the experience sent me into a depressed state as I walked home.

Another psychological hurdle was the prospect of teaching with a decidedly evangelical group of churchmen. I sang in the choir at Sewanee and in law school, but I never attended Sunday school, men's club meetings, or desired to be on the vestry of any church I attended. I liked the Book of Common Prayer and the conservative liturgical practices and hymns of the Episcopal Church. I did not feel comfortable singing hymns such as "The Old Rugged Cross" or "There Is a Fountain Filled with Blood." It seemed to be what one of my college professors referred to as "raw meat religion." To add to my misgivings was the fact that I had never taught school, either secular or religious, and I did not know what kind of reception I would receive from juvenile delinquents.

My apprehensions were misplaced, and the experience of teaching at the Florence Industrial School for nearly twenty-three years has influenced the course of my life. I came to the conclusion John Morley expressed in his *Life of Gladstone*: "The building up of the inner man in all of his parts, faculties and aspirations was seen [by Gladstone] to be, what in every generation it is, the problem of problems." I also recalled what I had heard at a lecture at Harvard given by William Ernest Hocking, that the greatest civil right is the freedom to become what one is capable of becoming without unduly interfering with others' right to do the same.

Armed with these noble sentiments, I began to teach Sunday school, but found the literature from which we were asked to teach not suitable for the instruction of teenage boys. I exercised much ingenuity in going from the text of the lesson plan to what I thought would engage the interest of my class. It was a matter of concern that someone might accuse me not only of being nonorthodox but also of teaching philosophy instead of religion. My fears were without foundation because I was never reproached by my fellow teachers. I told people that I was enjoying the spiritual benefits of two worlds: I taught for the Baptists and sang for the Episcopalians.

It did not take me long, however, to get into trouble with the authorities at the school. Early on I realized that many unnecessary repressive measures were taken to maintain order. After one of my classes a boy of about fifteen asked me if I could get him a rosary. He told me that he had endeavored to get one, but the officials at the school discouraged his doing so. Although I am not a Roman Catholic, I told the boy I would get him a rosary. I contacted Father William Tobin, the priest in charge of St. Anthony's

Church, and he brought a rosary to my office. I took it to the dormitory where the boy lived and delivered it to the adult in charge. What I regarded as a fundamental right and duty was disparaged by the person to whom I delivered the rosary. He seemed to feel that conversion to Protestantism might be better for the boy concerned. My response was that the boy had problems enough, and if his particular brand of religion was important in his life, it should be encouraged. It was probably unwise of me to elaborate by saying that if the boy were a Muslim, I would attempt to secure a prayer rug for him if he asked me to do so.

Word made its way up to the top of the school administration, and Judge Wylie H. Caldwell Sr., chairman of the Board of Juvenile Corrections, took me aside and told me that the superintendent had requested the board ask me to cease visiting the school's property because I was interfering with the school's management. Judge Caldwell assured me that the board was not going to grant the request. Despite that assurance I went to the superintendent and explained my course of action in the rosary case and told him of other, less dramatic wrongful actions by the school. Although my visit smoothed things over, I continued as probationer on the premises. I was determined, however, to help these young people as much as I could without getting into further trouble.

A big change took place in January 1953, when federal judge Ashton Williams appointed me to a committee to study ways to prevent juvenile delinquency. President Truman had appointed Judge Williams to a federal judgeship the year before. Williams was a man of deep feeling for other human beings, an intelligent man with a heart of gold. He served as a state senator from Florence County. He called a meeting in the courtroom of the federal building and appointed a committee of six people that included Jack O'Dowd and me. He told the group assembled that "young people did not become criminals if they received proper interest and attention. . . . It is my intention to devote the rest of my life to trying to assist these unfortunate men and women who need my help. They need your help. It is difficult for the court and its officers to accomplish much without the help of the good people of each community." Judge Williams asked the committee to study the matter and come back with a report. The committee elected me its chairman.

My connection with the Florence Industrial School proved helpful. One of the brightest lights in the administration was a new employee, Ellis MacDougall. Ellis had a degree in criminology from a great northern university, and he brought a new level of professionalism and understanding to the criminal justice system in South Carolina. We met and rapidly became friends. I explained to him my dilemma with regard to chairing the committee and asked if he had any books I could read on criminology. He gave me several, and I soon discovered I was dealing with "the problem of problems."

I learned that good intentions and good will are not enough in dealing with juvenile delinquency. Also, there are a limited number of areas in which volunteers can be useful or effective. In my reading I discovered the Big Brothers of America, an organization established in 1904 to help young boys who lacked father figures in their lives. I became convinced that the one man–one boy concept of Big Brothers afforded the best, most effective way of involving people of good will to deal with juveniles.

Ellis MacDougall later became the head of the South Carolina correctional system and an instructor at the University of South Carolina. I was fortunate that he was in Florence at the time to guide me.

I convinced the committee that there was a limited area in which volunteers could become involved in helping young people who needed guidance and that any group seeking to help others needed the guidance of people trained in the social sciences. Big Brothers of America had found, from experience, that assigning one man to one boy under the supervision of a trained social worker was a model that worked. The committee gave me authority to contact the national office of Big Brothers in Philadelphia and to investigate their program. I received an immediate response from their national director, Felix Gentile.

I have had the good fortune to meet and work with several people whom I liked immediately and whose influence on my life has been enduring. Such a man was Felix Gentile, who combined the qualities of urbanity, intelligence, and sensitivity to the problems of others. He volunteered to come to Florence to discuss the matter with me. We were the first group from the South that had asked to become a member of the national organization and the first group of any kind from a predominately rural area.

My report recommended incorporating a Big Brothers chapter for the nine counties that bordered the Great Pee Dee River. While the objective of the organization was to work in all nine counties, the main thrust was to organize in Darlington, Florence, and Marion. Once incorporated, we would be admitted to membership in the national organization and would be its fiftieth member.

Judge Williams called a meeting on July 2, 1953, and I presented the report of the committee. I sensed that Williams was disappointed that the committee had not proposed something more dramatic. With some difficulty I persuaded him that it was not only ineffective but perhaps dangerous to involve lay people in dealing with criminal offenders, young or old. What we proposed was a plan that had been tried and proven successful. An ounce of prevention is worth a pound of cure. Williams reluctantly approved our plan, but several weeks later he called a meeting in Charleston and set up a plan in which volunteers would aid young parolees. That group did not survive long.

Our group went forward, and we determined that the first board would be racially integrated. John Buchanan, a well-known tailor and leader among the area's black citizens, agreed to serve on the board. On July 17 at St. John's Episcopal Church, the Pee Dee Big Brothers held its organizational meeting. Seventy-five people attended, including Judge Williams, Felix Gentile, and Charles Berwind, president of the national Big Brothers.

In the first year of operation the organization had 126 referrals, 76 of which were considered appropriate for consideration, and of these 34 were assigned a big brother. My little brother was the first case assigned. He is now a substantial citizen of Florence. Working with him became a special project for me and my wife. In effect it provided a prelude to our own parenthood.

Serious problems arose after the U.S. Supreme Court desegregation decision in 1954. The Pee Dee Big Brothers was racially integrated from the outset, a fact that did not escape the notice of militant segregationists. In the April 9, 1955, issue of the *Charleston News and Courier* an article appeared under the headline "Florence Group Attacks Agencies":

Florence, April 8—Rep. G. S. Harrell of Florence County promised the local States Rights chapter today "the South Carolina General Assembly will stay in session the year around if necessary to keep state schools segregated."

The States Rights chapter, meeting to elect officers, leveled attacks on a local hospital, the United Fund and Big brothers, Inc. . . .

Jack Rains, a member of the Florence chapter, told the group a local hospital "is mixing babies in its nursery." Mr. Rains said the nursery is being attended by a white nurse.

Mr. Ivey told the group Big Brothers, Inc., one of the organizations included in the United Fund drive here, "is an interracial organization."

George Waring of Darlington leveled an attack on the Red Cross program. Waring said the Red Cross discontinued segregation of blood in 1951 under the advice of both "medical and non-medical groups." Waring said he was going to investigate the nonmedical group that gave the advice.

State representative George Sam Harrell, referred to in the article, was the dean of Florence County's House delegation and regularly introduced a bill in the General Assembly that would require the segregation of Negro blood from white blood. He referred to it as his "nigger blood bill."

In the fall of 1954 Anne got a job as a teacher in the junior high school in Florence. In addition to teaching math, she taught general science. There was a chapter on Darwin's theory of evolution in the general science textbook that was prescribed for use in the school. In order to do a thorough job in covering the subject, Anne ordered slides from the American Museum of Natural History. I warned Anne that there might be trouble if she went too thoroughly into the subject of evolution and briefed her on how to reconcile evolution with the biblical account of creation: "A thousand ages in thy sight are as a moment gone, etc." It was all to no avail.

A group of outraged parents petitioned the school board to have Anne fired. The principal suggested that Anne tell her classes that she did not believe in evolution and that it was only a theory. This she refused to do. Anne asked other science teachers how they dealt with the chapter on evolution in the state-approved textbook. They replied that they just skipped over it. It seemed inevitable that I would have to play Clarence Darrow in a replay of the Tennessee "monkey trial." Fortunately Hazel Gee came to Anne's rescue and sidetracked the demand that she be fired. The matter was resolved when it was discovered that Anne was pregnant, and she had to resign for that reason. Pregnant women were not allowed to teach at that time.

Our first child, Belton Townsend, was born on June 13, 1955, our second wedding anniversary. It became obvious when Anne was again pregnant that the two-room garage apartment would not be adequate for our growing family. My mother and Aunt Deda agreed to sell the Darlington Highway house to us and move into town. The move was accomplished by March 1956. Our second child, Helen Townsend, was born on May 11, 1956. Anne's father sent her a telegram congratulating her on the birth "of a second twin."

Once we were established in our new home, the garage apartment stood vacant. It weighed heavy on my conscience that some of the boys in the Florence Industrial School had to remain in the institution over the Christmas and Easter holidays, so Anne and I agreed to invite two brothers who had no place to go to stay in the garage apartment during these holidays. We made the mistake of putting in a supply of cold drinks, candy, and cookies for their consumption during the week. Unfortunately they ate most of the supply on the first night of their visit and became ill, requiring a trip to the doctor.

Charles W. Fleming, the first director, by his skill and enery, gave the organization a sound foundation. There is no sure way to judge the success or failure of any program like Big Brothers. We know there have been success stories and there have been failures, but the good will and resources of the community were marshaled in an intelligent way to solve the "problem of problems." The organization I helped create has lasted more than fifty years, and approximately six thousand boys have been given the care it provides. That means that at least six thousand men have been involved in the effort to help other human beings. When the organization celebrated its fiftieth year, my little brother, now a grown man, told the press that I had saved his life. I needed no more reward than that.

15
The Carney Case

It made me sick to talk to him, but I could not avoid it. Along with C. C. "Cubby" McDonald and Rogers Kirven, I was assigned to defend Raymond Carney on the charge of murdering Harvey B. Allen and Betty Clair Cain on December 6, 1953. It was a crime that had all of the gruesome details necessary to set the entire community in a state of frenzy and fury. Carney was a black man, and the victims were both white. The decapitated body of Betty Cain, who was only fifteen, was found buried in a shallow grave on a bank overlooking the Pee Dee River, and her severed head and Harvey Allen's body were found in a well on an abandoned house site about a mile from the grave. Anyone who committed these terrible acts seemed to me to have forfeited his claim to be a member of the human race.

For a period of nearly two weeks between the discovery of the bodies and the murderer's capture there was a period of intense apprehension. The authorities designated Carney as the prime suspect, and a reward of thirty-five hundred dollars was offered for information leading to his apprehension. In the poster offering the reward he was described as being thirty-eight years of age, "Height 6′2″; weight, 170 pounds; build, medium; hair black, with graying spots, may be wearing long sideburns; Eyes, brown; Complexion, dark brown; occupations, carpenter's helper, cook, laborer, painter;— Remarks, stammers and mouth twitches when talking, may be wearing a mustache."

Three hunters captured Carney in late December near Johnsonville, approximately sixteen miles from the scene of the murders. He stated that he had stayed in that area during the entire time of the manhunt. Carney first attempted to conceal his real identity when taken to the city jail in Johnsonville. He made one desperate, unsuccessful attempt to escape during the time his identity was being checked, using an iron bar he had concealed in his clothing. After about two hours in jail he admitted who he was and was immediately taken to the South Carolina State Penitentiary in

Columbia to avoid the danger of lynching by the outraged citizens of Florence County. He remained there until he was brought to Florence for arraignment in the court of general sessions on January 4, 1954.

Carney would need legal counsel. Even in 1954, South Carolina required that a lawyer be provided to any man on trial for his life, but it was a task that no lawyer sought. When the court convened, Judge Steve C. Griffith, who presided over Carney's arraignment, immediately appointed T. Kenneth Summerford as counsel. Summerford stated in open court and in the presence of prospective jurors that "he felt he could not and should not serve" as defense counsel.

Judge Griffith then appointed another Florence lawyer, Richard Dusenbury, to the case, but Dusenbury told the judge in chambers that his brother was an elected official and to serve as defense counsel for Carney would be detrimental to his brother's political career. For that reason he asked the judge to excuse him, and the judge did.

Judge Griffith expressed dismay at the difficulty in getting members of the Florence County bar to defend Carney, so he did something unusual. He directed the clerk of court to call all of the members of the Florence County bar to meet him that evening in the grand jury room of the courthouse. Notification was no big problem since there were only about fifty lawyers practicing in Florence County at that time. Of this number only about twenty were known as "courtroom lawyers," or—in today's terminology—litigators.

As a young courtroom lawyer I attended the meeting. There were about twenty-five lawyers in attendance. When we assembled in the grand jury room, Judge Griffith came in and asked us to move over in a group to one end of the room. He then made a short speech, saying he was disappointed that he had difficulty in finding a lawyer willing to defend Raymond Carney and stressing that under our system of jurisprudence every defendant had the right to have counsel in a criminal case. The case against Carney was not only a criminal case but also potentially involved imposition of the death penalty. Judge Griffith pointed out that lawyers take an oath upon admission to the bar agreeing to do their duty when the requested by the court.

Griffith said sternly, "I could make the lawyers I appoint do their duty whether they want to or not, but since this is a case in which the death penalty is a possibility, I do not think it would be fair to the defendant to have defense counsel who cannot give their best professional effort in defending the case." He expressed again his disappointment in the attitude of the Florence bar and stated firmly, "All of you who cannot do your duty if I appoint you to defend in this case, please move to the other side of the room." To my dismay, more than two-thirds of the Florence bar moved to the opposite side of the room, leaving me and three or four others standing helplessly in place.

Judge Griffith wasted no time: "Mr. Zeigler, I appoint you to defend Carney, and I appoint C. C. McDonald and Rogers Kirven to assist you. Thank you for coming, gentlemen, that is all." I was stunned. I did not move while the members of the bar filed out of the room. When I started toward the door, Judge Griffith stopped me and offered his hand. While I was shaking his hand, he said, "Mr. Zeigler, no matter how hard this may seem to you now, in the long run people will think more of you for being willing to do your duty." I thanked him and left in a daze.

The next day I told Uncle Peter what had happened. "This is the kind of case that, no matter how great the fee offered might be, you would have to decline it," I observed. Uncle Peter said wryly, "There may be a case like that, but I've never heard of it." I was learning rapidly, but what was most unexpected, I would learn a great lesson from Raymond Carney.

Carney was thoroughly demonized in both my and the public's mind. Who was this monster no lawyer anxious for the good will of the public wished to defend? His presence in Florence for the arraignment gave my associates and me our first opportunity to interview him. He was brought by two deputy sheriffs to an office in the courthouse, and I struggled to overcome my instinctive loathing for someone who could commit such a horrible crime. I found it difficult to maintain eye contact with him and suppress my feeling of revulsion.

The first conversation was primarily devoted to finding out who he was, where he had been, and what he expected our representation could do for him. Two things emerged immediately from our conversations. Carney stammered occasionally, and he had been previously treated for syphilis. Did he have mental problems that possibly might be associated with syphilis?

Relating the bare facts of his life was like probing a festering sore on the body of the South. It contained all of the degrading effects of racial segregation, poverty, lack of economic incentives, and the hypocrisy of separate but equal education. Carney was born in Wilson County, North Carolina, on January 4, 1915. He recalled that his father made twenty-five cents a day as a laborer, and prior to 1924 Carney attended school for only half a year. As a boy Carney drove a "fish wagon," for which he received some small amount of money and candy for his service.

When he was nine years old, Carney's family moved to Tarboro, North Carolina, where they remained until 1927. During this period Carney attended school and made it to the fourth grade. He earned money for the family by "chopping cotton." The family moved in and around Tarboro during the period 1927–32. Carney seems not to have attended school during this time but did carpentry work, earning a maximum of seventy-five cents a day as the South was entering the depths of the Depression. In 1932 they had a fight, and his father beat him and "ran him off."

In 1933 Carney joined the Civilian Conservation Corps, which had a camp at Fort Bragg, North Carolina. He was with the CCC for nine months, and on leaving in 1934 he married Rebecca Bridges and began living in the house with his wife's father. Carney and Rebecca had one child, a daughter, born in 1935. That year he was arrested on the day after Christmas for being drunk. Carney's life from this point on is punctuated by arrests, imprisonments, and drifting between and within North Carolina and South Carolina. In 1938 he was arrested for stealing a bicycle and sentenced to eighteen months in prison. In 1939 he separated from his wife and went to Wilmington to work for a sawmill. In 1941 he moved to Dillon, South Carolina, and worked on a farm until he was convicted of breaking into a store. For that offense he spent seventeen months and six days in prison in Columbia, South Carolina.

Upon his release Carney returned to Tarboro, North Carolina, and resumed cohabitation with Rebecca while he worked in a tent factory. He left and returned to Wilmington to work in a shipyard for six months but returned to Rebecca and Tarboro in 1944. This ended when he broke into the post office at Pollockville, North Carolina. For this offense he was tried in federal court and sentenced to five years in the Atlanta federal prison.

Released from federal prison in 1949, Carney went to Wilson, North Carolina, and lived with his uncle Elijah. There Carney was again arrested and sentenced to do time on the chain gang in Wilson County in 1950. One report stated that he had a record of eleven arrests in North Carolina.

In March 1953 Carney escaped from the Wilson County chain gang and came to Florence County, South Carolina, where he got employment with the Willow Creek Lumber Company. In July 1953 Carney moved in with Margaret Smith, who lived near Pamplico and soon became deeply involved in bootlegging whiskey. The vast swamps of the Great Pee Dee River and its tributaries, which had shielded Francis Marion during the American Revolution, provided a perfect hiding place for illicit liquor stills. No doubt Carney became intimately familiar with this river swamp and with the landing at DeWitt's Bluff, just down the road from Margaret Smith's house, where the tragic events of December 6, 1953, took place.

The story Carney told of the murders was striking for its horrible simplicity. On the evening of December 6, 1953, he was engaged to go on a "run" to deliver bootleg whiskey. He and two others went to Georgetown and returned to Pamplico about seven o'clock in the evening. Carney asked his companions to drive him to the end of the pavement on the Old River Road near the entrance to DeWitt's Bluff, where Carney said he had to meet a man. They saw the pistol Carney was carrying and watched him walk down the road leading to DeWitt's Bluff.

According to Carney his motive was robbery. He had observed couples parked at DeWitt's Bluff, which had the reputation of being a local lovers' lane. Carney waited a couple of hours for a victim, but no cars came. He was walking away when he saw a car turn into the road leading to the bluff.

Carney returned and concealed himself near the car. He listened for conversation in the car, and when it stopped, he crept up to the car. He intended to open the driver's door and thrust his hand with the gun into the car. Instead, Carney stated, he opened the passenger's door and announced that this was "a stickup."

According to Carney, Allen grabbed his arm and the gun fired twice. It was not clear whether Allen had been wounded, but he emerged from the car and fought Carney. Carney struck Allen's head several times with the gun, and Allen fell. Carney fired again to make sure that Allen was dead.

Cain asked if Allen was dead. Carney replied that he didn't know and grabbed her by the arm. According to Carney, she said, "I thought you wanted money." Carney replied that he did want money and proceeded to take Allen's wallet. Carney then pushed Cain down and told her to pull down her pants. She replied that she would not. Carney then pulled down her undergarments and endeavored to rape her but was unable to have an erection. He said Cain begged him not to shoot her, but he knew that she would tell, and the penalty for rape was electrocution. So Carney deliberately brought the pistol to her head and fired. She died instantly. Carney had only gained fourteen dollars and Allen's wristwatch.

Carney was then confronted with the problem of what to do with the bodies. That was the most bizarre and horrifying part of the story. Carney put both bodies in the trunk of Allen's car and drove toward the River Road using an old road that was overgrown with weeds. About a mile from the bluff the car bogged down. It was about midnight on a blustery winter night. Carney left the car and walked to his house—about a mile away—to get croaker sacks, wooden planks, and a shovel to use in getting Allen's car unstuck.

Carney returned on foot to the car, which had stood unattended. He had no idea if anyone else had come up to it in his absence. He got the car out of the bog and returned to DeWitt's Bluff. There he removed Cain's body from the trunk. According to Carney, he had read about a murder in the Bahama Islands where the murderer had escaped detection by dismembering the victim's body and burying the parts in different places. Carney claimed that on the basis of this book he decided to dismember the bodies of Betty Cain and Harvey Allen.

With only a pocket knife, he decapitated the girl. He intended to decapitate Harvey Allen but later claimed that he lost his nerve or perhaps his stomach. Instead Carney decided he would bury the girl's body in a stump-hole left by "a harrican tree," a hole formed by the uprooting of a large tree during a hurricane.

Carney used the shovel that he had brought to free the car from the bog and took the body to the hole, which was about five feet deep. He dug a grave in the bottom of the hole and buried the girl's headless body.

Having accomplished this task, Carney pulled himself out of the hole and stood there on its edge briefly. As the cold wind increased, a dead tree fell nearby. It was so close that Carney was struck by a limb of the tree, knocking him back into the hole and on top of the grave he had dug. It seemed to me that this was a symbolic if not a prophetic event that would have unhinged any ordinary mind. But Carney's was no ordinary mind. His life experiences had so brutalized and dehumanized him that he emerged from the hurricane tree hole, brushed himself off, and proceeded with the business of disposing of Betty Cain's head and Harvey Allen's body.

Carney remembered that there was an old abandoned house that had a deep well a mile or so from the bluff. He drove the car down abandoned roads to the nearest point to the house. Carney then went to a nearby tobacco barn and got what was known as a tobacco drag, a sled pulled by a mule and used to drag cropped tobacco from the fields to the curing barn. He put Allen's body and the girl's head in the drag and transported them to the well. Carney put them in the bottom of the well and shoveled in enough dirt to cover them. Having done this, he endeavored to camouflage the well by covering it with large weeds and cornstalks.

Carney then drove Allen's car to a "colored school house," abandoned it, and walked to his own house. According to Margaret he arrived at the house between 4:00 A.M. and "just before daylight," but she also made the statement that he got home at about 2:00 A.M., apparently in an attempt to provide an alibi. Carney told Margaret that he had been out with some girls, and to explain his bloodied condition, he said he had gotten into a fight. The next day Carney resumed working on another liquor run, but Margaret apparently suspected something and spent Monday night at her father's house. When she returned the next day, Carney was gone.

Incredible as it seemed, there was nothing in Carney's statement that indicated that anyone else had helped him either before or after the fact. We pointed out to him that we could make a better case for leniency if other people had been involved, but Carney was adamant, insisting that he had acted alone.

We had been furnished with a written confession, a typewritten document dated January 2, 1954, and signed by Carney, certifying that the two pages were "a true copy of [a] statement which I wrote in pencil in my own handwriting, and I have received a copy of same." He verified to us that the statement was essentially correct so far as the events surrounding the deaths of Allen and Cain.

I tried as best I could to explain to Carney the difficult position we were placed in as his defense counsel. He had confirmed to us that he and he alone had murdered both victims, and he had signed a written confession to that effect. Carney's response was frustratingly simple: "I want you to save my life if you can." It struck me as ironic that Carney, in effect, wanted mercy, but he had shown no mercy to Allen and Cain.

After the conference with Carney, Cubby McDonald, Rogers Kirven, and I went back to my office and agreed to move for a continuance of the trial. The case could be called within three days for trial but was too complicated to expect counsel to prepare an effective defense within that time. I suggested that we also make a motion to have Carney sent to the South Carolina State Hospital for a psychiatric examination, and it was agreed that I prepare the appropriate motion immediately. The grounds stated in the motion dated January 5, 1954, were that counsel did not have sufficient time to prepare a defense and that Carney should have an examination to determine his mental capacity.

In the motion for the continuance and the motion to have the defendant examined at the state hospital, we summarized our belief that there was a question of the defendant's mental competence because he had been treated for syphilis, had a pronounced speech impediment, and his powers of mental association appeared to be erratic. We argued that these facts raised the possibility that the defendant had a mental disease. The petition further stated that even if the court excluded the possibility of the defendant's basing his defense upon insanity, a relationship of the disease to the crime would have a distinct bearing upon the degree of guilt.

Judge Griffith heard the motion on the following day, January 6, 1954. The scene in the courtroom was dramatic. Carney, dressed in the same shabby clothes he had been wearing when he was captured, was seated beside me with other counsel at the defense table. Such was the hostility of the community toward Carney that sheriff's deputies and highway patrolmen were lined up, shoulder to shoulder, facing the spectators in the courtroom. I argued the motion, and counsel for the state immediately stated their opposition to both a continuance and the examination at the state hospital. Griffith asked that counsel come to his chambers to discuss the matter further before he made a ruling.

All counsel dutifully filed out of the courtroom to the judge's chambers. On my way there, George Keels, who was retained by the Allen family to assist the solicitor (the elected prosecutor) in trying the defendant, came up beside me, and we walked together down the hall to the judge's chambers.

Keels was one of the most flamboyant members of the Florence bar. He had never gone to law school, and my Aunt Deda had coached him in the early 1930s so that he was able to pass the bar examination. He was one of the last lawyers to be admitted to the South Carolina bar without having attended law school. He had a booming voice and the physical appearance of a man so full of energy he might explode at any minute. His addresses to Florence County juries provided entertainment because of their ingenuity and ferocity. Keels made no secret of the fact that he was an active member of the Ku Klux Klan.

"Nick," George said in a loud voice, "I'll tell you why I opposed your motions." I said nothing, and he continued, "They should take the son of a bitch and burn him right now." I was in no mood for this sort of exchange and replied stiffly, "That would hardly be in the great tradition of Anglo-American jurisprudence." By that time we had reached the judge's chambers, and there was no more said between us.

Judge Griffith stated almost immediately that he was going to grant both motions. He did not feel that counsel had sufficient time to prepare an effective defense and thought a mental examination was in order. He stated, however, that the case would be tried at the March term and that the order for a mental examination should provide that any examination of Carney by the South Carolina State Hospital would have to be completed by March 1, 1954. I prepared the necessary orders, and Griffith signed them.

When Griffith announced his decision in open court, he alluded to the fact that the jury panel may have been tainted by the original counsel's stating in open court that he could and would not defend Carney. The judge added, however, that he was granting the continuance on the grounds that defendant's counsel had argued.

It should be remembered that in 1954 there was no fund to reimburse counsel assigned to defend an accused in court and no provision for fees and expenses. If counsel wished to consult with Carney, we had to make arrangements with the state hospital or the Department of Corrections and pay our own expenses to get to Columbia and back.

To add to our vexation in the Carney case, community hostility was so intense that it was difficult to get law enforcement officials to cooperate with defense counsel. The matter came to a head when we requested that the sheriff's office take defense counsel to the Pamplico area to view the sites associated the crime. Sheriff John Hanna categorically refused to ride in the same car with us. He felt that to be seen riding with us would injure him politically and damage the state's case. Finally a deputy, who later became sheriff, agreed to drive us to various places mentioned in the accounts of the murders.

The threats to kill Carney in the courtroom became so persistent in Florence that some of my friends suggested I purchase a bulletproof vest. They pointed out that inevitably I would have to sit next to Carney during the trial, and if someone tried to shoot Carney, he might miss and shoot me. The fact that I had gone north to law school was thrown into the fermenting agitation, and some speculated that I was somehow connected with Yankee agitation to give civil rights to African Americans. The less charitable said I was "a nigger lover at heart."

Cubby McDonald, Rogers Kirven, and I visited Carney at least twice in the state penitentiary and once at the state hospital. We continued to stress the fact that if he had not acted alone, that if anyone else had been involved, it might make it easier for us to plead for mercy and avoid the death penalty. Carney steadfastly maintained that he had acted alone, although on one visit he indicated that he had received help from a white man. My recollection is that the name he gave the man had no significance for us. It was not a name that any of the three of us recognized as connected with anyone we knew in the Pamplico community. We immediately reported this information to the captain of the guard at the penitentiary however, so that it could be properly investigated.

It all came to naught. Following this visit an article appeared in Columbia's *State* newspaper on March 5, 1954:

CARNEY, SLEEPLESS AFTER LIE,

REPUDIATES TALE OF ACCOMPLICE

"I couldn't sleep last night after I had lied to you," Raymond Carney, confessed slayer of a Pamplico couple told officers yesterday morning. Before repudiating a statement involving another person in the crime [*sic*].

We may have stressed too much the advantage to Carney's case if he had received assistance either before or after the murders. The events surrounding the murders seemed to us to require more than the stamina and effort of one person acting alone. However, my notes do not contain the name of the person who was named by Carney, and my recollection is that the only time he stated he had gotten help from a white man was on that first visit with him at the penitentiary.

The March 1954 issue of *Official Detective Stories* magazine carried a story about the murders, adding fuel to the speculation that Carney had not acted alone. The article insinuated that Miss Cain had dated a young farmer who lived three miles from Pamplico while Allen was in the service. Using a fictitious name, "Lignone," for the estranged boyfriend, ostensibly "to protect the innocent," the magazine article stated that "Lignone was a moody fellow who seldom left his farm but he was interested in Betty [Cain] and when she stopped dating him after Allen returned he had withdrawn even further into his shell." The magazine article added cryptically, "Hanna [the county sheriff] and Williams [the state law enforcement agent] filed away in their minds that name." If they did, they never revealed that name to defense counsel.

In all of the interviews we had with Carney before his trial, it was repeatedly pointed out to him that he should reveal to us the identity of any person, black or white, who might have given him assistance before, during, or after the murders. The importance of such a revelation was depicted in the strongest terms. It might mean the difference between his going to the electric chair or receiving a life sentence. But after his initial "lie," Carney resolutely maintained that he acted entirely alone.

On February 27, 1954, William S. Hall, superintendent of the South Carolina State Hospital, wrote to the solicitor, with a copy of the letter to the clerk of court and Carney's counsel, stating, "Psychiatric examination does not reveal evidence of mental illness (insanity), and the members of the Medical Staff making this examination diagnosed Raymond Carney as not insane." The letter included a statement that examination of Carney revealed there was no evidence of neurosyphillis. It also stated, "Psychological examination reveals that Raymond Carney is functioning at an intellectual level commensurate with the average of his race, age, and educational opportunities."

Hostility toward Carney grew in the months before the trial and began spilling over onto those who represented him. I was told that if I had any future political ambitions, I would do well merely to sit by Carney and do nothing to help him in the courtroom. Threats were made to shoot him and us either on the way to the courthouse or in the courtroom.

We were concerned about Carney's appearance to a jury. He had no clothes other than the rags he was wearing when he was captured, and none of his family would go near him in the penitentiary. We decided that he should be presentable when he appeared in the courtroom for trial, so I agreed to give him a pair of trousers, a shirt, and a tie, and the three of us would pay for shaving cream, a safety razor, soap, a toothbrush, and toothpaste.

When Carney was brought to the Florence County Jail the Sunday before court, I took the clothes and toilet items to him. The jail was in a separate building behind the Florence County Courthouse. The cells on the second floor had access to windows so that passersby in the parking lot between the jail and the courthouse were frequently regaled by shouts and pleas from prisoners who sought attention and possible aid. The first floor, where the jailer and sheriff had an office, smelled of stale cooking and urine. It took one's breath away on entering, and it required some minutes to adjust to the odor.

Sheriff Hanna was a large, raw-boned man who looked as though he might have come from central casting to play the part of a southern sheriff. He was at the office desk when I entered and said that I had something I wished to deliver to Carney. Hanna eyed my shopping bag suspiciously, and I took the items out one by one. When the safety razor was produced, Sheriff Hanna, holding up the razor, said somewhat triumphantly, "What if he kills himself with this?" I could not resist being impertinent, and replied, "That would save both you and me a lot of trouble, wouldn't it, Sheriff?" I was allowed to deliver the package to Carney.

Since Carney had admitted to us that he had committed the two murders and had signed two confessions, putting him on the witness stand was fraught with danger. In our planning for the trial we decided not to put Carney on the stand and to offer no testimony. Under our court rules, the defense would then have the last argument to the jury. That last plea would be for mercy.

There was also the problem of the signed confessions. Since the murder of Harvey Allen was scheduled for trial first, we decided to make every effort to keep out any reference to the murder of Betty Cain. In that effort we were successful. Judge Griffith ruled with us that no statement Carney had made with regard to the murder of Cain would be admissible.

The day of the trial was filled with tension. The courtroom crowd was huge. All the seats were filled; spectators lined the sides of the courtroom and stood in the hall leading to the stairs. Sheriff's deputies and highway patrolmen lined up shoulder to shoulder facing the audience. So much hostility was directed toward us that when we entered the courtroom I had the sensation of a hot blast issuing from an open furnace door. Carney made his entrance heavily guarded and clean shaven. A newspaper account of the trial stated that "Carney, clad in blue overall trousers, a white shirt and green tie, spoke softly, barely audibly." His appearance was much improved since his arraignment.

The selection of a jury proceeded normally. According to the practice of the time, there were no women in the jury pool—women were not permitted to serve on juries—but two black men were included. Judge Griffith excluded three potential jurors for cause since they stated they had already made up their minds with regard to the defendant's guilt. One prospective juror was excused because he was opposed to capital punishment. The state, exercising its right to peremptory challenges, struck the two black men from the jury pool. Our system of justice had not advanced to the point where peremptory challenges based solely on race were not permitted. Counsel for the defense exercised ten peremptory challenges.

The trial proceeded in a subdued manner. Most of the details of Betty Cain's death were not mentioned. The state put into evidence the discovery of Allen's wristwatch at Carney's house, as well as the discovery of the pistol used in the murder of Allen where Carney indicated he had buried it.

Carney's bootlegging companions testified that they were supposed to "make a run that night" and that their still was in the direction of DeWitt's Bluff. They testified that when they left Carney, he was proceeding toward the bluff. One bootlegger testified that on leaving them that night, Carney said that he was going to meet a man. We did not place much significance in the statement. During prohibition and the 1930s, when a man wished to take a drink of whiskey, either alone or in the company of others, he made the excuse that he was "going to see a man about a dog." I did not believe Carney's statement had any other implication than that he had private business he did not wish to discuss.

During his testimony Sheriff Hanna stated that two or three weeks prior to the trial Carney had claimed that another man committed the murder. The next day, however, Carney retracted the statement and admitted that he alone had committed the murder. In view of Carney's repeated statements to counsel for the defense, it was—and is—my opinion that Carney acted alone in the commission of the murders.

The prosecution, sensing that our strategy was to make a plea for mercy, laid heavy emphasis on the fact that Carney had shown no mercy. All three defense lawyers made speeches to the jury. C. C. McDonald appealed for a merciful judgment if the jury decided that state proved its case beyond a reasonable doubt. Rogers Kirven praised the defendant's cooperation and repentance and appealed to the jury by reminding them that "forgiveness is divine." I appealed for mercy, noting that execution is not a deterrent and would have no effect on similar crimes. My recollection is that I used the quotation from the prophet Micah: "What doth the Lord require of thee, but to do justly, and to love mercy, and to walk humbly with thy God?" Several years later, when the old courtroom was being repainted, I employed my friend Everett Baker, who was in charge of the redecorating, to have the painters stencil the quotation in an empty panel in the plaster over the judge's bench.

Judge Griffith charged the jury, instructing them that they could not consider Carney's failure to take the stand as any evidence of guilt and that the state had the burden of proving his guilt beyond a reasonable doubt. The jury deliberated only fifty-five minutes before returning with a verdict of guilty.

Sentencing a person to death is a wrenching experience for all involved, no matter the circumstances of the murder. It proved so in this case. Griffith performed his duty in the traditional way and in conclusion stated, "May God have mercy on your soul." The deputy sheriffs moved in quickly, took Carney by both arms, and began leading him out of the courtroom. Carney had only taken a few steps from the defense counsels' table when he pulled back and turned toward us. He said simply, "Thank you." Cubby McDonald was more sensitive than Rogers and I were, and I could see tears welling up in his eyes.

I must confess that Carney's simple gesture made a profound impression on me as well. It made me realize that despite his horrible crime, he was still a human being. I was wrong in my initial belief that he had separated himself from the human race.

The action of Allen's uncle, a deputy sheriff in Dillon County, who sat with Allen's father during the trial, also touched me. When Carney had been removed, he came over to our table and thanked us for the manner in which we had conducted the defense.

One distressing incident took place as Carney was being led from the courthouse. A reporter asked if he was going to appeal the case, and Carney replied that he was. He did this, of course, without consulting us. In fact there was no basis for an appeal, and all the costs of appeal would have to be borne by the three of us. Judge Griffith had ruled in our favor on the motions we had made to protect Carney, and there was nothing in the record to contradict the evidence presented to the jury.

Carney was returned to the state penitentiary. The three of us decided that we had to make a trip to Columbia and tell Carney that there was no basis for an appeal. In effect it was our difficult task to tell him that he should accept the jury's verdict and reconcile himself to execution. We did this, and Carney took our advice. He said quietly, "If you tell me there is no reason to appeal, I accept it."

It made me wonder if there had been more kindness shown in his life by fate and other human beings whether he might have avoided this sad con- clusion. Carney had a certain amount of intelligence: he was rational when things were explained to him, and he was capable of showing gratitude. In fact he asked me to write to Judge Griffith and thank him for giving him a fair trial. I did this and received the following letter from Griffith:

April 6, 1954

E. N. Zeigler, Esq,
McEachin, Townsend and Zeigler
Florence, S. C.

Dear Mr. Zeigler:
    I have your letter of March 29th enclosing a copy of your letter
to Solicitor Long, advising him that you and your associates who
defended Raymond Carney have decided not to appeal his case
to the Supreme Court. You convey to me the thanks of Raymond
Carney for his receiving a fair trial. I appreciate this statement of
Carney's perhaps more than you realize. During my service on the
bench I have formed the opinion that nearly every defendant
appreciates a fair trial and realizes when he is getting one. I have been
astonished at the apparent ability of a totally ignorant defendant to
judge a trial with respect to its fairness. For this reason I make an effort
to try to convince the defendant that he is receiving a fair trial, and I
am very glad to know that Carney was so impressed in his case.
    I want to assure you again that I appreciate the services that
you and your associates rendered in this case, and I was particularly
pleased with the able manner with which you represented the
defendant. Your development that the defendant was sorry for his
crime and sought forgiveness and mercy was the only plea that could
have been justified under the evidence in the case, and while it availed
the defendant nothing, it was a credit to Carney and his attorneys.
Frankly and confidentially, I do not know whether the death penalty is
the proper remedy in such matters. I too think that thoughtful people
ought to think about it so long as capital punishment is imposed, and

your defense for Carney will keep people thinking about it in the way they should.

I have often said that one of the compensations of being a circuit Judge, and which I like very much, is that it gives the opportunity of becoming acquainted with the members of the Bar throughout the State, and particularly the younger members. I wish to assure you that it has been a pleasure to have become acquainted with you and to have known you, and I look forward with pleasure to following your career until you shall have reached a place of distinction that is the hope and aspiration of all young members of the Bar to attain.

> With warmest regards,
> Sincerely yours,
> Steve C. Griffith

In my letter conveying Carney's expression of gratitude for having had a fair trial, I told Judge Griffith my initial misgivings about defending Carney:

> I must confess that I was somewhat appalled by your selecting me to serve as counsel in this case, and approached the whole matter with the gravest misgivings as I was completely biased against the defendant from the reports which I had read in the newspaper. I have come to realize more than ever, as a result of your action in putting me into this case, that the true test of advocacy is the ability to represent a cause which does not seem meritorious to one personally.

The impact of the Carney trial on me extended far beyond an understanding of the role of an advocate. It deepened my understanding of what it meant to be a human being. The events following the trial would be as edifying as the trial itself.

Carney's execution was set for May 7. Since none of his family would go near him, I took it upon myself to correspond with him on a weekly basis until the time of his execution. Carney wished for a Bible and a hymnal. I sent him both. I made arrangements for his "wife" to visit him before his execution. I do not recall whether she did so.

As Carney's execution approached, I discussed with him whether he wished me to come to Columbia to advise him until the time of his execution. The tradition is that defense counsel of a condemned man walk the last mile with his client. I was relieved when Carney said he did not need me to do this. I feared I would not be emotionally strong enough to perform properly under the circumstances if he had said he wanted me there.

What shocked me was that it was announced that tickets to the execution would be available and that counsel for the defendant would be entitled to two of these tickets. The three counsel stated that they did not want tickets, but I received numerous telephone calls from acquaintances asking if I could arrange for them to get some. I did not oblige them.

The execution was something of an auto-da-fé. Approximately twenty-five spectators were allowed in the death chamber. They hurled insults at Carney as he was strapped in the electric chair and put to death. His final words were, "To the people that I have caused their hearts to mourn, I hope they will forgive me."

The *Florence Morning News*, which had supported the effort to give Carney a fair trial, expressed contempt for his death house repentance: "As in Carney's case, the hymn singing and the plea for forgiveness often come too late. Hymns a few feet from the electric chair sing not praise of the Almighty but of desperation." The story of the good thief on the cross teaches a different lesson.

I continue to grieve for the families whose children were so horribly murdered. Two innocent human beings were killed. Betty Clair Cain was a popular high school sophomore, and Harvey B. Allen was a respected U.S. Air Force veteran. The grief caused by their deaths was enormous.

My emotional journey during the five months of the Carney case led back to the question that Cain asked God after murdering his brother: "Am I my brother's keeper?" I believe that the answer God must have given was, "No, but you must never forget that he *is* your brother." Society may not have been Carney's keeper, but he was still our brother. I wish we had done better by him. It might have saved three lives.

Part II   *A Journey Outward*

"And the second is like unto it, Thou shalt love thy neighbor as thyself." A precondition to becoming what one is capable of becoming is not to hinder others from doing the same. The Christian's duty to love one's neighbor as one's self is more difficult to fulfill than the duty of self-discovery. It is only secondary to the first commandment, but "on these two commandments hang all the law and the prophets."

This part of my story covers the period from 1958 to 1990, when I retired from the South Carolina Board of Corrections. I perceived that my duty as a human being was, in the words of William Ernest Hocking, "to universalize myself." In the words of Jesus of Nazareth, "For whosoever will save his life shall lose it; but whosoever shall lose his life for my sake and the gospel's, the same shall save it." I take this saying to mean that once I reached my center, I had to lose myself in the service of others in order, more surely, to find myself.

16

My Political Novitiate

I never felt comfortable running for public office, and I dreaded and disliked doing what a politician must do to get elected. In a sense the same observation that my aunt Margaret McEachin had made about Uncle Peter was true of me: I was a "synthetic politician." It was always difficult for me to enjoy the chicken bogs, barbecues, and club meetings that are the lifeblood of a political campaign. After my defeat in 1958 one of my family friends said, "The trouble with Nick is he doesn't get out and cuss with the boys often enough." He was right; I did not enjoy getting out and cussing with the boys, and I regarded raising campaign funds with loathing. Alex Sanders was on the mark when he said that raising money as a candidate is the chemotherapy of politics. I always thought of it as the horsehair shirt of politics: necessary but uncomfortable. However, it was my fate to become a seeker of public office.

Although I was only nine years old at the time, I have a dim recollection of Uncle Peter's first election to the South Carolina Senate in 1930. The most vivid memory was the excitement of having the results of each county precinct projected on a large screen on one side of a building on Evans Street while a crowd milled about in the street that was closed to traffic, cheering when their favorite candidate received a majority. My uncle defeated the incumbent senator, Philip H. Arrowsmith Sr.

When Peter ran for reelection in 1934, I was thirteen years old and eager to become involved in his campaign. It was a great disappointment to me that my uncle did not have campaign cards printed. I thought that every serious politician was supposed to have cards for his supporters to distribute at stump speeches held throughout the county. To remedy the situation, I got a small hand-printing kit and printed some cards urging a vote for my uncle. My uncle was reelected, but I know my efforts had no influence on his success.

The next election was in the summer of 1938, when I had reached the advanced age of seventeen. This time I volunteered my services as a driver for one of his ward heelers who went into rural areas of Florence County touting my uncle's virtues as a senator. The Depression was still a real presence. Much of the county lacked electricity and could only be reached by traveling over unpaved roads that were either suffocatingly dusty in dry spells or quagmires in wet ones.

During this election I accompanied Uncle Peter to numerous stump speeches at various places around the county. They were usually all-day affairs with barbecue or chicken bog and a baseball game. Sometimes as many as a hundred people would be in attendance hoping for oratorical fireworks from the candidates. Among the candidates from Florence County seeking election to the House of Representatives was a man with dark hair and a mustache, Clyde Graham. I was struck by his appearance but had no intimation of the role he would later play in my political life.

In the 1938 Democrat primary, I was assigned to drive Montrose, a ward heeler, around Florence County. It was a revelation to me to be in an intimate association with a sharp-witted, down-to-earth, rural, politically savvy type like Montrose. I became quite attached to him and was fascinated by his rustic obliqueness as he tried to persuade doubtful contacts to commit to voting for Uncle Peter.

"Hit just won't do," he said frequently when talking about our opponent's lack of virtue. On one memorable occasion we were late in reaching a farmhouse with voters that my mentor thought particularly important. In fact it was "dusk dark" when we got there. There was no electricity, and lamps were being lighted when Montrose and I went up on the porch and the family came out to see who we were. Apparently Montrose was known to the father of a brood of children that included one buxom teenage daughter.

Montrose was invited into the house for serious discussion with the adult members of the family, and the young daughter, being my contemporary, was directed to sit with me in a porch swing and "entertain" me. We did as we were told, and as we swung back and forth I introduced several topics of conversation, but the only response I got from my companion was, "You're tellin' me." She ventured no other comment during our time together regardless of the subject matter I introduced. If amorous overtures were expected, I did not feel the urge to make any, and I was vastly relieved when eventually Montrose emerged from the house and we departed.

One of the most poignant episodes was during our travels near a community named Vox. Montrose went into a store to talk, and I remained in the car. I had the radio on, and part of a speech given by Adolph Hitler was being rebroadcast. It was bizarre to hear that strident voice in a foreign tongue while sitting in a car in a remote rural area facing a large pine forest.

My grandmother Leah McClenaghan Townsend McEachin was fearless when it came to confronting opposition. The stump speaking in Florence was at the Florence High School, and I was detailed to escort my grandmother there and sit with her.

My uncle had refused to appoint a brother of Roberta Muldrow Brown to some minor county office, and that had caused a rift in what had been a political alliance with the Muldrow family. Miss Roberta was another of those formidable female dreadnaughts like my grandmother. Feeling was running high after the political speeches ended, and since the auditorium was on the second floor of the building, the crowd had to descend by way of a split staircase to the ground floor. Unfortunately Miss Roberta was just ahead of us, and she was abusing my uncle in graphically defamatory language, of which she was a master.

My grandmother wasted no time in challenging her and said in a loud voice, "That's not my son you're talking about, Roberta." Miss Roberta turned and recounted how my uncle had perfidiously failed to appoint her brother to office. By that time Roberta was on the last section of the split stair and my grandmother was on the upper section. They were firing volley after volley at each other across the banisters. My grandmother stated in a loud voice that Roberta's brother was a drunken, no-account lout and unfit for public office. Roberta was firing back uncomplimentary remarks about Uncle Peter's character. I could not tell whether the crowd on the staircase was amused or horrified. The verbal battle continued until we reached the first floor and Roberta and my grandmother parted in opposite directions.

Before 1960 the Democrat primary in South Carolina was *the* election since there was no effective Republican Party to seriously challenge the Democratic Party's nominee. The primary was held in August, about thirty days before I was to enter college. Hauling voters to the polls was always a concern. There was an emergency, and I was told some voters needed to be hauled in a country precinct. It was my baptism of fire.

My uncle asked me to go to a crossroads store and ask for a person by name. That person would indicate where these potential voters were. I went to the store and met with a rather seedy looking man in his thirties. When he got in the car and I started driving away from the store, he asked if I had brought any money. I was surprised by the question but told him I had fifty cents. He seemed disappointed, but in 1938 fifty cents bought more.

We drove away from the store, and my passenger directed me to turn into a farm road that went through a field and to stop at the edge of the woods on the far side of the field. He told me to blow the horn twice. A figure emerged from the woods, and my passenger asked for the fifty cents. I gave it to him, and he and the stranger disappeared into the woods. In about ten minutes my passenger emerged with a quart jar filled with a clear fluid. I knew instinctively that it must be bootleg whiskey, and I was right.

My passenger got back in the car, and he unscrewed the top of the jar and offered me a drink. I faked taking a sip for I feared the consequences if we should be arrested smelling of alcohol. We drove on to a nearby house, and three or four disreputable looking men were invited to join us in the car. There were now three in the back seat and two in the front seat, all enjoying the libations my first passenger was offering. We drove to the polling place, and before we went in, my passengers stated that they did not know how to read. I told them I would go with them into the polling place to help them vote. I did so with great trepidation, however, because I thought the precinct manager might know who I was.

When we got into the polling place, I put on a brave front and stated that the five gentlemen had asked me to assist them in marking their ballots. To my surprise and relief the poll manager agreed. The five voters and I retired to another room. The poll manager came with us, and when I had secured the votes for my uncle, he stated that he was interested in a candidate in another race and asked if my companions would vote for his candidate. Since I had no interest in that race, I marked their ballots as the poll manager requested, and we departed. I took my passengers back to the crossroads store where they disembarked. My original passenger had one parting shot. "Son, next time bring more money."

I felt sure that I was in imminent peril of being arrested and drove immediately to my uncle's house and told him what I had done. I told him that I sincerely hoped that it would not cause a scandal that would deprive him of his office. He laughed and refunded me my fifty cents and told me not to worry. He got more votes than the two candidates opposing him but failed to get a majority. Thus there had to be a runoff election.

Roberta Brown lived on Irby Street one block across from the house where my grandmother and Uncle Peter lived. On the morning following the first balloting there was the end of a casket, apparently a drummer's sample, in the walkway to the front of my grandmother's house. The casket had a note attached to it that read, "May this receptacle contain the political remains of the late Senator McEachin." It was generally thought that Roberta had put it there.

My uncle won the runoff election, and when the result was known, Aunt Margaret and I took the casket to Roberta's house, although there was still some doubt that she was its owner. When we pulled up in front of her house, a man who worked for Roberta came out to see who it was. When we handed the casket to him, he said without hesitation, "You brought the casket back!" Aunt Margaret said to him, "Please give this to Miss Roberta as we have no use for it."

It is a matter of self-reproach that I never seriously questioned why black people did not vote in the Democrat primary. At one polling place during the 1938 election an elderly black man did come and present himself to vote, and he was allowed to do so. When I asked why he was allowed to vote, I was told his name was "Old '76," that he had voted for Wade Hampton in the election of 1876, and that in doing so he had gained the unquestioned right to vote in Democratic primaries thereafter.

When I returned to Florence to practice law, I took some interest in the organization of the county Democratic Party, partly out of curiosity about grass-roots democracy and partly because my uncle, though not a candidate, was still a person of political influence in the county. In 1950 I went to the Florence County Democratic Party's organizational meeting held in the courthouse. To my astonishment and dismay, I discovered that it was a completely disorganized affair. Although delegates from the various precincts were seated together in the courtroom, people wandered in and out and appeared to vote whether or not they were delegates.

Voting was done on scraps of paper on which the names of the candidates were written by the voter. Contested elections seemed to be almost fluid in the number of candidates and the method of casting votes. It was bad enough when the election was for one office, but the real problem came when electing delegates to the South Carolina Democratic Convention. Usually as many as fifteen delegates and alternates were to be elected. Delegates at the county convention were instructed to write on the ballot the names of the delegates to the state convention for whom they wished to vote. There was no prescribed order, and the names were written according to the whim of the voter with a multitude of misspellings. Counting ballots became a horrendous, time-consuming problem.

The next county meeting was better organized. When the nominations were made, we had the clerk list the nominations alphabetically. A stencil was cut, and only enough ballots for the number of delegates authorized to vote were printed. Although the change greatly improved the conduct of the convention, I received some angry inquiries by delegates about who authorized this strange innovation. They seemed to suspect that some political coup was being planned.

The next county Democratic Party meeting was in 1956, sufficiently after the school desegregation decision for community anger to have reached a boiling point. The place of the convention's meeting was changed to the

National Guard Armory on Evans Street. By that time I had recruited enough volunteers to help run the balloting and counting of the votes so that the convention, at least procedurally, went smoothly.

If I had to give a reason for abandoning my interests in the theater, the museum, and other cultural activities, I would probably say that after the school desegregation decision in 1954 I became painfully aware that the voice of moderation and reason was vital to preserve the honor of the state and the safety of my fellow citizens. The upheaval caused by the school desegregation decision and the resulting wild and irresponsible assertions made by the people of my community preyed on my conscience. There was talk of armed resistance by whites and the probability of bloodshed in the streets.

Edmund Burke's observation that all that is necessary for evil to prevail is for people of good will to do nothing nagged in my mind, and I was haunted by the martyrdom of my friend Jack O'Dowd, editor of the *Florence Morning News,* and Reverend Joseph Horn, the rector of St. John's Episcopal Church in Florence.

Jack O'Dowd took the forthright and sensible position that the ruling of the U.S. Supreme Court was the law of the land and would have to be obeyed. Nevertheless he was vilified and physically threatened for a stand that was only a plea for moderation in dealing with the crisis that arose in the wake of the Supreme Court's decision. On one occasion he was chased by what appeared to be members of the Ku Klux Klan. Fearful of what might happen if he went to his home, he took refuge with Anne and me in our apartment. In the county Democratic Party's convention in January 1956, the *Florence Morning News,* O'Dowd's paper, was condemned in a resolution as the "Carpetbagger Press."

Jack, who was among the helpers I had recruited to run the meeting, was nominated to be a delegate to the state Democratic Party's convention. Forty-five people were nominated, and Jack was forty-fifth in the number of votes received. As the *Florence Morning News* was beginning to lose subscribers, Jack's father told him he would have to resign as editor. He did so and left the state in the summer of 1956.

The following year Reverend Horn and four other Protestant ministers in the Pee Dee, including the Reverend Larry Jackson, a Florence native, published a pamphlet of twelve essays titled *South Carolinians Speak.* The pamphlet argued strongly in favor of peaceful desegregation and created so much controversy that the vestry of St. John's Parish, of which I was a member, was forced to issue a statement Horn and I composed. The statement declared that the question of segregation or integration should be judged by

Christians using the standard of whether a person was fulfilling the obligation to love his neighbor as himself.

Also in the fall of 1957 I directed and took the part of Barney Greenwald in *The Caine Mutiny Court-Martial* produced by the Florence Little Theatre. I was surprised when one of my Jewish friends thanked me for being willing to play the part of a Jew. I began to understand how deeply hurt some of my Jewish friends must have been by prejudice against them. The events of 1956–57 weighed heavily on my conscience. I found it more difficult to sit by and not participate actively in the effort to bring reason and moderation to the course of action the state must follow in order to survive the crisis. I decided to run for the South Carolina House of Representatives in the 1958 election.

Wearing a seersucker suit and bow tie, I made my first campaign trip to Johnsonville in the lower part of the county. There were no single-member districts and candidates because House seats were countywide. I did not have campaign posters printed, although I did have campaign cards without my picture. I avoided asking directly for votes and instead used the milquetoast statement, "Your support will be appreciated." In Johnsonville I went into a store and, after introducing myself to the proprietor, outlined some of the concerns I hoped I could help solve. I carefully avoided any reference to segregation or integration of the schools. When I finished making my pitch, I asked the proprietor if there was anything in particular he would like me to do in the legislature if I were elected. He replied, "If you get 'lected and go to Columbia, I'd be satisfied if you didn't do anything. I never feel safe when that crowd up there in Columbia is in session. You never know what fool thing they might do."

I also made an alliance with Karl G. Smith, who ran a feed, seed, and tractor store in Lake City. One of our mutual friends in Lake City said that Karl was like a diamond in the rough. He knew all of the farmers in the area and gave me an itinerary to follow each time I campaigned there. He had a large cage in his store with two fox squirrels with which I sometimes identified because I, like them, was trapped in a cage longing to be free. Karl told me after the election that it was inevitable that the racial issue would become a part of the campaign. It was widely publicized that I was "a nigger lover," that Anne and I had been married secretly by a Roman Catholic priest at her mother's house in Coward, and that "there were more niggers than white people at our wedding." The only thing missing in the rumors was an appeal to anti-Semitism. When I gave one of my cards to a stout white woman in a dry-cleaning establishment, she looked at the card and then scanned me from head to toe before saying, "I hear you favors the nigger." I replied that I favored everyone who needed help, but she only shrugged, and when I left, I saw her throw my card in a trash basket.

There were stump speeches all over the county, and each candidate was allowed five minutes to appeal for votes. I discovered that a short speech, particularly a five-minute one, is probably the hardest challenge of one's oratorical skills. I only blew my cool once, in a speech in Timmonsville, where I was asked if I was the troop leader of "a troop of nigger Boy Scouts." I replied that I was not, but I had been instrumental in founding the Big Brothers program, which was dedicated to helping both white and black boys. Falling back on my knowledge of Christian hymns, I said, "If we do not help both white and black boys who need our help, shame on us, or I should say, 'Thrice shame on us' if we refused to help them."

I lost the election. There were six candidates running for five seats, and although I got more than 50 percent of the vote, I was the lowest vote getter. The next highest, who was elected, was George Sam Harrell, a blatant racist. It was a blow to my ego and a shock to my belief in the fairness of democratic government. What disappointed me most was that the black vote was literally up for sale. Although I had taken a stand for moderation and acceptance of racial integration, I did not get the black vote; a racist did. I learned the hard way what "walking around money" meant in politics.

Several weeks after my defeat I was working in my herb garden when Sallyann Rogers came to call. We talked for a few minutes, and then I observed, "You know, I really enjoy gardening more than politics." Sallyann, one of the wittiest and most charming people I knew, said, "Of course you do. At least plants respond to kindness."

I bound up my wounds as best I could, but I had serious misgivings about being elected to public office given the climate of opinion in the county. A lucky break came in 1959. One of the issues in the 1958 election centered around the office of the county manager, Clyde Barnes. Barnes had been in charge of the chain gang before becoming county manager. The county manager was not an elective office but was employed by the Florence County Governing Board. This board was appointed by the governor on the recommendation of a majority of the county's legislative delegation. The board had only ministerial power, but the county manager had become such a powerful political figure that the legislative delegation grew apprehensive he might use his influence in the next election to defeat them. Three of the five House members, with the exception of Leroy Nettles and George Sam Harrell, introduced a bill that would make the county manager an appointee of the legislative delegation rather than an employee of the board.

Clyde Barnes and the board viewed this as an attempt by those legislators to grab power. During the 1958 campaign all of the elected members of the legislative delegation had openly expressed confidence in the board and Clyde Barnes.

I was still smarting from my defeat and particularly irked by the change of attitude by the majority of the legislative delegation, so I wrote a letter to the editor of the *Florence Morning News* in which I criticized the motives of the majority of the legislative delegation and their apparent attempt to grab power. Up until that time I had been treated with coolness by Barnes and the Florence County Governing Board, but after my letter appeared in the newspaper Barnes approached me and asked if I would consent to meet with the members of the board at a cabin on Willow Creek for lunch. I said I would be happy to do so.

The meeting was typical of the clandestine and vital gatherings that added mystery and excitement to politics. Although I had been through a countywide campaign, I could sense that the Florence County Governing Board regarded my political ability with misgivings. When I was campaigning in Lake City, one political activist and businessman asked me if I thought I could be elected. "I don't like to back no losers," he explained.

It was obvious to me that the board needed someone to defend their interests, but they didn't want to back a loser. I did my best to gain their confidence, and I succeeded. They gave me their blessing to act as their spokesman in opposing the action of the House members who sponsored the obnoxious legislation. For the first time I felt as though I had gained some traction as a politician. My association with Barnes and the board was rewarding, not only because it gave me the ability to be elected to the House of Representatives in 1960, but also because I got to know the man who made the political system work, Clyde Barnes. He was the quintessential political boss who knew how to get and wield power without running for elected office. He was the perfect eminence grise in county politics.

I mostly admired Barnes because he had qualities I lacked. There was a perceptible feeling of restrained potential for physical force in his personality. This was reinforced by the knowledge that he was always armed, although I never saw him put his hand on the pistol that was concealed at his side. I thought that the impression he might use force to get his way went back to the days when he supervised the chain gang in Florence County. That experience stood him in good stead when appealing to voters. The power to use county prisoners confined to the chain gang, to use county equipment to haul dirt, to scrape lanes leading from paved roads to residences, to install culverts for driveways, and to clear off weeds and brush from family graveyards gave Barnes leverage in getting and delivering votes. As county manager, Barnes used these tools to create a loyal voting block that could ensure victory or defeat in county elections. I did not have his support in my first political venture, and I was grateful to have it in the second.

The House members who introduced the objectionable county manager bill also introduced in 1959 a bill to create a lake, which eventually became Forest Lake, between Florence and Timmonsville. The problem with this legislation was that it claimed to be a bill to create a lake to irrigate farm-land, a public purpose, and therefore carried with it the potential to con-demn private property if necessary to create the lake. A large percentage of the rural community feared any legislation that gave that power—suppos-edly for a public purpose—to a governmental agency.

Foster Young had approximately twenty acres that might be condemned under the proposed legislation, and he retained me to challenge the consti-tutionality of that legislation. Young testified he was told by a legislator that if he did not go along voluntarily with the proposed lake, a center of a new real-estate development, a statute would give the commission developing the property the power to condemn his land. We succeeded in having the proposed action to condemn Young's and another landowner's property de-clared unconstitutional. This gave me a second string to my bow in attack-ing the incumbent House members.

However, my hopes for a political comeback had to be put on hold because of a traumatic development. Amid the exciting prospect of political redemption, my third child, Nina McClenaghan, was born in September 1959. Anne was in her seventh month of pregnancy, and the baby was deliv-ered by what Roland Zeigler, Anne's attending physician, called "dirty sur-gery." Because the umbilical chord had prolapsed, the baby had to be deliv-ered by Caesarian section.

Dr. Zeigler thought the fetus was too small to survive and urged me to authorize an abortion rather than risk Anne's life by performing a C-section. Hart, our pediatrician, urged us to save the baby's life if possible. Anne said she was willing to risk her life to save the baby. The C-section was per-formed, and when Hart emerged from the delivery room, he said, "Well, we've got more to work with than I thought, and it's good it's a girl because they have a better chance to survive than boys." I was shocked to see so tiny a baby but grateful that she was alive. "But what about Anne? How is she?" I asked. Hart said she would be fine, but they would have to keep her in the recovery room for a while. The baby was put in an incubator and remained there two months. The political campaign had to be put on hold while baby Nina and Anne recovered, but our troubles were not over.

While she was recovering, Anne had a hemorrhage and had to return to the hospital. When Anne arrived at the hospital, she was told that they were going to have to give her several blood transfusions. Anne asked where they were going to get the blood. Zeigler, aware of my position on civil rights and the legislative controversy about mixing white and black blood, replied, "From a big black buck." Anne survived the second ordeal, grateful for the blood, whatever its source, and we prepared for a second political campaign.

17

A Backbencher

It's better to win than lose elections. This truism, familiar to all politicians, was particularly true of my 1960 political campaign to be elected for a Florence County House seat and of my involvement in the presidential election that year. The opening salvo came at the Florence County Democratic Convention. The gauntlet had been thrown down by the incumbents, Ed Young, Barney Dusenbury, and C. Ray Parrott, who had introduced legislation seeking to make the county manager subject to their control. The legislation did not become law, but the plan to create a new power center in Florence County had been revealed, and I had assumed the role of the chief spokesman for the opponents of that group.

To add greater fuel to the coming election, Col. Frank Barnwell, who regarded himself as "Mr. Democrat" in Florence County, had been defeated by Julian Dusenbury as executive committeeman in the 1954 convention. He was itching for revenge. Julian Dusenbury, my contemporary, was a decorated war hero who had been so severely wounded in the Battle of Okinawa that he was confined to a wheelchair for the remainder of his life. Julian served several terms in the House and ran unsuccessfully against state senator Clyde Graham in 1954. His brothers, Barney and Dick, who practiced law together, were popular and active in politics. All three were close friends of Ed Young. Julian's personal charm and conspicuous gallantry made him a formidable political opponent. He was seeking reelection as executive committeeman of the Florence County Democratic Party in 1960. His opponents had to remove him from that office if they were going to quash the Young-Dusenbury group's attempt to control politics in the county.

The election of delegates to the county convention is usually a humdrum affair. But in 1960 there was so much interest in the power struggle between the Young-Dusenbury group and the Florence County Governing Board that the election of convention delegates was fiercely contested. It was the first time in my memory that there was a convention fight over which slate of precinct delegates would be seated.

When the convention convened in the National Guard Armory on Evans Street, one could sense the tension among the delegates. Julian Dusenbury called the convention to order and stated that he was appointing a credentials committee to hear contests between the contesting slates of delegates. This was my cue to raise a point of order to the effect that under the state law governing party conventions, the credentials committee had to be elected by the convention rather than appointed by the chairman. Our opponents were caught off guard, and we were primed to meet the challenge with a slate of nominees for the credentials committee. Our nominees were elected to the credentials committee and reported back to the convention that the committee had approved our slate of contested delegates.

The next order of business was the election of a permanent president of the convention. Uncle Peter had agreed to allow his name to be entered in nomination to oppose Julian Dusenbury. The election was close, but Uncle Peter was elected. When Dusenbury left the podium, it was clear that the Young-Dusenbury coup attempt was in trouble. Another important victory came when our candidate, Philip "Boobie" Arrowsmith Jr., was elected to the office of executive committeeman. Boobie was the son of Philip Arrowsmith Sr., who was defeated by my uncle in the 1930 senatorial election. Boobie had run unsuccessfully for the office of state senator against Clyde Graham in 1958.

During our strategic planning to dominate the county convention, I became friends with Peter D. Hyman. Unlike me, Pete relished every aspect of the political process, including going out and cussing with the boys. He had been elected to the office of magistrate soon after coming to Florence as an attorney and longed for higher office. Pete saw the Young-Dusenbury coalition as an obstacle to his gaining higher office. He and I agreed that we would offer for election to the House. It was not clear whether Ed Young would seek reelection; however, Barney Dusenbury and Ray Parrott both indicated they would do so. After the county convention Young announced he would not seek reelection. That meant our chief opponents would be Barney Dusenbury and Ray Parrott. Leroy Nettles and George Sam Harrell had not joined the Young-Dusenbury revolt.

The time for holding primaries had been moved from August to June, so the House campaign got under way almost immediately after the county convention. There were five seats to be filled in the House with eleven candidates giving that election the aspect of a free-for-all. The major contest was the challenge Pete Hyman and I presented to Barney Dusenbury and Ray Parrott.

Various strategy sessions were held, and Pete and I agreed we would conduct an aggressive campaign against the incumbents. At the stump speeches held across the county the speaking order rotated, so that sometimes I spoke after Barney and Ray and at other times before. When I spoke last, I would vigorously attack the records of the two incumbents, and when I spoke ahead of them and Pete spoke last, he would lead the assault with a vigorous attack. The attacks were not personal but were on their records. Pete did not live up to the agreement by leading the attack when he spoke after Barney and Ray. I accused him of hunting with the hounds and running with the hares. It was the beginning of a feeling of distrust between us that continued over many years.

It took only one defeat to cure me of the notion that I should not advertise or ask directly for someone's vote. This time I printed cards with my picture and a statement that "your vote will be appreciated." I printed posters with my picture. Leo Poston told me that he put one of the posters on the outside of his rural store and one of his dogs howled every time he passed it. I even bought TV time—a fifteen-minute program in which my family participated.

The election produced an odd result. Leroy Nettles, Pete Hyman, George Sam Harrell, and I were elected on the first ballot. The runoff election would have pitted Barney Dusenbury against Ray Parrott. In this unfortunate situation Barney withdrew from the contest, and the runoff election was between Odell Venters and Parrott. In the runoff election Venters defeated Parrott. The revolt had failed.

During the campaign I made a statement I later regretted. I said that I thought segregation was best for both races. When called to account for this statement in a later election, I stated frankly that I had been a hypocrite in making the statement. My actions prior to that time clearly indicated that I felt racial segregation was no longer possible in the South. I also felt that the black electorate had behaved shamefully in the past by allowing their leaders to be bought and by voting for open racists like George Sam Harrell. I knew I would be able to do more for black citizens if I were elected to the legislature. If I were defeated a second time, I would probably have no viable political career ahead of me. I was also convinced that given the rash threats of violence coming from both sides, a cooling off period would be helpful in making an orderly transition to an integrated society.

As further evidence of where my sentiments were, I resisted efforts by both friends and foes to get me to join the White Citizens Council. Not only did I resist doing so, but I stated at a council meeting to which the candidates were invited that I was not a member of their organization. After the election I told a Jewish friend of mine, who was the CEO of a manufacturing company, that I had refused to be pressured into joining the White Citizens Council because I did not see how I could face my Jewish, Catholic, and black friends if I did so. To my astonishment my friend stated sheepishly that he had succumbed to pressure and joined the council.

The nominees in the Democrat primary faced no real opposition in the general election, so I became deeply involved in the effort to carry the state for John F. Kennedy. At that time I did not admire Lyndon Johnson, although I saw the political wisdom in having him on the ticket with Kennedy. I never met Johnson, but Anne and I had an encounter of sorts with him in Washington. Early in 1960, before the Democratic Convention was held, we were asked by a friend to come to Washington for dinner at the Press Club. After dinner we toured the large banquet room where luminaries spoke. The banquet room was empty except for a knot of men who were talking loudly. We gave them a wide berth and made our way toward the elevator. Before we reached the elevator, the men left the banquet hall and reached the elevator ahead of us. The central figure in the group was Senator Johnson, and I could hear someone urging him, "Come on, Senator, let's go. Let's go."

Anne and I tried to avoid getting into the middle of the effort to subdue the senator by deliberately hanging back some twenty feet. Suddenly Johnson broke loose from his companions and started lurching down the hall toward us. He was a large man and had obviously had too much to drink. Anne and I instinctively gave way and pressed ourselves against the wall to let him charge by us like a Texas longhorn. After he passed, I said to Anne, "Do you think that man might become president of the United States?"

During the presidential campaign the successful candidates for the legislature were invited to a barbecue at Rocky Bottom in Pickens County to hear Lyndon Johnson make a campaign speech. Several banners proclaiming this to be Bobby Baker Day caught my attention. I had no idea who Bobby Baker was. I found a place to sit by Grady Patterson, who was then in the attorney general's office. He seemed to be as ignorant as I was about the identity of Bobby Baker. The mystery was solved after the arrival of Senator Johnson. Earle Morris, the state senator from Pickens County, was master of ceremonies and introduced Johnson. In his opening observations Johnson said that if South Carolina had done nothing else but produce Bobby Baker, our existence as a state would be justified. He then observed that Baker was the last man he saw at night and the first man he saw in the morning.

Anne and I became involved in the local campaign to elect John Kennedy, and I assumed the role of de facto campaign chairman in Florence and the upper Pee Dee area. We got an empty store on Evans Street and began assembling volunteers to keep it open. We were agreeably surprised to find that there was strong support for him. One of the people who came in to help was Mary Cameron, the business agent of the International Ladies' Garment Workers' Union (ILGWU) in South Carolina. It was a contact that would influence my future practice of law.

I also did something for which I had little experience or training; I produced a television ad for the Democratic Party. The ad drove home the necessity of having a president who was sympathetic to the problems of tobacco and cotton farmers, and local panelists on the ad opined that it was safest to entrust the Democratic Party with the future of agriculture. The ad was filmed live and came off well. So well, in fact, that federal judge Robert Martin, who was holding court in Florence, stated that it was the best political advertisement for the Democratic Party he had seen.

Anne, Sallyann Rogers, and I went to Columbia for a Democratic Party rally at which Kennedy was going to speak. Since Sallyann was a Republican, I was surprised that she agreed to go. We had seats on the Gervais Street side of the capitol. It was an electric moment when Kennedy appeared, framed by the columns of the building; the crowd, including Sallyann, immediately surged forward to shake his hand or just to touch him. I told Sallyann I was surprised that she would demonstrate such enthusiasm for a Democrat. Her response was, "You can tell a lot about a man when you shake his hand."

The gratifying result in Florence County was that Kennedy received 6,090 votes to Nixon's 5,815. Kennedy captured the state's electoral vote by a narrow margin. I was deeply moved by the outcome and felt that perhaps a new day was dawning in the rather dismal politics I had experienced in previous elections. I was reminded of Wordsworth's quote about the French Revolution: "Bliss was it in that dawn to be alive, / But to be young was very heaven!"

I never felt comfortable during the two years I served in the House. Sol Blatt Sr., who knew of my connection with Senator McEachin, never put me in any position of importance. It seemed when we made eye contact that I could see question marks displayed in the pupils of his eyes. Consequently I was assigned to one of the least important committees, the Municipal Affairs Committee.

I quickly observed a lack of consistency in the conduct of many legislators, who would oppose a measure one day and vote for it the next. The best explanation I got was from Pete Hyman, who said cryptically, "The Big Possum walks late at night." I figured I would never gain the confidence of marsupial politicians or be a part of their nocturnal maneuvers.

It also became apparent that legislative service would result in serious financial problems. To leave on Tuesday mornings and spend two nights in Columbia took the heart out of the time I spent practicing law. When I was discussing the problem with Heyward Belser, then a member of the House from Richland County, he quoted his father, who said the real problem with being in the legislature was that it took "the cream of one's energy." I never was able to make any money while serving in the legislature. Membership was always a luxury that made it difficult to support a growing family.

Service in the South Carolina General Assembly for many was a wonderful way to escape the humdrum burden of ordinary living. It was an enormous boost to one's ego. In Columbia a struggling lawyer or a food store manager could feel important because there was the prestige of sensing that his or her life and work had special meaning. Legislators received deference, and the lobbyists were always around to praise and entertain even the least important members.

In my House years there was no ethics law that proscribed the receipt of favors from groups and individuals. Treats were available on every hand. Even dinners at the Market Restaurant with lobster Newburg accompanied by wine were not uncommon. Many General Assembly leaders who were lawyers received retainer fees from important people and businesses whose interests needed protection. This put pressure on lowly backbenchers, like me, who had to worry about getting home to try cases and attend to clients' business. I tried to entertain myself by renewing my interest in the game of squash. I played regularly in the YMCA and renewed friendships or made friends with many people I would not have had opportunity to know.

In those two years there were a few events in which I had a major role. Foremost was the statute to remove the Florence Public Library from the jurisdiction of Florence School District 1. Second was the election of James Spruill Sr. to the judgeship of the Fourth Circuit. Last of all there was the centennial celebration of the Civil War.

My relationship with the legislative delegation was never an easy one. Leroy Nettles and Odell Venters were from the lower part of Florence County, Lynches River being the dividing line, and their attention was directed more to particular concerns and problems in that area. That left me, Pete Hyman, and George Sam Harrell as the representatives chiefly concerned with problems in the city of Florence.

One of the first to raise its head was the integration of the Florence Library. When the library was created in 1924–25, it was placed under the trustees of the Florence School District (later Florence School District 1). That area included the city of Florence and a large portion of the upper part of Florence County. A separate library board ran the public library, subject to the control of the school district. Consistent with separate schools for white and black children, the library building at the corner of Irby and Pine Streets was for the exclusive use of white citizens, and the fiction of equal treatment was that a library for black citizens was maintained at Wilson High School. This was consistent with the false rationalization that separate but equal library facilities were open to black citizens of the school district. It was an intellectually dishonest policy because the library for the use of black citizens was never equal to the one available to white citizens.

The library for white citizens opened with approximately six thousand books. Four years later the state and the Florence area entered the era of the Great Depression. Although there was a fine building for white use, the collection of books increased at a snail's pace. The public library was at the bottom of a list of priorities of a school system that had difficulty paying teachers. During the 1930s the major acquisitions the library received were the Book-of-the-Month Club selections, for which there was a waiting list.

The 1954 court decision mandating desegregation of the public schools posed a problem for the board of Florence School District 1, the successor of the Florence School District. O. S. Aiken Sr., a good friend of mine, was chairman of the board. I was not surprised when I received a letter from him early in March 1961 asking if he could come to Columbia to meet with the legislative delegation about problems that had arisen in connection with the library. The problem was that black people had applied for library cards at the white library. If a library card was issued, did that immediately precipitate a demand to integrate the public schools because the library was part of the school system? The black applicants had been denied a card but were persistent. All chairs were removed from the reading room so, if the worse came to worst, there could only be vertical integration. In desperation the school board finally closed the library and sought the advice of the legislative delegation.

Knowing what the problem was, we asked Dave Robinson, the counsel for the Gressette committee, to attend the meeting. Until then I had never met Robinson, but he and Peter McEachin knew each other. Both had served as counsel for the Gressette committee, chaired by Senator Marion Gressette, whose principal duty was to advise the legislature and state officials about the impending racial integration of the public schools.

The Florence County delegation met in a conference room in the State House with O. S. Aiken and Dave Robinson. Dave Robinson said the answer to our problem was simple. The library would either have to be integrated or remain closed. I said it was unthinkable that the city of Florence would not have a public library, and it was agreed to introduce a House bill to remove the library from the control of the school board and create a separate library board. On March 31, 1961, my bill to do this was introduced in the House.

Senator Clyde Graham was a shrewd man whose basic instincts with regard to integration were good. He trusted me but deeply distrusted Pete Hyman, especially in this situation, because Pete's uncle, George Sam Harrell, was a blatant racist. Senator Graham and I agreed that integration of the library was inevitable and should be accomplished without any violence. The real problem was to appoint library board members who would agree to integration. Graham left it to me to assemble the new board members if and when the legislation became law. To my surprise the bill passed without any great controversy, and I talked several of my friends into joining the new library board with the clear understanding that they would not oppose racial integration of the library. They agreed, and the library was racially integrated for the first time in 1961.

The second most important action in which I became closely involved was the election of James Spruill Sr. to the bench. South Carolina requires that judges to state courts be elected by voice vote in a joint session of the House and Senate. The system has been criticized and has many faults, but as Winston Churchill observed about democracy, it may be the worst system, but it is better than the others that have been tried. The voice vote affords one of the few moments of truth in the General Assembly; in it secret alliances and agendas become exposed for public inspection.

I knew James Spruill chiefly through my good friend Lucas Dargan, who was his first cousin. Lucas admired him greatly and told stories of Spruill's being a Rhodes Scholar at Keble College, Oxford. I met Spruill when I was a candidate for a Rhodes Scholarship in December 1948. He was a member of the committee that interviewed me. I did not get the appointment, but my disappointment did not diminish my respect for Spruill.

Spruill had been a House member from Chesterfield County and gained the respect of many of the present members, including Speaker Sol Blatt Sr. Blatt's firm support of Spruill was critical since there were two other sitting members of the House, Jack Gardner and Jack Lindsay, who were nominated. Senator James P. "Spot" Mozingo nominated Gardner, and Senator Paul Arant nominated Spruill. Eventually a fourth candidate emerged, Herbert Britt of Dillon, but support for him was limited. Senator William C. Goldberg was nominated during the course of the election but withdrew his name. The real contest came down to a battle between Spruill and Gardner. Gardner had the support of Senator Mozingo and many of the trial lawyers who were legislators. This was a great advantage because there was an abiding enmity between Mozingo and Spruill. Spruill was viewed by Mozingo and his admirers as too intellectual, aloof, and unsympathetic to plaintiffs and their counsel.

The joint session convened on March 15, 1961. On the first ballot Gardner received sixty-nine votes, Spruill received fifty-eight votes, Lindsay received twenty-eight votes, and Britt received seven votes. Three more ballots were taken; Spruill was gaining support. The result was sixty-nine votes for Gardner, sixty-eight for Spruill, twenty-two for Lindsay, and three for Britt. The number required for election was eighty-two votes. A recess was called until 3:00 P.M. Senator Arant and Faye Bell of the Chesterfield delegation asked me to go with them to the north portico of the State House for a conference. When we got there, Senator Arant turned to me and said, "Nick, what do you think we should do next?" I was appalled and alarmed because I was both a backbencher and a complete novice at this kind of maneuvering. I protested my inexperience but said that we should move to have the next balloting postponed until the following day so that we might have time to assess our strength. The joint assembly reconvened at three o'clock that afternoon and resumed balloting, only adjourning after the eleventh ballot in which Spruill received sixty-eight votes; Gardner, sixty-five; Lindsay, nineteen; and Britt, five. It was clear that Spruill was pulling ahead in the race.

The joint assembly resumed voting on March 16. On the twelfth ballot Spruill received seventy-three votes; Gardner took sixty-three; Lindsay, twenty-four; and Britt, three. I was the only member of the Florence County delegation and the upper Pee Dee voting for Spruill. His reputation and record, however, had gained him strong support statewide. I telephoned Lucas Dargan and some of my friends and urged them to send telegrams to their senators and representatives to change their votes to Spruill. Pete Hyman, who supported Lindsay, gleefully took the telegrams he received and showed them to Mozingo, who made a speech denouncing "corporations and kinfolks" who were trying to influence the election.

There was great excitement in the State House. The galleries were filled, and numerous friends of the candidates were gaining entrance to the House floor where the voting was taking place. There were demands that the president of the joint assembly enforce Rule 10 prohibiting anyone on the floor but senators and representatives. The president sustained the point of order, and the floor was ordered cleared. The Mozingo forces sensed they were losing and wished to adjourn in order to garner more support. All of their efforts failed; the joint assembly continued to vote until on the seventeenth ballot Spruill was elected by a majority of one vote. This was heady stuff, I thought.

April 12, 1961, was the hundredth anniversary of the bombardment of Fort Sumter, generally regarded as the beginning of the Civil War. The members of the House and Senate "and their attachés" were invited to attend a reenactment of this momentous event. The General Assembly had previously created a centennial commission to commemorate the anniversary of the Civil War and, without thinking of the future consequences, had authorized the raising of the Confederate flag beneath the U.S. and state flags on the dome of the State House. In our enthusiasm to promote events to attract tourists, the legislature created a problem that has plagued the state for thirty years and seems never to die: there was no provision in the resolution to remove the Confederate flag after the celebration was over, and it became the center of a future controversy that had nothing to do with the centennial celebration. Sinister motives were attributed to those of us who had supported the celebration, but I was never aware of such motives, and later those involved repudiated the idea.

My first legislative year ended on an upbeat note, but the school desegregation decision had brought on the prospect of a second Reconstruction. The Confederate flag was flying over the State House. The members of the General Assembly had enjoyed cocktails on a balcony of the Fort Sumter Hotel and, to the accompaniment of "Tara's Theme" from *Gone with the Wind*, watched a spectacular fireworks display reenacting the assault on the fort. But storm clouds of another war were gathering, this time in Asia.

18

Political and Judicial Defeat
1962–1963

After the first year I found being a House backbencher tedious and financially ruinous. I did not have the confidence of the speaker and leaders in the House, and the politicians who ran things in both Florence County and Columbia regarded me as an outsider or as a stick-in-the-mud. Edmund Burke's term "village vexation" seemed to describe the major portion of my legislative duties.

The lack of any systematic county government was particularly troubling. The Florence County Governing Board, the titular governing body of the county, was without any real power except to supervise the use of road equipment and disburse funds appropriated by the legislature to run the county government. The board was unable to enact ordinances or perform any of the functions that municipal corporations are generally empowered to do. Every year it was necessary to pass a "supply bill" for each county that included all of the money thought necessary to operate the county government for the next fiscal year. The accepted legislative practice was to permit only the delegation from each county to vote on its particular supply bill, giving the senator from the county an absolute veto on every item in the bill. There were no provisions for unforeseen items that might arise during the next fiscal year, and the governing board had no authority to spend money not appropriated in the supply bill.

This archaic, cumbersome arrangement led to what I considered the most troubling and dangerous procedure that a conscientious legislator had to face. When the legislature adjourned or before the supply bill was enacted, if some financial emergency required money, members of the county delegation signed "authorizations," which permitted the expenditure of funds on the legislators' unanimous promise to appropriate funds when the General Assembly reconvened. Demands for signatures on authorizations went far beyond necessary items. Groups seeking aid for favorite projects such as schools, bridges, baseball teams, civic organizations' charitable projects, and similar nongovernmental activities would seek money through an authorization. It was not clear to me that when the authorizations were signed the money was actually included in the next supply bill, where its inclusion was legally required.

The procedure was subject to every kind of abuse and opened the door to corruption. I therefore began to resist signing authorizations presented to me. This led potential opponents to devise a scheme to force my hand by wedging me into awkward positions. Without previous notice or discussion with me, an authorization would be drawn up and the senator and other House members would sign it. Only my signature was then required. I recall several times when the delegation was entertained with strong drink at an evening fish fry at someone's creek or river cabin. I would be invited to come over to the hood of a pickup truck and in the full glare of headlights would be asked to sign an authorization. I was like a deer caught in the lights, uncertain whether to freeze, fight, or flee.

Surrounded by eager proponents of the expenditure, I was often told, "We just need your name on this. All the rest of the delegation has signed." A pen was thrust into my hand, and a hushed quiet would fall over the group. On most occasions I signed, but at least once I refused, begging for time to think about it and thereby earning the disgust and anger of my hospitable constituents. I firmly resolved that if I were ever elected to the Senate, I would work to change that wretched system.

I do not mean to imply that I was devoid of political ambition. To be a successful politician, one must have ambition and zeal. To put it in the vernacular, one must have "fire in one's belly." I wanted to see how far I could advance, and I hoped that electoral success would help my legal practice. I therefore succumbed to the temptation to run for election to the state senate.

To win, I had to defeat Senator Clyde Graham, against whom I felt no personal animosity. In fact I discovered that he would usually make the right decision on important issues such as the integration of the public library. Graham was a seasoned politician who had served many years in the House before taking the Senate seat that Uncle Peter had held until 1950. He had become entrenched in office, and the political bosses felt they could bend him to their will.

Clyde Graham's shortcomings were well known. He lived in a rural area more than ten miles from the county seat and had no telephone in his residence. The only way to contact him at his home was to call the police station in Pamplico and have a deputy sheriff drive five miles to Senator

Graham's house and deliver a message. Graham would have to drive to Pamplico to use a telephone there if the message required a response.

Graham was notorious for promising before elections to pave rural roads for constituents, even having the South Carolina Highway Department put up stakes marking the area for paving, but never fulfilling the promise. He could do foolish things such as instructing the county tax assessor not to put a value of more than a certain amount on farmland in the county no matter how much its value exceeded that figure. This resulted in the disallowance of the tax valuation process in the county by the South Carolina Tax Commission, and the whole process would have to be repeated. Graham was an excellent farmer, but with Florence County poised on the threshold of industrialization, he seemed an anachronism.

I felt I had ingratiated myself with the tobacco farmers and warehousemen by representing them in suits against the federal Department of Agriculture. In the late 1950s I represented farmers protesting the marking of warehouse tickets placed on certain tobacco varieties. These varieties produced a greater volume of tobacco, but the tobacco companies claimed that these varieties lacked the aroma and flavor they desired and that they were unable to distinguish them from other desirable varieties on the warehouse floor when bidding on them. The undesirable tobacco was marked with a warehouse ticket that had red lines printed diagonally across it. One of my tobacco farmers when testifying complained that they put "one of them streaked tickets on my tobacco." We lost the suit in the federal court, but I became known as the champion of the tobacco farmers in the county.

The next big issue, and one on which we were able eventually to prevail, was revocation of the tobacco companies' requirement that flue-cured tobacco raised in any state other than Georgia had to be graded and tied before it was placed on the auction warehouse floor. This arbitrary requirement was reinforced by the federal government's refusal to grant price support unless tobacco farmers complied. One of my constituents called it "baby-dolling" tobacco. The controversy continued during the early 1960s and was resolved in 1965, when the grading and tying requirement to get price support was revoked.

One issue on which Senator Graham and I clashed was the use of a former tuberculosis sanatorium that was owned jointly by Florence and Darlington counties. Graham engaged in an unsuccessful effort to get the state to purchase the hospital and one hundred acres of land for use as a mental health facility. The Senate rejected Graham's proposal to have the state pay four hundred thousand dollars for the property; Graham dropped the price to three hundred thousand dollars, but that was voted down. Graham opposed the joint use of the property by the hospitals in Florence and Darlington as a convalescent center, in order to reduce the pressure on the hospitals for more beds. Eventually the property was leased to McLeod Infirmary for that purpose.

I grew increasingly aware of the lack of sufficient financing for public schools and reluctantly allowed my name to go on a bill proposing a referendum to permit horse racing in counties that wanted to use racing as a tourist attraction, provided the moneys were used for school purposes. The proposal was voted down, but Senator Graham later accused me on the stump of being in favor of "horse bittin." When he accused me of this, I was unsure whether he was referring to horse races or horse bites.

The omens seemed propitious, and I announced that I would be a candidate for the South Carolina Senate. A grueling pace was set, with eight stump speeches over the county.

I ran a hard campaign but never engaged in any personal attack on Senator Graham or his family. He did not show me the same courtesy. In one speech he insinuated that when Uncle Peter was senator he bestowed favors on his family. I publicly denied this and asked for any instances in which this was true. Graham never responded.

I challenged Graham to a television debate. He refused to accept and wrote a letter published in the newspapers stating that he would not debate on television. Graham said he would "speak to the people in clear, simple *American language* as it is taught in South Carolina. You [can speak] English as it is spoken and taught at Harvard, your choice of an institution." I replied, "In this country we don't judge people by where they went to school or if they went to school at all. I went to Harvard on the GI bill, and I make no apology for it." I also pointed out that the founders of Winthrop and Clemson, as well as many historically famous South Carolinians such as John C. Calhoun, went to colleges outside of South Carolina.

The fact that my uncle's law firm represented the *Florence Morning News* became an issue. Senator Graham repeatedly brought up the law firm's connection with the newspaper. He was appealing to lingering anger over the paper's stand on desegregating the public schools. In one speech Graham said, "If you elect me your senator, I will not have to swing on the coattails of the *Florence Morning News* and follow their dictates." My response on the stump, speaking in Florence, was that "my law firm represents the *Morning News* when lawsuits are brought against it. It is a client just as many of you are. I have no control over their editorial policy or any of their business affairs, just as I have no control over those of you who are also clients of my law firm." James Rogers, editor of the *Florence Morning News,* told me that the paper would come out for me or against me, whichever would do the most good.

Senator Graham attacked me for introducing a bill that would have removed the sovereign rights of cities. What he referred to was a bill I introduced—and subsequently withdrew—to permit lawsuits against municipalities' insurance coverage in cases in which a person suffered physical injury because of the negligence of city employees. The defense of sovereign immunity would be waived only to the value of the insurance coverage that municipalities had in place. If there was no insurance coverage, there could be no lawsuit. I wrote the bill because I brought a lawsuit against the city of Florence on behalf of a prisoner who was beaten with such force that his hip was broken. He was dragged from his cell to the municipal court twice for trial but was in such pain that the judge ordered him to be returned to his cell, where he lay most of the time on the floor instead of in a bed. It was five days before his jailors sought medical help, and he was permanently crippled because of the neglect. The city of Florence had an insurance policy that covered such injuries but asserted the defense of sovereign immunity. The courts agreed that in the absence of a statute the defense of sovereign immunity had not been waived when the city provided insurance coverage for such eventualities. Opposition in committee was so vehement that I withdrew it. The South Carolina Supreme Court ruled some thirty years later that I was correct, and because the legislature had been given the opportunity but failed to act, the court ruled in favor of a waiver where insurance had been provided.

Senator Graham belittled my record in the House, saying that if you took all of the ink that was used to write the bills I authored it would not be enough to dot a small *I*. My response was it depended on how big the *I* was. If it was a capital like the one Graham used in trying to take credit for acts with which he had nothing to do, then it would take several gallons of ink to dot it.

The voter registration system used in the early 1960s invited disaster. The registration books had the entries in handwriting and were not alphabetized in any manner. The only way a candidate could get a copy of the registration books was to have someone copy them by hand. It was a tedious and time-consuming process, but my wife, Anne, bravely undertook to do it. I determined that if I were ever elected to the legislature, I would work to reform the state's registration and election laws.

My biggest campaign mistake was my inability to "handle" the black vote. Uncle Peter advised me not to go to a meeting of black voters because I was regarded by white voters as a "nigger lover." I was dismayed by the fact that the lawyers in Florence almost unanimously opposed me because, as one of their leaders once said, "he'll be just like his uncle and use the office to monopolize the legal business."

Another disappointment was that the politicians I had helped two years earlier did not reciprocate. Either I had failed to earn their confidence, or they felt I could not be controlled as easily as they had controlled Senator Graham.

The fact that Graham had introduced the county manager bill in the Senate was forgiven. He told one audience that the only explanation for his allowing the controversial bill to be introduced was that "I was sitting over in the Senate one day and some House members brought a paper in and said this is a little bill we want you to pass. I said to them 'put it on my desk and I didn't read it.'" After it was introduced, he "got around to reading it, and decided it was unconstitutional."

The primary election was held on June 12, 1962. In the voting Senator Graham got overwhelming support from the rural areas, and my vote in the upper part of the county could not compensate for it. The final count was 6,693 votes for Graham and 6,283 votes for Zeigler. When it was clear that I had been defeated, I went to the courthouse where the balloting was being officially received and made a concession speech:

> On the basis of the unofficial returns in thus far, it appears that
> Senator Graham has been reelected. I want to thank those of you who
> helped me and those who didn't help me. I hope that you can change
> over to my side four years from now because I intend to run again at
> that time. I intend to live the rest of my life in Florence County. I think
> we have a wonderful county and it's a good place to live. Thank you.

I sensed that the contest between Senator Graham and me was the beginning of a sea change in local politics. A substantial number of potential voters did not vote in the Democrat primary because there was a loyalty oath that pledged a voter in the primary to support the Democratic Party's nominees in the general election. By the general election there was Republican opposition to Graham, and people questioned, in view of my criticism of him in the primary, whether I would support Graham or switch parties and support a Republican against him. I came out publicly in support of Graham's candidacy because I wanted to make it clear that my allegiance to the Democratic Party was not opportunistic but based on my firm conviction of what governmental policy and our society should be.

Some people criticized my support of Senator Graham in the general election as inconsistent with my position in the primary. One critic not only accused me of supporting Graham but also asserted that I was his campaign manager. I replied that this was not true and I did not "want to take credit where credit was not due." Graham won the election and boasted to his Senate colleagues that he "beat a Harvard man and a Republican."

Greater disappointment was in store for me. Anne's sisters and Mrs. Lide customarily rented cottages at the same beach so that the cousins would grow up knowing each other. In the summer of 1962 Anne and I, along with Florence and Bill Snider, were staying at what was affectionately known as the "old gray barn" on Pawleys Island. One hot afternoon, while most of the group was taking afternoon naps, there was a knock on the back door. A reporter wanted to talk with me, and to my surprise he turned out to be Charlie Wickenberg of Columbia's main newspaper, the *State*. I was startled when he said that it was his understanding that I was a leading candidate for appointment to the federal bench to replace Judge Ashton Williams, who had recently died. It was the first I had heard of this, and I was overcome by the information. I asked what his source was, and he replied that he had talked with Judge Robert Martin, who offered his opinion that because I had actively supported President John F. Kennedy, I would be a leading contender for appointment to the federal district judgeship. This was the beginning of a different sort of political campaign, but one that also ended in disappointment.

Terrell Glenn Sr., who was a U.S. attorney for South Carolina, confirmed Judge Martin's opinion that I was high on the list of candidates. All omens seemed good, and we began contacting friends to write letters to the senators and to Attorney General Robert F. Kennedy on my behalf.

A November 29, 1962, article in the *Charleston News and Courier* stated that the appointment of federal judges was likely to "kick up a storm." There were two vacancies when Judge George Bell Timmerman retired, and the list of possible candidates continued to grow. They included Dean Robert Figg, Charles Simons, Roy A. Powell, Representative Robert W. Hemphill, and Ted Riley. The article commented on my chances:

> On the other hand, Sen. Johnston may be able to stop the appointment of either Mr. Figg or Mr. Simons, and still not be able to put his long-time aid and supporter, Mr. Powell, on the bench. He may find himself compromising on the issue by naming someone like Nick Zeigler of Florence, a Harvard Law School graduate close to sources of power in the justice department.

The "sources of power" included not only Terrell Glenn but also William A. Geoghegan. Bill was from Cincinnati, Ohio, and we became friends through the Lincoln's Inn Society at Harvard. He had become an assistant to Nicholas Katzenbach, chief assistant to Attorney General Robert Kennedy. This gave me entrée into the inner sanctum of the Justice Department.

As time passed, the list of possible candidates increased to twelve. A prominent Richmond lawyer, Lewis F. Powell Jr., who later became a U.S. Supreme Court justice, interviewed me on behalf of the American Bar Association. Powell was interested in my participation in the Carney case and asked if I had read *To Kill a Mockingbird.* I replied that I had, and he said that my experience must have been similar to that of Atticus Finch in the book.

Eventually Senator Olin D. Johnston submitted my and Charles Simons's names to the president. Senator Thurmond submitted only the name of his former law partner, Charles Simons. The contest boiled down to a choice between Charles Simons and me. Terrell Glenn, who was close to Robert Kennedy, adamantly opposed the appointment of Simons. He stated to me and to the Justice Department that when he was attending court in Aiken at the time of the presidential election in 1960, he heard Simons say that he would not support John Kennedy. Judge G. Badger Baker of Florence said that Simons told him that he would not vote for Kennedy and confirmed Glenn's recollection of the conversation.

I of course knew nothing about this, but Judge Baker told me that he had received a telephone call from Bobby Kennedy and confirmed the information Glenn had given Kennedy. It bothered Simons that the Justice Department gave this information weight. When we met in the future, he persistently and aggressively pressed me to say how and from what source this information came to the notice of the attorney general. My last conversation with him was at the Florence Country Club, when he came over to my table and, in a belligerent manner, said, "I would just like to know who made those statements!" I did not answer; I changed the subject because I did not wish to get into a controversy with him on that subject, and he left abruptly. Judge Simons once got in a fight in a parking lot with a stranger who had a Charles "Pug" Ravenel bumper sticker on his car during the 1978 Senate race in which Ravenel opposed Strom Thurmond.

The most interesting event in the entire effort came when Anne and I went to Washington in the fall of 1962 to visit her father. I telephoned Bill Geoghegan, and he invited me to come up to the Justice Department for a visit. There I met with Bill and Nicholas Katzenbach and discussed the prospects of my getting the appointment. It was only about a month after Katzenbach had confronted Governor George Wallace at the schoolhouse door, and I told Katzenbach that I thought he handled himself well. Bill remarked that Katzenbach looked like a "pouter pidgin" on the television. I learned

how carefully Governor Wallace had choreographed the entire event. Katzenbach said that circles had been drawn on the pavement where he and each of
the participants were to stand. When we finished talking, Katzenbach asked
if I would like to speak to Robert Kennedy, and naturally I said I would.

When I entered the attorney general's office, I was struck by the size of
the room and its ornate decoration. Bobby Kennedy sat behind his desk,
and I stood in front of him. He rose, and we shook hands. I felt extremely
uncomfortable because immediately behind me a full-sized stuffed Bengal
tiger, a gift from some Indian potentate, was baring its fangs at my behind.

Kennedy was one of the most intense people I ever met. He paced
around and seemed almost to disappear in the vastness of the office. Then
he would come quickly toward me, almost belligerently, and get "in my
face," asking question after question. He wanted to know if I had any personal knowledge about Charles Earl Simons having supported Nixon, and I
said I did not, but I could not resist adding that I had headed his brother's
campaign in my part of South Carolina. The interview lasted only about ten
minutes, and I was enough of a politician to know that there were a lot more
factors being considered than whether Charles Simons or I had supported
John Kennedy's election to the presidency.

There were rumors for almost a year, until the morning of November
22, 1963, when I received a telephone call from Terrell Glenn telling me
that when President Kennedy returned from Texas, I would be appointed to
a federal judgeship. This was welcome news, and Anne and I, contrary to
our custom, had a glass of wine with our lunch. The telephone rang again.
It was a friend calling to tell us that Kennedy had been shot in Texas. We
were stunned and followed the terrible events on television.

I had to go back to my office, but I was in a daze following the emotional
roller-coaster ride of the past several hours. I had to attend to some business
at the courthouse, and when I emerged onto the street, I met a prominent
businessman who greeted me with an air of jubilation. He made the shocking statement, "One down, and two to go!"

My depression went beyond my disappointment in not being made a
federal judge. Although I had suffered a political defeat, I felt upbeat about
politics because I had sensed, in Kennedy's election, an elevation in the
character of politics that compensated for the pain of running for office.
Part of it may have been the sophistication and style Kennedy represented.
His death and my disappointment brought a sense of loss that I struggled to
overcome.

The appointment of federal judges then rested with President Johnson
and became an entirely different situation. My connections in the attorney

general's office would count for nothing since relations between Robert Kennedy and the new president were strained if not hostile. I do not know what took place, but Governor John West told me that President Johnson talked with Strom Thurmond and asked him for his assurance that he would not bolt the Democratic Party. With that assurance Johnson agreed to appoint Thurmond's former law partner, Charles Simons, to the judgeship. Some thirty days later, after the Senate approved Simons's appointment, Thurmond announced that he was changing parties. According to the stories reported by others, Lyndon Johnson cursed and swore for twenty-four hours after he received news that Thurmond had become a Republican.

It was ironic that the following year I was elected a delegate to the 1964 Democratic Party National Convention in Atlantic City, New Jersey. Governor Donald Russell and Lieutenant Governor Robert McNair headed the delegation. The company was excellent, but the experience was dismal. I have never felt so much as though I was part of a cattle drive as when the delegates were herded in and out of the convention hall. Lyndon Johnson's nomination was never in doubt, and only the contrived suspense of who would be his vice presidential nominee provided any excitement. I think most delegates knew it would be Hubert H. Humphrey. When I escaped Atlantic City, I promised the good Lord that I would never again attend one of those conventions.

Governor Russell backed Lyndon Johnson in 1964, at a time when the southern Democratic Party was about to be shorn of its white voters because of the Voting Rights Act and the Civil Rights Act. Since I had been a delegate to the national convention, Russell asked me to serve as a presidential elector for Johnson. It was not a popular stance to take, and Barry Goldwater carried South Carolina, the first Republican to do so since 1876.

I came in for a good deal of criticism because I had been a presidential elector for Johnson. I was not surprised when, following the passage of the Civil Rights Act, one of my constituents telephoned me and, without introducing himself, said, "Well what do you think about your president now?" As calmly as I could, I said, "I think he is president of the United States."

There was a pause, and then the caller said, "The next time you see him, tell him his Civil Rights Act stinks." With great relief I replied, "The very next time I see President Johnson I will be sure to relay your message." I had never met, nor would I ever meet, Lyndon Johnson.

19

Repairing a Law Practice

When the tumult and political shouting had ended in November 1962, it was not easy to repair a fractured law practice. My position in the firm of McEachin, Townsend, and Zeigler remained the same so far as compensation was concerned: I received only one-third of the fees I brought into the office. Uncle Peter's health began to deteriorate. My aunt, Leah Townsend, received the same salary she had received in 1932. There were bright spots, however, since I represented several steady, paying clients. Notable among these were the Sexton Dental Clinic, the R. P. Byrd Estate, the International Ladies' Garment Workers' Union, and the United Furniture Workers of America, the union at La-Z-Boy's factory in Florence. It was a strange, diverse assortment, but the different legal problems were frequently stimulating and provided a steady flow of fees. There was a great deal of day-to-day legal business, of course, like drafting wills, drawing up deeds, and handling minor claims that might be settled without a jury trial.

Sexton Dental Clinic required a great deal of legal advice. Uncle Peter represented Claude Lee Sexton when he had difficulty with the Internal Revenue Service in 1953–54, and the Sexton Dental Clinic remained a client of the firm thereafter. It was about the same time, around 1953, that Sexton decided to open a clinic in which patients could get immediate and permanent dentures at the lowest price. To do this he brought in William Shealey as a partner, and they developed an assembly-line method in which patients had their teeth extracted and dentures were made on the premises and placed in the patient's mouth—all in one day's time. This made it possible for low-income patients to have dentures made by Sexton Dental Clinic for fifty dollars, a procedure for which a regular dentist would charge three to four hundred dollars.

Sexton, a North Carolina native and a graduate of Emory University, came to practice dentistry in Florence in 1925. I recall as a young boy having a tooth extracted by Sexton when he was located in a simple second-story office in the building next to my uncle's law firm. When he organized the clinic in 1953, he moved the operation to a one-story building on Palmetto Street. The system he initiated did not change dental practice methods but merely focused on one aspect of it and skillfully organized it on an assembly-line model. Sexton Dental Clinic was a success from its opening days.

The clinic was not popular with local dentists or with the South Carolina Dental Association. There were periodic attempts to find some violation of the state's dental regulations and to close the clinic, but all these efforts failed. I recall one instance in which the South Carolina Dental Association brought an action against the clinic, seeking an injunction for violating dental regulations, but the judge hearing the case happened to have teeth made by Sexton Dental Clinic in his mouth. The injunction was not granted.

The number of patients increased from thirty-five or forty a day to between four hundred and five hundred by 1977. The patients came from every part of the United States as well as from foreign countries. It was not unusual to see busloads of Amish folk from Pennsylvania, in their distinctive black dress, and tattooed motorcyclists in town to have dental work done at Sexton's Clinic. During the first thirty years there was no advertising except from the patients themselves. The numbers seeking dental work at the clinic increased so dramatically that Florence became known as "Tooth City, USA," making it hard for critics of the clinic to argue against thousands of satisfied patients. The Florence Chamber of Commerce estimated that the clinic's contribution to the city's income was between $4 million and $5 million a year. The clinic and staff of dentists, technicians, nurses, and office workers rose to more than one hundred.

A big jump in the number of patients came after an NBC television documentary in 1976. The producers wished to do a program about the unique success of the Sexton Dental Clinic, and Sexton asked me to accompany the NBC people at all times when they were on the clinic's property interviewing patients and filming. It was a grueling routine. I reported to the clinic at 4:00 A.M. and met the television crew. We followed the entire procedure, from the extracting of teeth to the fitting of dentures. Only about one-third of the clinic's patients had this done, but the procedure by which patients could accomplish this in a single day was the story that interested the television crew.

I recall one man, of spartan constitution, who had all of his teeth, nearly twenty, extracted and was waiting for his new dentures. The television interviewer asked him what it was like to have so many teeth extracted at one time. His response was that there was nothing to it, "it was just like shucking corn." The television broadcast caused the patient load at Sexton's to jump dramatically.

Sexton, who was a self-effacing person, never spared himself the rigors of the system that he devised and supervised. He rose every morning at 3:00 and went to the clinic, where he was a hands-on supervisor of the operation. There were occasional difficulties between the dentists employed by the clinic. One event in particular remains vivid in my memory. Sexton called me and said that two dentists working at the clinic had engaged in a dispute that resulted in a fistfight. He wanted me to come over immediately and "straighten them out." Drawing on my navy background, I conceived the notion that I was being asked to conduct a "captain's mast" for the clinic.

When I arrived, Sexton was in his extremely small office. After he told me what had happened, he summoned the two fractious dentists to his office, and I told them how unprofessional their conduct had been and asked them to apologize to each other and shake hands. They meekly complied, and my services were no longer needed. I was greatly relieved because we were so jammed into the office space that if they had resumed throwing punches, Sexton and I might have not escaped unscathed.

My association with the clinic continued after Sexton's death because he designated the Guaranty Bank and Trust Company as executor of his will. O. S. "Sandy" Aiken Jr. was the trust officer for the Guaranty Bank and

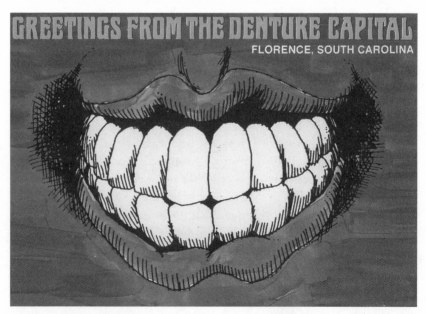

Postcard advertising the Sexton Dental Clinic, 1965. Collection of the author

Trust Company, and I assisted him with legal advice. I also became the lawyer for Sexton's successor, Hoyt L. Eagerton Jr., and for the clinic that came under his supervision and continued to prosper after Sexton's death.

The coming of Interstates 95 and 20 changed the complexion of Florence. R. P. Byrd Sr.'s estate involved me in another and more complex field of probate and trust law. Byrd was a substantial farmer and owner of three tracts of land near Florence, the chief parcel containing approximately 1,439 acres. He died testate on March 9, 1928, and the devisees under his will were his wife, to whom he left a life estate in all of his property, and his two sons, R. P. Byrd Jr. and George S. Byrd, whom he made beneficiaries of a trust in his real property for their lifetimes. Upon the death of his sons, their portion of the land was devised to their children and, if there were none, then to Epworth Orphanage. His wife died in 1936, and the lands in which she had a life estate passed to trustees for her two sons. The major portion of the 1,439-acre tract was generally described as the "Home Place" and contained approximately 1,000 acres. It constituted the corpus of the trust held for the benefit of R. P. Byrd Jr. The remaining part of the 1,439-acre tract, approximately 450 acres, was known as the "Powers Place" and was held in trust for George Byrd. The original trustees appointed by the probate court resigned, and George McCown and James W. Parker Sr. were appointed trustees in 1940. James Parker Sr. was the brother-in-law of George McCown, who handled the moneys coming in from the lands, while Parker supervised the land and the trust properties.

What would have been a run-of-the-mill administration of an estate and trusteeship became complicated. In 1946 George Byrd, in order to get money, conveyed his interest in the two separate parcels of land in which he had a beneficial interest to the wife of George McCown, and in 1950 R. P. Byrd Jr. sold his beneficial interest in the Home Place to her. Mrs. George McCown now held the beneficial interest in all of the lands except for the Powers Place. Mrs. McCown died in 1954, and her husband died in 1956. Their heirs were the beneficiaries of the remainder interest in the Home Place during the life of R. P. Byrd Jr.

It was not the quality of the farmland that made the Byrd land valuable and catapulted it into a multitude of controversies and lawsuits. The proposed Interstate 95 passed through the farm, and the northeastern terminus of Interstate 20 was located on it. A lawsuit was filed by R. P. Byrd Jr. in October 1960 against the McCown heirs and James W. Parker Sr. seeking to set aside the deed by which Byrd had conveyed his interest in the Home Place to Mrs. George McCown and to hold the trustees, that is, James W. Parker Sr. and the heirs of George McCown and Mrs. McCown, liable to him for an accounting.

The case was heard by J. W. Clements, the Florence County master in equity, in 1961. During the course of the litigation James W. Parker Sr. died, and his daughter Suzanne Parker Smith and son James W. Parker Jr. were substituted as defendants in the lawsuit, and the Guaranty Bank and Trust Company was appointed substitute trustee under the will of R. P. Byrd Sr. I became counsel for the Guaranty Bank and Trust Company as trustee.

The master in equity decided the case in favor of my clients, and counsel for R. P. Byrd Jr. appealed to the circuit court. Judge James Spruill in an adjoining circuit heard the appeal and confirmed the master in equity's findings in 1963. Counsel for R. P. Byrd Jr. appealed to the South Carolina Supreme Court, and the opinion of the circuit court was upheld in 1965.

The connecting of I-20 with I-95 took place on land entirely within the Home Place. What would have normally been a family land dispute affected the future development of Florence. The most significant series of events in which I played a part was as counsel for the Guaranty Bank and Trust Company as "Substitute Trustee under the Will of R. P. Byrd." It came with the development of the land held by the trustee containing all four quadrants of the land surrounding the interchange created by I-20 and the spur leading to Florence (later David McLeod Boulevard) and I-95. Its development over the next twenty years, in effect, moved the business center of Florence to a location outside the city limits.

In the summer of 1970 Mayor Cooper Tedder and Lewis Vickers, head of the Florence County Loan and Development Commission, approached me and stated that a major industry wished to purchase a site in the southeastern quadrant of the interstate located on the Home Place. The industry was not interested in leasing any land but wished to purchase the site on the Byrd estate. The difficulty was that the will of R. P. Byrd Sr., which created the trust, specifically limited the power of the trustees to hold the land for leasing or renting "the arable land." The trustees were not given the power to sell any of the land held in trust.

The identity of the industry that wished to purchase the land was cloaked in mystery. It was described as "a large, financially stable manufacturing company, which intends to build a facility for the manufacture of electronic components and equipment." Anne and I invited two unknown representatives who came to Florence for dinner at our house, but they gave us assumed names and would not tell us for whom they worked. Unquestionably the location of such an industry on the property would confer a benefit on the remainder of the trust lands because it would necessitate the extension of water, natural gas, and other utilities that federal grants would facilitate. If the sale of the property could not be arranged or approved, the overwhelming consensus was that there would be "a terrific financial loss" to the trust lands.

The Guaranty Bank, as trustee and on my advice, filed a suit that asked the court to allow it to deviate from the terms of the trust created by R. P. Byrd Sr. on the grounds that the trust would suffer financial loss if such deviation was not approved. By this time the number of defendants who had to be made parties to the suit was over fourteen, and in addition, John Doe and Mary Roe, as "Unknown, Unborn, Incompetent Contingent Unknown Remaindermen," had to be made parties.

I persuaded my friend John McGowan to be attorney for John Doe and Mary Roe. The usual procedure was followed with a hearing before the master in equity, and he issued a report that recommended approval and the circuit judge approved the report. The mysterious industry let it be known, however, that it would not go through with the transaction unless the South Carolina Supreme Court approved the deviation from the wording of the trust. This necessitated an appeal and the writing of briefs. I agreed with John McGowan that we would file an appeal in the names of John Doe and Mary Roe to the South Carolina Supreme Court.

The Supreme Court decided in favor of giving the trustee the power to sell land to this unidentified industry. South Carolina case law was not clear on the power of a trustee to deviate from the terms of the trust instrument, so our favorable decision was seen as a landmark decision in the state's trust law. It produced the benefits that had been anticipated. The federal government assisted the city with grants, and water and sewer lines were extended to the site. But first the site had to be incorporated into the city of Florence, so a figurative umbilical cord was created along the spur of I-20 from the city limits and the site became a part of the city. The mysterious industry exercised its option to purchase the site consisting of 128 acres by paying $473,960. The company's name was revealed to be General Electric.

General Electric's coming accelerated development of the remainder of the Home Place because the northeastern quadrant was an ideal site for a shopping center. The GE ruling approving the sale had limited application unless it was possible to show that there would be irreparable harm to the remainder of the trust property if a sale of land was not allowed. The prospective developer of the property as a mall was willing to accept a ground lease. Thus I entered into a long and protracted negotiation for the leasing of the northeastern quadrant to be used for the construction of a shopping mall. This eventually became Magnolia Mall.

The last hurrah in which I was engaged as counsel for the trustee, now the First Union Bank as successor of the Guaranty Bank and Trust Company, was the building of a civic center on a part of the borrow pit from which the South Carolina Highway Department had excavated soil to build the interchange at I-95 and I-20. Sandy Aiken and I had always regarded the borrow pit as a liability rather than an asset of the trust. It was partially filled with water and had become a dumping ground for people seeking to rid themselves of junk.

Suddenly there was a movement to put a civic center on the site and use a large portion of the borrow pit as a parking area. There is no question that a civic center is an asset to a growing city, but experience shows that one has never been able to support itself financially.

The proposition to build it aroused strong opposition from many citizens of Florence. One opponent, a prominent dentist, said that if the proposed building with a seating capacity of ten thousand was approved and built, and the seats were filled to capacity, he would walk across the stage naked and "ass backward" to celebrate the event.

The controversy got so heated that the officials of First Union Bank directed me not to make any statements either for or against the civic center's construction. A question, however, was raised publicly about the

The intersection of I-95 and I-20 on the estate of R. P. Byrd Sr. Center left: Magnolia Mall; center right: General Electric; center right rear: Wal-Mart and the borrow pit. Collection of the author

signatures of some of the beneficiaries of the trust on the deeds of conveyance to the commission charged with its construction. Ed Young, who was now the principal owner of the beneficial interests, asked that I consent to an interview on the radio and clarify the situation. First Union approved his request and I did so, and the question about signatures was resolved.

Eventually the civic center was built with the aid of a five-hundred-thousand-dollar grant from the legislature, although the dentist who opposed construction has never been called upon to make his stage debut. R. P. Byrd Jr. died, and the trusteeship came to an end. Sandy Aiken and I have had the satisfaction of having steered the trust through many years of difficulty, have made the holders of the beneficial interests rich, and have changed the face of the city of Florence forever.

The third group of clients I represented were labor unions. One of my critics once said, "If you would stop representing blacks and labor unions, you could be a rich man." This was probably true, but I would not have been able to be a part of two movements that transformed the South into a modern and vital part of this nation, nor would I have been able to help people who needed their interests protected. I have no regrets about having been part of the civil rights movement, which integrated blacks into southern society, or about being part of the labor unions' struggle to solve problems created by industries that moved into the South promising financial security.

My connection with labor unions really began when I met Mary Cameron at the headquarters that Anne and I helped open for the election of John Kennedy in 1960. A year or so later Wentworth Manufacturing Company moved from New England to South Carolina. It brought the ILGWU with them, and Anne and I became friends with the manager of the company, Ronald Sopkin, and his wife, Doris. All was well until there was a strike and some of the strikers were arrested and put in the county jail. Mary Cameron came to me and asked if I would serve as counsel and arrange bond for their release. I did this, and I recall that Doris Sopkin told me I should be flattered that the ILGWU wanted me to represent them because it was the most respected union in the garment industry.

Doris was right. The lawyers with whom I associated in the nearly thirty years I acted as local counsel for the ILGWU have been examples of the best virtues of the legal profession—intelligent, compassionate, and ethical.

The situation was ironic. In the South's zeal to get out of economic doldrums, it fell into the trap of giving community support to sewing plants—many of which exploited women laborers—while their exploiters enjoyed the accolades of gullible civic leaders and politicians. Communities built sewing plants to lease them with the keen expectation of bringing money into the community. One manager said in response to criticism of the working hours and conditions in his plant, "We stretch these women like rubber bands. It's too bad if some of them break."

Union organizers, who helped workers to organize for better pay and working conditions, were subjected to physical abuse and imprisonment, often with the approval of the supervisors and managers of some of these plants. I frequently went down to jails at night to secure the release of organizers who had been arrested on some flimsy pretext.

I was impressed with the tenacity and spirit of some of the women who were subject to harsh treatment by their employers. During a strike at a sewing plant a picket line was established, and eggs and balloons filled with water were thrown by nonstriking employees at the pickets. I met with some of the women who were picketing, and I told them I knew how difficult it was at times not to retaliate when they were being provoked and harassed but explained the importance of their not giving the company an excuse to have them arrested. One high-spirited young woman in the group seemed to have a fiery temper. She said, "Mr. Zeigler, if they higher ass me, I'll higher ass them right back!"

The fortitude and perseverance of some of these women astounded me. In one case a young woman, a sewing-machine operator, was seen by company agents going to an ILGWU meeting. She was an outstanding operator and never failed to make her production quotas. In order to fire her without the reason being obvious—that she had attended a union meeting—she was transferred to a defective sewing machine that constantly broke down. It was hoped she would fail to meet production quotas. Despite the loss of time on the defective machine she managed to make her quota. She was then transferred to a machine with even more defects and that required more maintenance. She told me that she sat at her machine and wept, but through the tears she struggled to make the production quota. As she struggled, she kept repeating to herself, "I will not let them break me down." In the end she was discharged.

Most of the sewing plants built in the 1950s and 1960s now stand empty. The "runaway industry" that was welcomed in the 1950s and 1960s as it fled northern states has now run away to foreign countries. The sewing industry is almost dead in our area; the jobs have been sent offshore, where it is easier to pay workers less.

The other union I represented, but on a different level, was the United Furniture Workers of America, which had a union at the La-Z-Boy plant in Florence. The plant manufactured furniture, and the workers with whom I dealt were predominantly men and were of both races. The legal problems for which they sought my help were almost entirely individual grievances under the collective bargaining agreement already in existence between the industry and its employees. This representation caused me to become familiar with arbitration procedure, since the collective bargaining agreement called for arbitration under the rules of the American Arbitration Association.

I was greatly heartened by the fact that there were both white and black officials in the local union and that they seemed to work together in harmony. It also impressed me that they seemed genuinely to care for each other when difficulties arose with regard to production quotas, leaves of absence, unjustified firings, and other complaints their members brought to them for arbitration. Many of the complaints had little merit, and some were obviously "gold bricking," but I am convinced that in an industrial democracy even these seemingly frivolous complaints must be adjudicated in such a way that the aggrieved party feels he or she has had a day in court.

The story of my representation of unions would not be complete if I did not acknowledge that I have been subject to criticism and opprobrium for having represented them. It was acceptable in the public mind to represent murderers and thieves, but not labor unions. Despite this hostility I attained some status in the legal profession. In 1963 and 1965 Governors Russell and McNair, respectively, appointed me to be a special judge and hold equity hearings in Columbia.

20

A Redeemed Promise

1966–1967

I was determined to redeem the promise made in 1962 that I would run for the South Carolina Senate in the next election. The political alliances in Florence County had changed little, and there was no guarantee I would succeed. Encouraged by the belief that many thought I had paid my dues and deserved to be elected on a second try, I took the plunge. Because apportionment of the Senate was mandated, there would be two senators from Florence County; running against Senator Graham would not be a problem.

I also played a role in the lawsuit brought in the federal court to enforce the "one man, one vote" rule. The Senate was tied up in a filibuster through which the small counties sought to increase the size of the Senate from forty-six to fifty-six members so that they could retain a resident senator. The compromise was a plan to increase the Senate to fifty members, but the resolution could not be made law without recourse to the federal courts.

A group of senators from small counties decided to intervene and pressed their plan for a fifty-nine-seat Senate in a suit in the federal court. Ralph Gasque was the senator of Marion County, one of the small counties. When Senator Gasque was in trouble with the South Carolina Department of Revenue, Uncle Peter represented him. This contact led the small county senators to retain me to represent them before a three panel court of federal judges convened to review the various plans to reapportion the Senate.

On February 14, 1966, I argued before the panel of judges in Columbia, with Judge Clement Haynsworth as presiding judge. I made an emotional appeal to the court to understand the dilemma in which the legislature found itself and asked that it seriously consider the fifty-nine-seat plan. I concluded by asking that the panel "temper the wind to the new shorn lamb." The final result of the combined actions of the Senate and the court was approval of the fifty-seat plan, which would give two senators to Florence

County for two years to allow time to enact a plan more in conformity with the "one man, one vote" standards.

I announced early in March 1966 that I would seek the new seat for Florence County. This would avoid another race with Senator Clyde Graham, but it soon became known that Representative David Harwell intended to run for the same seat. David was a friend of mine and a political ally, so I was eager to avoid a conflict between us. The Florence County Democratic Party Convention was held on March 7, 1966, and I was elected president. The next day the *Florence Morning News* account of the convention gave this report: "Florence attorney E. N. (Nick) Zeigler, an announced candidate and president of the convention, set the tone for the biennial gatherings at Florence's armory with a shouted declaration that he had 'rather fight than switch,' an obvious reference to a sprinkling of state Democrats who have defected to the Republican Camp."

The main theme of the meeting was for the party to maintain unity. When the convention adjourned, I went to David Harwell's office to talk about the harmful effect of a campaign between us for the Senate seat. After our conference David announced that he would seek reelection to the South Carolina House of Representatives. No one else announced for the Senate in the Democratic Party's June primary, so the Democrats nominated both Senator Graham and me.

Storm clouds were gathering however. The county Republicans met on March 18, 1966, and nominated former Democrat Julian Dusenbury to oppose Graham and Dennis O'Brian to oppose me. Dusenbury had run unsuccessfully against Clyde Graham in 1954, and Dennis O'Brian was a member of the Florence City Council. A full slate of Republican candidates for the House was nominated. Dusenbury in his acceptance speech stated prophetically, "We must have a positive attitude and behind the leadership of Thurmond and [Harry] Dent and others we cannot fail."

In early May 1966 O'Brian suffered a heart attack and withdrew his name from nomination. The county Republican Party reconvened and nominated Stanley Baldwin, an employee of DuPont and executive committeeman for the county Republican Party. He had many contacts in Florence County but had never before been a candidate for public office.

The election was heated because this was the first serious attempt by the Republican Party to defeat Fritz Hollings, South Carolina's junior senator in the U.S. Senate. State senator Bradley Morrah took on Senator Thurmond. The local Democrats opened a campaign headquarters and began a united effort to defeat the Republican candidates. Public speeches were organized by the Democrats, and at one held in Timmonsville I said, "We accept the Republican Party's suggestion that you vote for the man instead of the party. Man for man there can be no doubt that the Democratic Party's nominees are better qualified than their Republican opponents."

Whatever Senator Graham's basic virtues were, public speaking was not one of them. I recall one gathering at the Johnsonville VFW hut organized by the Democrats and attended by fifty hardworking, sunburned, thin-lipped, stony-faced men. Senator Graham spoke ahead of me, and I was chafing at the bit to lay out our case against the Republican candidates. Senator Graham strayed into a long discourse about the venerable history of the Democratic Party. As he got deeper and deeper into the story, he began to pile hyperbole on hyperbole. "The Medes and Persians were Democrats," he said. "The Greeks and Romans were Democrats. The Democrats were at Runnymede." I wondered who the audience thought the Medes were. Perhaps they thought they were a Mead family living across the Pee Dee River. I feel certain few in the audience knew much about Runnymede or understood what relevance it had in this election.

The Republicans attacked me in a handout titled "Had Enuf," which alleged that I roomed with Robert Kennedy when I was at Harvard Law School. It made no difference that Robert Kennedy went to the University of Virginia Law School, not Harvard. Above all it was boldly and frequently asserted that I was a liberal. At the opening of the Democratic headquarters, county chairman Ralph Anderson came to my defense by urging the Republicans to "stop trying to slander Democrats with irresponsible charges."

Although little had changed with regard to the internal political alliances within Florence County, there was a gradual lessening of tension about the integration of the public schools. In November 1963 a group of civic and religious leaders organized a retreat for fifty Florence citizens to form a consensus about how to handle racial integration peacefully. The group met at the Litchfield Inn, and I suggested that we call the resulting movement for moderation "The Spirit of Litchfield."

The result of the election was a resounding victory for the county Democrats. I received 10,980 votes and Baldwin received 5,195. Graham defeated Dusenbury, receiving 9,577 votes to Dusenbury's 6,638. All of the Democratic House candidates were elected, and Hollings was reelected. The only ominous note was that Thurmond was also reelected to the U.S. Senate, but Democrats McNair and West were elected as governor and lieutenant governor together with the constitutional officers.

It was generally a joyous time and caused me to recall something Col. John Moore once said: "Everyone needs to have a victory experience now and then." I was grateful for my chance to win. For the first time in politics, I felt I was performing in a theater that demanded all of my energy and talents.

There was great anxiety in the South Carolina Senate about the number of newcomers who had been elected. Twenty-two who were elected had not served in the Senate previously. Six of these were Republicans, and one was an Independent. It was feared that there were so many newly elected members they might be inclined to rebel against the seniority system. We were all invited to lunch at the Palmetto Club before the legislature convened, and Lovick Thomas, the longtime clerk of the Senate, beseeched us not to attempt such drastic actions. I grew fond of Lovick, who took his job seriously, sometimes appearing to be an anxious private school headmaster endeavoring to control unruly pupils and sometimes an outraged drillmaster enraged by his recruits' lack of decorum. He fretted constantly over the Senate's public image being tarnished by the disreputable conduct of some senators, and he frequently had ample reason to do so. Howard McClain, executive director of the Christian Action Council, once told me that when he made one of his infrequent visits to the State House, he felt as though he was among "burley sinners." I understood how he might come to that conclusion, for on one occasion Senator Ralph Gasque, in a speech on the Senate floor and only partially in jest, said, "I don't smoke. I don't drink. I save myself for major vices."

I felt exhilarated to be a member of the Senate, having spent two uninspiring years in the House. Instead of being a backbencher, I fought toe to toe with the entrenched senatorial leaders. Conspicuous in this group were Senators Edgar Brown, Marion Gressette, Rembert Dennis, James P. Mozingo, and Ralph Gasque. They were a fascinating and frequently exasperating group to deal with. In their amiable moods they were prima donnas, and in their menacing aspects they were warlords. I knew that one of them had exhausted all reasonable arguments in any debate, when he asserted that you could not put any credence in legislation sponsored by a Harvard man. This prompted me to reply on one occasion that some of us are born lame, some are born blind, and some go to Harvard, but we all struggle hard to overcome our disabilities.

It also helped my advancement to have Lieutenant Governor John West as a friend and as presiding officer in the Senate. In December, before the legislature convened, West showed his confidence in me by appointing me to the special joint committee of the Senate and House to study the state's election laws. On December 29, 1966, J. Clator Arrants, a former senator and former House member from Kershaw, was elected chairman. In a burst of enthusiasm over my selection, I had Judge G. Badger Baker administer the oath of office to me on December 28, prior to the committee meeting the next day. The Senate, however, did not recognize that as giving me any seniority over the others elected at the same time.

It was difficult to grasp that my duty as a senator was divided between responsibility for the smooth operation of county government and the need to address larger statewide issues. I had made a firm resolve after my experience in the House to reform county government and free the legislature from the responsibility of passing separate budgets for each county. The effort to accomplish this was referred to as "home rule." I was equally committed to pushing for reform of the state election laws.

These interests, however, had to be deferred while the pressing issue of Senate reapportionment was resolved. My maiden speech was on the thorny subject of reapportionment. It was gratifying to receive a letter from John West on January 25, 1967. It read in part, "I want to congratulate you on your maiden speech to the Senate. Your comments on the reapportionment question showed an excellent understanding and analysis of the problem. Your thoughts were unusually well presented and I, along with your colleagues in the Senate, were most impressed."

Reapportionment would be among the most vexing and time-consuming of my activities. When a joint committee of the House and Senate was created to study the matter and propose legislation, West appointed me a member. The other Senate members were Marion Gressette, Jack Lindsay, and Dick Riley.

My appointments to the Election Law Study Committee and to the Reapportionment Committee were the most important and demanding tasks I faced in the two-year term of office in the Senate. These committees produced major pieces of legislation with statewide implications and effect.

The Reapportionment Committee began meeting early in February 1967, and it was clear from the outset that Senator Gressette now had another Ivy League stalking horse besides me: Heyward Belser, a member of the House from Richland County, was a graduate of Yale Law School. The two seldom agreed on any proposal, and they exchanged sharp rhetorical barbs in our discussions. I recall a special meeting of the committee that lasted past midnight; finally Senator Gressette said he was leaving even though the rest of the committee stated it would not leave until some agreement was reached. Gressette got up and walked out of the committee room, leaving Heyward Belser, the vice chairman, to preside. Five minutes elapsed before Gressette returned to the committee room and resumed the chair. He said he felt he could not trust the committee to proceed properly in his absence. We continued for about another hour without reaching an agreement and finally adjourned. Senator Gressette frequently complained that his task was complicated by having to deal with both a Yale and a Harvard graduate.

Senator Riley and I felt that the reapportionment problem could best be solved by adopting a fifty-seat Senate and passing a bill calling for an amendment to the state constitution to reflect that change. We thought that Senator Gressette was in agreement with us, but in the time it took to get from the third floor conference room to the Senate chamber, he had changed his mind. Despite this setback Dick Riley and I introduced a bill in late February calling for a constitutional referendum to change the number of senators from forty-six to fifty. I argued that the federal court had approved a plan allowing fifty senatorial seats and indicated that this would give the legislature "ample time" to adopt a permanent reapportionment plan, including the submission of a constitutional amendment to the people.

The bill to submit a constitutional amendment to the people was recommitted, and a suit was filed in the state court for a declaratory judgment that the state's constitution mandated a forty-six-seat Senate. In late March the South Carolina Supreme Court ruled that the state's constitution mandated a forty-six-seat Senate. I then proposed that the Senate adopt two plans—one calling for a fifty-seat Senate and the other for a forty-six-seat Senate—together with a bill calling for a referendum on the issue of changing the state's constitution to allow for fifty senators.

This was not acceptable, and only a forty-six-seat Senate was debated. Senator Jack Lindsay and I incurred the wrath of Senator Ralph Gasque. Glaring at me with the television cameras running, Gasque said, "Senator Zeigler, I'll cut your throat from ear to ear." He was referring to the fact that under the forty-six-seat plan Darlington, Florence, and Marion counties would be grouped together with only three senators as opposed to the four senators under the fifty-seat plan. My wife was watching television that night and called my hotel to inquire about what was going on and whether my life was in danger. I assured her that Gasque was only speaking of my political throat. The end result was the passage of a bill for a forty-six-seat Senate that grouped Florence, Marion, and Williamsburg counties in the same district with three senators. This was not the end of the controversy, however, and the method of filing proved another thorny issue. My woes continued because I was a member of the Election Law Study Committee and the method of filing in multiseat districts would come under that committee's responsibility in the next session.

The senatorial members of the Election Law Study Committee were me, Senator Marshall B. Williams, and Senator Eugene C. Griffith, a Republican and the son of the judge who had presided over the Carney case. The bills the committee filed in the Senate carried all three names, but we frequently disagreed with each other during debates. The first reform I pushed was for a centralized, computerized registration of voters. I felt I owed it to my wife to get this done after she had spent endless hours hand copying lists of names from county precinct lists when I ran for the House. The second reform I championed was the creation of a bipartisan election commission that would be responsible for enforcing election laws. This was an attempt to remove enforcement from the jurisdiction of the secretary of state, which is an elective office. Usually the party powerful enough to elect the governor is also able to elect the secretary of state. It is, in short, a political office and subject to the influence of party politics.

I fully believe that the democratic process is flawed when the election process is not fairly administered. The only solace a defeated candidate for public office has is the knowledge that a majority of voters did not want him or her elected. That in and of itself is a stinging blow to the ego, but it is intolerable when the result is not the true verdict of a popular majority. It endangers the very democratic process itself.

The three of us on the committee introduced the first bill to begin centralizing registration on February 15, 1967, and it was referred to the Judiciary Committee. The Senate bill was matched by an identical House bill to ensure that one or the other would make it through the legislative process before the General Assembly adjourned. The House version moved more quickly, and it became the one that, after amendment, was eventually enacted. I assumed the primary responsibility for getting the House version of election reform through the Senate. The difficulty arose when I proposed to amend the bill to allow voter registration certificates to be valid though December 1968. It was my opinion that the drastic changes in the registration system under the new law did not allow sufficient time for voters to reregister in compliance with the constitutional requirement to reregister every ten years. The amendment passed on first reading with only six Republican senators voting against it. The bill was then given its crucial second reading and was on the calendar for its third reading—it was not customary to amend bills on third reading.

Senator Gressette was not present when the amendment was adopted and therefore did not vote either way. The Republican senators, however, threatened lawsuits and filibusters to prevent the extension of the voters' certificates. Senator Marion H. Smoak was quoted as saying, "This amendment is obviously designed to protect the Democrat vote in this state for Lyndon Johnson in 1968, which may be reduced as a result of problems the Democrats will have in registering some of their members." The racist nature of the Republican objections was openly stated. In a June 1, 1967, *Charleston News and Courier* article, the racial bias was made abundantly clear:

> Sen. John E. Bourne, R-Charleston, said passing the bill would be giving federal registrars (who registered thousands of Negroes last year in Clarendon and Dorchester counties) "a pat on the back."
>
> "We've got a lot of people who were bused in on the rolls. Don't you think its time to get rid of them rather than keep them?" Bourne said.

A headline in the *Charleston News and Courier* made no bones about it: "GOP Loses Fight to Cut Negro Vote." The headline in the *Charlotte Observer* stated, "Republicans Threaten New Filibuster to Stop Zeigler." Senator Floyd Spence, who later became a U.S. congressman, was quoted as saying that validity of the registration certificates was being extended so that "all the illiterate voters presently on the rolls will be sure to vote in the 1968 election for Lyndon Johnson and—Democrat officeholders."

The Republican senators charged that what I proposed was unconstitutional. I tried to squelch that argument by getting an opinion from Attorney General Daniel R. McLeod that there was nothing unconstitutional in the proposed amendment. McLeod, the brother of David McLeod, who was criticizing me in Florence, came under attack by the Republicans as being a partisan Democrat and unworthy of being taken seriously.

All seemed well until the bill came up for its third reading on June 14, 1967. The House version, which had been amended to extend the validity of registration certificates until December 31, 1968, had been debated only briefly on June 13. In the meantime it was reported on the news services that President Johnson had nominated Thurgood Marshall to fill a vacancy on the U.S. Supreme Court. I encountered Senator Gressette on the Senate floor before the afternoon's session began. He was in a towering rage. He said he would not vote for any measure that would give Johnson any advantage in the election and he would support an amendment to make recertification mandatory before the November 1968 election.

Forewarned is forearmed. I went to Dan McLeod's office and told him of the new development. He told me that voting certificates had been extended in 1948 and suggested that I get the original bill from the archives and see whose names were on it. I did so and found many surprising facts. Thus I prepared myself for the onslaught of Gressette and the Republican senators.

The bill as amended came up for debate, and Senator Smoak introduced an amendment to strike the year 1968 and insert the year 1967, but he withdrew his amendment in favor of one offered by Senators Smoak, Gressette, Spence, James Stevens, and Claymon Grimes by striking "December 31, 1968" and inserting "July 1968." Gressette now was the main spokesman for the amendment and argued in its favor. I was prepared but felt that I had little chance of carrying the day against so formidable a foe as Senator Gressette.

I began by quoting from Thomas Babington Macaulay's *Horatius at the Bridge*: "Then none was for a party, / Then all were for the State . . . The Romans were like brothers / in the brave days of old." I pointed out that things had changed, but in 1948 the Romans were still like brothers and "none was for a party." I had with me the original bill, passed in 1948, that extended the voting certificates past the election in 1948. I pointed out that the bill had been introduced and passed in the House of Representatives. Senator Nathaniel W. Cabell, Republican from Charleston, who was vocal in his opposition to my amendment, was a member of the House Judiciary Committee in 1948 and had apparently made no objection to the constitutionality of the extension at that time. The bill sailed through the House of Representatives without opposition and came to the Senate. Senator Gressette, who had spoken eloquently in arguing the unconstitutionality of my amendment, was a member of the Senate in 1948 and a member of the Judiciary Committee that reported on the extension favorably. It had passed the Senate. Two current South Carolina Supreme Court justices, Joseph Moss and James Brailsford, and two current circuit judges, J. H. McFadden and George Bell Timmerman, had been members of the 1948 Senate: they had then failed to see any constitutional impediment to extension's passage.

When Senator Griffith rose to question me, I pointed out that his distinguished uncle's name appeared on the original bill as one of its draftsmen. One by one I hushed every critic by pointing to some connection they had with the legislature that had passed the bill in 1948. I brought my argument to a conclusion by stating that it was reassuring to me to find that the governor of the state also had signed the bill. In a thinly veiled allusion to Senator Gressette's nickname, I pointed out that it was the wily Br'er Fox who devised the tar baby that gave so much trouble. I brought my speech to a conclusion by holding up the original 1948 bill and calling attention to the fact that the governor's signature was written on that bill so large that it filled an entire line. "There it is," I said, holding it up. "J. Strom Thurmond! How many times has the senator from South Carolina lectured us on strict construction and constitutional law! He found nothing unconstitutional in the extension of voting certificates in 1948. Why should we do so now?"

Gressette, in his own inimitable manner, answered my argument, saying that he had read where the senator from Florence had described himself as a lamb and Senator Gasque from Marion was a lion. The writer of the article added that "the Old Grey Fox [Gressette] was busy taking care of both of them." He finished with several salvos fired at me.

I moved to table the amendment. The vote was close, but the Gressette amendment was tabled by a vote of twenty-two to twenty. I felt some satisfaction in having challenged and defeated the establishment.

John West, who was presiding, was kind enough to write a note to my wife, Anne, who was in the chamber:

Anne:

Lovick [Thomas] & I agreed that Nick's Speech was the best either of us have ever heard in this chamber—

John

I was not deceived, however, for I knew that Big Possums were walking at night, and I knew the effectiveness of their nocturnal maneuvers. On June 20, 1967, Senator Gressette and his coalition were prepared to amend the bill by having my amendment stricken. Dick Riley and I had anticipated this action and prepared a motion that Dick filed that would strike my amendment and replace it with a section greatly increasing the ease with which voting certificates could be renewed and acquired for the first time. These drastic changes liberalizing registration included the authority to mail applications for the granting of renewal certificates without having to fill out an application and allowing the certificates to be notarized before a notary public rather than a registration board member, deputy, or clerk; only requiring a proof of residency rather than proving qualification for renewing a certificate; and making applications for certificates available at places other than at the registration office. Our reasoning was that under the state's constitution voting certificates had to be renewed every ten years, and if the renewal process was made easier, we would accomplish more than just extending the requirement for renewal for a few months. Our compromise greatly expanded the opportunities for disfranchised voters to get certificates.

We got Dick Riley's motion filed before Gressette's motion to strike my amendment, and when Gressette attempted to have his motion heard ahead of ours, I raised the point of order that Riley's motion took precedence. My motion was granted, and Senator Gressette withdrew his motion. Dick Riley's motion to amend passed without argument.

Senate Republicans hailed this as a victory, but when the bill was returned to the House and the Republican members had time to digest the full implications of our amendment, one of them remarked, "Our Republican senators are not as smart as they think they are." Our compromise had added provisions to the election law bill that would have been unthinkable to Republicans at the beginning of the session. The bill became law, but I was determined that in the next session I would back a provision creating an election commission with bipartisan representation.

My last confrontation with a Senate warlord came with the passage of the arts commission bill. I introduced a bill on February 9, 1967, to create a state arts commission. I had no difficulty in getting twenty senators, including Senator Gressette, to cosponsor it. It was logical that I should be the chief proponent of the legislation since I had served in 1966 as chairman of the state's Interagency Committee on the Arts and Humanities before I was elected to the state senate. I made a speech describing the bill and its purpose and pointed out that creative artists and art patrons are the most neglected and misunderstood people in South Carolina. I added that eggheads

South Carolina Senate debate, 1970. Left to right: *Senator Nick Zeigler, Senator (later Governor) Richard W. Riley, Senator Paul M. Moore, and Senator James B. Stephen;* background: *Lovick Thomas, Senate clerk. Collection of the author*

were not doing too well in South Carolina, either. I then told the story about Adlai Stevenson, who, after one of his defeats for the presidency, addressed an audience at Harvard. He said that this was the most intelligent audience that he had faced for a long time and he was reminded of a quotation that probably never occurred to Horace: "Via ovicipitum dura est." He said, for the benefit of the engineers among you, "The way of the egghead is hard."

John West, in wondering out loud to which Senate committee the bill should be sent, remarked that he didn't know which committee had the most eggheads on it or which committee would do the most for the eggheads. He decided to send the bill to the Judiciary Committee of which Senator Gressette was chairman. The bill had no difficulty in passing both the Senate and the House, and it became law on June 6, 1967. The real reason for its unobstructed journey was that it appropriated no money.

I was led to believe that a small appropriation for that purpose would be added to the general appropriations bill. However no item for an arts commission came out of the House Ways and Means Committee's version of the general appropriations bill, and none was added to that bill when it passed the House. In dismay I inquired why this was omitted and was told that it would be added in the Senate Finance Committee's report on the bill. The bill emerged from the Senate Finance Committee without an appropriations for the newly authorized Arts Commission, and the only alternative left to me was to propose an amendment to the general appropriations bill when it came up for debate on the Senate floor. Senator Edgar Brown told me in no uncertain terms that he would oppose its addition. His opposition was generally regarded as the death knell for any addition to the appropriations bill.

I persuaded Senator Hyman Rubin of Columbia to put his name on my proposed amendment to the appropriations bill to grant the commission sixty-five thousand dollars. Senator Brown stated his objection and remarked that the Arts Commission was "just another gadget." Luck was with me; just as Senator Brown finished speaking, a group of school children were ushered into the Senate gallery. I seized the opportunity to make my point by stating that creation of the Arts Commission was just as important as anything else we were considering. Turning to Senator Brown, I said, "Senator Brown, turn around and face those children in the gallery and tell them that you are not willing to appropriate sixty-five thousand dollars to expand their horizons and give them opportunities that more fortunate children have." Senator Brown glanced up at the gallery and said, "All right, put it in." It was one of the few times that I felt my presence was vital to the passage of a major piece of legislation. The Arts Commission survived by the skin of its teeth. The effort that brought me the most pleasure was the successful sponsorship of the legislation creating that commission.

The session was plagued by filibusters, chiefly the long filibuster over the consolidation of Charleston County schools. I was successful in getting a rule change that required the participants in a filibuster to answer roll calls or forfeit the right to speak for more than one hour. I introduced a bill to study the need for a legislative definition for permissible conduct and practice of General Assembly members in appearing before state agencies, but it got nowhere.

The *State* newspaper of Columbia issued its judgment when the session finally adjourned on July 14, 1967:

> Weary South Carolina legislators went home Thursday after the longest—and perhaps the most controversial—General Assembly in the state's history.
>
> When adjournment comes next Friday for local and uncontested matters, the session will have lasted 109 days, 10 days longer than the previous record set in 1939. During those days, state lawmakers have confronted some of the thorniest problems ever facing the legislature.

I was happy to leave the thorny jungle of Columbia for the less threatening briar patch at Florence.

21

Complex Village Vexation

My service on the Senate Election Law Study Committee and on the Reapportionment Committee produced major pieces of legislation of statewide importance, but I had a major problem that had to be dealt with in Florence County. It was a virulent case of complex village vexation.

In 1966 the city and county of Florence reached a turning point in their relationship. The city council was made up of young, energetic entrepreneurs and businessmen who were attempting to transform Florence from a railroad town to a metropolitan center. In their impatience to do so, they encountered the obstacle of the Florence County Council, the members of which were predominantly conservative rural farmers. The county council had no real municipal powers, yet the demands of metropolitan expansion required them to move out from their dependence on the legislative delegation. Good government required that the two governmental bodies find a basis to cooperate with each other.

One aspect of that cooperation would be the sharing of physical facilities. It was generally agreed that a combination of city and county offices in one building or group of buildings would result in great savings. Like most issues involving the expenditure of public funds, the devil was in the details. Although the voters of Florence County had approved a constitutional amendment in the November 1966 election allowing an increase in the limit of the county's bonded indebtedness in order to finance a joint structure, the decision on how much to allow the building commission to spend and what powers the building commission would have would become controversial.

There was a continuing suspicion by the city council that it was bearing an unfair tax burden in financing the construction of the complex as well as discontent with the archaic manner in which the county governing board was organized. This was matched by the suspicion of the rural areas that they were being taken advantage of by the "city folks" in Florence. Senator Graham was essentially the spokesperson for the rural voters in the county.

I assumed the role of the go-between in a confrontation between Benny McCutcheon (the chairman of county council) and Mayor David McLeod.

The festering enmity between the Florence City Council and Florence County Governing Board had come to a head in 1966 with a report commissioned by the City-County Building Commission. Walter C. Jacobs of Space Utilization Analysis, Inc., in Beverly Hills, California, authored the report. It went beyond space analysis and was highly critical of how county government operated in Florence County. Singled out for criticism in the Jacobs report was Clyde Barnes, the county manager. The report charged that Barnes had too much power and his duties should be more clearly defined.

While many of the expert's opinions were true, it was obvious that Jacobs and the City-County Building Commission did not understand the consequences of the controversial report and its disparaging remarks about the Florence County government. The task of mending relationships between the two governmental bodies and beginning reform of county government in Florence County was a difficult task that required more tact and understanding of local politics than the expert in Beverly Hills could be expected to have. The chairman of the commission appeared before county council and asked for a vote of confidence. The council refused to give it, and all of the members of the City-County Building Commission resigned.

In the first two months of the session, which began in January 1967, there were threats by city officials that Senator Graham and Representative Harwell and I would be "dumped" in the next election because we took the position that there must be a realistic limit on how much the building commission could spend on the complex. The county council announced that it felt an advisory referendum should be held to determine the amount that would be authorized. This angered the city council, and Mayor McLeod appeared before the county council and announced that city council had voted to withdraw from the project.

I began working behind the scenes to keep the two governing bodies from destroying the idea of a joint city-county facility. The members of the House of Representatives passed a bill that limited spending for the construction to $4,097,440, and Senator Graham and I reduced the amount to $3,700,000. In a joint press release I quoted Edmund Burke: "Your representative owes you not his industry only, but his judgment; and he betrays instead of serving you if he sacrifices it to your opinion." We pointed out that not one square foot of floor space requested by the city of Florence had been eliminated.

One of the issues behind the position taken by the city of Florence was the unfairness of the makeup of the county council. I agreed that reapportionment of the council should be undertaken, and I promised to get it done as soon as possible. Despite my efforts to bridge the gap between the county and the city, the city of Florence withdrew from the plan after the members of the City-County Building Commission resigned. It would be my duty when the legislature adjourned to revive the idea of a city-county complex.

A great deal of foolish talk had been engaged in by both sides. The members of the building commission had referred to themselves as "untouchable," indicating that they considered themselves not subject to any governmental control. Most commission members were my friends, so I tried to convince them that there was no such thing as an untouchable commission created by governmental action and that they must understand that they were working for both the county and city governments.

I had little success in persuading the leaders of the two governments to deal with each other's concerns. As an alternative a Justice Center that would provide a joint city-county jail and courtrooms was proposed. The cost of the proposed building was $1.8 million. Painful experience had taught me that tact and patience were required to accomplish any major reform. I felt I had secured the confidence of the county officials by defending them in the 1960 election. I could, with patience, begin the process of reform without offending either group.

I told the city leaders that I would work toward the reapportionment of the Florence County Governing Board. My experience with Senate reapportionment had given me enough confidence to believe that I could do this using the voter registration lists since the census figures did not reflect the districts into which the county would be divided for the county council election. It was the position of Mayor McLeod and the Florence City Council that the rural areas of the county had a disproportionately larger representation than the city of Florence. A lawsuit was threatened by city council to force a reapportionment of county council, thus strengthening my hand in persuading them to agree to reapportionment.

In early May 1968 a public hearing was held on a reapportionment plan that I drafted based on voter registration, which had been deemed to be the proper base for reapportionment in some federal court battles. The *Charleston News and Courier* ran a story on May 14, 1968, about the meeting under the headline "Council Apportionment Sparks Debate." It quoted me: "'Reapportionment has gotten to be an ugly word and none of us are here by choice,' Zeigler said. 'Nobody, no matter how sick he is, likes the surgeon when he puts on the rubber gloves, no matter how much he needs the operation.'"

I used the prospect of a lawsuit to force reapportionment as an argument to get the county council to agree to reapportion itself voluntarily and not wait until ordered to do so. This would open the way to establishing "home rule" in Florence County years before a statewide law was passed. Senator Graham and I introduced a bill on May 14, 1968, to reapportion the county council in Florence County, and the House members introduced the same bill. It was passed in the House first and sent to the Senate. Senator Graham and I reported out the House bill and amended it to reflect the method used and variance per council member. There would be nine county council members: four would come from the greater Florence area and the remaining five from the rest of the county. It became law without controversy. One advance was made in the appointment of a new county councilman. I insisted that one appointee be an African American. Although there was some controversy with the remainder of the delegation, I was able to get Jerry Keith, an African American, appointed to one of the county council seats.

Having demonstrated good faith in seeking to reform county government, I went to Weston Houck, who later became a federal judge, and asked him to reconsider becoming a member of the newly appointed City-County Building Commission. He agreed to do so, and the commission was back in business again.

I did not understand, initially, that the commission planned to destroy the old courthouse, built in 1891, for the very term *complex* implied more than one building. The commission, however, decided to raze the old courthouse and have only one building. I was adamantly opposed to their doing this. My mother made an impassioned plea at a public hearing against the courthouse's destruction. I told someone that the result of having only one building called a complex indicated that the complexity would not apply to a group of buildings but to the complex task of getting two governmental agencies to cooperate with each other in the same building.

Trouble was brewing in another sector of local government. On February 10, 1970, I introduced a bill that would eliminate the requirement that only those with a valid tax receipt would be allowed to vote on the millage levied for schools in Florence School District 1, which included the city of Florence and upper portions of the county. This bill was passed by the House of Representatives and signed into law by the governor. Almost as soon as it became law, June O. Yarborough published an ad in the March 8, 1970, edition of the *Florence Morning News*. Although the bill was approved by the House members, Yarborough's attack was an ad hominem attack on me. The opening sentence of his "Notice to Property Owners of Florence County" was "You have been taken for a ride and it is *not* a *free* one." He continued by saying, "Senator Zeigler has introduced and passed Senate Bill No. 572, which allows *all voters, whether they own property or not, to vote at*

Citizen's School Meetings to increase your school millage. . . . Whether you be for the increased millage or not please be there and vote." The attack on me came as a surprise.

The idea of a town meeting for the purpose of electing school board members and setting the tax millage was antiquated and completely unmanageable for a municipality and county like Florence. Restricting the right to vote on the millage that supported the public school system to real property owners harked back to the eighteenth century, when ownership of property was regarded as a prerequisite for voting and holding office. Yarborough argued that at a town meeting the non-property-owning citizens attending could vote for the election of board members but could not vote on the question of tax millage for school purposes. It was completely unmanageable. Approximately four thousand people attended the town meeting for Florence School District 1 held on March 24. The crowd was larger than the auditorium at McClenaghan High School in Florence could accommodate, so the overflow was disbursed to the gymnasium and classrooms throughout the building with the meeting being conducted via closed circuit television. Yarborough's fears of having those who did not own property vote for extravagant taxes were unfounded. By a vote of three thousand to nine hundred, a proposed increase in taxes for school purposes was defeated. The meeting, which lasted until after midnight, elected the first black member, Theodore Lester, to the school board.

The crisis created by the problem of electing board members and setting the millage for school taxes was so great that I proposed that the House members join me in introducing legislation that would call for a referendum on how this important function of government would be conducted. We held an open forum at the county courthouse on March 27 at which we outlined the legislation we intended to introduce in both the Senate and the House. The bill called for a special election to be conducted annually for the election of school board members and the approval or disapproval of millage increases proposed by the school board, and it became law in 1971—in time for the election of school board members that year.

After the dust had settled, I was told by some of my political supporters that I had done great damage to my political reputation by sponsoring this legislation. Nevertheless I regarded it as an essential reform for the progress of the city and county of Florence. The town meeting system was impossibly antiquated. And seen in the most unflattering light, it was just another shabby way to prevent blacks and poor whites from having any voice in school affairs.

The *Florence Morning News* and the *State* began a series of investigative reports on the inefficiency and probable illegality of county government.

The editor of the *Morning News,* James Rogers, had an abiding distrust of
Clyde Barnes. The two newspapers began to urge a grand jury investigation
of the accounting and purchasing practices of the Florence County Council
and the county manager. This placed me in a delicate position because the
county council and Clyde Barnes were my political allies and the *Morning
News* was my client. I told James Rogers that I appreciated his unsolicited
advice and that I would do everything I could to bring about reform, but
that I would have to do it my way. There was a public meeting on April 8,
and as a result of that meeting, the county council authorized the formation
of a committee to investigate the charges.

In late September 1971 I called the county council together in the office
of the county attorney, Philip Arrowsmith Jr., and told them that if any of
them were involved in any illegal or unethical practices, I wanted to be told
immediately, because it was my intention to go before the grand jury of Florence County and ask for a thorough investigation of the charges and for the
indictment of any council member who engaged in illegal or unethical practices. They assured me that none of them were guilty of such practices, and
I prepared a petition to be signed by the county council and the legislative
delegation asking for a grand jury investigation. I went before the judge of
the court of general sessions and asked for an investigation and indictment
of the guilty. The grand jury investigation was not completed until the following year. It found no evidence of wrongdoing and issued no indictments
but added parenthetically, "Don't do it again." The operation of the chain
gang was the most criticized activity, and as a result of the investigation, the
county abandoned the chain-gang operation and declined to institute in its
place a public works program, as other counties had done.

During the fall session of the legislature in 1971, I was reminded that in
politics one has to be constantly aware there are those who wish to see you
defeated either to advance themselves or to settle old scores. On September
14 I was startled to find one of the House members from Florence County
seated next to me in the Senate. After we exchanged greetings, he leaned
close to me and said, "Do you want me to kiss you?" I don't know which was
greater, my shock or my indignation. "Absolutely not!" I said. "Why should
you make such an outrageous suggestion?"

"Well," he said, "I thought it was customary to kiss someone you have
just fucked."

My incredulity and outrage continued. "I have no notion of what you
are talking about."

"We have just passed in the House a bill that would make it legal to use county equipment on private property. We know that you will have to kill it and suffer the consequences."

, "You go back and tell your fellow House members, who I thought were my friends, that I will take care of the situation." He left confident that I had been placed in an untenable position.

To solve my problem, I went down to Governor West's office and explained the situation to him. I said I would let the House bill go through the Senate if he would promise me to veto it. He agreed to do that.

The dilemma in which the House members sought to place me arose from the open controversy in Florence County about the use of county equipment on private property, chiefly for plowing private driveways, hauling dirt and making culverts for driveways, and cleaning private burial grounds.

It had long been believed that Clyde Barnes, the county manager, used his power to provide these services as a means of controlling politics in Florence County. It was clearly an unconstitutional use of public funds and equipment, and it aroused the ire of James Rogers. Periodically the *Florence Morning News* would run an editorial about the misuse of county equipment and money for political purposes with such headlines as "The Trucks Are Rolling Again."

"What's all this about unconstitutionality in Florence County?" Senator Gasque asked me one day in the Senate. I explained what the problem was and that the *Morning News* was correct in pointing out that the use of county equipment and money for work on private property was unconstitutional.

"Well, its not unconstitutional in Marion County," Senator Gasque replied. I did not argue with him.

I found I was liable to attack by those espousing a sullen conservatism that frequently masked racism. I regularly received defamatory telephone calls, letters, and occasional death threats. Two instances of this harassment are memorable.

One evening a telephone call came to my home. A male voice inquired, "Are you Senator Zeigler?"

I answered that I was.

"You're a nigger-loving son of a bitch," the voice said.

"How did you find out?" I responded.

The caller hung up abruptly. I don't recall hearing from him again.

The other instance had a more sinister tone.

I answered the telephone one evening, and the male voice asked if I was Senator Zeigler. I replied that I was. The caller then said, "I'm going to shoot you, your wife, and your children."

"You're going to do what?" I responded.

"I'm going to kill you and your family. I am up in one of the trees in front of your house with a high-powered rifle and will shoot you and your family when you come out."

I exploded with rage and cursed him. I was even rash enough to suggest that we meet and have this out man to man. He did not reply and hung up. I felt sure that if an assassin were going to kill me, he would not call in advance to warn me, but I did scan the treetops in front of my house for some weeks thereafter to reassure myself that no sniper was there.

The Florence City-County Complex was completed and opened in 1972. Architecturally it is probably one of the ugliest buildings that could be imagined. Someone referred to it as "Post Stalinist Modern." Despite its lack of charm, it has performed the useful purpose of economy and has served as a unifying force for the city and county for more than thirty years. On the plaque in the lobby of the complex commemorating its construction, Senator Graham and I are stripped of our titles as senators and, apparently as a mark of disapproval, are merely listed alphabetically with the House members as part of a group designated as the legislative delegation. *Sic transit gloria mundi.*

22

The Double Shuffle

1967–1968

Everyone should have the experience of building a house, but only once in a lifetime. Anne and I realized that the house on Darlington Highway in which we were living was inadequate. With a growing family, we knew that eventually we would have to move. In March 1962 our friend Sallyann Rogers told us she had found the perfect lot for us on Greenway Drive in Florence. It had been rented by Charlie Womack as part of his nursery. We borrowed money to buy the lot but had to wait five years to build the house.

Early in the 1960s we engaged our friend Jack Dowis to draw plans for a house. I had grandiose ideas about a house whose exterior was modeled after colonial buildings of the Carolina lowcountry, but Jack wisely advised us to concentrate on what the interior should look like rather than on the exterior. What we wanted was a sense of openness in which there would be vistas from each room and, as nearly as possible, a sense of bringing the outdoors inside. The ideal would be a contemporary house in which furniture and decoration from any period could be made to fit and be esthetically pleasing.

I was somewhat disappointed in the exterior design. I told Jack his design looked like "beach cottage modern." The interior, however, had what we most desired: openness. It had large windows, and the stair steps projected out from an interior brick wall and were flanked by a railing of iron rods, giving the impression of a gigantic harp.

There was a great deal of heartache as the years went by and we realized that construction would have to be delayed until our financial position grew more secure. When some light at the end of the tunnel of financial gloom appeared after I was elected to the state senate, we asked Jack Dowis to put out bids for the construction of the house. When the bids came back, I was astonished by the fact that the lowest bid was fifteen dollars a square foot. I told Anne that nobody could afford such extravagance and that we should wait until the price of construction came down. Anne was adamant. She said that we were going to build the house and risk financial ruin by paying the inflated price. She was wiser than I, because the price of construction never came down and in fact increased dramatically over the next twenty years.

Construction began in June 1967, and we moved into the house at the end of September. I repeatedly said that this was to be my final resting place. I didn't know whether the undertaker or the sheriff would take me out, but those were the only options for vacating the premises.

There was real trauma at the end of January 1968. Florence suffered one of the worst ice storms I can remember. Trees, especially tall pine trees, covered with ice began crashing down; transformers exploded like bombs; and limbs cracked and fell with the sound of artillery blasts. It was freezing cold, and the power went off. Five tall pine trees fell on our new house, and we had no water, lights, or heat. Fortunately we had two open fireplaces downstairs. The difficulty was that the downstairs was open. There was no way to close off a room. We could not leave the house because fallen trees blocked our driveway and Cherokee Road was impassable. It was almost a week before we were able to leave the premises.

Meanwhile, in Columbia the Joint Committee of the House and Senate to reform election laws had been meeting regularly since the General Assembly had adjourned. I was determined that the state should have an election commission that would have bipartisan representation and employ an executive director who was not an elected official. The bill introduced in the names of the three senators on the Election Law Study Committee (Williams, Griffith, and Zeigler) was forty-four pages long. Its title filled more than one page of the original printed bill. Besides creating an election commission, the bill dealt with the method of filing election protests, required adequate poll managers, prohibited the distribution of campaign literature within a certain distance of the polling place, and provided a method for replacing a candidate who died or withdrew. It was reported out of the Judiciary Committee the following day with only minor amendments and ordered for consideration on the following day. It was given second reading on February 1, 1968.

There followed a delay while I tried to find a way for candidates from multicounty districts to file in an orderly manner without engaging in a footrace to the secretary of state's office in an effort to file first. I called the plan an attempt to banish the last ghost of reapportionment. The press promptly named my proposed amendment the "Zeigler double shuffle." It was hard to understand, and I requested that my proposed amendment be printed and mailed to each senator before the vote on third reading of the bill. Even so, there was controversy.

At one point I had a blackboard brought into the Senate chamber and went though the procedural process that my amendment called for. At last a majority of the Senate understood that it was necessary to pass the amendment or there would be chaos in the next election. The bill was given third reading on Valentine's Day and sent to the House.

A new source of trouble, which the Election Law Study Committee thought had been settled, surfaced. The secretary of state, Frank Thornton, let it be known that he still wanted to be the head of the newly formed election commission. This would have defeated the purpose of creating a commission free from the taint of political influence. When I went to his office and explained the purpose of a bipartisan commission, Governor Robert McNair told me he opposed having Republicans on the election commission. He named some Republicans who were anathema to him and whose presence on such a commission would not be acceptable, and he said that he was contemplating a veto of the bill. I pointed out that too much was at stake for him seriously to consider doing that. He reluctantly agreed that he would not veto the bill if both houses of the legislature passed it.

There was also trouble brewing in the House. There had been a provision in my original bill to change the date of the primary election from June to August. Senator Gressette adamantly opposed this provision, and it was deleted from the bill by an amendment when it reached the Senate floor. For some reason the House was equally determined to change the primary election's date. The House had passed a bill in 1967 that would have changed the date to August, but the bill was bottled up in Senator Gressette's Judiciary Committee. Realizing that it might be able to force a change of the date, the House approved the massive election law bill but amended it to alter the primary election's date to August.

It was returned to the Senate on February 29 with the amendment Senator Gressette opposed. John West asked Senator Dennis and me to promise the House leadership that if they would agree to eliminate the change of date, we would in the next week make an effort to get the House bill changing the date out of the Judiciary Committee. This worked, and the Senate by vote refused to accept the amendment to change the date and sent the bill back to the House.

The whole election process was teetering on the verge of disaster because the filing date for statewide offices was scheduled to begin on Monday, March 4. Only one senator held out, Senator William C. Dobbins from Laurens County, who opposed being forced to run against Senator John Long of Union County. He planned to filibuster the whole election law bill. Immediately upon the Senate's refusal to accept the House changes in the bill, Lieutenant Governor John West and Lovick Thomas handed the bill to a Senate page, who literally sprinted across the lobby to deliver it to the House. Senator Dobbins got up to make his protest but was ruled out of order since the bill was no longer in the Senate. The March 1, 1968, edition of Columbia's *State* newspaper recorded Senator Dobbins's frustration: "Dobbins threw up his hands and said, 'That's the fastest I've ever seen a bill taken out of here. It must have been gone before Zeigler (Sen. E. N. Nick Zeigler, supporter of the bill) even got back to his seat.'"

Only the fast work of John West saved the Senate from failing to pass the measure. But the fight was not over. The House acceded in the Senate's action, and the bill received final passage at 6:00 P.M. on February 29. I was unable to get the House bill changing the date of the primaries out of the Senate Judiciary Committee, and Senator Dennis's motion to recall the bill from the Judiciary Committee failed.

Pete Hyman took an active part in the dangerous action of the House by putting the entire election law bill in peril over the change of the primaries' date. I felt that his active opposition to so vital a piece of legislation with which I was so clearly identified was somehow intended to embarrass me. It further widened the growing gap between us. His close friendship with Governor McNair, who reluctantly signed the bill into law, further caused me to suspect his motives.

The "Zeigler double shuffle," or "double lottery," took place on March 4, 1968. The process was complicated since the candidates were filing for some senatorial districts that embraced three counties. Florence, Marion, and Williamsburg were grouped together and allotted three senators. The three seats were numbered, but Florence County was large enough to claim two of the three seats. The secretary of state first drew the name of the county that would have first choice of a numbered seat. Florence County was drawn, but Senator Graham and I had agreed that in this event we would pass and let the field of candidates become clear before we acted. Marion County was drawn next, and Senator Gasque chose to run for seat number 1. That left Williamsburg County, and Senator LaNue Floyd chose to run for seat number 3. The drawing then came back to Florence County and to Senator Graham and me. The second phase of the lottery, then, was to draw the name of a candidate. My name was drawn, and I chose to run for seat number 2. Senator Graham then had to choose between running against me, Senator Gasque, or LaNue Floyd. He chose to run for seat number 3 and against Floyd. He told me that he was confident his strength in the rural areas would make it likely that he would defeat Senator Floyd. I was lucky. I had no opposition in either the Democrat primary or the general election.

The move to establish a four-year college in the Pee Dee was given a boost by the Moody Report, which recommended it. Both Senator Graham and I had been vocal about the need for a four-year college in the Pee Dee. On April 2, 1968, we introduced a bill to create the Central Pee Dee College District and provide a governing body for it. It also gave authority to levy taxes to finance the board. The bill passed the Senate and House and was ratified on June 7, 1968. It was essentially the beginning of Francis Marion College.

While there were troubles inside the General Assembly, there were even greater troubles brewing outside. On February 8, 1968, state law enforcement agents killed three black students during a protest at South Carolina State College. The incident came to be known as the Orangeburg Massacre, and the next six months saw more violence and riots across the state and the country, including the assassinations of Martin Luther King Jr. and Robert F. Kennedy. The incident at Orangeburg took place during the period in which I was shepherding the election law reform bill through the Senate. There was little that any of us in the legislature could have done to prevent the death of the students, and I was not aware of the approaching crisis. My energy was being spent trying to reform the whole election process and opening elections to disenfranchised minorities.

I was not present in the Senate chamber when Steve Moore, the cofounder of the Black Awareness Coordinating Committee, tried to read a petition from the visitor's gallery and had to be removed. I had left to attend a meeting of the Public Service Commission. I returned and learned that there had been a demonstration of black students and that some had asked that I meet with them but were told I was not in the capitol building. When I went to my car, which was parked on the street during the protest, I found a handwritten note stuck under the windshield wiper that read, "SLED killed us dead." I have kept that bit of paper among my records to remind myself not only of the tragedy that took place but also of my own and the state's failure to prevent it from happening.

The installation of Maceo Nance Jr. as president of South Carolina State College was scheduled to take place on November 27, 1968. It was decided that it was too dangerous for Governor McNair to attend, but Senator John Drummond and I felt that some representation from the legislature was necessary. We went separately, and when I arrived at the college for the ceremony, I identified myself as a state senator and was immediately ushered down to the first row of seats and seated next to Nance's wife. I formed a friendship with Nance that continued until his death. Someone sent me a photo of the audience at that ceremony with the notation "I understand the third party to your right is the wife of Cleveland Sellers." Cleveland Sellers of Denmark, South Carolina, was made the scapegoat for the riot as an "outside agitator." The Senate and House passed a joint resolution commending Senator Thurmond for introducing "legislation that would make it a federal crime to cross a state line for the purpose of inciting or participating in violence."

The murder of Martin Luther King Jr. on April 4, 1968, came at a time when tensions between the races in South Carolina were near the breaking point. The threat of race riots was so great that Columbia declared a curfew from six at night until six in the morning. I recall the eerie feeling I had when the Senate sessions lasted beyond the curfew hour and Columbia seemed a ghost town. The Highway Patrol transported senators back and forth to their lodgings, and on one occasion during the curfew I was transported to Florence in a patrol car.

The Democrats' primary election was held on June 11, 1968. Although Senator Graham carried Florence County, he lost to Floyd in Williamsburg and Marion counties. The final vote was 13,886 votes for Floyd and 11,806 votes for Graham. I was unopposed.

Senator Graham was an unusual man, and in many ways our service together in the Senate healed many of the wounds caused by past political battles. He did me the compliment of listening to my advice on matters affecting the city and county of Florence during our joint service. Graham was an ardent conservationist and was given the nickname "Shad" because of his vigorous defense of that fish in the Pee Dee River.

I was determined to do something to correct the inadequacies that existed in the juvenile reform system of the state. My years of teaching at the Florence Industrial School for Boys had convinced me that I had an obligation to correct a system that did not accomplish reform. On April 17, 1968, I introduced a bill to create by concurrent resolution the Committee to Study the Problems of Juvenile Offenders. It passed the Senate and was concurred in by the House. The committee, created on May 14, 1968, consisted of three senators, three House members, and three members appointed by the governor. The committee named me chairman and Representative Travis Medlock vice chairman.

In June 1968 Terrell Glenn, who had been a U.S. attorney and was a friend of Robert Kennedy's, called and asked if I would consider heading up a committee in South Carolina to support Kennedy's bid for the Democratic Party's nomination. Since I had no opposition in the general election and because I felt chagrin at the way things had gone in the state with regard to race relations, I agreed to do so. I knew that the political fallout of an association with Robert Kennedy would be great, but it was worth the risk for the sake of my own conscience and for the honor of the state. I met with Terrell in the library of the South Carolina Supreme Court, which then occupied the basement of the capitol building. He asked me to compose a letter for Kennedy to sign addressed to the voters of South Carolina. I did so, and the opening line of that letter was, "Liberty is the word which South Carolinians put on their flag when they were defending Fort Moultrie against the British." The letter tied this devotion to liberty to the need for modern-day South Carolinians to fight for liberty for all its citizens. The letter was never sent because Robert Kennedy was assassinated on June 5, 1968.

His sudden death was almost as painful a blow as the death of his brother John. I was attending a hearing before a National Labor Relations Board trial examiner in Waynesville, North Carolina, on June 4 and was scheduled to appear at a banquet in Myrtle Beach for the South Carolina Tobacco Warehouse Association on the evening of June 5. On the long drive from North Carolina to Myrtle Beach I listened sorrowfully to the bulletins about the condition of Bobby Kennedy, and when I arrived at the Ocean Forest Hotel for the banquet, he was dead. I wondered if my friend in Florence was going down Evans Street triumphantly proclaiming, "Two down, one to go!"

At the 1968 Democratic National Convention, I was appalled and disheartened by the outpouring of anger and violence. I admired Hubert Humphrey, but I felt it would be difficult to elect him president. I had a deep distrust of Richard Nixon that bordered on loathing. The "southern strategy" Strom Thurmond was given credit for helping devise appeared to me to be nothing more than thinly disguised racism. If the Republican Party could force all blacks into the Democratic Party, the Republican Party in the South would become the political party for "whites only." It was the antithesis of the idea of racial integration that I understood to be the goal of our national policy. I felt pride in the manner in which integration was being achieved in South Carolina despite the growing opposition of the state Republican Party.

Part and parcel of the southern strategy was the idea of single-member districts. The goal was to have more black faces in public offices. To that end election districts would be gerrymandered to create a few districts with a majority of black voters. I regarded this as the opposite of integration. It forced a minority of white Democrats into districts composed predominately of black voters and decreased the influence of black voters in districts of predominately white Republicans.

I publicly announced that I would support Hubert Humphrey, who in the fall election faced both Richard Nixon and George Wallace. Since I was one of a few public officials in the state who openly supported the Democratic Party, I was called upon to speak at various party gatherings. On one occasion I was asked to speak at a political rally at Furman University. I appeared on the stage with Harry Dent, who was representing Richard Nixon, and a representative from George Wallace's campaign. The audience was excited and vigorous in its demonstrations of approval and disapproval.

When my turn came to speak, I stated that I was there on behalf of Hubert Humphrey. A loud and prolonged booing arose from the audience. When the clamor ceased, I lectured the students. You can boo me as much as you wish, I said, but any man or woman who seeks to be president of the United States deserves your respect and I don't want to hear you boo his name again. It worked, and the shamed audience calmed down. The thing that intrigued me most was the animosity between the Nixon and the Wallace camps. At the reception that followed I was virtually ignored, and large groups were pursuing and haranguing the Nixon and Wallace speakers.

My son Belton, who was only thirteen years old and a public school student, adopted my political ideas and gave voice to them at his school. He came home one day and said, "Dad, it's tough to be a Democrat. I got beat up three times today for speaking out for Humphrey." He was right. It was tough to be a Democrat in those days.

23

Corrections and Indians

1969

The first year of my four-year term as a state senator was full of contradictions, conflicts, and curiosities. John West appointed me to two more important committees: the Tricentennial Commission and the Constitution Study Committee. Work on the Election Law Study Committee continued, and the Committee to Study the Problems of Juvenile Offenders brought heightened importance and additional work early in the year.

The Committee to Study the Problems of Juvenile Offenders had conducted hearings during the fall of the previous year, discovering that the South Carolina Department of Education had made a study of the inadequacies of the educational program at the Florence Industrial School for Boys. The 1967 report was made available to the committee, and many of its proposals were incorporated in the legislation the committee was preparing. The report found that the South Carolina Board of Education did not accredit the schools of the Department of Juvenile Corrections.

On March 27, 1969, I introduced the first piece of legislation approved by the Committee to Study the Problems of Juvenile Offenders. The bill provided for a complete restructuring of the Board of Juvenile Corrections; the addition to the board of the state superintendent of education and the supervising chaplain of the Department of Juvenile Corrections, ex officio; giving certain responsibilities relating to academic and vocational training to the state Department of Education; limiting commitment authority to certain judges; and the creation of a separate Board and Division of Juvenile Placement and Aftercare for children committed to the Board of Corrections. The bill was so sweeping and complicated that I moved, successfully, to have copies printed and mailed to all members of the Senate so that they would have a better knowledge of it when the matter came up for debate. The bill received third reading on May 6, 1969, and was sent to the House.

218 A Journey Outward

To complicate the problem, the integration of the prisons, including the juvenile corrections' "schools," became a burning issue. In 1968 there were four separate institutions—the one in Florence for white boys and three in the Columbia area—one for African American boys, one for African American girls, and one for white girls. It was obvious that this arrangement had to change not only because of the Supreme Court's rulings but also on the grounds of economy and efficiency.

The *Christian Science Monitor* published on March 31, 1969, a report by Howard James on the juvenile corrections system in South Carolina. James wrote, "In a South Carolina reform school I found, among other things, boys being beaten with fists, rubber hoses, ropes, broken hoe handles and broom handles, and other weapons. Beatings were administered both by staff members and by large bully-boys appointed to do the job."

Attention over the deplorable state of affairs in the state's juvenile corrections system focused on the John G. Richards Industrial Training School for Negro Boys in Columbia. Governor McNair reacted defensively. In the *State* newspaper of April 2, 1969, under the headline "Reports of Brutality Exaggerated—McNair," the governor was quoted as saying that he had not changed his original opinion that improvements are being made at the institutions and that further investigations are not necessary. The article also quoted Governor McNair as saying there is a difference between beatings and "brutal beatings."

I received a letter from Judge Wylie H. Caldwell Sr., chairman of the Board of Juvenile Corrections, which asked for an investigation of the institutions by the committee already in place. I read the letter to the Senate on April 1, 1969, and asked that it be referred to the Senate Judiciary Committee for appropriate action. Despite Governor McNair's opposition, the committee presented a joint resolution on April 2, 1969, to "provide for an investigation of specific acts of wrongdoing and malfeasance at institutions maintained by the State Board of Juvenile Corrections and to provide a penalty." It gave the joint committee already created subpoena power. The joint resolution passed both the Senate and House and was ratified on May 14, 1969. The committee, with the assistance of the attorney general's office, conducted full hearings based on that report. I presided over these hearings.

The hearings began on June 2, 1969, and continued through August 6, 1969. The unanimous conclusion was that the problems that existed in the state's Department of Juvenile Corrections were the result of two great failings. First, there was an almost complete failure by the board to direct the Department of Juvenile Corrections to formulate regulations, principles, and policy for the management of the four correctional facilities as well as a lack of effective direction, coordination, and management by the officials. Second, there was a failure by government to provide adequate financial support for the Department of Juvenile Corrections and a general lack of sensitivity on the part of governors, legislators, law enforcement officials, judges, and members of the South Carolina Budget and Control Board to the complex and difficult problem of controlling crime and rehabilitating youthful offenders.

The testimony was shocking. It was hard to believe that the people of South Carolina and their elected officials allowed such a wretched system to exist. The Florence Industrial School elicited the fewest number of horror stories, but the John G. Richards School for Negro Boys and the school for black girls were beyond belief in their callous treatment of children. The youths at these two institutions were frequently put in solitary confinement, sometimes for as long as forty-five days. Some of the girls burned the initials of their lesbian lovers on their arms with cigarettes or cut them into their arms with knives. Homosexuality was prevalent at all institutions, and venereal diseases were not uncommon. The committee held one of the meetings at the John G. Richards School; the buildings looked alarmingly like a set for Dickens's *Oliver Twist*. The school had been named to honor Governor Richards, a distinguished public servant. After the hearing a reporter came up to me and said, "Just think, if you are successful in getting elected governor, you might have a place like this named after you!"

One of the most disturbing bits of testimony about the staff of John G. Richards School came from the superintendent of the school, who stated that the swine supervisors on the farm run by the school got paid more than the "cottage parents" because "the swine supervisors have more responsibility." The final committee report in 1971 listed in some detail many of the worst abuses, all of which were addressed in the 1969 legislation. The bill passed the Senate and went over to the House of Representatives. The best accolade I received when the hearings were finished came from Attorney General Dan McLeod, who told me that it was the only controversial investigation conducted by a legislative committee to which his office had given assistance in which there were no complaints made claiming unfair treatment.

Travis Medlock and I were taken somewhat by surprise by opposition, primarily from the governor's office, to some parts of our reform package. Governor McNair took the position that the legislation unnecessarily created two separate entities: the Custodial Board of Juvenile Corrections and the Board of Placement and Aftercare. He argued that this division was not administratively or economically necessary. The purpose of separating the two functions was to break through the bureaucratic callousness that had allowed young people to be treated with such shameful insensitivity. The bill made the chaplain a nonvoting member of the Board of Juvenile Corrections to ensure that some humane influence would be present during their deliberations. Past experience indicated that children were discharged not because they had been reformed or did not need more custodial care but to make beds available for incoming inmates. The committee felt the board should understand that it was not dealing with apples and oranges. These were human beings. Administrative efficiency and economy should not take precedence over humane treatment.

One important provision of the new legislation was that juvenile corrections schools were made a separate school district under the supervision of the state superintendent of education. This addressed the anomalous situation of having a child sent to a corrections facility for truancy and not being able to attend a state certified school while there.

A great flurry of activity followed the Senate's approval of the bill after it was sent to the House. The governor actively opposed the decentralization Travis and I felt was a vital response to the scandalous conditions in the state's juvenile corrections institutions. It was the position of the governor that the entire Department of Juvenile Corrections should be merged with the adult Department of Corrections and that the chaplain's position as a nonvoting member of the juvenile board be eliminated.

The governor sought to amend the bill in the House by the unusual procedure of having it sent to the Ways and Means Committee. The House rejected the governor's proposals. Our version of the bill passed and became law.

I was absent from the state when the House passed our version because I had gone with Lieutenant Governor John West to a conference in Denver, Colorado. Travis sent me a wire reporting our victory. The *State* ran an article on June 16, 1969, noting my absence. "Senator Eugene N. Zeigler, D-Florence, was not around Wednesday to savor what must certainly be one of his finest political hours," it began.

The trip to Denver proved memorable. West was attending a national meeting of lieutenant governors and asked me, Senator William J. Brockington of Richland County, Senator James M. Waddell Jr. of Beaufort, former senator T. Allen Legare Jr. of Charleston County, and our wives to accompany him and his wife, Lois. The main speaker at the convention was Senator Edmund Muskie of Maine, who seemed to be the Democratic frontrunner for the presidential nomination in 1972.

It was Anne's first trip to the western part of the country. There was much to see and do. We rented a car with Senator and Margaret Legare and drove though Estes Park and attended a performance of *Die Fledermaus* at the Central City Opera House. Despite the pleasant distractions Anne continued to feel sick and was told that this frequently happened to people who were not used to high altitudes. When we returned to Florence, Anne went to her doctor and, to my great surprise, came home from the visit and told me she was pregnant. Our fourth child, Benjamin Turner, was born on February 17, 1970. My colleagues in the Senate insisted on referring to him as "Little Denver."

On May 27, 1969, I had introduced fourteen separate bills that had been prepared by the Election Law Study Committee. One of the bills made it clear that candidates for statewide offices were to file with the newly formed Election Commission rather than with the secretary of state. Here I ran into trouble with the governor's office. Secretary of State Thornton wanted to preside over the newly formed Election Commission, but the purpose of the legislation was to get politics out of the election process as much as possible. Thornton had appeared before the committee in January 1969 and asked it to put in a provision that would make the secretary of state chairman of the proposed election commission. The committee rejected his request. The House did not change the Senate-passed bill, but Thornton sought to have the Senate Finance Committee put such a provision in the permanent section of the annual appropriations bill. He stated that both Governor McNair and Senator Edgar Brown approved making him chairman. I was quoted in the press as saying that this was not the way to change election laws. It was an attempt to get something in through the back door when it couldn't get though the front. The Election Law Study Committee had been created the previous year. It was a bipartisan group, and the legislation the committee proposed had as one of its objectives to make the election process as nonpartisan as possible. The Senate Finance Committee did not insert the secretary of state's proposed change in the general appropriations bill. That ended the matter.

Among the other bills were proposals to make the general election day a state holiday and to give eighteen-year-olds the right to vote. These did not make it through the legislative process. One of the election bills that made it through the legislature limited the number of registered voters at each precinct. Its purpose was to eliminate long lines of voters at the polls. Strangely this reform stimulated a lot of controversy. On one occasion I went over to the House and spoke with the Speaker, Sol Blatt, who asked me if I had not been elected under the election laws that existed in 1968. I replied that I had. He immediately said, "Then why do you want to change the election laws if you were successful in winning?"

Another bill called for the authorized use of "Votermatic machines," or punch-card voting machines. The punch cards would be machine readable, faster to tabulate, and capable of being manually recounted, and we thought punch-card machines were a great idea. All of this was clearly before the danger of hanging chads were revealed in Florida. Eight of the fourteen bills introduced, including the punch-card voting bill, became law in the 1970 session. The additional bills were carried over to the next session.

Lieutenant Governor West put me on the Tricentennial Commission to replace Senator Graham. I consented to the appointment thinking that the work of celebrating the three-hundredth anniversary of the founding of the state had been completed and all that remained would be the social events surrounding the celebration. Nothing could have been further from the truth. The main focus of the celebration would be the site of the 1670 English settlement on the Ashley River above Charleston. But jealousy reared its ugly head: Columbia wanted to have its own tricentennial center, and Greenville followed suit. This meant the need for more funds and controversy within the legislature. The centennial site in Columbia was fixed at the Hampton-Preston House, which in the antebellum period had had a fine garden surrounding it.

Greenville proposed a tricentennial center on Roper Mountain. This building would be a geodesic dome constructed from a framework of interlocking aluminum parts and enclosed by glass. It would be a striking object for tourists traveling on Interstate 85. To accomplish this modern marvel, the services and advice of one of the outstanding modern architects, Buckminster Fuller, were secured.

At one point the need for more funds made it necessary to go to the legislature for an additional appropriation. In the debate Senator Mozingo, who rarely attended sessions of the Senate, came in with a flourish and argued that the whole project should be abandoned. He argued that we were now going to spend about $1 million dollars more than the original appropriation of $10 million. There were approximately 250,000 adult inhabitants in the state, so we could avoid a great deal of trouble if we simply bought every citizen in the state a fifth of good whiskey and let them get drunk while wishing the state "happy birthday." The next day there might be a lot of hangovers, but it would be better than the problems the Tricentennial Commission was encountering. His advice did not prevail.

I was honored to serve with the distinguished group that composed the Tricentennial Commission, and they did me the honor of putting me on the commission's executive committee. One member was a person for whom I had great admiration and respect, Tom Pope of Newberry. Tom was a descendent of John Belton O'Neall, a friend of my great-grandfather,

Benjamin D. Townsend. O'Neall had no sons, so my great-grandfather named one of his sons Belton O'Neall as a compliment to his friend.

The main cause for our disagreement came with the location of a pavilion on the Charleston site, named Charles Towne Landing. There had been an ongoing argument with the Charleston group over the development of Charles Towne Landing. I was surprised when I first became a member of the commission to learn that the Charleston group wanted to build a Disneyland-like reconstruction of what they thought might have been on the site. I objected and asked that the state archaeologist, Robert L. Stephenson, be consulted about the development of this important site. I was again surprised that many commissioners had so little regard for archaeological evidence, but upon my insistence they agreed that an archaeological survey should be undertaken of the site where the town had originally existed. I believe the proper procedure would have been to have an archaeological survey of the entire site before anything else was done. My insistence that nothing be done to the site that could not be justified by the archaeological evidence brought down criticism from the Charleston group, who began calling me a "purist."

The excavation at Old Towne was the first important project the Department of Archaeology had undertaken. It revealed that settlers had built a moat and a palisade of wooden logs for protection, but there was no evidence of the type of structures that the Charleston group wanted to put there. I was able to prevent the commission from doing anything more than reconstructing the moat and a part of the palisade. Almost as an afterthought I suggested that archaeologists excavate the site of a pavilion planned for another part of the land before construction on it began.

If many members of the commission had very little regard for archaeology, they had less for the archaeology of American Indian sites. This became clear when Robert Stephenson and Stanley South of the University of South Carolina discovered evidence of a unique building exactly where the pavilion was to be built. In their opinion they had uncovered an Indian great house roughly two hundred feet by two hundred feet, almost identical in dimensions to the planned tricentennial pavilion.

I felt the pavilion should be moved to another site, even though that might delay the opening celebration of the state's three-hundredth birthday. In one stormy session Tom Pope had a handful of beads the archaeologists had uncovered and said it was not worth moving the pavilion for such trifles as these. I replied that there was more information in that handful of beads than in the pavilion planned for the site. In another exchange Tom said that if we moved the pavilion site because of what the archaeologist had

uncovered, it would be like the tail wagging the dog. I replied that the tricentennial celebration was a "son of a bitch" but denied archaeology was its
tail. Some of the academic members of the commission visited the excavation site and reported that they saw nothing but holes in the ground.

The preservation of the great house became a matter of public debate.
Letters were written to the editors of newspapers, and a lawsuit threatened.
Indian burials were found on the site, and it became clear that the great
house was roughly contemporaneous with the Charles Towne colony. It
may have been abandoned at the time of the settlement, but it was in all
likelihood associated with the Kiawah Indians, who befriended the English
settlers and persuaded them to settle on the Ashley River. Stephenson
described the discovery of a great house with associated Indian burials
as unique. Its reconstruction would attract great public interest. One newspaper account quoted me: "'We are not dealing with purely scientific interest but public interest,' he [Zeigler] said. 'A sense of history is the really
important thing.' There is nothing better to instill this, he said, than the
knowledge that 'you have stood where someone in the past stood—on the
very ground seeing the very objects you see.'"

I failed to persuade the commission to move the pavilion. The site of the
great house was destroyed, although we were able to get emergency funds to
complete the site work and preserve the information and the artifacts discovered there. I warned the commission that if it destroyed the great house,
the roof of the pavilion would fall in. I meant that figuratively, but Mayor J.
Palmer Gaillard Jr. of Charleston, who was a member of the commission,
recalled my impassioned plea to move the pavilion in his book *Boards to
Boardrooms*:

> Senator Eugene N. (Nick) Zeigler from Florence County, a member
> of the Commission, was adamant that we not build over the burial
> site. He made an impassioned plea for us to move the building or, if
> that was not possible, do not build it at all. . . .
> After the vote [to construct the pavilion], the Senator made
> another impassioned speech in which he asked us to reconsider our
> action. He closed the remarks by pounding the table and said, "If the
> building is built over those Indian remains, the roof will surely cave
> in!" He certainly got our attention but we did not listen. The building
> was built over the burial site and sure enough "the roof caved in!"

Discounting the mystical explanation, the roof collapse was due to
economies attempted in construction. It was agreed that the cast-aluminum

members manufactured for the geodesic dome in Greenville would be used for the roof of the pavilion at Charles Towne Landing. The contract to build the pavilion was let in August 1969 with a promised completion date of February 15, 1970. Difficulties, however, immediately arose as the roof was being assembled. The structural members would not stay together, or as I joking put it, "The hip bone wouldn't stay connected to the thigh bone." That was bad news for Charles Town Landing but worse news for the geodesic dome just under way in Greenville. To keep the roof of the pavilion at Charles Towne Landing together, supports had to be placed at regular intervals, and instead of a sweeping view provided by an open-air structure, there was a maze of support columns. The really bad news, however, was that the Greenville geodesic dome had to be abandoned.

Amid the disputes over juvenile corrections, election laws, and archaeology, I began to get deeply involved in the committee to study revision of the state's constitution. The Senate was plagued by filibusters. On April 3, 1968, Senator Jack Lindsay proposed changing the Senate rules so that any senator who absented himself from the Senate chamber after Rule 4 had been invoked and was not present for two roll calls more than two hours apart would forfeit the right to speak on any bill then being debated.

During one filibuster by Senator Long, I had made a point of order to cut off his speaking because his remarks were "superfluous and tedious," citing *Jefferson's Manual.* This aroused Senator Gressette's ire, and there was a confrontation between him and John West, who ruled in my favor.

A serious filibuster was organized to prevent a change in the rules, but we were determined to succeed in changing them. I teamed up with Lindsay to break the filibuster because we had the votes to change the rules, but to accomplish this, we had to keep a majority of our supporters in the Senate chamber at all times. I stood in the anteroom and kept track of all senators' comings and goings. At one point a fellow senator, one of our supporters, was leaving, and I stopped to inquire when we could expect him to be back. He confided he had a woman waiting for him in his hotel room. I callously asked how long his assignation would take, and he replied an hour. I told him we could not spare him for an hour and asked if he could be back in forty-five minutes. He reluctantly said he could. He kept his word and returned, looking somewhat sheepish. We prevailed, and the rules were changed making it a little more difficult to filibuster successfully.

A survival kit for filibusters was left for me in the Judiciary Committee room. It was sent anonymously, but I later learned it was the work of Dave Sennema, director of the South Carolina Arts Commission. I reported to the Senate that it contained both offensive and defensive weapons "for use during the tedious and superfluous debates." The weapons of attack included a bottle of laryngitis pills with instructions to slip them in the speaker's water glass, a half pint of scotch whiskey, five hundred aspirin tablets, and a pamphlet prepared by the Federal Reserve Board to be read during filibusters.

The defensive weapons included a bottle of "sleeping pills" and a bottle of "happy pills" to keep the senators in good spirits. After I informed the Senate of my good fortune, Lieutenant Governor West remarked, "I hope this won't mean you're going to speak a filibuster because you are prepared."

With the help of Senators Dennis and Claymon Grimes, I got through the Senate amendments to a bill passed by the House that made the boards of Francis Marion College and Coastal Carolina College autonomous. I was also successful in getting an additional thirty thousand dollars added to the general appropriations bill for Francis Marion. In fact all of the legislation that dealt with Francis Marion College became my responsibility.

Things were not at all peaceful in my own county. Mayor David McLeod and I were called upon by black leaders to hear a list of grievances by black citizens against city and county government. The petition was read to us in front of the Florence City Hall early in October 1969 at the conclusion of a march by about one hundred black citizens from a black church to the city hall. It was a hot day, and the reading of the grievances, some of which were reasonable and some of little consequence, took over an hour. One of the grievances was a demand that Francis Marion State College (Francis Marion College) be renamed for "the black descendent of a black slave" rather than for Francis Marion, who was a slave owner.

Another demand was that the voting age for blacks be lowered from twenty-one to eighteen. I had previously endeavored to get the voting age reduced for both white and black citizens without success. Among the demands made were (1) that blacks be appointed to the vacancies on the South Carolina Highway Commission and the South Carolina Board of Education, (2) that secret meetings of city and county governing bodies end, (3) that a directory of all municipal jobs with photographs and background material showing who held them be published, (4) that the charges against one hundred black people arrested since August 18 be dismissed and the money collected as fines be turned over to the "SCLC Black Liberation Fund," (5) that an ordinance be passed requiring that half of the mannequins in store windows in Florence be black ones and that all-white beauty contests cease, (6) that transfer of the title to a bus company used for city transportation to black ownership be required, (7) that the city scrap its plans to modernize its garbage collection system to prevent loss of jobs by blacks, (8) that Southern Bell and Carolina Power and Light be required to employ blacks to fill 50 percent of their labor force "at all levels," (9) that the Florence Industrial School for Boys be integrated (this had been done already), (10) that blacks be allowed to own and rent property in white neighborhoods, and (11) that all media, including newspapers, be required to fill 50 percent of their workforce with blacks. Roswell N. Beck, a leader in the black community and a political supporter and friend of mine, read the demands. I was puzzled by some of the demands that involved action in areas where city and county governments had no authority.

The year ended with a change in the venue of my law practice. Several years earlier, during the summer of 1962, Uncle Peter had decided that Aunt Deda and I should separate ourselves from the old firm of McEachin, Townsend, and Zeigler but said we could remain in the same office building as long as we practiced as a separate firm. By then I was already deeply involved in politics, which took time away from the office. Aunt Deda's feelings were badly hurt by the manner in which her brother announced that he no longer needed her, and she was reluctant to remain in the same office building. My uncle had always taken a jaundiced view of my aunt's doing too much free legal work. He once said that she would undertake to change the name of the state of Arkansas for a fee of twenty-five dollars. I persuaded my aunt that there were too many clients who might go elsewhere if we left the building, so we remained, practicing under the firm name of Zeigler and Townsend.

In 1969 I came to realize that the arrangement of sharing the same office building with Uncle Peter and Dan McEachin had to cease. In one instance I was representing a client who was being sued by one of their clients, and the opposing parties met in our joint waiting room. They found it hard to understand the situation. I was fortunate that the Hubert Yarborough office at 246 West Evans Street was available, and I was able to rent it. In December we began preparing the new office space and moved into it on January 1, 1970, setting up practice under the name Zeigler Law Firm. Aunt Deda was eighty-one years old and in very good physical health, but she was slowly slipping mentally. She soon retired from the practice of law. She was as dear to me as my mother, and it broke my heart to see her give up the practice.

24

Vox Populi?

1970

The 1970 legislative session swung from dealing with matters of great pith and moment to handling the usual village vexations. On January 20, 1970, I introduced two bills, one that had been approved by the Committee to Study Juvenile Corrections and one by the Election Law Study Committee. The first prescribed the rules of procedure for legislative committees created by joint resolution that would have authority to subpoena and swear witnesses and to punish them for contempt. This was deemed necessary after a long hearing had taken place before the Committee to Study Juvenile Corrections in which it was discovered that there were no statutory guidelines for conducting that sort of hearing.

The second bill was designed to set out rules of procedure for the proposed article-by-article amending of the state constitution and for voting on all proposed amendments. I took the position that a constitution should not be amended by the legislature, even though the changes were submitted to the people for approval. It was my opinion, based on the history of state constitutions, that the proper method of changing the entire document was through a special convention called for that purpose. The logic behind my view was that a constitution should come from an authority higher than a legislative body. It should be the voice of the people. I did not, however, prevail in convincing the committee of this. I argued this position with Senator Gressette in private conversation, but he was firmly opposed to calling a constitutional convention. He remarked, "You never know what damn fool thing such a convention might do." So much for vox populi vox Dei.

On January 21, 1970, I introduced a bill on behalf of the Election Law Study Committee to provide for a uniform municipal election law, and I reported favorably to the Judiciary Committee on a bill clarifying the election law passed the previous year. The next day I introduced a bill dealing with the maximum number of voters who could be registered at any precinct. It was our intention to eliminate the problem of long lines at voting precincts. On February 3, 1970, a joint resolution was proposed to have the people vote to change the state's constitution to allow counties and municipalities to form regional councils of government.

One measure that received little notice was my success in getting $205,000 in the state's bond bill to improve the Florence Airport so that it could qualify as a jet port. The opportunity arose in a bill that originated in the House Ways and Means Committee to increase the amount of the state's capital improvement bonds. I persuaded Senators Gasque and Floyd to co-sponsor an amendment to the bill that would earmark $210,000 from the amount designated for the state's aeronautic commission "for the further development of the Florence Airport." This attempt failed. Undaunted, I moved to amend the bill by allotting $205,000 for the development of the airport. By that time I had persuaded Senator Dennis that the airport would lose federal funds if the improvement was not made. He joined with me arguing in favor of its adoption, but Senator Brown still opposed it. We were able, in the final effort, to get the amendment adopted. John West later jokingly said that I managed to "steal $200,000" from the state for Florence County.

Rembert Dennis was one of the more agreeable and less threatening Senate warlords. I never had any serious argument with him, and I believe one of the reasons I was able to persuade him to let the Florence Airport appropriation pass was because I attended the Berkeley County Tricentennial Ball in Moncks Corner.

There was an air of old-fashioned gallantry about Senator Dennis. When he spoke, I had a sense of the soft flow of air passing though Spanish moss in a cypress swamp. Once he defended his friend, former senator Legare, in a speech in the Senate and referred to him as one of the finest men "who ever put foot in shoe leather." The turn of phrase impressed me as one only a lowcountry gentleman would use. I only witnessed one time when Dennis lost his temper, and that was in the early morning hours of a filibuster. A few punches were exchanged with a fellow senator, but no one was seriously hurt. Lovick Thomas, the Senate's clerk, attributed the difficulty to "bad liquor."

It may have been presumptions on my part to take an active role in pushing through the various amendments to the constitution that were to be voted on in 1970 since I had only been on the joint committee to study revision for a little over a year. I was placed on a steering committee, however, to get the committee's proposed amendments approved by the Senate. By April, four of the seventeen amended articles had been introduced in the Senate and House. These included articles dealing with the functions of

government, charitable and penal institutions, impeachment of public officials, and declaration of rights. The *State,* whose editor, William D. Workman, was a member of the Constitution Study Committee, took the
General Assembly to task for moving too slowly on constitutional reform.
Both Dick Riley and I rose to defend the work of the committee, although
I had misgivings about the ultraconservative nature of the proposed reform
of the state's constitution.

The real controversy came with the proposed amendment dealing with
suffrage. The bill the committee reported out did not deal with the question
of giving eighteen-year-olds the right to vote. Senator Robert B. Scarborough and I offered an amendment to the article on suffrage that would have
reduced the voting age to eighteen. The argument was made that the inclusion of this provision might lead to its defeat when the article was submitted to a popular vote. Senator Gressette opposed letting eighteen-year-olds
vote because he felt more hippies than serious-minded young people would
be inclined to do so.

Although I was a member of the Constitution Study Committee, I criticized the article on suffrage as being merely a rearrangement of the words
in the 1895 constitution since it avoided dealing with anything controversial, such as giving voting rights to eighteen-year-olds. I asserted that any
high school student could have composed the new article on suffrage. My
friend and co-committee member, Senator Riley, hotly denied this. Senator
Scarborough and I offered an amendment to give suffrage to eighteen-year-
olds, but the measure was defeated by a vote of sixteen to twelve.

The tricentennial celebration opened with a flourish on April 5, 1970,
at Charles Towne Landing. The main speaker for the event was the astro-
naut Pete Conrad, but Congressman Mendel Rivers also spoke. The congressman was full of praise for Vice President Spiro Agnew, who at that time
was becoming conspicuous for his purple prose in condemning any critic of
the Nixon administration. Congressman Rivers said about the vice president, "I don't care who doesn't like Vice President Agnew, he's *my vice president.*" This brought thunderous applause from the audience, but I sat on my
hands. Some months later Spiro Agnew was investigated for income tax eva-
sion and bribery, which eventually led to his resignation.

The Tricentennial Commission went from crisis to crisis. After it was
discovered that the aluminum roof members in the Charleston pavilion
were defective, the question of the geodesic dome in Greenville came to the
fore. I proposed that the Greenville site be abandoned and that the commission use Walnut Grove Plantation in Spartanburg as the upcountry site
for the tricentennial celebration. To that end I made a formal visit to the site

accompanied by Joab Lesesne Jr., president of Wofford and member of the Tricentennial Commission. Walnut Grove is a model of historic preservation, and it was feared that using it as the tricentennial site, and constructing the necessary parking facilities and support buildings, would jeopardize the integrity of the restoration. The idea was abandoned.

I grew concerned about the increasing expense of the Tricentennial Commission, which was constantly coming to the General Assembly for additional funds. When the subject of more money for the tricentennial came up in the 1970 appropriations bill, I voted against it. I had my reasons for doing so printed in the Senate's *Journal.*

There were many disappointments about the tricentennial, but none was greater than the failure to produce a new history of the state. Before I became a member of the commission, three prominent historians were given ten thousand dollars each to write a new history divided conveniently into three parts, each covering one hundred years. Nothing came of the venture, and no history was published. The commission was successful, however, in publishing several short histories of lasting value and importance.

One commission publication that fortunately received little attention was *A Tricentennial Anthology of South Carolina Literature, 1670–1970.* Along with selections by Henry Laurens, Eliza Lucas Pinckney, John C. Calhoun, and Henry Timrod, it includes poems by James Dickey. Dickey was unquestionably one of the outstanding figures in modern American literature, but his poem "The Sheep Child" was shocking. It describes a coupling between a farm boy and a sheep that produces a stillborn fetus, which is then preserved in an Atlanta museum to serve as a deterrent for other boys so inclined. The opening lines are arresting: "Farm boys wild to couple / With anything with soft-wooded trees . . ." I feel sure there are themes and subthemes that transcend the bare outline of the poem's framework, but I shuddered to think of my fellow legislators' reaction if they read this poem printed at the state's expense. I need not have worried, for apparently no legislator got anywhere near page 559, where the poem appeared.

I persuaded the commission to get South Carolina native Carlisle Floyd to compose an overture for the tricentennial observance. He did so, but it was largely ignored, although the symphony orchestra in Florence did play it in one of its concerts. In another musical area we were more successful. The Tricentennial Commission sponsored a production of DuBose Heyward and George Gershwin's *Porgy and Bess.* It was the first performance of the opera in the state, where the action was set, and there was some trepidation among the commission members about the reception it would receive as there would be a racially integrated cast playing before a racially integrated audience. It was performed to enthusiastic audiences and was a resounding success. In the words of Jack Bass's book, Porgy had come home.

The South Carolina Arts Commission prospered under the able direction of David Sennema. So much so that it attracted the attention of the National Endowment for the Arts, whose director had the intriguing name of Nancy Hanks. The commission invited Hanks to come to Columbia and address a joint session of the General Assembly. I was asked to introduce her. A large package containing biographical material was mailed to my Florence office; in the press of other matters I put it aside unexamined.

In the meantime the political situation was heating up. John West was planning to run for governor, and he asked me to be on an advisory committee to give him help and ideas about the coming election. The state's Democratic Party Convention was to meet in Columbia on the same day as the proposed joint session. It was thought prudent to withdraw the invitation and cancel the joint session of the assembly, and I was left thinking it would not be necessary for me to introduce the NEA director after all. Other activities were planned to honor Hanks, and I was included in these festivities. The convention was unusually controversial and drawn out. By three o'clock in the afternoon I left and went to the motel where I was staying with Anne to dress for a black-tie reception at the residence of the president of the University of South Carolina. I was tired but in good spirits because the prospects of electing West governor seemed good and we were celebrating the success of the South Carolina Arts Commission I had struggled to create. I recall that when Anne and I went down the receiving line at the USC president's house I endeavored to make some flattering remark about the success of the South Carolina basketball team, the Gamecocks. I knew absolutely nothing about the Gamecocks except what I had overheard other people say in conversation. To my astonishment President Thomas Jones looked me steadily in the eyes for several moments and then suddenly threw back his head and crowed loudly, like a rooster. I was uncertain whether I was expected to respond with the same crowing sound to add verisimilitude to my comments, but I restrained myself.

After the cocktail party we went to the banquet, which was attended by approximately one hundred guests, including Governor McNair, most of the state's constitutional officers, the members of the Arts Commission, and many faculty members, all in black tie. Anne and I sat at the head table across from Governor McNair and other state officials.

The university's choral group gave a moving short concert before dinner was served. I was in high spirits and thoroughly enjoying myself when the program began. David Sennema presided and said that he was going to introduce the person who would introduce the distinguished guest and speaker. It crossed my mind that this was somewhat unusual, but I settled back to hear who this person was. The "introducer of the introducer" thanked everyone who had come to participate in this wonderful occasion and said what an honor it was for him to introduce the person who was going to introduce the speaker. He then said something that caused my blood to freeze. He said, "It is very unusual to have a state senator who is interested in the arts." I knew he was introducing me, and I was supposed to introduce the speaker. I thought of that unopened envelope on my desk in Florence.

I sometimes have a nightmare in which I am entering a classroom to take an examination in a subject and realize that I have never attended any of the classes or read any of the textbooks. The same feeling of panic now possessed me. The speaker chronicled my various supposed accomplishments as my mind raced ahead trying to imagine how I might extricate myself from the situation. I could not embarrass myself by saying that I had forgotten to read the biographical material sent to me or try to excuse myself by saying that when the joint session was canceled I forgot I was asked, in addition, to introduce Hanks at this function. The applause that followed my introduction only added to my embarrassment.

I made a bold decision. I thanked the South Carolina Arts Commission for its fine work and for bringing a distinguished guest to South Carolina. Then I said, "I have spent most of the day at the state Democratic Party's Convention, and I am worn out by hearing speaker after speaker introduced by saying that he was born at such and such a place, educated at such and such a school, married such and such a person etc., etc." I then said, "I am not going to subject you to that. I don't propose to bore you with these details about our distinguished guest. She is here because of the wonderful things she is doing for art in this country, and we are profoundly grateful to her for what she has done to help us in South Carolina." I then briefly described the work of the National Endowment for the Arts and what it had done to help the South Carolina Arts Commission and concluded by stating I was happy to present her to this audience. It crossed my mind to say that the first Nancy Hanks had given us Abraham Lincoln, but I did not know how well that would go over.

I felt that I managed to salvage a few shreds of my dignity and had escaped the complete disgrace of an egregious social blunder. There was a reception after dinner at the Columbia Museum of Art. A faculty member sought me out and said, "That was the most unusual introduction of a speaker I think I've heard." It was a remark loaded with insinuation, but I smiled and said nothing. What I wanted to say was, "Amen, brother. You don't know how unusual it was for me to give it."

The legislative session was criticized for being unproductive. It had not been as productive as the previous two years, but I was determined to make light of the criticism. I brought my nine-week-old son, Ben, to the Senate chamber on April 23, 1970, took him in my arms to the speaker's lectern, and said I was determined "to squelch reports that this has been an unproductive session. Here was the evidence that it was productive." Ben bawled into the microphone. Then I said, "He obviously doesn't believe in the cloture rule." I soon received a letter from family court judge Wylie Caldwell Sr., who suggested I might be prosecuted for contributing to the delinquency of a minor by exposing my infant son to the baleful influence of the South Carolina Senate.

The fear that there would be too few students registered at Francis Marion College to generate sufficient income was unfounded. By September 1970 the enrollment was over 906. But there were problems. Although the recruitment of teachers had been going forward, there were still some gaps in the faculty that had to be filled. Olin Sansbury, who was teaching at the

Benjamin T. Zeigler, son of the author, introduced to the South Carolina Senate, 1970. Left to right: Senator Eugene N. Zeigler, Benjamin T. Zeigler, Lovick Thomas (Senate clerk), and Lieutenant Governor John West. Collection of the author

college, called me in early August and asked if I would consider teaching Political Science 101. He said that it was the beginning course, and I would probably not have a large number of students.

Olin had touched a sensitive weakness in my psyche. When I was released from active duty in the U.S. Navy, I seriously considered going to graduate school and getting a degree in history. That would have meant devoting my life to teaching. I reluctantly abandoned the yearning to be a historian and became a lawyer instead, yet I had always wondered if I would have been happier as a teacher than as a lawyer. The opportunity to teach at Francis Marion gave me the chance to determine whether I had made the right decision.

I told Olin I would have to teach early in the morning so I could get to my office as soon as possible, and if I taught in the spring of the following year, I would have to get to Columbia in time to attend sessions of the Senate. It was agreed I would teach twice a week. I pointed out to Olin that I had no previous experience as a teacher, but he assured me that the classes would be small since they were scheduled so early in the morning. I agreed to become a teacher at the new college and in due course received my comeuppance for being so presumptuous.

The classroom I was assigned was in an abandoned school building about a quarter of mile from what would become the main campus. The grounds around the school building had grown up in weeds and sandspurs, creating a hazard to anyone trying to get access to the classrooms. When I arrived on my first day as a professor, I was greeted by a class of fifty-five students. "Is this considered a small number of students?" I inquired. I was assured that the number of students should be regarded as a compliment to me, but I had doubts about the veracity of that statement.

One aspect of my new role as a college professor struck me almost immediately. Male students appeared barefooted, in very brief shorts, and with shirts opened down to the navel. I knew the parents of some of these barefooted, scantily clad students and knew they had the means to provide appropriate footwear and clothing for their sons. In addition I did not see how it was possible to walk through the sandspurs barefooted without extreme pain. I regarded their attire as more a case of perversity than poverty.

I resolved to find out what the dress code at Francis Marion was, so I got directions to the dean's office and went to have a conference with him. This was my first meeting with John W. Baker, a delightful man and a fine musician. He had been at Winthrop College as dean of the College of Arts and Sciences. I introduced myself to Jack Baker and after a few pleasantries asked, "What is the dress code at Francis Marion College?"

"Dress code?" he responded as though it was a novel idea.

"Yes," I said, and I described the lack of sartorial standards and my confusion at having to instruct such scantily attired students.

"Well," Jack replied with a tone of tolerant amusement, "just so long as they are decent, don't say anything." It was my first lesson in modern academic tolerance.

The second shock I experienced was the discovery that 90 percent of the students in the class could not write a sentence of English. I gave my first quiz and included a question that required a paragraph-long written answer. I graded papers until three o'clock in the morning, trying to decide whether the responses contained any indication of knowledge about the subject or just the inability to express ideas in the English language. I resolved to never again give questions that required a written response.

The third shock came when I found that only 10 percent of the class had made a passing grade on a quiz, even though I used a sliding scale in which I put the best grade at 100. I said, however, that I would give a second test on which a passing grade would be the maximum that could be attained no matter what grade was made on an absolute scale. The first two weeks of the class I had tried to put political theory into perspective by giving them lectures on Greek and Roman political history, which include a little Aristotle and Plato. I gave the second test on an extra unscheduled class day. Everything went well until the end of the period. One student, a charming woman whom I shall call Miss Sully, kept agonizing over her paper. Miss Sully had an ingratiating smile and manner that melted my heart. She was a teacher's aide and wanted to become a teacher. I was prepared to do anything I could to help her.

She was the last student in the room, and I told her I would have to take the paper because I had to get to my office in town. She kept shaking her head, seemingly in agony, causing me to ask, "Miss Sully, is there anything I can do to help you?"

"No, sir," she replied. "I guess that encyclopedia I've got is just out of date."

"Out of date?" I responded. "I don't understand what you mean."

"Well, I keep looking for that fellow Pluto you talk about, and I can't find him."

By that time she was rising from her desk, and in desperation and dismay I said, "Just give me your paper, Miss Sully."

She was not able to pass the class that semester and took it again the following semester, barely making a passing grade. I suppose she eventually found out who "that fellow Pluto" was.

25

Nature, Art, and Strife
1971

My penultimate year of service in the South Carolina Senate was the longest and least interesting of my six years of service. The session opened on January 12, 1971, and adjourned on July 2, 1971, only to reconvene on September 14, 1971, and adjourn sine die on November 9, 1971. My greatest preoccupation was the passage of resolutions to submit the revised articles of the state's constitution to the people for a vote. The admission of male students at Winthrop College occasioned the liveliest debates, primarily between Senator Gressette and Senator Lew Wallace, and reapportionment plagued the session.

I took an active part in John West's campaign for governor. The race was hotly contested by a former colleague of mine in the House of Representatives, Albert Watson. Watson was an able man, but unfortunately he was lured into the trap of playing the race card to get elected. In this tactic he was fully supported by Senator Strom Thurmond, who actively campaigned on his behalf. The worst incident took place at Lamar, only twelve miles from Florence, when, following a speech by Watson advocating resistance to federally mandated school busing, a group of citizens attacked and damaged local buses carrying students to school. The incident was so violent and prolonged that state highway patrolmen were sent to make arrests and stop the violence. It backfired, and even conservative newspapers such as Columbia's *State* endorsed West's candidacy.

John West's election was a dual turning point for the political history of the state. It marked the end of race as the sine qua non of elections, and Strom Thurmond, ever the master politician and opportunist, began a slow and politically expedient retreat from his previous militant advocacy of white supremacy. It was a difficult and dangerous time, when strong leadership in the highest offices was needed to call out the best instincts of South Carolinians to establish a stable, integrated society. Men like John West and Fritz Hollings were doing that; Thurmond was not.

The first speech I made that session was on January 13, a memorial address honoring Senator Clyde W. Graham, who had died on January 2, 1971. My remarks made reference to my first seeing Graham in the 1930s, when he was a vigorous young man running for the House. I noted that Graham served in the South Carolina General Assembly for thirty years.

The first order of business was to enact five revisions of the state constitution that had been approved in the 1970 general election. These were Article I (declaration of rights), Article XVII (suffrage), Article XII (charitable and penal institutions), Article IX (corporations), and Article V (impeachment). My objection to the legislature's revising the constitution by submitting articles to the electorate for approval was vindicated during the election in 1970. More than 50 percent of those voting simply ignored the constitutional ballot, and the polling booths were littered with printed copies of the amendments discarded by voters. It seemed patently absurd to ask a voter in the heat of an election to vote yes or no on a constitutional amendment that sometimes ran seven or eight pages and about which there were divided opinions about wording and meaning.

On January 20, 1971, I joined Senators Marshall B. Williams and Kenneth Rentiers in introducing seven bills dealing with election laws. Three were passed, and the others were either retained in the House or held up in conference. The fact that an Election Commission with an executive director was now functioning made it easier to fine tune the details of the election laws.

While Anne and I were on a trip to Tobago, West Indies, I received a telephone message that my uncle, Peter McEachin, had died on February 1. It was sad but not unexpected news. The man who had been my mentor in law and politics was gone. When I returned to the Senate, I gave a memorial address about my uncle that was printed in the Senate's *Journal.*

On February 9 Senator Frank C. Owens and Senator Brockington of Richland County asked me to cosponsor a bill that, by joint resolution, would create a committee to study the feasibility of establishing a state museum. The resolution passed the House, and I along with Senators Owens and Gordon Garrett were appointed committee members. We made a report to the General Assembly on May 23, 1972. Owens immediately introduced a bill that led to the creation of the South Carolina Museum Commission and, eventually, to the establishment of the South Carolina State Museum.

Trouble of a different nature was brewing. The question of the appointment of female pages was raised, and in 1970 Senator Brockington appointed Carrington Salley as the first female page. I followed suit by appointing Susan Scott. Lovick Thomas, guardian of the Senate's public image, took alarm that the use of female pages might further encourage senatorial vices. When Victoria Eslinger, an outspoken feminist, applied for appointment, Lovick felt that the Senate rules had to be changed to prevent female pages from going to the motel rooms of senators. Only by consent of the entire Senate would the clerk appoint a female page. Such consent would have not been possible in the case of Eslinger, and her name was withdrawn.

Eslinger filed suit against Thomas and the Senate in the federal court. I was appointed to assist the attorney general in defending the case and to serve without compensation. It was felt that since I had appointed a female page, I would be less vulnerable to feminist criticism for representing the Senate in the lawsuit. After the preliminary hearing before Judge Robert Hemphill, I advised the Senate that its refusal to employ female pages was unconstitutional. The rules of the Senate were changed to make it possible for them to serve. By the end of 1970 eight females were serving as pages in the Senate; none were serving in the House.

At the initial hearing before Judge Hemphill, Eslinger was represented by Jean Hoefer Toal, who later became chief justice of the South Carolina Supreme Court. In direct examination one of the witnesses stated that she felt there was nothing wrong in a female page going to the motel room of a senator and there was no reason to believe that anything of a sexual nature would transpire. Judge Hemphill, who frequently shot from the hip, said that perhaps the female page wanted something of that nature to happen. This brought down a storm of protest, and Hemphill recused himself from trying the case. It was turned over to Judge Robert F. Chapman, who decided the Senate could legally, by rule, require that no female pages be sent on personal errands by senators. The case was appealed to the Fourth Circuit Court of Appeals, which reversed Chapman's ruling.

Amid all of this trouble I saw a way to increase the powers of the Florence County Council and, in effect, complete the granting of home rule to the council. The state constitution of 1895 gave no powers to a county governing board, and the need for extending water and sewer lines into areas outside municipalities was becoming increasingly problematic. Such elementary and necessary functions like trash collection and disposal were beyond the power of a county council to provide or regulate. It had always troubled me that county government was in a straitjacket; it had been one of the causes of the conflict between city and county governments in Florence County.

On March 23, 1971, I introduced an act that created the Florence Regional Council of Government, which authorized the county and city of Florence and any other municipality in Florence County to study and make recommendations on "matters affecting the public health, safety, general welfare, education, recreation, pollution control, planning, development and such other matters as the common interests of the participating governments may require." Most important of all, the act permitted the expenditure of funds by the participating governing bodies to carry out the recommendations.

My bill brought forth loud protest from the original sponsors of the councils of governments act, who contended that the act was meant to apply to larger areas than counties. I pointed out that the language of the act permitted the type of organization that I devised for Florence County.

One morning I found on my desk a quart jar of dead flies with a note that read, "These bothered me when they were alive, and I want them to bother you now that they are dead." I knew who had sent them. The sentiment was clearly identifiable as that of a longtime client, Sonny Buck Cook. A serious health problem was thus brought forcefully to my attention by a colorful political ally.

Cook's story is fascinating. He came along as a young man during the Depression when he said he worked for fifty cents a day, but he amassed a large tract of land in Vox, a community in the lower part of Florence County. I asked a longtime resident of Vox if the name came from the Latin maxim "vox populi vox Dei." No, he said; they had a postmaster who could only make a *V*, an *O*, and an *X*, so they named the community post office Vox.

Sonny Buck's farm was like a caravanserai with numerous tenants and hangers-on either standing or running about. He and his wife, Miss Leola, did us the honor of asking Anne and me to dinner once. Only the four of us were seated at table, but five or six women stood around prepared to bring whatever the guests requested. Hunting was one of the main diversions on Sonny Buck's place, and he kept a kennel of some fifty hounds in addition to a menagerie of other farm animals. During every political campaign Sonny Buck would hold a barbecue to which all candidates were invited and at which they were expected to make short speeches. It was strictly a men's party. I was always impressed not only by the quantity of barbecue that was served but also by its presentation in a hand-hewn, six-foot-long wooden bowl. These raucous events provided the hot spice of local politics.

My first professional relationship with Sonny Buck came when he was prosecuted in federal court under the peonage statute, which had been passed during Reconstruction. It was alleged that Sonny Buck had threatened certain of his tenants with a pistol and forced them to gather tobacco at gunpoint. The trial, one of the first such brought since Reconstruction, attracted media attention. When Sonny Buck and I approached the federal building in Florence, newspaper reporters, television cameramen, and photographers pressed in on us for a statement and to get photographs, effectively blocking our entrance into the federal building. When one aggressive reporter blocked our path, Sonny Buck, who was a large man, said, "If I wasn't all suited up, I would bust you one." A path was made for us through the crowd.

When we went up to the courtroom on the second floor, we began hearing a loud noise on the street outside. Sonny Buck and I went to a window to see what it was all about and saw a band coming down the street playing a stirring march. Now thoroughly intimidated, Sonny Buck believed that the parade had something to do with his trial. He turned to me and said, "Lord, Mr. Nick, what has I done?" The parade was celebrating fire prevention week, not Sonny Buck's trial.

The trial ended in an acquittal, for which Sonny Buck was eternally grateful to me. When one of my political detractors tried to persuade him to vote against me in an election he replied, "I can't vote against Mr. Nick. Me and him has been through them tribulation days together."

A large chicken farm near his land was the source of his latest problem. The swarms of flies were indeed horrendous. I got the message and pushed through the General Assembly a bill to empower the Florence County Health Department to make rules and regulations governing the sanitary operation of poultry houses. Sonny Buck was a constituent who demanded—and received—immediate attention.

The admission of male students to Winthrop College caused the greatest controversy and debate during the session. Senator Lewis "Lew" Wallace of York County was determined to get a bill passed that would open Winthrop to male students. Senator Marion Gressette was equally determined to prevent the enactment of any legislation that would admit male students to that college. The debates excited great public interest. I supported Wallace's endeavor to open Winthrop to men because I felt it was inevitable that all state supported institutions would have to be made available to both male and female students.

Senator LaNue Floyd was a different type of senator. He was, in the parlance of modern young people, "laid back." LaNue was a lawyer living in Kingstree, the county seat of Williamsburg County. Hunting and fishing took up most of his leisure time. His desk in the Senate was next to mine, and he would seldom attend the first months of a session and only appeared when the season for hunting birds had closed. After Senator Graham's defeat, LaNue took over the duty of protecting wildlife in the Pee Dee, particularly the shad fish in its rivers. He frequently introduced legislation to

limit the length of legislative sessions because he found it difficult to understand why it took so long to get things done. When I was first elected to the
House I was told by a wise older member not to put my name on any bill
that had scales, feathers, or fur in it, so I was happy to defer to LaNue on legislation dealing with those issues.

The Constitution Study Committee produced four or five more revised
articles for submission to the electorate in 1972. The only one that occasioned an argument between me and Senators Gressette and Riley related to
the term of office for the governor. The committee had debated the proposal
to allow a governor to succeed himself for one term following the precedent
established in the U.S. Constitution. An amendment to the bill was reported out of committee and was offered by Senators Scarborough and
James B. Stephens:

> Section 3. The governor shall be elected by the qualified voters of the
> State at the regular election every other even-numbered year after 1970.
> No person may succeed himself in the office but shall be re-eligible.

The amendment was adopted. Then, with Senator Robert C. Lake, I
moved to amend Section 4, which provided for a term of four years to give
the governor a six-year term of office. The amendment was tabled. I then
had the Senate's *Journal* record my reasons for having moved to make the
governor's term six years.

The Tricentennial Commission was scheduled to conclude on June 1,
1971, and the assets were to be conveyed to the Department of Parks,
Recreation and Tourism. I successfully amended the bill to provide that no
permanent improvement or construction would be erected or placed upon
those properties until the department has requested a written opinion from
the state archaeologist regarding the impact of such construction or
improvement upon the archaeological value of the property.

When I left the Senate, I had no further connection with the Tricentennial Commission. I did go to Charleston at the request of the Charleston
legislative delegation to persuade the Rebecca Motte Chapter of the DAR to
allow the state and federal governments to spend several million restoring
the Old Exchange Building. The building had been turned over to the DAR
in the 1930s by the federal government when it ceased to be used as a post
office. I regard it as one of the most, if not the most, historically important
buildings in the state. I had set my winning high school drama there. For
two hours I caught the devil from these ladies, who seemed adamant in their

opposition to anyone other than DAR members having access to the building. When I left the Old Exchange after the stormy session, I ran into a friend on Broad Street who inquired what I was doing in Charleston. I replied that I had been storming the "breastworks of the DAR" and that it was not an enviable task.

In the summer months between the sessions of the legislature, I received a telephone call from a man named J. C. Truluck, who asked to visit me in my Florence office. I agreed, and we met. He said that he wanted me to sponsor legislation to preserve a unique natural site known as Woods Bay. I was unfamiliar with Woods Bay, but he explained that it is located at the junction of three counties, Florence, Clarendon, and Sumter. He asked if I would go with him and see for myself what a wonderful natural asset the bay was, and I agreed to meet on a Saturday morning. I was told to wear old clothes and tennis shoes as I might get my feet wet.

On the agreed upon Saturday morning, Truluck appeared, looking very much like Mr. Clean in the television ads. We drove to Woods Bay. It is a Carolina bay, a topographical phenomenon that occurs on the coastal plains of North and South Carolina. This one is very large and had, at one time, been used as the source of water to turn a grist mill. The center of the pond or lake that covered the bay was so remote and inaccessible that virgin cypress trees survived there. Wild life was abundant there, especially what Truluck called water turkeys, which I have since identified as anhingas, or snakebirds.

To show me some of the wonders in the lake or pond, Truluck asked if I would mind wading out into the water with him. I consented and followed him until we got waist deep. It was then that I enquired whether there were alligators in Woods Bay. "Oh, yes," he said cheerfully. "I see them frequently out here." If I could have walked on water, I would have done so, such was the speed with which I endeavored to reach the shore again.

I was impressed by the natural beauty of Woods Bay and promised Truluck I would try to have the state acquire it. A portion of the bay is in Sumter County, and R. James Aycock was a longtime House member from Sumter County and chairman of the House Ways and Means Committee. I told him about the bay and the necessity to act quickly to preserve it. He arranged to meet me there, but I did not propose that we wade out into the lake. He was impressed and said he would do what he could to get an appropriation in the 1972 session to acquire it as a state park. Jim followed through, and an appropriation of $200,000 was passed the following year. Woods Bay is now a valuable part of the state park system.

At the end of the exhausting session of 1971, I could not say with Walter Savage Landor, "I strove with none, for none was worth my strife." I had striven with about everybody in the General Assembly, and the causes that I espoused, in my opinion, were worth the strife. To my great satisfaction I had saved Woods Bay, and the South Carolina Arts Commission had been firmly established. I did agree, however, with the poet's next line: "Nature I loved and, next to Nature, Art."

26

Into Deep Political Water
Primary Election for the U.S. Senate

Aunt Deda used to admonish me that "intelligent people are never bored." Despite her sage words, after five years in the South Carolina Senate, I was bored. But the fact of the matter was I was more exhausted and frustrated than bored. The mechanics of driving to and from Columbia each week for three days of legislative sessions and being forced to spend at least one night away from home in a motel had become tedious. The last session, which lasted for almost eight months, had played havoc with my law practice. I made up my mind that I would either become a full-time officeholder or I would give up elective office.

The reasons for engaging in self-promotion are manifold. My friend Bertram Cooper once told me that I suffered from having both a large ego and a low self-image. My response was that I was thankful it was not the other way around. Bertram's analysis, however, came very close to the mark. I felt I had the ability to lead and to accomplish a number of good things for the public, but I doubted my ability to succeed as a politician.

The person whose advice I valued most was John West, for I felt he was one of the few people in public office who took me seriously. He thought Strom Thurmond could be defeated and encouraged me to consider taking him on. John overestimated my ability to conduct a successful campaign for statewide office, but I was flattered by his confidence. I even asked Senator Edgar Brown what advice he might share with me about running against Thurmond. His response was, "I could write a whole book about running against Strom Thurmond." He never wrote the book, and I never got his advice.

Before I could make up my mind to enter the race for the U.S. Senate, I first had to fulfill my obligation as a member of the South Carolina Senate. The session began on January 11 and ended on July 28, 1972. Thirty-three bills or resolutions bore my name, about the same number as in the previous year. Of those, ten were resolutions that carried multiple sponsors, four dealt primarily with local matters, four dealt with election laws, several dealt with constitutional revision, and the rest were generic resolutions of congratulations or condolences. One bill that dealt with Florence County proposed a referendum on creating a county museum commission that would transfer ownership of the museum to Florence County, but the referendum failed to approve the transfer.

A project that had come to my attention earlier involved an 1860 painting of Francis Marion that was now being offered for sale. John R. Craft of the Columbia Museum of Art contacted me and inquired whether the Florence Museum would be interested in acquiring the painting. The asking price was ten thousand dollars, far out of range of the Florence Museum, which was having a difficult time getting enough money to survive. In addition, it was a large painting, about eight feet high and twelve feet long, but it was unframed and in poor condition. I began exploring ways and means for the state to purchase the painting. I went to Governor West, who said he might be able to get various departments that had not spent all their appropriations to remit the balance to the state and thus acquire funds to buy the painting and to pay for its restoration and framing. My recollection is that approximately twenty thousand dollars was put together in this fashion, and the painting became property of the state.

The painting is by an artist with the fascinating name of William DeHartburn Washington (1834–1870). It depicts an event in the life of Francis Marion in which he defends Captain Butler, a notorious Tory during the Revolutionary War, from his own men, who probably intended to lynch him. The incident took place at Burch's Mill in what is now Florence County. Restored and framed, the painting was unveiled on March 22, 1972, in the lobby of the State House. I gave an address on Marion in which I stressed his courage and fairness when he affirmed the rule of law and order over vengeance and vendetta. It gave me some satisfaction that the acquisition of this painting began a process by which the state acquired other paintings depicting the part South Carolina played in the American Revolution.

My sense of obligation to restore the memory of our state before the American Revolution led to another bill I introduced. This one created the Long Bluff Historical and Recreational District in Darlington, Florence, Marlboro, and Chesterfield counties. The purpose of the district was to acquire the land on which the first courthouse in the upper Pee Dee region had been built in 1770 and to begin an interpretive preservation of the site. It has been a disappointment to me that after I left office the legislators from those counties allowed the district to dwindle to nothing. Although the land was purchased and one archaeological survey was made, little else has been done.

The main legislation that occupied my time was the revision of the state constitution. The record was poor in getting action on any of the five bills that dealt with constitutional amendments. The amended Article X, which dealt with finance, taxation, and bonded indebtedness, was never brought to second reading in the Senate. Article XI on public education, which had passed the Senate, was returned from the House with extensive amendments but passed without argument in the Senate. Article XVII, which related to miscellaneous matters, was passed, whereas an amendment to the constitution regarding elections was not acted on. It was a relief not to be facing reelection from the new district, which included Florence, Marion, Horry, and Williamsburg counties.

Turf battles were increasingly bogging down the process of amending the 1895 constitution. I recall that there was an act to remove the office of sheriff from the constitution and make it simply an office over which the county council had control. This was bitterly opposed by the Sheriffs' Association, and the legislature backed down in the face of its opposition. The perennial argument about whether the adjutant general should be an elective constitutional office or merely an appointee of the governor continues to be debated although logic is clearly on the side of the job being appointive.

In March I called a press conference and announced that I would not seek reelection to the South Carolina Senate. This seemed only fair to those who were anxious to replace me in that office. I confess I did not regret leaving office, although I had and continue to have profound respect for those who have served in there. When Charles "Pug" Ravenel in the campaign of 1974 attacked the Senate as a den of thieves, or words to that effect, I felt my hackles rise, although I was painfully aware of the vices and shortcomings of certain members.

One thing I vowed not to do was to become a lobbyist after I left office. I saw so many men whose friendship I valued become ghosts haunting the capitol building, attempting to influence the votes of legislators not on the basis of reason or conviction but because they were getting paid to do so.

I never found a way to make money while serving in the South Carolina General Assembly. It was a luxury hard to sustain while practicing law and raising a family. In eight years I was never offered a bribe. One person remarked that it could be explained one of two ways—either I was a "ding-a-ling" whose vote was unimportant or it was regarded as futile to offer me a bribe. I hope it was the latter, although I must confess I have felt some disappointment that I was not put to the test.

I have frequently compared the situation of a legislator's being offered a bribe to that of a big-game hunter in Africa. It seems to me that the important point of big-game hunting is to confirm one's manhood. If the game being hunted is a rhinoceros and the hunter is being charged and is in imminent peril, he must remain cool and collected, raise his gun, and fire a fatal shot so that the rhino falls dead at his feet. My courage was never tested, and I never experienced the exhilaration of downing a charging lobbyist.

While the speculation continued about my running against Strom Thurmond, I received a telephone call. The operator said that it was a call from the White House. I had become used to pranksters continually calling, pretending to be Nicholas Katzenbach, Bobby Kennedy's assistant, or some other notable, so I assumed that this was another of those prank calls.

To my surprise, it was Harry Dent calling me. I knew Harry and was familiar with his voice. He identified himself and asked if I was seriously considering running against Strom Thurmond. I replied that I was. He then asked if I knew what "grantsmanship" was. I replied that I was unfamiliar with the term, and Harry explained to me that President Nixon and his administration had held back numerous grants to communities in South Carolina so that Thurmond could announce them during his campaign for reelection. Although he did not put it in these terms, he indicated that the announcement of these grants would have the effect of a tidal wave and drown any opponent foolish enough to challenge Thurmond's reelection. I thanked him for his warning, and I said I would take it under consideration. It, in fact, had the opposite effect on me. I was firm in my conviction that this type of political power should be opposed.

On March 27, 1972, I announced that I would be a candidate for the U.S. Senate. The statement I made on that occasion presents my platform in some detail. I used a cartoon that appeared in the *State* as the point of departure for my announcement.

The cartoon seemed to establish clearly the nature of the political situation in which I found myself. It depicts a wintery scene in which snow is falling and gloomy forests and snow-covered mountains fill the background. In the foreground, deeply imprinted in the snow, are two footprints of a gigantic human creature. To the left of the footprints are two little people, one an Indian and the other a cowboy or hunter labeled "Thurmond opponent." Boldly lettered across one footprint is the name "Thurmond." The caption is "Are you sure you want to chase him?" What the artist and the *State* must have had in mind, I said, was that legendary creature that inhabits the snow-covered mountains of central Asia. Supposedly this creature lived in another age—centuries ago—but is now a mere oddity, out of touch with the world in which we live. People have called this elusive creature the abominable snowman, although no one has proved that he really exists.

I said it would be unkind to call the senior Republican senator from South Carolina an abominable snowman, but I thought, with some political accuracy, we could call him the "intolerable no man." His record showed that he had consistently voted no on almost every measure seeking to help people struggling with the problems of our complex society. I listed over thirty measures that Thurmond had voted against (see appendix A).

Cartoon by Walt Lardner in Columbia's State *newspaper predicting the difficulties a Thurmond opponent would face, March 23, 1972. Courtesy of Walt Lardner*

I stated that the cream of the jest is that Thurmond claimed to be in favor of conservative, responsible government and yet had taken every opportunity to state that if the people wanted him to "shake the money tree," he would shake until he shook it down.

I answered yes to the question posed by the *State* newspaper. I wanted to track down and retire South Carolina's "intolerable no man." I wanted to show the people what he really was—a myth, a political opportunist who belonged to the past. No amount of image changing could alter this. The advertising men and pollsters, on whom the senator placed so much reliance, were only mythmakers. They could not fool South Carolinians, who have traditionally taken a commonsense approach in sizing up politicians for what they really are.

I said that if the Indian in the cartoon was supposed to be Tonto, then I cheerfully accepted the role of the Lone Ranger, for in truth that was what I was in this fight. As usual, the establishment would not be on the side of the little people. But whatever the odds, truth and courage would come together as an irresistible force. I called for positive leadership and action for this decade because the people of South Carolina could not wait. The future was now. Together, I said, we would win this victory.

On April 10, 1972, I named Patton Adams my campaign manager. With limited funds we put together a campaign staff and opened a headquarters on Lady Street in Columbia. My wife's niece, Margaret Stanback (now White), a graduate of Radcliffe, kindly came to South Carolina to help manage the campaign. Her intelligent and skillful assistance was invaluable during the entire campaign.

One of the first problems that Patton Adams faced was reshaping my image. He felt that I appeared to be an Ivy League intellectual and that I had to adopt a more folksy southern persona. The first recommendation was that I abandon dark pinstriped suits and buy a more fashionable double-knit suit. I protested, saying, "You are trying to make me into a double nitwit!" Reason prevailed, and I purchased one of the double-knit suits.

The initial problem was to win the primary with sufficient strength to demonstrate to the Republicans that I was a serious threat. To do so, I had to face a perennial gadfly and office seeker, John Bolt Culbertson. He took pride in being a member of the extreme left wing of South Carolina's Democratic Party. My first recollection of his style of politics was in Fritz Hollings's first race for the U.S. Senate. Hollings had a fund-raising dinner at the Wade Hampton Hotel, and Culbertson, after the event, went through the hotel's trash bins and gathered up all of the empty liquor bottles and lined them up in a television ad to demonstrate the reckless drinking habits of Hollings and his supporters. He was a master of the bare-knuckles style of stump speaking and prided himself on the number of prominent politicians he had debunked, if not insulted, during his campaigns.

On April 10, 1972, I stated that two radicals, one in the Democrat primary and the other in the general election, opposed me: "I stand between a radical on the right and a radical on the left. Their candidacy divides people—mine seeks to unify. Their candidacy recalls old bitterness—mine seeks to reconcile our people. Their candidacy speaks the cold language of ideology—mine the language of human sympathy and common sense. I hold the middle ground. This is where most South Carolinians are and will be on election day."

I recall that at one of the first stump speeches held in each congressional district in the state, Culbertson said I did not understand what it meant to go through a campaign against him. He said it reminded him of his friend who was a fisherman; when time came to clean the freshly caught fish, he would say, "Hold still little friend, I am not going to hurt you, I'm just gonna gut you."

Gut me Culbertson earnestly tried to do. Among the various epithets he hurled at me was "panty-waist Sunday-school teacher." Perhaps the unkindest cut of all was his saying that I was nothing more than "another two-bit Strom Thurmond." My strategy was to keep my cool and concentrate on Thurmond's record. I would say that so far as our personal political views went, there was not much difference between me and John Bolt Culbertson, and that the real race was going to be the contest between me and Strom Thurmond. This did not deter Culbertson. He and the Republicans discovered that in 1960 I had stated that segregation was best for both races. In fact I felt both sides needed time to cool down their rhetoric. I admitted making the statement but said that my record proved I believed otherwise. The statement had been made during the heat of my campaign for the South Carolina House, and I had known I did not mean it when I said it. I had been a hypocrite trying to win votes. Culbertson never set forth any coherent platform for change, he just attacked mine. It was almost as if he was determined that no one should defeat Strom Thurmond. My campaign began to wonder if there was any connivance between him and Thurmond, but there was no evidence to prove it. At one point I said that if Culbertson were the nominee of the Democratic Party, I would support him. He never said he would support me if I were the nominee.

I had a friend and client, Robert Harris, who owned a twin-engine Aztec plane with the call number 85-Yankee. He provided me with transportation to and from many speeches since I had not realized how taxing it would be to

Cartoon by Kate S. Palmer depicting John Bolt Culbertson causing problems for Zeigler in the Democratic primary for the U.S. Senate, 1972. Courtesy of Kate S. Palmer

cover the state. At first I made the mistake of believing I did not need a driver when traveling by automobile. One afternoon, however, as I was driving myself from one engagement to another, I dozed for only a second or two and veered into the median of an interstate highway. After that I never drove myself. One of the few pleasant aspects of the campaign was that I got to know several fine young men who had volunteered to drive me around the state.

Nick and Anne Zeigler after winning the U.S. Senate primary, 1972. Collection of the author

A Journey Outward

Money was always a problem. I tried, without any great success, to make contacts that would produce income for the campaign. Ann Springs Close, who had served with me on the Tricentennial Commission, was the largest individual donor, and various labor unions sent in money, but we were always operating on a shoestring budget. People just don't like to back a loser, and no matter how hard I tried, I was perceived as a loser.

To make a virtue out of necessity and, in a sense, to emphasize the Lone Ranger theme, we adopted a red *Z* as the symbol of our campaign. This also partly evoked the image of the Greek novel *Z* by Vassilis Vassilikos and, probably more understandable to the general public, the mark of Zorro. Campaign buttons featured a red *Z* with "Zeigler" in smaller blue letters across the main figure. The campaign also put out "Z-grams," which expanded the issues against Strom Thurmond.

The greatest effort on behalf of Culbertson came from a weekly newspaper, the *Osceola,* which took a radical left-wing position on all issues.

I defeated Culbertson in the primary, but with only approximately 63 percent of the Democratic vote. We had hoped to get 68 percent, but we believed that many Republicans voted for Culbertson in the Democrat primary to weaken me. The real task, however, came in running against Senator Thurmond.

27

Taking on Strom Thurmond

1972

"Most of my friends have done prospered themselves out of the Democratic Party," said former governor Marvin Griffin of Georgia. His statement proved to be true in my campaign against Senator Strom Thurmond. An editorial in the *State* commenting on the announcement of my candidacy said that "the issue is joined fairly and squarely in the tradition of the American party system." Unfortunately this was not true. The campaign lacked many of the features of the "tradition of the American party system." Harry Dent was right when he warned of the danger of trying to survive the tidal wave of grants with which Senator Thurmond, with President Nixon's help, would flood the state. Even less in the tradition of American politics, Senator Thurmond would not debate the issues with me. He conducted a campaign not on the issues but on personalities and treated me as a nonperson because I had the temerity to challenge him on his dismal voting record. The greatest disappointment for me was the cupidity of the electorate, allowing their votes to be, in effect, "bought" with taxpayers' dollars. The quid pro quo for federal grant money would be votes. I had become accustomed to a candidate's "buying" votes with campaign funds, euphemistically called "walking around money," but this was a vastly larger, more brazen variation on an old theme carried out with little camouflage.

My platform spelled out what I considered to be the important issues— tax reform, busing, health care, housing, gun-control legislation, crime, the Vietnam War, amnesty, welfare, Social Security, government spending, the vote for eighteen-year-olds, voting rights, and state colleges—and my positions on them. (The full text of my platform is in appendix B.)

At my first press conference I laid out my position on the issues and then asked for questions from reporters. One of the first questions was about my position on the removal of the Confederate flag from the capitol building. I confess I had not thought of this as a major issue and was somewhat taken aback. After a few moments I said that I agreed with Father Abram Ryan, poet laureate of the Confederacy, when he wrote, "Furl that banner, . . . let it rest."

Fortunately the reporter did not pursue the matter. I had a premonition that the removal of the Confederate flag would become an issue that had little to do with the Confederacy and a lot to do with achieving racial integration and understanding.

Soon after I won the primary election, I challenged Thurmond to a debate over the issues. He refused, and my campaign issued a Z-gram:

WHY WON'T STROM THURMOND FACE THE PEOPLE OF SOUTH CAROLINA?

I stand ready to debate Thurmond. I welcome the opportunity.
You and I know that there are many issues which need to be
debated—tax reform, health care, education, rising grocery prices and
jobs, just to name a few.
The next time you see Thurmond, ask him why he refuses to
debate Nick Zeigler. Ask him why he refuses to defend his record.
ASK HIM WHAT HE IS HIDING FROM.
Tell him to come down off his pedestal and out of the smoke-filled
rooms. Tell him to stop his political double-talk.

TELL HIM TO FACE NICK ZEIGLER AND THE PEOPLE OF SOUTH CAROLINA

Not only did Thurmond refuse to engage in a debate, but he made every effort to prevent any personal contact with me during the campaign. There were numerous occasions in which Senator Thurmond and I would be close to each other and, invariably, his aides would get between us to prevent us from being photographed together. In all of the campaign there was only one instance, at Indian Field Campground, in which a photograph showed both of us at some distance apart. I thought perhaps our age difference would not help Thurmond's campaign, but after the Hampton Watermelon Festival I surmised that Thurmond was camera shy because of the hair-transplant procedure he underwent during the campaign.

The Watermelon Festival was in July, and the heat was overpowering. The candidates were driven in open cars, in the midday heat, down the parade route and, by tradition, were bareheaded to aid recognition. To camouflage the hair transplant in progress, someone had drawn lines on Senator Thurmond's head with an eyebrow pencil or magic marker. The sun bore down mercilessly, and his perspiration dissolved the simulated hair, which began to run in streaks down Thurmond's face. When the issue came up at campaign headquarters, I ordered that no comment be made about his hair transplant and expressly prohibited any speculation about the source of the hair being transplanted to his head.

Senator Hollings supported me and was invited to introduce me at a fund-raising event in York County. Several hundred people were in attendance. To everyone's surprise a Ku Klux Klan grand dragon, resplendent in purple regalia, attended with two lieutenants in white robes. They were not masked since there is a state law that prevents wearing masks in public.

The presence of the Klan members caused considerable apprehension about what they might attempt to do. The dinner went off well, and Senator Hollings got up to introduce me. He talked for about fifteen minutes without mentioning either me or my campaign and sat down. The master of ceremonies reminded him that he was supposed to introduce me. He got up and did so without any apparent embarrassment. I could not resist the opportunity to say that it was my ambition, *with the cooperation of Senator Hollings*, to make him the senior senator from South Carolina. When I began to speak the grand dragon rose and shouted a question he wanted me to answer. I replied that this was not a forum in which questions and answers were permitted, but if he would remain after the meal, I would

Senator Strom Thurmond and candidate Nick Zeigler in the only photograph of them together, taken accidently, 1972. Collection of the author

meet with him to answer any questions he might wish to ask. To my relief he sat down, and I continued my speech.

After dinner I went to the table where the grand dragon was seated with his lieutenants. He said he was a minister of the gospel and believed the KKK was doing the Lord's work. The two lieutenants seated on either side of him kept their beady eyes on me with an unblinking gaze. They had such hard, mean, and unsmiling faces that I was certain they might literally gut me if I incurred the displeasure of the grand dragon. I was glad newspaper and television reporters were present to deter this unhappy possibility.

The conversation got into the area of miscegenation, and the grand dragon waxed eloquent on the God-given rule that red birds did not mate with blue birds and white folks should not mate with black folks or socialize with them. Several biblical texts were cited, and I ventured to say that I found it difficult to believe that anyone who was a Christian minister could take such a harsh view of the relationship between white and black people. I think I quoted the 133rd Psalm: "Behold, how good and how pleasant it is for brethren to dwell together in unity!" His idea of unity and mine were not the same, however. I wonder what his reaction would have been if he had known that Thurmond had fathered a child with a sixteen-year-old black girl.

Nick Zeigler confronted by a Ku Klux Klan grand dragon and his lieutenants during the general election, 1972. Collection of the author

I did not want and did not expect the endorsement of the KKK, whose activities and views I regarded as repugnant to civilized people and downright unpatriotic. In October the grand dragon of a splinter group of the KKK, Robert Scoggin of Spartanburg, reportedly announced at a Rock Hill rally that his organization had endorsed Strom Thurmond. I immediately called on Senator Thurmond and his campaign to disavow their support. As reported in the October 24, 1972, *State,* Thurmond's response was equivocal. He stated, "I have not contacted any Ku Klux Klan leaders. I have been contacted by no Ku Klux Klan leaders and I do not expect to be contacted by any Ku Klux Klan leaders. Any individual who wants to support me is a different thing." He did not say whether his campaign had been contacted by the Klan or whether the endorsement of an individual wearing the purple or white Klan robes would be welcomed. Thurmond stated that the endorsement of his candidacy for the U.S. Senate by the Klan was "concocted [by my campaign] to scare off" the Negro vote he was attracting. This was a blatant falsehood.

There was considerable discussion about Thurmond's apparent change of heart in his relationship with black Americans. Was it a matter of conviction or of political expediency? One fact is undisputed. Thurmond never apologized for his years of racist rhetoric and opposition to civil rights legislation. Thurmond also remained a senior member of the board of trustees of Bob Jones University, which was racially segregated but still sought to receive federal funds. In an article published in the *State* on October 31, 1972, Don Fowler, chairman of the South Carolina Democratic Party, pointed out the inconsistency of Thurmond's position:

> According to Fowler, Thurmond, through his membership on the Senate Armed Services Committee and the Senate Veterans Affairs Committee has tried to get the Veterans Administration to adopt a policy which would approve the segregation policies of Bob Jones. Fowler said the VA has refused this.
>
> The college has brought suit against the VA for refusing aid to veterans on its campus because of the policy against admitting Negroes.
>
> The suit says the policy is based on its "belief that God meant for the races to be separate, and the VA action restricts the college's religious freedom."

This reasoning sounds a great deal like the grand dragon's "blue bird and red bird" argument.

There seemed to be no danger of scaring off the "Negro vote" so long as the grant money held out. As early as March 1972 an op-ed piece by Victor Riesel appeared in the *State* newspaper, stating that the White House believed that Strom Thurmond had more black approval than disapproval:

> "He has been delivering," said the White House chap, "announcing and awarding grants of aid, child care, his black aide, Thomas Moss, has made a very strong push to get black projects approved. For example, a couple of months ago Thurmond took an assistant secretary of HUD with him for a survey of a black area of Columbia, S.C.
> "The next day, he announced a $2 million grant to clean up the area. And he got a telegram from a very prominent black leader, Matthew Perry, saying in effect—some people talk, you deliver. 'Congratulations.'"

I pointed out that Senator Thurmond "talked" against the bill that made the money available for the clean-up in Columbia.

One of the most revealing contacts I made during the campaign was with Victoria DeLee and the mayor of Lincolnville. Lincolnville is an almost completely black municipality near Charleston. I asked to meet with DeLee and the mayor after it was reported that she had gone to Washington, D.C., and been taken to dinner by Senator Thurmond. I had read about DeLee in the *New Yorker* magazine and was aware that she undoubtedly suffered much and accomplished much during the 1950s and 1960s as a civil rights leader. Her work attracted national attention to the extent that she was given an honorary degree by Amherst College.

We met on the front porch of DeLee's house. From the beginning of our interview I sensed a lack of frankness. When I had finished making my speech about the dismal record of Senator Thurmond on every issue that would help black people, including day-care centers such as DeLee's, which Thurmond had called "dangerous," I said that I had read about DeLee's visit with him in Washington. She then opened up and said, "Yes, I'm gonna eat them steaks with Senator Thurmond." The mayor maintained an ominous silence. I said, "Well, I hope that the other black voters do not feel that way." DeLee replied, "Mr. Zeigler, don't worry about the black voters. You just worry about them big white Democrats." It was later reported that the mayor had received a grant for Lincolnville and endorsed Thurmond. DeLee also received a federal grant for her day-care center.

One interesting and more encouraging encounter with a prominent African American came when I received an invitation to visit and have dinner at

Bruton, the antebellum plantation near Beaufort then owned by Joe Frazier, the world heavyweight boxing champion. I assume that the contact was initiated because I had previously represented Frazier's sister in a labor dispute. Frazier was quoted as saying, "After rapping with my sister, who believes in you, I wish you all the luck in the world."

I was accompanied by one campaign worker. We were admitted to the plantation grounds, and Joe Frazier greeted me. A newspaper reporter from the *State* covered the meeting, and the lead sentence of the article published on October 26, 1972, was "The politician and the pugilist broke bread together Tuesday night in the moss-hung splendor of South Carolina's Lowcountry."

Frazier's staff made it clear that he wanted no announcement and that he had not endorsed my candidacy because there would be ramifications if he became involved in politics. But he left no doubt that he regarded my candidacy with favor; hence the invitation to have dinner with him. We had a formal dinner in the plantation's dining room that would have been in keeping with the wealth and manners of its original builders. George C. Rogers, a University of South Carolina history professor, stated that my visit with Frazier was symbolic of the fact that the Civil War and Reconstruction were over.

From the outset we had an African American assistant campaign manager, Jerry Keith. Jerry and I spent a great deal of time together. A graduate of Voorhees College, he subsequently became a lawyer. On one occasion when he drove me to a speaking engagement in a rural area, he parked the car very close to a ditch that ran along the setback so that when I opened the door of the car I fell into the ditch. Jerry Keith came rushing to my aid and said, "I don't know what folks are going to say about a lame duck and a dark horse out politicking together." I also had the help of James Clyburn, who worked in John West's office.

Inevitably the grisly issue of the death penalty entered the questions asked of Thurmond and me. Thurmond endorsed the necessity of the death penalty as a deterrent to crime, whereas I had some difficulty endorsing it without qualification. From my experience in defending those accused of murder, it seemed to me the death penalty should continue to be an option only in certain cases: sexual assault, kidnapping, the homicide of a police officer or prison guard while acting in his or her official duties, and mass murder. It is my belief that the death penalty does not really serve as a deterrent, but the victim of a crime should be armed with the argument that if his or her life were spared, the possibility of the death penalty would be removed. Thurmond's position met with greater public approval than mine.

As the campaign entered the final month, the Nixon administration and the senator's campaign got bolder in using federal money and federal employees to advance his reelection campaign. In a studied attempt to embarrass and insult me, I was not given an invitation to a dedication of the Lake City Housing Authority, a project that used federal funds, although all other members of the legislative delegation were invited. Lake City is in Florence County, where I have lived nearly all my life and which I still represented in the South Carolina Senate. To add insult to injury, Thurmond was invited to be the speaker for the occasion. Patton Adams took offense at the political implications of the insulting slight to me. There was a halfhearted reply to his objection in a letter to the editor of the *State* written by the executive director of the Lake City Housing Authority to which Adams replied, detailing the facts supporting his charge that federal money was being used to elect Thurmond.

In the final week before the general election, James V. Smith, national administrator of the Farmers Home Administration, toured with Thurmond, ostensibly for the purpose of inspecting a proposed $4.2 million domestic water project in the Babon Creek Rural District in Laurens County, a $355,700 water project for the Cassatt Water Company, Inc., and a $1 million water project for the Valley Public Service Authority in Aiken County. It was supposed to be a nonpolitical tour, but at the meetings in Camden and Aiken, Smith said that Thurmond was a "man who can call the president, and not only that, the president calls him." It was almost on a par with the statement of President Johnson about Bobby Baker.

As reported by the *State* newspaper on October 31, 1972, Thurmond acknowledged the truth of these political events in an astounding spirit of braggadocio and frankness:

> Thurmond told the group attending the Camden appreciation luncheon that his opponent, state Sen. Eugene N. Zeigler, D-Florence, had said Thurmond voted against programs in Washington, "then comes down here and distributes it."
>
> "That is exactly right," the Senator said.
>
> He said he often voted against programs he thought might not be in the country's interest or were inflationary.
>
> "But if the money is there and it's going to California or somewhere, I'm going to see that South Carolina gets its share."

I had underestimated the unquenchable thirst of mayors and municipal officeholders for federal funds. By the time the campaign reached its last days, over one hundred and fifty mayors of both races had endorsed Senator Thurmond. At almost every speaking engagement, Thurmond announced another grant. So many grants to municipalities were for sewage disposal that I quipped, "You might think Strom Thurmond is running for the head of the Sanitation Department."

It also astounded me that Thurmond claimed that through his influence South Carolina was getting more than its share of federal grants. In the first place I believe it is irresponsible for a U.S. senator to brag about depriving any state of its share of federal funds. In the second place the figures proved the contrary. South Carolina ranked thirtieth in the amount of taxes it paid into the federal government and thirty-first in the amount of money it received from the federal government. The timing of the announcement of the awards was the critical factor since the grant money was deliberately held back by the Nixon administration to make it appear that Senator Thurmond was getting more than the state was entitled to during his campaign for reelection. Harry Dent was correct in warning me of a tidal wave of funds that would flood the state.

In a speech in Spartanburg I pointed out this discrepancy and the misleading impression that Senator Thurmond was getting more for the state than it was entitled to get. I said, "Senator Thurmond wants to be Scrooge in Washington and Santa Claus in South Carolina, but we are not going to let him get away with it."

After the speech a reporter asked if he had heard me correctly. He said his notes showed that I had said, "Senator Thurmond wants to be *screwed* in Washington." I promptly interrupted. "I did not say that. I said he wants to be 'Scrooge' in Washington. The word is 'Scrooge,' as in Dickens's *A Christmas Carol.*" I hope he got it right.

In October the editor of the *Edgefield Advertiser*, W. W. Mims, published a story in his paper and paid for two television commercials that claimed Strom Thurmond had "colored offspring." The newspaper's headline of October 11 read:

THURMOND UNQUALIFIED

SEN. THURMOND IS UNPRINCIPLED

WITH COLORED OFFSPRING

WHILE PARADING

AS A DEVOUT

SEGREGATIONIST

The charge was true, but in reviewing it I am reminded of lines from Oscar Wilde's *The Importance of Being Earnest,* in which one character, after an attempt to explain his role in an embarrassing situation, says, "That . . . is the whole truth, pure and simple." His friend responds, "The truth is rarely pure and never simple." The truth that Thurmond had an illegitimate child by a sixteen-year-old black girl was not pure, and its eventual revelation was not simple.

No one connected with my campaign had anything to do with the startling headline and story. When I campaigned in Orangeburg, I talked with a classmate of Essie Mae Washington's at South Carolina State College. She said that all of Essie Mae's classmates believed she was Strom Thurmond's daughter. I made the decision, however, that my campaign would be conducted on issues, not personalities. In the first place our information was that both Strom Thurmond and Essie Mae Washington denied that Thurmond was Essie Mae's father, and there was no way to prove otherwise, even if we were tempted to do so. Nor I did not wish to engage in this type of campaign. I stated publicly that the charges were "scurrilous," and I completely disassociated myself from any such attack on any candidate. The public statement reported in a November 4, 1972, *State* story was clear and unequivocal:

> [Zeigler] said, "I can assure you that no one connected with my staff has had anything to do with distribution of any [Mims] material to my knowledge—and if anyone has any knowledge, Sen. Thurmond or anyone else, I wish them to make that information available to me and I'll take such action as necessary."
>
> Zeigler also called on Thurmond to make public any information he has connecting Zeigler's aides with Mims and said his opponent should apologize if he can't produce such proof.

When asked if he thought I had anything to do with Mims and the article in the *Edgefield Advertiser*, Thurmond had given equivocal answers as reported by the *State* on November 3, 1972:

> Thurmond blasted Zeigler Thursday for running a "scurrilous" campaign that involves "malicious falsehood."
>
> "I am utterly amazed at the depths to which he and his cohorts have taken this campaign," he said.
>
> Asked for an example, Thurmond said, "You know what I mean."
>
> Asked if he thought Zeigler was linked to charges by the editor of the small weekly *Edgefield Advertiser*, Thurmond told reporters to "draw your own conclusions." . . .

Asked again if he thought Zeigler was linked to Mims, Thurmond said, "Ask Mr. Fowler. He can probably give you that whole story," referring to Don Fowler, chairman of the State Democratic party.

Thurmond gave no information connecting anyone with my campaign to Mims, who announced that he was a write-in candidate for the U.S. Senate in the general election, and Thurmond never apologized for accusing me and my campaign of being connected with Mims. I can only speculate that it must have been a heavy burden for Thurmond to conceal, with such bravado, his guilty secret that Mims's charges were true.

One incident caused me to believe that the Thurmond campaign was seeking to make political capital out of the Mims's accusation. A newspaper reporter who was an active Republican with ties to the Thurmond campaign said that he had found a copy of the *Edgefield Advertiser* with the offensive headline in the waiting room of our Columbia headquarters. It is my belief that it was planted there by Thurmond supporters in their strategy to make it appear that my campaign was connected with Mims. The Republican Party nationally was engaging in "dirty tricks" on an unprecedented scale. Because the master of that political technique, Lee Atwater, was a former employee of Strom Thurmond, I am inclined to believe that the newspaper was deliberately planted by supporters of Thurmond.

The Thurmond campaign attacked me for having the support of labor unions in South Carolina, principally the ILGWU and the International Brotherhood of Electrical Workers (IBEW). On one occasion ILGWU members distributed a single sheet of paper that contained ten questions to ask Senator Thurmond. There was nothing on the sheet but the ten questions about his voting record. A spokesman for Re-Elect Thurmond was quoted in the October 4, 1972, *State* as saying, "It appears that labor unions and their bosses are mounting an all out effort for State Senator Eugene N. Zeigler" and that the "people realized that these tactics are underhanded and cheap." My response was that there was nothing cheap or underhanded in seeking answers to the questions that were relevant to the election issues in the campaign, especially since Thurmond had refused to debate these issues. It might have been said that the discredited Teamsters Union was supporting President Nixon, who had paroled former Teamster president Jimmy Hoffa from prison.

Increasingly I began to feel like a social pariah. One day a member of the Florence Country Club spotted a car parked there with a Zeigler sticker displayed on its bumper. He inquired suspiciously of members of the club about whose car it might be. The response he got was that the car probably belonged to the help employed by the club.

Our campaign was vastly outspent. The Thurmond campaign spent $666,372, without having a primary election to finance, while my total expenditure for both the primary and general elections was only $167,750. People and organizations in other states contributed large amounts of money to Thurmond. One of the most unusual contributors was Gene Autry, the singing cowboy, who lived in California. Thurmond refused to list the contributions his campaign had received before April 7, when the campaign disclosure law went into effect.

A generous fund-raising dinner and art auction for me was sponsored by an outstanding group of state artists. If I had to point out any one political action in which I take unqualified satisfaction and pride, it would be the role I played in the formation of the South Carolina Arts Commission. The commission established the Elizabeth O'Neill Verner Award honoring individuals, organizations, businesses, artists, and public officials who have made significant contributions to the arts in the state. In 1972 they presented the award to me as an individual who had made such a contribution to the arts. The symbol of the honor is a statue designed by South Carolina artist Jean McWhorter.

The Vietnam War was also a troublesome issue. Senator Thurmond spent much of his time castigating actress Jane Fonda. I am not a great moviegoer, and I had no particular regard for Fonda, but she seemed entirely irrelevant to the issues facing us in South Carolina. It was obvious to everyone that President Nixon was going to end the war in Vietnam, and we had failed in what we were trying to accomplish there. Thurmond was reported by the press as wearing an American flag pin in his lapel, a necktie resembling the flag, and American flag cufflinks. I don't wear my patriotism on my sleeve or on my coat's lapel or display it in my neckwear.

During World War II, I served three and a half years on board four aircraft carriers, a good part of the time under combat conditions, and I remained active in the Naval Reserve for over twenty years until I had to retire. Being in the active Naval Reserve, I was required to sign an agreement that if I were called to active duty, I would not seek deferment. I never changed my designation from deck officer to legal officer. I attended the Naval War College and took correspondence courses to maintain my active status in the reserves. If Strom Thurmond was seeking to question my patriotism by attacking Senator McGovern and Jane Fonda as surrogates, he was barking up the wrong tree.

I was surprised when I discussed the Vietnam War with college students that they seemed to be untroubled by the fact that during the Nixon presidency we had dropped more bombs on Vietnam than had been dropped on Germany in World War II.

There was some concern that Robert G. Liming, who the *State* assigned to accompany me during that last week of the campaign, had connections with the Republican Party and Senator Thurmond. Liming had been Albert Watson's press secretary in his campaign for the governorship, and his father had been active in the Republican Party in Abbeville County. After a conference with the editors of the *State*, I agreed that we had been wrong in judging that he would not cover our campaign fairly. His report in the November 5, 1972, issue of the *State*, during the last week of the campaign, gave a favorable impression of my campaign:

> An avid campaigner, Zeigler takes great personal delight in shaking hands with workers at industrial plants and textile mills. He enjoys passing out his Z-grams, legal size sheets dealing with his proposals on a wide range of issues from the need for tax reform, health care, and gun control to adequate housing for all income and age groups.
>
> He openly discusses the issues and his views with friend and foe on college campuses, mill lines, drugstores and city streets in hopes of swinging more voters to his side.

In an article three days earlier, Liming had described the grueling pace I maintained during the last week of the campaign:

> By the end of the day, Zeigler's right hand had a long red bruise from shaking the hands of well over 2,000 prospective voters. Toward late afternoon, he began to show signs of tiring under the grueling pace but during one stop, he was greeted with a spirit-lifter when an aid, bringing campaign literature from Columbia gave him a package of jelly candies from one of his daughters.
>
> Throughout most of the tiring day, his tall, poised, dark haired wife, Anne, accompanied him on most of the campaign stops and shows herself to be a hardy campaigner, helping to hand out literature and greet would-be voters.

In a desperate last-minute effort to get votes, John West persuaded Governor George Wallace, in a letter addressed to him, to state that he would vote for me if he were living in South Carolina. I sincerely appreciated West's efforts to stem the tide running against me, but the letter, when reproduced and distributed as campaign material, probably had no effect on the election. I was placed in the awkward position of stating that while I disagreed with Governor Wallace on many issues, I agreed with him that we need more open and honest government and that the poor people and the little man had been terribly neglected by the Republicans. Senator Thurmond asserted that he was more entitled to Wallace's endorsement than I was. "I think Governor Wallace's philosophy is more in line with mine," he was quoted in the November 2 *State* as saying. He concluded by saying that Wallace would vote for him although Wallace said he would not.

It came as a disappointment but not as a surprise that John Bolt Culbertson publicly endorsed Strom Thurmond, although he claimed to be a double-dipped Democrat who would vote for McGovern. His reason for doing so was that I was a "hypocrite." Even more disappointing was the open endorsement of Nixon, and by clear inference Thurmond, by former Democratic colleagues, including Peter Hyman.

All of the major newspapers endorsed Thurmond. The *State*, while endorsing Thurmond on October 21, 1972, shed a few crocodile tears over my departure from the state legislature:

> One flaw in the American system of representative government is the winner-take-all nature of the elective process since there is no prize for the runner-up in an election. The public is deprived of the services of able persons who fail to break into the winner's circle.
>
> Just such an event is likely in the current race for the United States Senate. As South Carolina's senior senator, Strom Thurmond, enjoys a deserved advantage over his challenger, State Sen. Eugene N. "Nick" Zeigler of Florence, and in all probability will be returned to Congress. But it must be counted as a loss to the state that Senator Zeigler will not be back in the General Assembly to continue his effective service at the state level. . . .
>
> We like to think that the future holds for Nick Zeigler a useful role of service for South Carolina. But perish the thought that he could be the instrument through which the Palmetto State—and the nation— would lose that strong voice in public affairs now exercised by Strom Thurmond.

I got clobbered. Thurmond got 63 percent of the vote, and I got 37 percent. What hurt the most was that Thurmond got more votes in Florence County than I did. The vote in Florence County, where I had worked and suffered for almost twenty years was Thurmond 14,832 to my 10,274. I did, however, run 3,000 votes ahead of McGovern, and Thurmond ran over 3,000 votes behind President Nixon. Almost a quarter of a million South Carolinians thought I was worthy of their vote for the U.S. Senate.

I did not call Senator Thurmond or visit his campaign's victory celebration. He had, in effect, treated me as a nonperson, and I resolved to return the compliment. Anne and I went to several television stations and broadcast my concession statement and congratulated Senator Thurmond on his victory. At ten o'clock on election night, November 7, 1972, I issued the following concession statement:

> Tonight my personal thanks go to the people of South Carolina who have supported me in my bid for the United States Senate.
>
> Thousands of people throughout our great state gave their time and energies on behalf of my candidacy and to each of them I extend my grateful appreciation.
>
> I congratulate Sen. Thurmond on his reelection, and wish him God-speed as he returns to Washington.

28

Human Affairs, and
I Get Clobbered Again

1973–1974

If the archangel Gabriel had descended from heaven and endorsed my candidacy in the race against Strom Thurmond, I don't believe it would have
made any difference. The people had spoken and the matter was closed. I
accepted the result. In a democratic republic such as ours, the voice of the
people is the final word. The people are entitled to have the leadership they
wish and deserve what they get.

No one likes a bad loser, and I hope that any comments on my defeat in
the 1972 general election will not be viewed in that light. It goes without
saying that I wanted to win the election, but win or lose I felt strongly that
Senator Thurmond should not be reelected unopposed and that he should
be opposed on issues, not personality. Thurmond did much for many people, helping them when in personal distress and browbeating federal
bureaucratic employees on their behalf. He was a master of the art of constituent service.

I was frequently referred to in the press and in conversation as "a sacrificial lamb" for the Democratic Party. In a sense I was, but I accepted the role,
for I felt it important to establish on the record that one-third of the state's
electorate disagreed with Thurmond's position on issues important to
the state and nation. It was remarkable that this one-third stood firm and
resisted the blandishments of money and power that Thurmond represented. On a personal note, I never heard from Senator Thurmond after the
election, either orally or in writing, and I never asked Thurmond for or
expected any favors from him.

When my teenage son Ben visited Washington over a decade after the
election, the group he was with visited Senator Thurmond's office. Ben

identified himself as Nick Zeigler's son, to which Thurmond replied, "Tell your daddy I'm not mad with him for running against me." I could not have cared less whether Senator Thurmond was mad with me because I did not run against *him,* I ran against the position he had taken on issues. I hoped that my candidacy had made that point, but it hardly drew a line in the sand that anyone regarded as important. In subsequent years Democrats who supported me sought favors from Thurmond and endorsed his candidacy in other elections. As one of my supporters put it, "We'll have Thurmond 'til death do us part." We nearly did.

A political defeat is like a death in the family, but in some ways it is worse, for it not only leaves an empty space but creates a keen sense of personal failure and anxiety about what future, if any, one might have in public life. There is a passage in Paul Tillich's sermon "Our Ultimate Concern" that describes the depth of anxiety I felt after the unsuccessful campaign in 1972: "Do you know the agony of those who want to heal but know it is too late; of those who want to educate and meet with stupidity, wickedness and hatred; of those who are obliged to lead and are worn out by the people's ignorance, by the ambitions of their opponents, by bad institutions and bad luck? These anxieties are greater than those about our daily life."

My adrenaline pumped too strongly to exclude myself from any form of public service, and I sought to overcome my anxiety by taking a hair of the dog that bit me—a nonelective public job. It was fortunate that Governor West asked if I would take the chairmanship of the Human Affairs Commission, a nonpaying job. The Human Affairs Commission, created by the legislature, came into existence on June 23, 1972, at a time when I was deeply involved in the Democratic Party primary, so that I did not have any part in its creation. There were problems integrating state agencies, and Governor West flattered me by believing that my type of leadership was needed to overcome some of them.

Integration of the public schools was the hot political issue of the 1950s; busing was the hot political issue of the 1960s. Affirmative action became the hot political issue of the 1970s and continues to be so. Affirmative action was at the heart of the difficulty with the Human Affairs Commission. The amendment to the federal Civil Rights Act passed in March 1972 gave the Equal Employment Opportunity Commission the authority to investigate and litigate all civil rights complaints filed against state and local governments. Most South Carolina agencies, in fact practically all of them, had done nothing to implement affirmative action in the employment of personnel. This set a bad example for the civilian sector of our state and had to be remedied. The recognition of merit and competence in employment, without regard to race, sex, or age, was a pressing problem. Every effort had to be made to level the playing field.

During the 1972 campaign I addressed a group of African American leaders in Columbia and stated that it was indefensible that qualified black men and women were not given the opportunity to be employed by the state. Modjeska Simkins, matriarch of Columbia's black community, warned me not to use the word "qualified," for as she put it, "This word has been used to discriminate against blacks for a long time." The word may have been unfortunate, but it is indefensible to put people on the public payroll who are not capable of performing the requirements of the job. There is a duty, however, to seek out and encourage those who are capable or who can become capable of performing specified requirements regardless of race and sex. The heart of the matter was to achieve simple fairness.

Governor West appointed me chairman of the Human Affairs Commission in April 1973, and I served until November 1974. Several of his friends were members of the commission—John Lumpkin; Arthur M. Williams; Mrs. Charles Wickenberg; Joab Lesesne Jr., president of Wofford, with whom I had served on the Tricentennial Commission; and Jean Hoefer Toal, who later became chief justice of the South Carolina Supreme Court.

The executive director at the time was George Hamilton, a black man who carried out his duties in a conscientious manner. I did not always agree with him on the permanent nature of affirmative action, but I wholeheartedly supported him on the necessity to get it started, particularly in state agencies. I recall going with him to make a speech at Benedict College in Columbia to explain the work of the commission. In his remarks he attacked the establishment in South Carolina for its insistence that state employees have certain academic requirements he regarded as irrelevant. Hamilton became carried away in his argument for relaxed academic standards for state employees and disparaged general cultural courses, which he asserted only taught students about Mozart and Beethoven's "Mickey Mouse music." I understood where he was coming from, but it was hard for me as an admirer of classical music, particularly Mozart's and Beethoven's, to hear their music thus denigrated. Hamilton had to walk a very fine line between the black and white communities.

The failure of state agencies to develop affirmative action plans became such an impediment to the success of the commission that I went to Governor West and told him something drastic had to be done. He agreed and said that he would summon all of the heads of state agencies to a meeting and read the riot act to them. True to his word a meeting was called, and the heads of all eighty-eight agencies were assembled. West told them that they would comply with the commission's request that they develop a plan for affirmative action within their agencies or suffer the consequences. The consequences would be that when they came under scrutiny and investigation by the federal government, he would not come to their assistance.

It worked, and within several months the commission had on file plans for a program of affirmative action from all eighty-eight state agencies except one: the South Carolina Judicial Department, headed by Chief Justice Joseph R. Moss. Moss took the position that the judicial branch of government was not subject to the orders of the legislative or executive branches, that is, the Human Affairs Commission could not require the state's judicial branch to do anything it did not want to do. While I was on the commission, I don't recall our doing anything to force the Judicial Department to comply. By January 1974 of the eighty-seven affirmative action plans filed by state agencies, sixty had been approved by the commission, twenty-three were in the process of being revised, and only four were considered delinquent.

From June 1972 to October 1974 the commission had received 192 complaints—103 in the public sector and 89 in the private sector. Under the commission's action, 84 of the public sector complaints and 35 in the private sector were resolved, conciliated, and closed. In my appearance before the Budget and Control Board in 1974 asking for additional funds to continue and expand the work of the commission, I said, "We feel that we have saved and are continuing to save the state thousands of dollars that would be spent in court costs and litigation in the federal courts if it were not for this agency's resolving these complaints. In addition to this saving of state money is the possible loss of millions of dollars that may have been taken away from the various agencies because of their lack of compliance with federal regulations."

George Hamilton resigned as director on August 9, 1974, and the commission elected James Clyburn his successor. I was familiar with Clyburn, who had worked in Governor West's office, and considered him an intelligent, able man. Clyburn had also helped in my campaign in 1972. He was later elected congressman for the Sixth Congressional District and presently is the national Democratic Party's majority whip.

I entered the 1974 race for the governorship reluctantly and against my better judgment. It seemed a way to gain some leverage to extricate myself from the debt of my previous campaign. I considered running for the office of lieutenant governor, but that would be getting back into the same trap of having a part-time job while trying to earn a living practicing law.

It was a mistake to end my political career as a miserable failure, or as T. S. Eliot put it, "not with a bang but a whimper." In the first place I had no money and no prospects of raising any significant amount on which to conduct a statewide campaign. In the second place I had the mistaken idea that I had built up a statewide constituency in the race against Strom Thurmond. Not only was there no residual group that could constitute a constituency to support my candidacy, but my Florence associates, one by one, deserted me. I recall going to Clyde Barnes and asking if he was going to support me, and he said quite frankly that he was not. I asked why. His response was that I had no reasonable expectation of being elected and that he was not going to support a candidate who did not have a chance of winning. It was bad news, but I understood the realities of politics and remained on friendly terms with Barnes until his death in 1980.

With no money and few prominent people supporting me, becoming involved in a statewide race was a great gamble. I made a speech to the Mental Health Association on January 22, 1974:

> I feel a little shy about appearing before you tonight in view of the fact that a political cartoon recently appeared in the *State* newspaper depicting me as naked with only a barrel covering my nakedness. The words "Old Political Debts" are inscribed on the barrel. There is more truth than poetry in the cartoon. However, I am reminded of a famous scene between Julius Caesar and his British slave, Britannus, in which Caesar asks why the natives of Great Britain paint their bodies blue. To which Britannus answers, "In war we stain our bodies blue, so that though our enemies strip us of our clothes and lives, they cannot strip us of our respectability." I take great comfort that although the campaign of 1972 may have stripped me of everything but a barrel covering my nakedness, it did not strip me of my respectability.

After my reluctant entrance into the primary, the contest rapidly became something between a comic opera and a depressing satire. I gambled on the long chance that so many candidates were vying for the office I would be a logical compromise candidate. I was wrong. In my opinion the disarray of the Democratic Party in that election caused its collapse as an effective political organization in South Carolina.

The Republican Party's slate consisted of Gen. William Westmoreland of Vietnam War fame and state senator James Edwards, an oral surgeon from Charleston. There were seven candidates in the Democrat primary: William Jennings Bryan Dorn, a former congressman; Earle Morris, then serving as lieutenant governor; Charles D. (Pug) Ravenel, who had a devoted following of young people; Maurice Bessinger, a Columbia restaurateur; John Bolt Culbertson, who had given me so much grief in the 1972 election; Milton J. Dukes, a former Baptist minister turned restaurateur; and me. Pug Ravenel took center stage and was the main cause of an unexpected and devastating setback for the Democrats.

My first meeting with Pug Ravenel took place during the primary contest in 1972. I was scheduled to go to a political gathering outside Charleston, and Bo Morrison volunteered to take me there. I sent a strange message back to my headquarters in Columbia: "I have gone to Wadmalaw Island with Bo, Booper and Pug." William G. "Bo" Morrison and Eddie "Booper" Prichard Jr. were both lawyers. Pug Ravenel, who had moved back to Charleston from New York in early 1972, had supported my candidacy against Thurmond.

Pug Ravenel has genuine charisma. That, combined with intelligence and an engaging manner, makes it virtually impossible not to like him. We have remained friends, even through the travails of the 1974 Democratic

A bipartisan group of candidates for governor at the Peach Festival in Gilbert, South Carolina, 1974. Left to right: Maurice Bessinger, Earle Morris, Eugene N. Zeigler, James Edwards, William Jennings Bryan Dorn, Gen. William Westmoreland, and John Bolt Culbertson. Missing in this photograph are Charles "Pug" Ravenel and Milton J. Dukes. Collection of the author

primary. I envied his vigorous campaigning and athletic prowess. One of his campaign leaflets featured a glamorous picture of Pug in a football uniform, raised right arm holding a football, just moments before throwing a pass. Pug was—and still is—an excellent athlete, and it was disconcerting when the two of us happened to be at the same gathering during the primary and he began to demonstrate his athletic skills by driving a few golf balls or playing several games of tennis, both done with a skill I admired and envied.

The consensus of the other candidates in 1974, however, was that as attractive as Pug was, he had not paid his political dues. He had not, in fact, run for any public office in South Carolina or elsewhere previously. He also suffered to a lesser degree from my handicap: he had gone to Harvard. It was remarkable that he overcame that disability by reason of his record as a football quarterback. I, on the other hand, came away "sickled o'er with the pale cast of thought" from my three years at Harvard Law School. His greatest handicap, one that proved fatal to his campaign, was that he had not been a resident of the state of South Carolina for five years as required by the state's constitution. His enthusiastic determination blurred the deep significance of that problem.

In the early days of the campaign it occurred to me that I should make some overtures to Pug. I was convinced there was no way he could be qualified for the governorship under the state's residential requirements. Since he and I held similar views and represented a new type of political leadership in South Carolina, I believed that for either of us to prevail we should join forces. To do this I sent a message through a mutual friend to the effect that if Pug would withdraw from this contest and throw his support to me, I would do the same in the next election for him. If I were successful in being elected governor, we would be a much stronger political force. The whole suggestion of a coalition was based on my firm conviction that Pug inevitably would be disqualified by the residency requirement contained in Article IV, Section 2, of the state's constitution, which provides that no person shall be eligible to the office of governor who "shall not have been . . . a citizen and resident of this State for five years next preceding the day of election."

It seemed clear to me that Pug Ravenel's life in New York and Washington disqualified him, but a message came back from Ravenel that he was not interested in my proposal. He felt he had momentum and was confident he could secure a judicial decision finding that he met the residency requirements. Although the word "resident" is somewhat vague in its meaning, there are certain well-established indices of residency in the law, including a driver's license, paying taxes, and voter registration. Unfortunately Pug could not show anything but a mental intention to return to live in South Carolina.

Ravenel had a friendly lawsuit brought on March 28, 1974, to have himself declared a resident of South Carolina and thus eligible to run for governor. The suit was brought by a plaintiff whose only standing was that of a taxpayer and citizen of South Carolina. The case law is firmly established in this state that only a person who has a direct interest, as a candidate, in a contested office has standing to bring a suit against another candidate seeking that office.

It was ironic that Culbertson had brought suit against Sol Blatt Sr. and other officials alleging dual officeholding. *Culbertson v. Blatt et al.,* 194 S.C. 105, 9 S. E. 2d 218 (1940) was a case in which Culbertson sought to have Blatt and others disqualified from holding office as trustees of the University of South Carolina because they held elective offices. Culbertson had standing only as a citizen and taxpayer and could show no interest in the office of trustee of the University of South Carolina. The court ruled that only a person interested as a candidate could challenge the right of an official to an elective office.

Despite the clear precedent established by the *Culbertson* case, on April 29, 1974, Judge John Grimball ruled that Ravenel was eligible under the state constitution to be elected governor. It was an unsupportable decision, as future events proved, and as the primary approached the probability of someone's bringing a proper suit to question his eligibility increased. I believed the Democrats were headed for disaster.

With little money to run a campaign, I had to rely on friends to help. Steve Skardon Jr., who had been a volunteer in the 1972 campaign, agreed to be my campaign manager in Florence. Lucta Allen and James "Jim" W. Parker Jr. drove in Jim's truck to various campaign speeches to distribute campaign material. The truck had a big sign that urged voters to PICK NICK. My son Belton, my daughter Helen, and my wife helped campaign for me, and Bob Harris made his Aztec plane available. Total campaign expenses came to less than thirty thousand dollars.

Since there were seven candidates competing for the governorship, the stump speeches sometimes took on a carnival atmosphere. Milton J. Dukes would appear riding a bicycle, and Maurice Bessinger frequently appeared at these gatherings riding a big white horse. At a gathering and parade at the Gilbert Peach Festival, it began raining and all of the participants had to seek refuge under a funeral tent that had been provided in case of emergency. The tent under which I took cover was also the refuge of General Westmoreland, Senator Edwards, and Bessinger and his horse.

This campaign was not like the one against Strom Thurmond in which there were controversial issues to run on and discuss. But one issue that attracted attention was the legislature's reenactment of the death penalty statute. Governor West vetoed it, and the General Assembly overrode his veto. All of the candidates had to take a position on the death penalty. Culbertson stated that he opposed the death penalty, as did Ravenel. I had stated my position on the death penalty in the 1972 campaign: it should be reserved for those cases in which it possibly arms a crime victim with an argument to save his or her life. The rest were either noncommittal or in favor of the death penalty. The other issues I raised were ignored.

On May 27, 1974, I wrote an open letter to Governor John West in which I urged that he address the General Assembly and seek their support in solving some of the real issues facing the state. The *State* ran an editorial on June 3, 1974, commenting on my letter to the governor:

ZEIGLER PUTS GOVERNOR AND RIVALS ON A SPOT

Whether he wins or loses the Democratic nomination for governor, Eugene N. Zeigler has rendered a conspicuous service to South Carolina by spelling out 11 issues which should be—but generally are not—discussed by all gubernatorial candidates in 1974.

Mr. Zeigler has thus, in one imaginative gesture, put not only the present Governor, but all prospective governors (including himself) on the spot. That is where they should be.

The primary came down to a political beauty contest, that is, a question of which candidate had the experience and personality the voters believed made him the best choice for governor. The issues I raised were ignored. Dorn and Morris were regarded as frontrunners, but Ravenel, who spent $325,000 on a television campaign, was overtaking them.

There was an ominous article in the *State's* July 12, 1974, issue in which Dukes said that he would "go to court to keep Charles Ravenel, 'Pug,' out of the governor's mansion." The article quotes Dukes as saying, "I'm going to solicit the services of an attorney—like John Bolt Culbertson":

According to Dukes, who spent some time pasting a "Dukes for Governor" sign on the back wheel of his faded red bicycle, said [*sic*], "I feel like the people are being taken. . . . Ravenel doesn't have any more right to run than John West."

Dukes said he didn't "give a rip what every cotton pickin' judge" in the state says about Ravenel's eligibility. As far as Dukes is concerned, Ravenel is not constitutionally eligible to run for governor.

Several weeks before the voting was to take place, Ravenel sent me a letter asking if we could arrange a meeting. He came to Florence, and we talked. His proposal was that I withdraw from the primary and throw what support I had to him. Even though I was way down in the polls, I was reluctant to do this because I felt sure that Pug would ultimately be declared ineligible. It was a friendly conversation, and I told him I would think about it and consult some of my friends and supporters.

The following day I got a call from a supporter in Greenville who said that Ravenel's people were saying that Pug had conferred with me and that I was withdrawing from the contest and throwing my support to him. I said this was not true and assured my caller I was still a candidate.

The following day there was a news article in which a reporter asked Pug if he had talked to me about my withdrawal. Pug denied he had any such conversation. There had been an understanding between us about confidentiality. It had been breached by the Ravenel campaign, so when I got a call from a reporter, I confirmed that there had been a conversation between us on the subject, but I had not agreed to withdraw. Pug's explanation of his misleading the press was that he was endeavoring to protect the confidentiality of the meeting, but his staff had already breached that confidentiality. The next day I got a telephone call from Pug's campaign manager, who asked how I thought we should handle the matter. By that time I was angry and said that since their campaign had created the problem, I would leave it to him to figure out how to deal with it. I could not desert the people who had been working for me throughout the state, so I remained in the race.

In the first balloting in the Democrat primary on July 16, 1974, no candidate got a majority of the votes. The results were 32 percent for Ravenel, 31 percent for Dorn, 25 percent for Morris, 3 percent for Zeigler, 2 percent for Bessinger, and less that 1 percent each for Culbertson and Dukes. The top vote getters were William Jennings Bryan Dorn and Pug Ravenel, but neither had a majority. A runoff was held on July 30, 1974, and Pug Ravenel got a majority of the votes. It was a pyrrhic victory for Ravenel.

On August 10, 1974, Dukes and Ben Dekle, a radio announcer from Cayce, filed suit against Ravenel to declare him ineligible. Both Dukes and Dekle had standing to bring the suit, Dukes having run in the primary for the governorship and Dekle because he was campaigning to become a write-in candidate in the general election. Ravenel's attorneys moved to have the suit enjoined by the South Carolina Supreme Court, and that court took jurisdiction.

The suit brought by Ravenel in March 1974 was conceded by his attorneys in the new lawsuit to be invalid so far as determining the issues raised by Dukes and Dekle. Since the new suit eventually ended up in the original jurisdiction of the South Carolina Supreme Court, the court directed Judge J. B. "Bubba" Ness to take the testimony and report it with exhibits to the Supreme Court without recommendation.

The South Carolina Supreme Court heard the case on September 23, 1974, and ruled immediately and unanimously that Pug Ravenel was ineligible to be a candidate for the office of governor. A written opinion was filed by the court almost a year later in *Ravenel v. Dekle et al.*, 265 S.C. 364, 218 S. E. 2d 521 (1975).

Ravenel's magnificent, expensive campaign came crashing down. Its death throes were heart-rending and gargantuan in scope. A suit was filed immediately in the federal court, and a three-judge panel presided over by Judge Clement Haynsworth ruled that the state's constitutional provision for a five-year residency was reasonable and that Ravenel was not eligible. A petition filed with a justice of the U.S. Supreme Court to enjoin the election was refused. Petitions were circulated asking that a special session of the legislature be called to amend the state's constitution to make Ravenel eligible, but there was no time for that extreme measure, even if that were politically possible before the general election on November 4, 1974.

The Democratic Party was thrown into turmoil. A party convention was hastily called to meet on October 1, 1974. Numerous people were nominated to fill the vacancy, and my friend Jim Parker nominated me. It was difficult to conceal how one was voting in a convention where the chairman of the delegation had to announce the results. Alas, nearly all of the delegates from Florence County decided not to support my candidacy. Out of thirteen delegates from Florence County I received only two votes. I learned anew that gratitude is a perishable commodity in politics. Or I should have recalled that gratitude in politics is the keen anticipation of future favors. I had reached bottom and had no future favors to disburse. In the final vote William Jennings Bryan Dorn was selected to fill the vacancy.

There was one poignant scene at the convention held at Columbia's Township auditorium. I left the convention and went outside to get something from my car. Pug Ravenel came around the corner of the building at that moment, and we met face to face. No one else was present. We greeted each other by name and shook hands. Neither of us could articulate our shared feelings of disappointment and hurt, so we stood for a moment or two without saying anything and then went our separate ways in silence.

I felt that the three of us, Ravenel, Culbertson and me, represented a different vision for the state of South Carolina. Each had a separate approach. Culbertson was a liberal with leanings to the left, Ravenel a liberal with leanings to the right, and I was, in a sense, the middleman. I continued to admire and respect the other two; in fact I remained friends with all of the candidates throughout the campaign. It was sad that the election of 1974 turned out to be nearly the death knell of the Democratic Party's dominance in state government.

It was the end of my political struggles and very near the end for John Bolt Culbertson, although he ran again in the 1978 primary against Ravenel for the U.S. Senate. He had almost finished his turbulent career in politics. During the 1974 primary campaign Culbertson and I became fairly friendly because most of his wrath was expended on Earle Morris and Pug Ravenel. He referred to himself in the campaign as being like a bastard at a family reunion.

A few words should be said by way of a requiem for John Bolt Culbertson (1908–1983). I felt he had abused and betrayed me terribly in the 1972 election, but in the helter-skelter governor's election in 1974, he and I came to understand each other better. He told me when the campaign was over that I was the only person he had run against who had treated him as a gentleman. After the election Anne and I invited him and his wife to have dinner with us in Florence, and we spent a pleasant evening together. They reciprocated by inviting us to their home in Greenville. It was a strange house built underground as though it was a bomb shelter but very elaborate in its layout and decoration. I was surprised to learn that he collected fine china, and even more surprised to learn that my aunt Leah Townsend had taught Culbertson history when he was a student at the University of South Carolina. I don't know where his soul is now, but I am sure that wherever it is, there will be turbulence.

The general election on November 4, 1974, resulted in the election of James Edwards, the first Republican governor since Reconstruction. The wounds inflicted on Dorn, the Democratic candidate, in the primary were not healed. It should be remembered that the whole primary campaign was carried on in the shadow of the Watergate hearings. President Nixon resigned his office on August 9, and South Carolinians, along with the rest of the nation, were disillusioned by politics and political leaders. They wanted a change, even if it meant electing a Republican. Had I received the Democratic nomination, I doubt that I could have defeated Edwards, who stated publicly that he opposed the Civil Rights Act on which affirmative action was based. In the Republican Party's book, I was a dangerous liberal.

Culbertson scorned my type of liberalism as not being radical enough, and I feel certain he would have agreed with my liberal labor lawyer friends who reproached me as being "a Burke-type liberal." He went for the jugular in politics and would not suffer fools gladly when they advocated moderation. I empathized with his frustration in trying to make the establishment, or Victoria DeLee's "big white Democrats," more sympathetic toward the working men and women, black and white, young and old in South Carolina. I appreciated the courage it took to espouse the radical positions he advocated, but I questioned his judgment in his attempt to pull down the temple that cast him out.

There was no question in my mind that I would never run for political office again. I had given politics my best effort and had not succeeded. There was a small consolation prize however. In November 1974 the Human Affairs Commission presented me with a plaque that, to some degree, softened the pain of my second defeat.

THE STATE HUMAN AFFAIRS COMMISSION

AND ITS STAFF

PRESENTS

THIS TOKEN OF APPRECIATION TO

EUGENE N. ZEIGLER

WHO AS ITS CHAIRMAN

HAS ACTED DYNAMICALLY

TO PROMOTE HARMONY,

ENCOURAGE FAIR TREATMENT FOR, AND

ELIMINATE DISCRIMINATION AMONG

ALL CITIZENS OF THE STATE

AND WHOSE WORK HAS ADDED

A NEW SENSE OF DIGNITY TO

AND FOSTERED A NEW LEVEL OF

MUTUAL UNDERSTANDING AMONG ALL

PEOPLE IN SOUTH CAROLINA

29

Tobacco and Prisons

Where there's smoke, there's fire. There had been fire in the first round of the Democratic primary that ended for me on July 16, but now it was tobacco smoke coming from troubles tobacco farmers were experiencing, and there was a lot of emotional fire beneath that. When the tobacco marketing season opened on July 15, 1974, the prices tobacco farmers received were so low that they either barely broke even or, in some cases, went further into debt. As one farmer said to me about the low prices he received, "I didn't know whether to cry or fight."

I returned to my law office in an effort to repair the damage caused by the time I had time spent on the political trail. One of the congressional candidates, John W. Jenrette Jr., was running as a Democrat for the Sixth Congressional District seat that included my county. I was invited to a fund raiser at the Florence Country Club. Former governor Jimmy Carter of Georgia was to be present. I went somewhat reluctantly since I was hardly in a position to contribute to any candidate. As I approached the front door of the club a television reporter and a newspaper reporter greeted me. "We understand that you are going to bring a lawsuit against the tobacco companies," they said. I was taken aback since that was the first I had heard of it. The reporters then explained to me that Jenrette had made a little speech in which he deplored the low prices tobacco farmers were being paid for their product and stated that he was going to ask Nick Zeigler to sue the companies for price fixing.

I entered the main ballroom of the club and met Jenrette, who confirmed what the reporters were saying. I knew Jenrette from when he was a House member in Columbia but had not had much association with him. He had a disconcerting way of greeting me in the State House lobby, usually asking, "What have you done for me today?" I generally replied, "Absolutely nothing."

He had mastered the "good ol' boy" style of politics with a pronounced populist bent. On this occasion I explained to John that the engagement of a lawyer to bring a lawsuit required a client to come to the lawyer's office, sit down, and discuss the matter in detail. I was not prepared to make a commitment to bring an antitrust suit unless that procedure was followed. At that moment Jimmy Carter came up and spoke to me. Anne and I had escorted his wife and son in Columbia during the inauguration of John West in January 1970. He recalled his wife telling him of our doing this and said he was pleased to meet me. He then said that he would be glad to be of assistance if I needed to make tobacco growers in Georgia a part of the lawsuit. I thanked him, and we parted.

Jenrette came to my office the next day, and we discussed the difficulties that would be encountered in bringing a lawsuit against the large tobacco companies. I explained that I could not go out and recruit plaintiffs for a lawsuit against the tobacco companies. If he knew any farmers who might be willing to become plaintiffs in such a suit, he must tell them to come to my office and talk with me before I could put them down as plaintiffs.

I surmised that because of my experience over twenty years, I had established a good reputation for representing tobacco farmers and had included in my campaign speeches and literature reference to my experience in helping tobacco farmers in getting fair treatment and prices. To establish my credentials I frequently said that I had sued every secretary of agriculture from Benson to Butz to get fair treatment for farmers and that I would do it again if I had to.

In 1957 I had represented tobacco farmers who had raised a variety of tobacco that nearly doubled their poundage output. These seeds had been developed at Coker Pedigreed Seed Company in Hartsville, and I had the opportunity to become acquainted with the company's owner, Robert Coker, who supported the position that my clients took. Another problem for which I took a prominent part in finding a solution was to secure price support for loose leaf tobacco in South Carolina. In the Georgia markets, which were controlled by the tobacco companies, price support was offered on tobacco auctioned as loose leaves, but in the rest of the flue-cured tobacco growing states, which included South and North Carolina and Virginia, the farmers had to grade and tie tobacco offered for sale in small bundles of leaves for it to receive price support.

After my conversation with John Jenrette, I agreed to bring an antitrust lawsuit against twenty-two major tobacco companies to end what almost everyone involved in raising tobacco agreed was price fixing. True to his agreement, Jenrette asked several tobacco farmers, primarily from Horry County, to come to my office and discuss bringing a lawsuit in their names. Several tobacco farmers came in of their own accord.

After the lawsuit was filed, the tobacco companies were eager to explore whether I had committed barratry, or solicited clients in order to bring a lawsuit. But I had carefully refrained from recruiting anyone as a plaintiff. One plaintiff, when being deposed, was asked how he learned that a lawsuit was being planned. The farmer replied that he was down at the crossroads at Dog Bluff in Horry County "eatin' a Moon Pie and drinkin' a Pepsi when Jenrette come in and says, 'Nick Zeigler is gonna bring a lawsuit against the tobacco companies' and would I be willing to go talk to him about it."

The lawsuit with six tobacco farmers as plaintiffs was filed on July 27, 1974. A great deal was made over the fact that Jenrette announced on television that a lawsuit had been filed. The matter had already become a political issue in which both Jenrette and the Republican incumbent urged action to solve the problem. The Democrat backed the lawsuit, and the Republican called for an investigation by the Department of Agriculture. The lawsuit, however, alleged that the Department of Agriculture was in the conspiracy with the tobacco companies.

The lawsuit received extensive media coverage, as a result of which I received a telephone call from John A. Cochrane, a lawyer in St. Paul, Minnesota, expressing interest in helping to manage the action. Cochrane was a lawyer with wide experience in antitrust actions, and I knew that my small-town practice was not going to be a match for the law talent on the other side. Page Dees, a woman who had become an associate in my law firm, and John E. Thomas, an associate in Cochrane's office, made up the plaintiffs' team.

There were usually about thirty or more lawyers representing the defendant tobacco companies and the secretary of agriculture. The defense team was headed by counsel from Arnold and Porter of Washington, D.C., and Davis, Polk and Wardwell of New York City. When hearings were held, frequently all of the seats—including those usually occupied by nonlawyers—were filled by defense counsel. One judge remarked that I had done more to enrich lawyers than any other attorney practicing in South Carolina.

After extensive discovery and depositions the matter came for a hearing before Judge Robert F. Chapman on June 19, 1975. On September 26, 1975, Judge Chapman issued an order denying class action status to the lawsuit. Only when a class action is authorized can sufficient funds be raised to pay the expenses necessary to fight large corporations with their millions of dollars and the largest law firms in the country behind them. The influence of big tobacco companies was omnipresent and bipartisan since they gave liberally to both Democrats and Republicans.

Chapman denied class action status because the trial of the case would be, in his opinion, "unmanageable." One of my clients summed up the situation in which we found ourselves: "If you are going to be crooked, be crooked in a big way, then the court will say that your lawsuit is 'unmanageable.'"

We appealed Chapman's decision to the Fourth Circuit Court of Appeals. In the meantime a second action had been filed in North Carolina that included all of the remaining tobacco-growing states. Counsel for that suit were J. Nat Hamrick of Rutherfordton, North Carolina; Robert C. Howison Jr. of Raleigh; and Frank M. Wooton Jr. of Greenville, North Carolina. It was decided to keep the lawsuits separate but that counsel in both cases would cooperate in any action.

I went to Raleigh and conferred with North Carolina counsel about their lawsuit, and they asked if I knew of any Georgia tobacco farmers who might be willing to be plaintiffs in the North Carolina suit. I recalled my conversation with Jimmy Carter and said that I would contact him to see if he could help us. By that time Jimmy Carter had begun his campaign to win the presidency, so I called his headquarters in Atlanta. One of his campaign managers told me that he would take it up with Carter and get back to me. I waited for over a week and, having heard nothing, called again. This time I was told that Carter was no longer interested in helping tobacco farmers in a lawsuit against tobacco companies. Obviously the tobacco companies were too rich and powerful for a candidate to make them his enemies.

A panel of three judges heard the appeal of the South Carolina farmers in the Fourth Circuit Court of Appeals—senior circuit judge Albert V. Bryan, Braxton Craven Jr., and Charles E. Wyzanski Jr., senior district judge, District Court of Massachusetts. Judge Wyzanski was a graduate of Harvard Law School and as a judge had participated in some of the moot courts. In the cases I observed, he was merciless in showing how foolish some of the students' arguments were, which caused me to feel that he was as mean as a snake. I changed my mind during the oral argument in our case, for he clearly sided with the tobacco farmers by persistently asking the lawyer from the tobacco companies what the difference in the quantum and character would be in a trial on the issue of conspiracy if there were six or twenty thousand plaintiffs. They were not able to answer the question. At one point Judge Wyzanski asked me why I thought the tobacco companies had done certain reprehensible things. I replied that I thought it impolite to say what I really thought their motives were because I believed them to be so unworthy. This resulted in general laughter, even from opposing counsel.

On July 16, 1976, the court of appeals reversed Judge Chapman's order as being "plainly wrong" and an "abuse of discretion." The majority opinion was written by Judge Wyzanski and joined in by Judge Craven; Judge Bryan dissented.

The tobacco companies filed a motion for a rehearing en banc, which means that all of the judges on the Fourth Circuit Court of Appeals would listen to arguments in favor of reversing the decision. The court of appeals granted the motion, and the case was heard on February 14, 1977, before seven justices presided over by Judge Clement Haynsworth. Judge Craven, who had joined Judge Wyzanski in deciding for the tobacco farmers, was a member of the en banc panel, but unfortunately he died in May 1977. The court rendered its opinion, written by Judge Donald Russell, on October 22, 1977. Judge Russell's opinion reversed the opinion of the three-judge panel, but Judge Butzner filed a dissenting opinion and it was assumed that Craven would have also dissented.

A petition for a writ of certiorari was filed with the U.S. Supreme Court in October 1977, but the Court denied certiorari and the class action status of the complaint was denied. The action in which the six farmers were plaintiffs was still alive, but the prospect of these tobacco farmers being financially able to carry the lawsuit through was conceded to be remote. There was a hearing before Judge Chapman on the question of the continuation of the action, at which time I moved that he now declare this to be a class action. Chapman said he was surprised I had the nerve to make such a motion, given all that had transpired in the case. I then quoted Shakespeare: "Sweet are the uses of adversity; / Which, like the toad, ugly and venomous, / Wears yet a precious jewel in its head."

I argued that the jewel in the toad's head would be a declaration that the lawsuit could be continued as a class action. Chapman was not moved by my poetic allusion and did not grant my motion. The North Carolina lawsuit suffered the same fate. Cochrane had decided the matter was not worth his time, trouble, and expense, and he withdrew from the case, which was eventually settled by the payment of a small sum to cover the costs and attorneys' fees of the plaintiffs. I did point out to Chapman that one of the reasons for bringing the suit was to get the tobacco companies to pay more for the tobacco they purchased, and the price being paid became substantially higher after the suit was initiated. Thirty years later, when my son Ben had the privilege of clerking for Judge Russell, I had a conversation with Judge Russell in which he said, "Nick, you were ahead of your time in bringing that lawsuit against the tobacco companies." This was cold comfort since my prospect of a large monetary judgment and attorneys' fees vanished as a result of his opinion.

One amusing incident resulted from a misapprehension by the court reporter who was transcribing my argument before Judge Chapman. I got a telephone call from the reporter, who said that his notes contained something that did not make sense. "I have it in my notes that you said 'Sweet are juices of diversity,'" the reporter told me. I got him straight on Shakespearean poetry.

I have always had a feeling of ambivalence about tobacco farming. Flue-cured tobacco is the essential ingredient of cigarettes. Beginning in the late nineteenth century, flue-cured tobacco rapidly replaced cotton as the chief money crop in the Pee Dee. Its cultivation provided a lucrative occupation for small farmers and provided a distinctive atmosphere and character to the Pee Dee section of South Carolina in which I live. Tobacco farming rapidly spread after the Depression and was strengthened by the government's system of acreage allotments and marketing quotas.

Whatever its harmful effect on the human body, tobacco in its raw, cured state smells good. A trip to a tobacco warehouse where piles of cured tobacco were waiting to be bought was always a treat. There was excitement as well as the heavy aroma, somewhat like incense, in the air. The chant of the tobacco auctioneer resembled the priestly incantation of a primitive religion. The whole scene made a fitting tribute to the god Mammon. "Ready cash," no matter how deficient from expectation, was the balm of the whole tobacco farming industry. When the auctioneer pronounced, "Sold to American" or some other tobacco company, it was like the denouement of a play in which the final message behind the author's writing is revealed.

It is all gone now. Tobacco is known to have caused pain and suffering to millions of smokers, and the warehouse auction system was something of a hoax. The tobacco companies, in my opinion, conspired to fix prices to their advantage, and the tobacco cooperative system was preempted by the tobacco companies and became a tool that gave them greater leverage to control the whole system. What was supposed to be a boon for the tobacco farmers turned out to be another way to deceive them.

The saddest change was the passing of the small tobacco farmer who could, with the expenditure of effort on the part of his entire family, make a living. Tobacco planting, gathering, and curing was a labor-intensive, hands-on effort. It brought thousands of people close to the earth and to growing things. The system sustained a whole class of yeoman farmers who have now yielded to large operations called agribusiness. No longer are the leaves of tobacco tied to sticks and cured in barns that required all-night vigils to prevent fires, as there are now mechanical bulk curing barns. The raising of tobacco for cigarettes, once the lifeblood of the rural community, is now relegated to contracts between farmers and tobacco companies. I cannot help but grieve over the passing of a way of life that provided so much good for the farmers involved, even when its final product caused so much harm.

My term of office on the Human Affairs Commission expired in November 1974, and though virtually impoverished, I still wished to be useful in some part of government. I had a meeting with Governor West and opened the conversation by saying that I had come to get his help in writing my political epitaph. He was sympathetic and said that he had been holding an appointment on the South Carolina Arts Commission for me. I thanked him but said I wanted something different and more robust and demanding than that. The chairman of the Board of Corrections had died in October, creating an opening on that board. I asked Governor West if he would consider appointing me to fill the unexpired portion of that term. In November I was appointed to the Board of Corrections and confirmed by the Senate.

The move from politics and the arts to adult prison reform caused some stir among my critics. The wisecrack that one of my former associates made when he heard I had been appointed to the Board of Corrections was, "Nick will get along better with prisoners than he did with politicians." It turned out to be true.

My interest in reform of correctional institutions was long-standing, and now that I had reached the bottom rung of the political ladder I knew that I could sympathize with the ultimate underdogs of our society, prisoners. I was convinced that the state's correctional system was antiquated and counterproductive since prisoners left the state's prisons worse than when they went in. The need for reform was clear to me not only for the sake of the human beings who were being wasted by the system but also because I agreed with Fyodor Dostoyevsky: "The degree of civilization in a society can be judged by entering its prisons."

Our prisons are a hopeless hodgepodge. I argued for a radical restructuring of the system. My opinion is that one-third of the prisoners we punish should be assigned work release and do time in halfway houses; one-third might be reformed if the funds, personnel, and the environment necessary for reform were available. The other one-third we should only expect to remove from society as long as possible and, in effect, merely warehouse them.

I refused to succumb to the temptation of trying to put a good face on prison conditions by using bureaucratic euphemisms. People sentenced to the custody of the Department of Corrections should be called *prisoners*, not *inmates*. The department should operate *prisons*, not *centers* or *institutions*. I thought the supreme euphemism was coined when a new building, specifically designed for executions, was called the *capital punishment facility* instead of the *death house*.

The difficulty that comes from the use of these fancy designations was illustrated on one occasion when I was invited to attend the correctional officers' annual banquet. The principal speaker was an aspiring politician for whom a speech had been written, which meant that he was probably only vaguely familiar with the words and ideas in it. Anne and I were seated at the head table so that we were facing the audience. The speaker may have taken several drinks to steady his nerves so that when he came upon the ultimate euphemism, *incarcerate,* he said, "incinerate." The assembled crowd who were engaged in running the prisons in South Carolina were told, "In this state we incinerate too many people." Images of Dachau and Auschwitz came to my mind, but my wife, who has difficulty in repressing her emotions, puffed up as she struggled to suppress her laughter. The dreadful malapropism was repeated twice more, and it was marvelous that the audience never so much as smiled.

In 1974 there were 3,482 prisoners in the custody of the Department of Corrections. Of that number 3,340 were males and 142 were females. The department was headed by William D. Leeke, and there were approximately 1,500 employees in the department. Bill Leeke was a capable, tough, humane director of the prison system with outstanding credentials. He exemplified for me the quality most desired in a prison official: compassionate firmness. His refreshing candor never ceased to amuse me. Once when asked by newspaper reporters why South Carolina imprisoned more people per capita than any other state in the union, Bill replied, "I guess we're just meaner than other people." In the fifteen years I served on the Board of Corrections, I developed a deep sense of respect for Bill Leeke, his staff, and most of the employees in the department.

The Board of Corrections consisted of six members, one from each congressional district, and the members served without pay. This made a compact group and was better than having a larger, unmanageable board. The governor was an ex officio member, but during the fifteen years I served on the board, I do not recall a governor actually attending a board meeting. He usually sent a representative who gave us the benefit of the governor's thinking and reported to the governor what we were doing.

I was shocked when I first visited the maximum security building where the hardcore criminals are kept. I had to surrender to the warden all sharp objects, such as pens, and I was warned not to get within fifteen feet of the bars on the cells. If I got close enough, I was told, a prisoner might reach through the bars, seize me by the throat, and strangle me to death before I could be rescued. An additional danger was the possibility that a prisoner might throw his feces or urine at me. This act was not uncommon in prisons. When I completed my visit, I felt I had a better idea of what the innermost circles of hell must be like.

When I became a member of the Board of Corrections there was an explosion of the prison population, making the building of new prisons mandatory. The architectural firms in the state were concerned that the money appropriated would not be spent wisely and would be subject to political favoritism. The board wisely devised a system by which all bids for new prisons would be reviewed by a subcommittee composed of staff employees, and at least one board member had to attend the presentation of plans from interested firms. The subgroup would then propose five firms for the board's approval, and again there would be full presentations made to the full board. This method successfully sanitized the selection of firms, and we had no more complaints of favoritism although millions of dollars would be spent on new prisons.

The Budget and Control Board approved $5,630,763 for fiscal year 1973–74 and $30,000,000 for 1974–75 for the building of new prisons, but the Budget and Control Board placed a moratorium on all construction projects financed with capital improvement bonds. By July 25, 1975, I had sufficiently familiarized myself with the serious problems facing the Department of Corrections and the prison system, and I wrote a letter to Governor Edwards outlining what I thought the main problems were and how they should be addressed. I explained that the increased overcrowding and the deteriorating conditions in the prison system invited intervention by the federal government. Such intervention would be both embarrassing and costly. Included in my letter was a list of specific things I wanted Edwards to consider: (1) the leasing of additional temporary facilities, (2) obtaining preengineered facilities for placement on state-owned or state-leased property to accommodate 240 minimum-security inmates, (3) increasing the number of inmates assigned to county facilities that met the minimum standards established by the Association of Counties, (4) releasing young offenders sentenced under the Youthful Offender Act, and (5) studying "the possibility of a complete change in the concept of criminal punishment in this State. It is imperative that we find alternatives to institutional confinement that does not reform, but in many instances trains criminals. The study of this is more of a long term solution but it should be seriously pursued." In 1982 I went so far as to draft a proposed law doing this for consideration by the legislature, but it got nowhere.

Nothing was done to improve the situation, so on February 27, 1976, I wrote to Governor Edwards again. I began the letter by saying, "No one really likes a Cassandra or a Jeremiah. However, at the risk of taking that role, let me again express my grave concern over the rapidly worsening overcrowding within the facilities of the South Carolina Department of Corrections."

I pointed out that the Department of Corrections facilities were then housing 1,636 prisoners more than their designed capacity. The letter continued: "Again, I urge that you support legislation to lift immediately the bond limit on $37,413,642.52 of capital improvement funds made available by lifting the bond ceiling for the South Carolina Department of Corrections."

I presume my suggestions fell on deaf ears, for when my term on the board was about to expire, I received a letter from Governor Edwards informing me in a patronizing tone that he was not going to reappoint me to another term. The reason he gave was that he felt members with new and innovative ideas should be on the board, or words to that effect, but I feel certain that the Republican administration regarded me as a dangerous liberal. One of my out-of-state friends, on learning of Edwards's action, asked if the title "oral surgeon" described political or dental skills. I suspect that it was not my lack of innovative ideas but my having too many of them that disturbed Governor Edwards.

In the long run the governor was thwarted in his attempt to replace me. The appointment had to be made with the advice and consent of the Senate, and my friends in the Senate held back on any action on my replacement until Dick Riley was elected governor in 1978. Governor Riley reappointed me, and the Senate immediately confirmed the appointment.

After Riley was elected governor, I felt comfortable enough to go to his office and discuss the prison system's problems with him face to face. Governor Riley had honored my daughter Helen by asking her to be legal counsel to the governor, and he and I had been close allies during the six years I served in the South Carolina Senate. After one of these meetings, when I had poured my heart out asking for more money for the Department of Corrections, Riley said, "Nick, I surely will try to help you with your problem." To which I replied, "Governor, its not 'my problem.' If there is a riot and people are killed, the problem is going to be right where you are sitting."

One of the beneficial services Board of Corrections members provided was in the area of community relations. Members were available in their separate districts to talk to troubled relatives of prisoners, and being unpaid employees, we were often both more approachable and less callous. One instance stands out in my memory. A young man had gotten into trouble of a nonviolent nature and was placed in the custody of the Department of Corrections. The first phase of his imprisonment was to go through an evaluation. Because of the severe overcrowding, the department had taken over the old city jail in Columbia for this purpose. His distressed mother told me that her son, along with numerous others, had a mattress in the hall of the city jail. Sleep was virtually impossible, and its possibility was made less likely because cockroaches crawled over him during the night.

I reassured her that I would personally visit the old jail and see what the situation was. I found conditions worse than the mother had described. I conferred with Bill Leeke and told him that if this situation was not corrected, I would file suit against the department and the state to correct it. Within a week additional space was found, and prisoners were no longer forced to sleep on the floor.

The situation reached crisis status in the 1980s. When I first became a member of the board a five-year plan had been drawn up in response to a lawsuit alleging that Central Correctional Institution (CCI) was dangerously overcrowded. CCI was the first state prison built, in 1866, by South Carolina, and in the twentieth century it had become a chamber of horrors. Funds to carry out the settlement in the case were frozen by the Budget and Control Board, and prisoners were moved out of CCI into other prisons, causing them in turn to become overcrowded. The department was told to create a ten-year plan, but no money for new prisons was appropriated to carry it out.

The two paths of action for relief provoked bitter debate. The first was a proposal to begin releasing prisoners before their parole date on what was called "supervised furlough." The Department of Parole and Community Corrections, the parole board, would administer the program. Fifth Circuit Solicitor James Anders filed suit in 1983 to prevent the early release of prisoners, and the state court enjoined the parole board from releasing prisoners before their parole dates. This caused a further backup in the number of prisoners who had to be housed by the state and had a chilling effect on the parole board as it considered granting paroles to eligible prisoners.

A second controversy developed around the proposed use of the old State Park Health Center by the Department of Corrections. This building, which had been constructed as a tuberculosis sanatorium, could be converted into a six-hundred-bed minimum-security prison for far less money than it would take to build a new prison. Opposition immediately appeared, chiefly from the Richland County delegation, the Department of Health and Environmental Control, and residents living in the area near the State Park Health Center. I appeared before the governor's Committee on Criminal Justice, Crime, and Delinquency to explain the urgent need for converting the old hospital into a minimum-security prison. There was some talk of having the Budget and Control Board reconsider its three-to-two vote for a moratorium and release funds to renovate the hospital, but that was not possible unless someone who voted in favor of doing so moved to reconsider. No one did.

Trouble then came when a legislative committee called the Joint Bond Review Committee voted against converting State Park Health Center into a prison. If six hundred inmate beds could be made available at the center, it would not solve the prison problem, but it would demonstrate good faith. I said, "If the legislature turns its back on this proposal, I suggest you are inviting federal take over of the prisons in this state." I persuaded the Board of Corrections to ask the attorney general to enter a lawsuit against the Joint Bond Review Committee alleging that it was unconstitutional since it was composed entirely of legislators and was exercising executive rather than legislative powers. We were never able to get the attorney general to bring the lawsuit. State representative Jarvis Klapman, a Republican from Lexington County, was quoted in the *State* newspaper as saying about me, "He is a do-gooding, bleeding heart when it comes to prisoners. . . . He would let them all go."

I confess that I became somewhat paranoid. I *was* quoted in the press as saying, "I would say that we're the least popular agency around. Everybody likes to kick the Department of Corrections—judges, legislators, anybody will give us a kick." I complained, "Nobody knows what we're trying to do with this prison system. We're just muddling around in a mess. Everywhere we turn, we're frustrated, baffled and rebuffed." I said that the crux of the problem was that the general population really demanded no more of its prisons than that they keep the convict problem out of sight and that included people who should know better. "I have talked to many circuit judges, whose mental ability I respect, who have no conception of the problems we face," I declared. Besides contacting judges and legislators, I began making speeches to any organization that was willing to hear about the prison system. Leeke commented wryly, "You could say we've been looking for love in all the wrong places."

In 1982 Gary Nelson, an inmate in CCI, filed the inevitable federal lawsuit against the Department of Corrections. The American Civil Liberties Union became involved, and the director of the state's affiliate, Melissa Metcalfe, said that if South Carolina wanted to feel more important than other states by locking more people up than them, then the state is going to have to pay for it. At that time the state was imprisoning 270 people per 100,000, compared with the national average of 160 people per 100,000. In August 1983 there were approximately 8,300 prisoners in prisons with a maximum design capacity totaling 6,293.

Deputy Attorney General C. T. "Bert" Goolsby Jr. was assigned to represent the Department of Corrections. After he finished saying that the state would allege that what it was doing in the prison system was constitutional and it did not transgress the constitutional prohibition against cruel and unusual punishment, I replied that I would not stoop to such a defense because I strongly believed that what the state was doing was unconstitutional. This shocked Bert, who was my friend and for whom my daughter Helen worked when she was in the attorney general's office. I stated that I would file a separate answer in which I would declare that I doubted that what was being done was constitutional, and I asked my friend who had labored with me in prison reform, Travis Medlock, to serve as my attorney.

The lawsuit dragged on until February 1984, by which time the attorneys representing the parties agreed to commit the state to making $75 million dollars in minimum improvements to the prison system. If the case had gone to trial, it was believed that the amount could easily have been $300 million. The settlement agreement required the signatures of each member of the Board of Corrections and would subject us personally to the possibility of fines if the agreement was not carried out. I would not sign until the attorney general, the governor, and the chairmen of the House Ways and Means Committee and the Senate Finance Committee signed also. It was important the legislature recognize that it now had the responsibility for carrying out the agreement. I said, "We're telling them, 'This is the best we can do.' If they don't want to fund [the settlement], then we can get on with contesting the lawsuit. But I'm not going to sign my name to something they [the legislature and Budget and Control Board] aren't going to back." They all signed, and the lawsuit was settled.

One deeply distressing event occurred during a time I was serving as chairman of the board. The death penalty had been reinstated in South Carolina, and Bill Leeke and the board had to draw up procedures by which it would be carried out. I am committed to there being the possibility of the death penalty in certain restricted circumstances, and I wrote Bill Leeke on December 30, 1979, giving my opinion on what these procedures should be. The last sentence of my letter sums up my deep feeling: "In everything we do in this ghastly business, I believe that we should be as liberal and compassionate as possible."

Leeke retired as commissioner of the Department of Corrections in 1988, and the election of his replacement became controversial. H. Parker Evatt, a Republican member of the House from Richland County, was interested in becoming commissioner. He had outstanding credentials that included being the executive director of the Alston Wilkes Society. All of my political friends expected that I would oppose him because of his party membership, but I declined to do so. I nominated him because of his outstanding credentials. He was elected by a vote of three to two. Governor Carroll Campbell was actively supporting Evatt for the job, and when the election was over I told the governor's representative, who was attending the meeting, that I hoped that it did not embarrass the governor that he and I had been on the same side in this election.

If I expected my support of Evatt would ingratiate me with the Republican leadership, I was mistaken. Several months before the expiration date of my term I got a "Dear John" letter from Governor Campbell, similar to the one Governor Edwards had written, stating that he was not going to reappoint me. If the governor had asked if I wished to be reappointed, I would have told him I did not. My mind was firmly set. After fifteen years of "penal servitude," I was entitled to a "parole," or at least to "extended work release."

30
Why I Am a Democrat

In the mid-1990s I was asked to speak to the Florence Rotary Club about the Democratic Party. I was told that someone would be speaking about the Republican Party at the preceding weekly meeting.

I am not a Rotarian, but I have for many years been a member of the Kiwanis Club, so I know one of the universal civic club rules: you may not make a speech for or against anyone running for political office at a service club luncheon meeting. This constituted no problem since no election was pending and I did not speak on behalf of any candidate. I told the Rotarians that I would simply tell them why I was a Democrat.

I began my speech by stating my belief that the health of our political system depended on its having two parties—one in power and one out of power ready to challenge the one in power. To have only one party is dangerous and an invitation to tyranny, and to have more than two parties leads to political chaos. It is important, at times, for the government be conservative in its actions, and at other times its actions should be liberal. Therefore the main political parties should recognize that division in political thought. The Republican Party is basically conservative and mistrusts government. The Democratic Party is basically liberal and less mistrusting of government. It is a citizen's duty to find one of these two parties in which to mold political action and serve as a guide in voting. No party has a monopoly on wisdom and virtue, and each must justify its stewardship. Having issued this disclaimer of narrow partisanship and ideological bias, I said that I would simply try to explain why all of my life I have been a supporter of the Democratic Party.

First, I said, I grew up during the Depression, and that had left in my mind the impression that the Republican Party had nearly brought an end to democratic government through its demonstrably unsound management. The United States was on the verge of revolution when Franklin D. Roosevelt became president. It has been indelibly impressed on my mind that in

1933–34 approximately three-fourths of the people in South Carolina were being fed by the federal government. The recollection of frantic people literally running down the streets of Florence in a futile effort to withdraw their earnings from busted banks in 1928 confirms my opinion of the danger in which the nation found itself. There are memories of crushing poverty throughout the state and of a pervading sense of hopelessness. The election of Franklin D. Roosevelt brought both hope and action. "We have nothing to fear but fear itself," will resound in my mind alongside the beginning of the revitalization of South Carolina and the nation. Electricity was made available, roads were paved, farming was put on a sound basis, attention was given to protecting the land, and Social Security gave the promise of an old age with some dignity. All of this was not enough, however, and it took a global war to bring about complete industrial recovery, but recover we did, with the Democratic Party in power. It was the Democratic Party that correctly perceived the danger of Hitler and began to prepare the nation for World War II over the opposition of the Republican Party.

Second, the critical issue of racial integration dominates all issues in the post–World War II South. The Republican Party has done little to aid in the critical transformation from racial segregation to integration. I reminded the Rotarians that one of the main burdens of southern history is to make African Americans feel that southern history is also their history, although their experience as slaves and as an oppressed race is different from the history of whites in the United States. It is the Democratic Party that has struggled to integrate the races both in education and in social affairs. I asked the audience to look at the composition of county political party conventions. When the Florence County Democratic Party meets almost half of the delegates are African American, but when the county Republican Party has its convention only 1 percent, if that, of the delegates are African American. Perhaps I should not have said so, but I pointed out that the southern strategy of the Republican Party essentially is racist in that it seeks to create a southern white Republican Party to oppose a racially integrated Democratic Party. The end result has been a politics of confrontation. There may be a time when an African American middle class will begin to vote for the Republican Party, but I have seen no evidence of an effort on the part of the Republican Party to hasten that day.

Third, I made several references to the highly touted "Contract with America" that recently had been advanced by Senator Newt Gingrich of Georgia and other Republicans in power. I said that it probably should be called "A Contract on America," so baleful were the implications of the program it advocated. The Democratic Party is ridiculed by Republicans for being the "tax and spend party." The Republican Party, I added, seemed to be the party that says, "Don't tax but spend." I summed up by repeating that everyone should find a place within a two party political system, even if it meant compromising some of one's pet theories and projects.

My remarks were overwhelmingly condemned by the club members, but the longtime African American maître d' of the Florence Country Club, Henry Blue, while supervising the cleaning of the head table where I was standing, leaned over and whispered, "Mr. Zeigler, you laid it on 'em." The repercussions of the speech echoed in the community for days. A prominent member who was a friend, told me that there was a movement to have the board of directors of the Rotary Club adopt a resolution that, in the future, I would not be asked to speak at its club luncheons. I went to the club president, a friend of mine, asked if the rumor were true.

I prefaced my inquiry by stating that my life would be just as complete if I were considered persona non grata and never asked to speak to the Rotary Club again. However, I was offended at being vilified by some club members for speaking on the subject of the Democratic Party, a topic my invitation specifically asked me to address. He assured me that he was aware of no movement to bar me from speaking, and I have been invited to speak at the Rotary Club several times since that controversial speech. When I made the same speech to the Kiwanis Club, it was received with polite but restrained approval. Perhaps they were just being "marvelously courteous."

The expression "marvelously courteous" comes from a remark made by an English newspaper correspondent after George McGovern's appearance in Columbia during the 1972 presidential election. One foreign reporter noted to his companions that he thought McGovern had gotten a surprisingly good reception in the state capital. The English newspaperman replied, "You can't tell. These people are so marvelously courteous."

In addition to approving generally of the policies of the Democratic Party, I believe that the party has produced many outstanding political leaders. I remember Eric Sevareid saying after Adlai Stevenson was defeated in 1952 that it is a mistake "to have a love affair with a politician." He explained that this was not disillusionment with the politician but disappointment in his own failed expectations after the public rejected a person who so embodied leadership. I too felt that Adlai Stevenson's defeat boded ill for the Democratic Party. He appealed to me because he was a sensitive, intelligent, and capable man whose leadership in the 1950s was sorely needed by this country. It was only during the confrontation in the UN Security Council during the Cuban missile crisis that the nation had a glimpse of Stevenson's leadership qualities.

The assassinations of the Kennedy brothers during the 1960s brought my emotional involvement with national politics to an end. I would never regain the enthusiasm I felt for John F. Kennedy and, to a lesser degree, Robert Kennedy. There is no question that Lyndon B. Johnson carried on with the programs the Kennedy brothers espoused and changed the racial situation in the South forever, and my wife and I even opened a headquarters for Johnson in Florence during the 1964 campaign, but none of the local politicians would come near it. Only Congressman John L. McMillan came to the opening and stated that he knew LBJ personally and endorsed his candidacy.

I made speeches for Hubert Humphrey, but I never had the same commitment to his candidacy as I had to those of the Kennedy brothers. The 1972 George McGovern campaign came to a climax at the time I was running against Senator Strom Thurmond. I stated that I supported him and the other candidates of the Democratic Party, which given the temper of the times probably hurt my own candidacy. It was ironic that Richard Nixon, who brought to my mind the biblical injunction against spiritual wickedness in high places, defeated a man of unquestioned honesty and integrity. Senator Thurmond took pride in being called the kingmaker of Richard Nixon.

Jimmy Carter was a good man and I supported him, but when he appeared on television for a chat holding hands with his wife, Rosalynn, and the Marine Corps band played "Always" instead of "Hail to the Chief," I felt we were going to have trouble. Eric Severeid's comment after the program was perceptive: "It is obvious that President Carter wants to be your friendly commander in chief." A graduate of the Naval Academy trained in nuclear submarine warfare, Carter was defeated by Ronald Reagan, a Hollywood movie star who spent World War II making training films.

Anne and I struggled through the campaigns of Walter Mondale and Michael Dukakis and opened headquarters for their campaigns in Florence. In 1992 we met Bill Clinton at the Florence Airport and worked for his election. I was on a local television program providing commentary the night of Clinton's first election. During a break in the local program, it was announced that Clinton had won the election. Although there were half dozen people in our group, only I rose from my chair and applauded while the others grimaced in disapproval.

I have no enthusiasm for George W. Bush. I feel that his campaign brought out the worst in Americans, both domestically and in foreign relations. Senator John Kerry spent the night in our house during the 2004 primary campaign. We hoped that we would be able to refer to our guest bedroom as "the presidential bedroom," but Kerry lost the election.

My detractors refer to me as a "yellow dog Democrat," meaning I would vote for a yellow dog just because he or she was a Democrat. My reply is that I vote for the party and not the person. Winston Churchill's response to someone who said that they voted for the person and not for the party was that it was like saying that you bet on the jockey and not on the horse.

My only reward for being a Democrat has been the satisfaction of feeling that I have been true to my convictions. I have never received any substantial office for being a faithful party member. The nonelective offices to which I was appointed by Governor John West, the Human Affairs Commission and the Board of Corrections, involved controversial work, the sting of unpopularity, and no pay. Twice I was passed over for appointment to the federal bench, but I have consistently repudiated the notion that my political convictions are based on personal opportunism.

It distresses me that the word "liberal" has fallen into bad repute. My definition of liberalism in politics is that it is the willingness to try new solutions to solve old problems. This involves taking risks such as spending money for projects that might fail and angering rich taxpayers who are naturally conservative in fiscal matters. Risk taking to help solve social problems and help the needy should be regarded highly in my opinion, yet the L-word has become the scarlet letter in politics. I recall a conversation I had with Governor Richard Riley in which I proposed that he take a certain position, and he replied that if he did, his political foes would call him a liberal. I responded that I had been called a liberal so often that now I don't flinch when the accusation is made.

Above all, in politics and government the art of compromise is critical. Without it humanity is left with growing fanaticism and chaos. I kept a quotation from Reinhold Niebuhr's *Moral Man and Immoral Society* in my desk in the Senate to remind me of the meaning and necessity of compromise: "Politics will, to the end of history, be an area where conscience and power meet, where the ethical and coercive factors in human life will interpenetrate and work out their tentative and uneasy compromises."

Part III *Pursuit of Happiness*

It is difficult to separate self-discovery, social conscience, and self-indulgence. It is virtually impossible to separate one's attempts at disinterested action and interest from one's own self-interest and eccentricities. A dear friend, May R. Coker, once advised me never to confuse my principles with my prejudices. I have tried to heed that advice.

This part carries my narrative from 1991 to the present. I have not saved the best for last, but I am convinced that without some chiefly personal details, the story would be incomplete. I agree with Aristotle that it is futile to pursue happiness. Happiness comes only when you have behaved in such a way that you deserve it. As Wordsworth said: "I could wish my days to be / Bound each to each by natural piety."

31

The Episcopal Church

When I left the Board of Corrections in 1990, I would not hold any public office again. Walking in the shade of private life, I am convinced that the two big disappointments of my old age are the Democratic Party and the Episcopal Church. I tried to reform both with little success. My hope is that I have planted enough good seed to help the next generation succeed where I failed.

American society and international society are suffering from the malady of excessive materialism. How do we solve the problem of problems that confronts every generation: building up the inner man in all of his parts, faculties, and aspirations? How do we heal the soul of our nation and other nations and treat all human beings as we would like to be treated ourselves? I am inclined to turn to religion as the institution that has traditionally performed this function. As a Christian and churchman I hope that God's kingdom will eventually come on earth. I believe that Jesus Christ revealed the way, the truth, and the life that leads to God, and in that sense he is my personal Savior.

As a Christian I believe that if my life is not day by day becoming more Christlike, doctrines such as transubstantiation or acceptance and justification by faith in Jesus Christ are meaningless. This statement, however, is not to be read backward. Transubstantiation and justification are symbols and teachings that stress the grace of God as revealed through Jesus Christ. They give eternal meaning to the inward and outward journeys I have experienced. Without faith in the grace of God, I could not have experienced either journey; for our ultimate goal is not human perfection but the peace of God, which passes all understanding.

The logical place to start looking for happiness and to attempt to remedy the disease that afflicts postmodern society is in churches, temples, mosques, and religious gatherings of all persuasions that teach the divine imperative of the inward and the outward journey. I do not believe, however, that faith can be of value without works.

While religious organizations are the prime source of spiritual growth, my religious belief is reinforced by the experience of art. Henry Bamford Parkes expressed this idea in his book *Gods and Men: The Origins of Western Culture*: "There are two kinds of human experience by which physical forms become charged with a value transcending rationalistic explanation; the experience of love and the experience of art."

In 1980 I became so aware of the need for this reinforcement of my religious convictions through art that I began singing with the Masterworks Choir in Florence. The choir has performed excellent renditions of some of the great religious oratorios; G. F. Handel's *Israel in Egypt* and *Messiah*, Joseph Haydn's *Creation*, and Felix Mendelssohn's *Elijah* all became a part of my life. Music speaks to the soul. The exultation of merely being a fractional contributor to the reproduction of the thoughts and emotions of great artists brings one close to the divine, and I am convinced that the great choruses of classical music are the true voice of humanity. The elevation of spirit that I have experienced singing in choirs has transcended rational explanation.

The Florence Industrial School for Boys closed in 1972, ending my twenty-one years of teaching Sunday school there. I then became one of a group that taught an adult Sunday school class at St. John's Episcopal Church, and I continue to do so. I had stopped trying to teach morals to juvenile delinquents and started the more difficult task of teaching religion to Episcopalians.

Although I have served on the vestry and as a lay reader in my parish church, I have not enjoyed helping with church business. The saga of my involvement in church business began in an unexpected way in a Columbia restaurant in the mid-1970s. I was counsel for a codefendant in the federal criminal case that ultimately resulted in the conviction of Senator Ralph Gasque, one of the most flamboyant warlords of the South Carolina Senate. The trial was being conducted in the federal building that adjoined the Columbia City Hall. During midday recess we went to lunch at the nearest restaurant.

The Elite Epicurean Restaurant across Main Street from city hall was the usual place where lawyers trying cases in the federal building would go for lunch, and we went there during a recess from the trial. My fellow attorneys and I were eventually seated in a booth, and I was discussing with cocounsel the latest turn in the trial's events. The restaurant was crowded and somewhat noisy. Suddenly I became aware that a clergyman, a man I would judge to be in his fifties, had come to our table and asked if I were Nick Zeigler. I replied that I was, and he introduced himself as FitzSimons Allison and stated that we had a mutual friend, Bertram Cooper. We shook hands, and

I explained to him that I was in the midst of a trial. We discussed briefly our mutual friend, and we parted.

On September 25, 1979, the Reverend Christopher FitzSimons "Fitz" Allison was consecrated bishop coadjutor of the Diocese of South Carolina. His election to the bishopric stimulated a great deal of discussion about him with my friend Bertram Cooper, who felt that the two of us would become good friends. This prediction became a reality when Bishop Allison made his first Episcopal visit to St. John's. We invited him and his wife, Martha, to have lunch with us. I told him later that I was so favorably impressed that I thought, in biblical terms, that our spirits had risen up to embrace each other. It had to be a spiritual embrace, for I shun the charismatic exuberance that condones masculine hugging.

Bishop Allison is a remarkably brilliant and attractive person. He was born in Columbia in 1927 and graduated from the University of the South, Sewanee, in 1949. He received a master of divinity degree from Virginia Theological Seminary in 1952 and a Ph.D. from Oxford University in 1956. Before becoming bishop of the Diocese of South Carolina, he was assistant rector at Trinity Cathedral, Columbia, and chaplain at the University of South Carolina. He was a professor of church history at the University of the South, 1956–57; professor of church history at Virginia Theological Seminary, 1967–75; and rector of Grace Church, New York,

The author at St. John's Church, Florence, 1967. Collection of the author

1975–80. He is the author of *Fear, Love and Worship; The Rise of Moralism; Guilt, Anger and God;* and *The Cruelty of Heresy.* In the preface to *Guilt, Anger and God,* he acknowledged his debt to the editorial help of "the sharp-tongued Bertram Cooper." Fitz's graciousness and charm make him one of the people whose friendship I value most. To his enemies, however, Fitz is a formidable opponent, as befits one noted for his intramural boxing prowess during his college days.

My friendship with Bishop Allison grew after he became bishop. Fitz telephoned me in early June 1984 and asked if I would consider being elected to the office of chancellor of the Diocese of South Carolina. The chancellor is the legal adviser to the bishop and diocesan officers. I told him I would like some time think about it. I telephoned our mutual friend Bertram Cooper, who urged me to accept the offer. Bertram said that the chancellorship is the highest office a layperson could hold in the Episcopal Church and that I should be flattered that Fitz had offered to nominate me.

Fitz wrote to me on June 25, 1984, and repeated his request to nominated me as assistant chancellor of the diocese with the understanding that Thomas S. "Tommy" Tisdale, who was then chancellor, would resign after I had learned the ropes. His concluding paragraph was flattering: "I will be most grateful if you will accept this role in the Diocese. I know we will greatly benefit from the contributions you can make, both with your legal expertise and with your vigorous intellect and commitment to the work of the Church." I find flattery hard to resist, especially when it comes from someone for whom I have great respect and warm friendship. I did resist, however, partly because I was not sure that I wanted to become that deeply involved in church business and partly because I did not want to offend Tommy Tisdale, who had supported me when I ran against Strom Thurmond. I declined Fitz's offer.

Fitz was persistent and continued to press me about becoming chancellor during the next year. He repeatedly assured me that the office was mostly honorary, that the only real function would be to assist him as presiding officer of the diocesan convention by ruling on points of order, and that he was asking me, as a friend, to agree to become chancellor. When he put it on the basis of asking me as a friend, I could not say no. In 1985 I gave in and agreed to his nominating me to be chancellor at the diocesan convention in September of that year. The convention elected me without a dissenting vote. After the election I told Fitz, "First, I want you to understand that I am doing this for you personally and, only secondly, for the church." It became one of the most tumultuous and demanding nonpaying jobs that I have undertaken.

Being chancellor, however, gave me the opportunity to develop a deep and abiding friendship with Fitz and his wife, Martha. That alone justified the struggles that ensued upon my taking office. It also opened the opportunity for me to become friends with the other chancellors and bishops in the Fourth Province of the Episcopal Church.

The Episcopal Church is divided into regional groupings of dioceses called provinces. The Diocese of South Carolina and the Upper Diocese of South Carolina are in the Fourth Province, which includes the Diocese of Louisiana, the Diocese of Kentucky, and the dioceses located in Mississippi, Alabama, Florida, Georgia, Tennessee, and North Carolina. The chancellors in the dioceses of the Fourth Province have a yearly conference of bishops and chancellors for the purpose of getting to know each other and discussing mutual problems. I found my fellow chancellors to be intelligent, committed men and women. It was a group with which I could talk about the problems of the church without getting entangled in theological controversy. I was also getting to know the bishops of the other Fourth Province dioceses.

In fall 1985 Anne and I attended the Fourth Province chancellors' meeting in Pensacola, Florida, and Fitz and Martha went with us. It was there that I heard of the controversy caused by the passage of the Dennis Canon by the 1979 General Convention of the Episcopal Church. A canon is the equivalent of a bylaw of a secular corporation. The purpose of the Dennis Canon was to prevent breakaway parishes from taking property that they had title to while the parishes were part of the Episcopal Church in the United States (ECUSA). It provides that all property held by parishes of the Episcopal Church is held in trust for the dioceses and the national church. In the discussion of the reasons for its passage by the General Convention of the Episcopal Church, it was argued that it merely put in written form what had always been assumed to be a trust relationship between the parishes, the dioceses, and the national church. The 1987 convention of the Diocese of South Carolina adopted the Dennis Canon, specifically naming the Diocese of South Carolina as cotrustee with ECUSA of property held by parishes in the diocese.

As chancellor I was distressed to discover that most of the diocesan canons were in need of revision and updating. This became abundantly clear when Bishop Allison said there was a possibility that the diocese might have to try a clergyman on charges that he had misappropriated moneys. The canon that set the procedure to be followed in this diocese was so out of date that I immediately began to draft its revision. I drew on my experience at Naval Justice School and began to structure a trial of the clergy on that model. It was fortunate that this revision was adopted as part of the canons of the diocese before anyone had to be tried. The clergyman who might have been tried first under this new canon died, so there was no trial. My work, however, was used to revise the diocesan canon in Louisiana and influenced the revision of Title IV of the canons of ECUSA, which deals with clerical trials.

Martha Allison had inherited land near Georgetown that contained the remains of an old rice plantation named Rosemont. Rosemont has all of the charm of the lowcountry concentrated in one place: magnificent oak trees and the wide expanse of tidal marshland where rice was grown before the Civil War. It also has the presence of lurking danger, adding an emotional dimension to its ambiance—alligators inhabit the marshes. Fitz is an enthusiastic landscape engineer and enjoys renting backhoes and earthmovers and operating them to improve the property and beautify the site of the home that they built there. On one occasion when he was working out in the marshes and needed to get some tool from his house, he decided to jog back through the heavy vegetation to get it. He turned a corner in the marsh and confronted a seven- or eight-foot alligator a short distance ahead of him in the path. It was a tense moment as the bishop and the alligator eyed each other. Fortunately the alligator sized Fitz up and decided he was no match for the bishop and slipped away into the marshland. Fitz's critics in the House of Bishops react in the same way—they just don't want to tangle with him.

I discovered quickly that the office of chancellor was not just honorary. There was a constant stream of humdrum, everyday affairs about which my advice was sought. Early in 1989 Fitz announced that he was going to retire as bishop in 1990. I was stunned. I had agreed to be chancellor as an act of friendship, not from any desire to get involved in church business. I sensed, however, that the transition from one bishop to another would be difficult and that some knowledgeable person would be needed to help when the new bishop came on board. Once a new bishop was consecrated, I could decide whether or not to resign as chancellor. On September 9, 1989, the Reverend Edward L. Salmon Jr. was elected the thirteenth bishop of the Diocese of South Carolina.

Bishop Salmon was born in Natchez, Mississippi, in 1934 and graduated from the University of the South in 1956 and Virginia Theological Seminary in 1960. He served in churches in Arkansas and Missouri and is chairman of the board of SPEAK, which publishes the *Anglican Digest,* and president of the board of Nashotah House Seminary, Nashotah, Wisconsin.

It is hard to imagine two men of more contrasting personalities than Bishop Allison and Bishop Salmon. Whereas Fitz is mercurial, energetic, and combative, Salmon is deliberate, contemplative, and conciliatory. Fitz has the jocular manner of an extrovert; Salmon's bearing has an aspect of old-fashioned gravitas reinforced by the presence of sideburns that would have done a nineteenth-century prelate proud. When Fitz retired, the diocese gave him a pickup truck as a farewell gift because of his fondness for earthmoving equipment, whereas Salmon has a museum-quality vintage Rolls Royce in his garage in St. Louis and is a connoisseur of antique automobiles and objects of art. Fitz spends his leisure time in strenuous activity in the woods and marshes; Ed Salmon is a skilled carpenter and remodeler of old houses. Bishop Salmon is an expert bridge player and shares his time and cardplaying skills with retired people.

Fitz and Martha live in the haunting landscape of the lowcountry, whereas Ed Salmon and his vivacious wife, Louise—when not in Charleston—live in a magnificent three-story mansion constructed of granite blocks in the heart of St. Louis, Missouri. Both men are graduates of the University of the South and Virginia Theological Seminary; both have unusual gifts for proclaiming the Gospel; both have been my friends during the strenuous years of their bishoprics; and both have had a profound influence on me.

After Bishop Salmon was consecrated in 1990, Fitz and Martha continued to make their home on Water Street in Charleston for several years. When Hurricane Hugo ravaged South Carolina in September 1989, it flooded the lower part of the Charleston peninsula. Fitz and Martha took refuge on the second floor of their Water Street home. The first floor was completely flooded, but they emerged unscathed.

Hurricane Hugo was particularly devastating north of Charleston, in the areas of Georgetown and Waccamaw Neck. One of the clergymen who played an active, conspicuous part in the relief effort on that part of the coast was the Revered Antoine L. Campbell, the priest in charge at Camp Baskerville just north of Pawleys Island. Camp Baskerville adjoins All Saints Parish, Waccamaw, and was established by the Diocese of South Carolina primarily to serve black Episcopalians and others in the area through educational programs, religious worship, and a health clinic. Cathcart Smith, a retired physician, directed the health clinic, donating his time and skill to help others.

It was a coincidence that the two priests who caused me to work hardest and suffer most, the Reverend Antoine "Tony" Campbell and the Reverend Charles "Chuck" Murphy, both had charges on Waccamaw Neck in Georgetown County. Both of them possessed charisma, extraordinary ability, and a zeal to serve God and the church. Both, for different reasons and under different circumstances, fell from favor in the Diocese of South

Carolina, and it was my duty to defend the interests and integrity of the diocese in the events surrounding their disassociation.

The Reverend Tony Campbell's rise to prominence in the Episcopal Church was meteoric. He is an African American, born in 1955 in Gary, Indiana, and both his parents were teachers. After graduation from high school he attended the United States Naval Academy and thereafter spent five years as an officer in the U.S. Marine Corps. When he was discharged from the military, Campbell attended Yale Divinity School. Upon graduation he was brought to the Diocese of South Carolina by Bishop Allison. White and black Episcopalians welcomed him with open hearts. His interracial marriage symbolized part of the closing of a racial gap.

When Hurricane Hugo struck, a great deal of money for relief was administered through Camp Baskervill, putting Campbell in the national spotlight. In fact President George H. W. Bush made him the 615th "Point of Light." This sparked a remarkable expansion of the services offered at Camp Baskervill. The staff was increased from one to twenty, and the annual budget grew from eighty thousand dollars to a million dollars. Campbell's work there was made the subject of a book and a documentary, and because of his relative young age he was regarded as a rising star in the Episcopal Church.

Although Bishop Allison had retired, his Georgetown residence was only about forty miles from Charleston, and he has remained an eminence grise in the diocese. I discovered that Fitz has an abiding distrust of ECUSA, which was headquartered at 815 Second Avenue, New York City. The numerals "815" became synonymous with everything Fitz found wrong and perverse in the actions of the national church. I came to think that "815" had become the "666," the modern equivalent of the mark of the beast in the Book of Revelation. He frequently said that if I wanted to know what was wrong with the Episcopal Church, "look at the House of Bishops."

After the hurricane Camp Baskervill was reorganized, and its management was put under the control of lay people while the priest in charge of the church at Camp Baskervill remained responsible to the bishop. Tony Campbell was transferred from Camp Baskervill and made canon missioner by Bishop Salmon with an office in the diocesan headquarters, further evidence that his star was rising.

The Allisons invited us to spend a weekend with them while the archbishop of Canterbury, John Carey, and his wife, Eileen, were guests at Rosemont. It was decided that the six of us would go to eight o'clock service at Prince George, Winyah, on Sunday morning. The archbishop did not wear ecclesiastical attire.

Prince George, Winyah, in Georgetown, is a lovely pre–Revolutionary War church with very uncomfortable pews that are self-contained units closed in by a door so that the six of us did not sit together. The assistant minister who conducted the service had no idea he was preaching to the archbishop of Canterbury. When the service was over, the minister stood at the church door to greet the congregation as it departed. The archbishop and his wife were directly ahead of Anne and me, but the minister gave them only perfunctory greetings. Instead the minister greeted me, as chancellor, with enthusiastic cordiality. I yearned to enlighten him on his misdirected attention, but it was too late. The archbishop and his wife were already at the car ready to leave.

On another occasion when the archbishop of Canterbury and his wife visited the Allisons, they wished to take a boat trip out into the marshes, perhaps hoping to see an alligator. Martha Allison had shopping to do in Georgetown, so she did not join the expedition. The embarkation proved difficult, so Fitz asked the archbishop's wife if she would mind pushing the boat off from the bank so that the outboard motor could be started. She did so, but in pushing the boat she lost her balance and fell forward into the marsh. The result was nearly total immersion, and she emerged encased from her chin to her feet in adhesive black mud. Being a considerate guest and a good sport, she went back to the front of the house, took off all of her clothes, and hosed herself down in the front yard.

When I first heard the story, I asked Fitz, "What would you have said if someone had driven up to your house and found a naked woman hosing herself down in the front yard?" Without cracking a smile Fitz said, "Oh, that's the wife of the archbishop of Canterbury." I am sure the startled, incredulous spectator would have thought or said, "Now I've heard everything."

The diocese seemed to be getting along well, but storm clouds began to gather at the diocesan convention in March 1992. Bishop Salmon had tried to prevent the diocesan conventions from considering and debating resolutions of a political nature. An argument developed in the convention centered around a resolution relating to the national church's position on ordination of homosexual and lesbian priests and on blessing same-sex marriages. In his address at the opening of the convention, Bishop Salmon described how the national church's House of Bishops was moving toward healing theological and philosophical rifts in the Episcopal Church. A sizable group of clergy did not agree that the House of Bishops was acting firmly enough regarding the issues facing the church and submitted a resolution, designated as "number nine," stating that scripture is to be interpreted in terms of apostolic teaching that affirms the Trinity, that Jesus is the only way to salvation, and that "genital sexual expression" is God's exclusive gift to married people. Some of the other eight resolutions dealt with social and political problems, and a few had racial overtones. It was the understanding that all nine would be tabled in order to prevent what the newspapers called a "shootout at the OK Corral."

The chairman of the Resolutions Committee, the Reverend Charles Murphy of Pawleys Island, presented the report of the committee. The first eight resolutions, by consent, were tabled, but when it came to the ninth, dealing with the House of Bishops' dialogue, it was presented to the convention for a vote. This excited a great deal of anger, and the Reverend Campbell went so far as openly to accuse the Resolutions Committee not only of betrayal but also of racism. Two motions to table the ninth resolution failed, and the delegates got more emotional and began shouting out their votes on various motions and shouting at each other as the debate continued. Bishop Salmon reiterated his position about this kind of debate:

> This situation illustrates what happens when you put people in a win-or-lose political situation. It makes enemies of people and it has just done that in this room. The amount of feeling people have about this has totally transformed this convention. . . .
>
> Everything was going along until you put a political resolution on the floor. All egos hit it. People began thinking about their own turf. It is this approach to doing the work of the Gospel that has practically killed the Church.

I had endeavored to keep the convention on the right track by ruling on various motions as they arose, but the debate grew so heated that at one point Bishop Salmon led the convention in prayer seeking guidance of the Holy Spirit. After that the convention took a recess while the Resolutions Committee went back into session to reconsider the matter.

When the committee finished deliberating, the chairman had a private conversation with Bishop Salmon and me in which he proposed recommending that the convention recess for thirty days and come back for a vote on the ninth resolution. I had reached the end of my patience. I said, "You must be mad to think that these delegates would come back to Charleston thirty days from now to vote on this one resolution. It is my opinion that it must be settled before the convention adjourns." Bishop Salmon agreed, and the committee went back into session. It returned with the recommendation that the eight resolutions that had been tabled be brought back for reconsideration and a vote. This was done, and only one of the eight resolutions previously tabled received a majority vote. The ninth resolution passed.

The *Coastal Observer's* account of the convention observed, "Soon, the convention was adjourned. The delegates apparently stunned by the lengthy process and tension, quickly left the church. Few seemed pleased by the turn of the events." The chief controversy was provoked by the ninth resolution, concerning human sexuality and the exclusive nature of Christianity. In an interview with the press, Bishop Salmon addressed both issues:

> I think the theological issue of the uniqueness of Christ is something that a lot of people don't understand. When you try to put that in a simplistic setting, it sounds like we're saying there's something wrong with other people.
>
> For example, I have respect for Judaism and Mohammedanism because of Christianity, not in spite of it.
>
> So, if Jesus is the unique revelation of God, then He is unique. I also think that Jesus is not coercive. There was nothing coercive about the crucifixion. It's an act of inspiration, not coercion. There have been plenty of Christians who were coercive, but Jesus wasn't so.
>
> The sexuality controversy is simply related to the cultural struggle we're going through now. We're living in a promiscuous culture that says sexuality is a right. Our culture doesn't understand the profound nature of human sexuality. There are some people who would like to see other people as fair game and want us to approve it.

On a more cheerful note, on May 1, 1993, the diocesan convention of the Diocese of Virginia elected the Reverend Tony Campbell a suffragan bishop. However, ominous clouds that would cause extraordinary trouble and grief were gathering on the horizon.

Two events dominated my service as chancellor: the trial of Canon Campbell by an ecclesiastical court and the litigation over the breakaway of All Saints Parish, Waccamaw, from the diocese. In the first instance the trial of Canon Campbell strained my relations with Bishop Salmon, and in the second the defense of the diocese against the breakaway group at All Saints Parish led by the Reverend Chuck Murphy put a strain on my relationship with Bishop Allison. I value my friendship with both bishops and have tried hard not to jeopardize it by faulty advice or by the position I took in both situations.

After the Reverend Campbell's 1993 election as a suffragan bishop of the Diocese of Virginia and before his consecration, a woman called the office of the presiding bishop in New York and claimed that she had engaged in an adulterous affair with Campbell that began in 1991 and continued over several months. The matter was not resolved by mediation.

On May 26, 1993, Campbell's accuser had her attorney write to the presiding bishop demanding, among other things, a donation of one hundred thousand dollars to the organization for which her client worked and one hundred thousand dollars as compensation and restitution for her. The letter also asked that "the Church acknowledge its shadow and honor [her client's] requests so that all those involved can heal."

The Diocese of South Carolina appeared to be a probable codefendant in any litigation that might commence against Canon Campbell. The Church Insurance Fund employed local counsel to act as defense counsel if and when litigation was instigated. That brought me into contact with Benjamin Allston Moore Jr. and Julius "Sam" Hines of the law firm, Buist, Moore, Smythe, and McGee in Charleston. It was the beginning of friendships that have been both professionally and personally rewarding; both Moore and Hines are devout churchmen, have a keen interest in history, and are delightful companions.

On June 8, 1993, the presiding bishop issued a press release stating that the consent process regarding the election of Canon Campbell had been suspended pending an investigation into allegations of sexual misconduct. The "consent process" requires that a majority of bishops and standing committees of the Episcopal Church give their consent before a bishop elect can be consecrated. At the same time the Diocese of Virginia created a subcommittee to deal with the problem of certifying Campbell following the allegations made against him.

This caused a storm of protest in the clergy of the Diocese of South Carolina. Fifty diocesan clergy, almost half of the number of resident clergy, came to Canon Campbell's defense. They signed a petition, dated July 7, 1993, addressed to the presiding bishop expressing their "unequivocal support for our brother [Campbell]" and belief that the charges against him were untrue. The main thrust of the petition was to protest the unfairness of giving public notice of the suspension of the consent process of the bishop-elect before the charges were officially investigated and resolved.

I advised Bishop Salmon that despite the Standing Committee of the Diocese of Virginia's meeting with Canon Campbell and his attorney, Tommy Tisdale, the Standing Committee of the Diocese of South Carolina should meet and be asked to investigate the charges. A standing committee fulfills roughly the function of a grand jury in secular criminal proceedings. It has both lay and clerical members, and it conducts an investigation into whether there is "probable cause" that the charges, if believed, would result in a finding of guilt. Finding probable cause would result in a presentment, and a trial would follow in an ecclesiastical court. The South Carolina Standing Committee, of which I was an ex officio, nonvoting member, met on July 20, 1993, and issued a presentment against Campbell. There was substantial evidence over and beyond the statements of the parties involved that the offenses had been committed.

It was my position that, given the threatened lawsuit, the charges against Canon Campbell had to be resolved by an ecclesiastical court. This began a vexing, time-consuming process because the diocese had not had an ecclesiastical trial for many years, and the canon I had revised prescribing the conduct of a trial had not been tested. It was almost like having to reinvent the wheel, and the burden of creating forms and procedures rested entirely on me.

Two aspects of the trial were exceedingly troublesome. The first was that only clergy resident in the diocese could serve on the ecclesiastical court, and 50 percent of them had stated in writing that they thought Campbell was innocent. I advised Bishop Salmon that those who signed the petition to the presiding bishop should not be considered eligible for service on the court to try the charges against Campbell.

Second, the burden of proof necessary to establish guilt was set traditionally as proof beyond a reasonable doubt. That is the standard of proof in criminal cases, and I argued that it was not appropriate in an ecclesiastical court not conducting a criminal proceeding. The court rejected my advice and adopted the standard of proof beyond a reasonable doubt to prove guilt.

I became somewhat paranoid in my dealings with the clergy, for I sensed a smoldering hostility toward me and my effort to have Campbell tried. At one point a clergyman member of the Standing Committee asked that I leave the room where the committee was meeting so I would not be privy to their discussion. Under the constitution of the diocese I was a member of the committee, and I had a right to be present during their deliberations. I did not leave the room.

Another circumstance that complicated my effort to create a court and have a fair trial for both Canon Campbell and his accuser was the fact that Campbell was on Bishop Salmon's staff and his office adjoined the bishop's office. On one occasion when I was endeavoring to untangle a complicated situation before the ecclesiastical court, I was seated in Bishop Salmon's outer office working with my lap full of papers. Campbell came into the room and said, "Nick, I'll pray for you, if you will pray for me." I was in no mood for jocularity, particularly about religion, so I replied, "Tony, I have too many sins to burden anyone else with them. I'll pray for myself and let you pray for yourself." There was no further conversation between us. On another occasion when I was working in the same outer office, Archdeacon Jack Beckwith, whose office was in the same building, came into the room and said, "Nick, I don't see how you can take so much time working on this case." I replied, jestingly, that I was counting on my reward not in this world but in the next. He responded, "You can't be sure of that either, can you?" I began to feel that in the eyes of the clergy I was literally the devil's advocate.

I was able to persuade Howell Morrison to be the church attorney (prosecutor) and Capers Barr Jr. to serve as lay adviser to the court. Once the court was formed, I had no further duties except to advise the court, if requested to do so, on canon law. The court, in fact, voted to deny me the right to be an observer during the trial.

Although I was not permitted to stay in the room while the court was in session, I remained in Charleston the first two days of the trial. After the first day of trial I told Bishop Salmon that in my opinion the court would find Canon Campbell not guilty, but that the Diocese of Virginia would withdraw its invitation to have him consecrated suffragan bishop. The bishop found it hard to believe, but that is what happened when the trial ended five days later.

But more difficulty lay ahead. Two other women, one a layperson and the other an Episcopal priest, made complaints against Canon Campbell. They advised Salmon that they had been subjected by Campbell to sexual harassment and inappropriate conduct. The laywoman stated in a letter to Salmon that Campbell, while serving as her spiritual adviser at a church retreat, had engaged in inappropriate body contact with her during the meeting.

I advised Salmon that even though Campbell had been found not guilty in the first trial, the Standing Committee should investigate the charges and, if probable cause was found, issue a presentment. In the event a presentment was issued, then a trial should be held to resolve the charges made in the two new complaints. There was even stiffer resistance on the part of the clergy to a second trial, but I insisted that in view of probable litigation the charges could not be ignored. Howell Morrison became discouraged by the diocesan response to the new charges and resigned as church attorney. Michael Battle of Conway agreed to replace him.

At one point it was suggested that the Standing Committee withdraw the presentments it had made on the last two charges, and I told the bishop that if this were done, I would resign as chancellor. The suggestion was made that if Canon Campbell were tried on the two additional complaints, he would probably be found not guilty. I responded to this suggestion in a letter to Bishop Salmon:

I regard it as a reproach to the diocese and the church that you are convinced that Canon Campbell will not be convicted if brought to trial regardless of the testimony against him. This is what critics of the church have been saying. Despite information given to you by your brother clergymen . . . [others] have been tried in other dioceses and been convicted on facts and charges similar to those pending against Canon Campbell, but as I have advised you, the two cases should be consolidated for a single trial if a trial becomes necessary.

The Standing Committee did not withdraw the presentments, and the two new cases were consolidated. The committee recommended and the bishop inhibited Canon Campbell (that is, he was not permitted to function as a priest on a temporary basis). A second court was convened. Before the trial on the two new charges, the parties compromised on terms agreeable to the church's attorney, the two complainants, Canon Campbell, and his attorney. Campbell received a call from St. James Episcopal Church in Houston, Texas, and left the diocese. It is my understanding that because of further difficulties similar to those in South Carolina, he has left the ministry of the Episcopal Church.

Trouble was brewing in another quarter. The national church was moving steadily away from theological orthodoxy and moving increasingly toward authorizing the blessing of same-sex marriages and the ordination and consecration of priests living in homosexual and lesbian relationships. The General Convention of the Episcopal Church met in Phoenix, Arizona, in 1991. Apparently some conversations took place in Phoenix between Bishop Salmon and the Reverend Charles Murphy that became the center of a controversy between them.

I first became aware of the difficulty between Salmon and Murphy at the 1997 diocesan convention held at All Saints Parish, Waccamaw, where Chuck Murphy would, in effect, be our host.

As chancellor, I was chairman of the Committee on the Constitution and Canons and had the obligation to meet and report on proposed changes to the convention. One proposed change in the canons was an addition to Section 1 of Canon XXXVI, "Prevention of Sexual Misconduct within the Diocese":

Pastoral Relationship. In addition, it is expected that all Members of the Clergy and Lay leadership of his diocese shall be under obligation to abstain from sexual relations outside of heterosexual Holy Matrimony.

The proposed changed had come from a clergyman.

Bishop Salmon considered the change redundant because he had already required all clergy in the diocese to sign an agreement that they would abstain from sexual relations outside marriage. When the committee met, I informed them of Salmon's opposition, and they voted to give the proposed change an unfavorable report.

I sensed that there might be trouble brewing, so I advised Salmon not to become entangled in the debate over the report but to let me handle it and bear the heat and burden of the argument. He agreed, and when the time came for me to make the report of the Constitution and Canons Committee, I informed the convention that the committee had given it an unfavorable report. Someone asked why, and I replied that it was the bishop's opinion that it was redundant. That provoked the question of why the bishop considered it to be redundant. Before I could answer the question, Bishop Salmon rose from the presiding officer's chair and stated that he would explain his position. He turned the convention chair over to Suffragan Bishop William J. Skilton.

The bishop, clad in his purple cassock and standing on the chancel steps of the new building, patiently began to explain all of the measures he had taken to ensure that the clergy in the diocese were committed to upholding matrimony as being only between male and female as well as the written commitment they had all made that they would not engage in "sexual relations outside of heterosexual Holy Matrimony."

Suddenly there was a commotion on the floor of the convention, and I saw the Reverend Murphy striding down the center aisle shouting at Bishop Salmon. A bitter exchange took place between them with regard to what had been said while they were attending the convention in Phoenix. It was never clear to me what the Phoenix conversation was about, but I gathered it had to do with the diocese's position opposing the national church on same sex relationships. At one point the Reverend Murphy said in a loud voice that reverberated throughout the church, "That's a lie!" The acrimonious exchange went on for several minutes before three hundred startled delegates.

Finally Bishop Salmon, without saying a word to me or to Suffragan Bishop Skilton, walked out of the chancel and retired to another room. The Reverend Murphy left the convention floor. There was stunned silence broken by a motion to table the proposed amendment. To the relief of all concerned, the motion to change the canon was tabled. Bishop Skilton and I carried on with the agenda of the convention until Bishop Salmon returned after an absence of about twenty minutes and resumed the presiding officer's chair. He gave no explanation to the convention or to me why he had absented himself. I sensed, however, that he was deeply hurt by the incident.

The 1998 diocesan convention was held at St. Andrew's Church in Mount Pleasant, South Carolina. This time the deans of the four deaneries and the dean of the cathedral offered an amendment similar to the one tabled the year before:

> Sexual Misconduct and Pastoral Relationship. In addition to the above definitions of sexual misconduct, the diocese and the congregations thereof affirm that Holy Matrimony is the context for sexual relations and the clergy shall not bless same-gender relationships as Holy Matrimony and they shall not condone same-gender sexual relationships by any official act.

In the hearing on the amendment before the Constitutions and Canons Committee, I had the committee add the following sentence: "Sexual relations outside marriage shall be deemed to be failure to set a wholesome example to other members of the church."

Any amendment to the constitution and canons requires a separate, two-thirds vote of approval by both the lay and clergy delegates. Bishop Salmon, as presiding officer, was seated at a table with me, as chancellor, on his right side and the archdeacon on his left side, enabling us to communicate with each other easily. As the vote was being tabulated, it appeared that the vote in clergy order would be one vote short for passage of the proposed change. Both Bishop Salmon and Archdeacon Beckwith had voted no because they regarded the amendment as redundant. I advised the bishop and the archdeacon, in a whispered conversation, that the provisions of the diocesan constitution required that if a change of canons received a majority vote but lacked a two-thirds vote, the proposed change had to be carried over for consideration at the next convention. In other words the failure to carry the change at this convention would only postpone the debate to the next convention, further prolonging the controversy. I suggested that if the bishop and archdeacon changed their votes before the result was announced, the necessary vote in the clergy order would be achieved. Both the bishop and archdeacon announced to the convention that they were changing their votes from no to aye. The result was then announced, and the motion to change the canon was adopted. A clergyman rose and asked Bishop Salmon why he had changed his vote. To my embarrassment he said, "The chancellor told me to do it."

Bishop Salmon counseled patience while trying to find some means of holding the diocese together and opposing the actions of the national church. In the 2000 general convention, resolution DO39, which stated a

desire "to support relationships of mutuality and fidelity other than marriage which mediate the Grace of God," directed the Standing Committee
on Liturgy and Music "to prepare for consideration by the Seventy-fourth
General Convention of rites for inclusion in the book of Occasional Services by means of which the Church may express that support." Both Salmon
and Skilton voted against it.

The prospect of its passage in 2003 was too much for Bishop Allison,
who accompanied the Reverends Murphy and John Rogers to Singapore,
where they were consecrated as bishops by the Anglican bishops of South-
east Asia and Rwanda. Their actions signaled their allegiance to a movement
named Anglican Mission in America (AMiA). Salmon ruled that Murphy
was no longer canonically resident in the Diocese of South Carolina when
he was consecrated a bishop in the Rwandan church. He agreed to give him
a license to continue as a priest, but only as a priest, in the diocese.

In fall 2000 the AMiA Church, now a mission in South Carolina led by
Bishop Murphy and part of the Episcopal Church in Rwanda, was aiding an
Episcopal parish in Morehead City, North Carolina, to break away from the
Diocese of North Carolina. Preparatory to making the break, the parish
vestry conveyed the parish property to another group and then announced
that the parish was leaving the diocese to join the Rwandan missionary
effort. The parish argued that since the canons of the national church that
prevented this were not recorded in the courthouse, there was no notice to
a proposed buyer that it was binding. When I learned what was going on in
North Carolina, I became concerned that All Saints Parish, Waccamaw,
might be contemplating similar action.

I discovered accidentally that the McNair Law Firm had been engaged
by All Saints Parish to make an exhaustive title search of the records in
Georgetown County. This caused additional concern because it is diocesan
policy to have all parishes own their own property, subject to the constitution and canons of the diocese and the national church. There would be no
need for one of the largest law firms in the state to do an exhaustive title
search, unless the same tactics the AMiA was encouraging in Morehead City
were being contemplated by All Saints Parish.

I telephoned Bishop Salmon and gave him my opinion that the constitutions and canons should now be recorded in each county where the Diocese of South Carolina had parishes and missions, beginning with Georgetown County. He agreed, and with his approval I drafted an affidavit that
quoted the canons of the diocese and the national church declaring that all
property held by diocesan parishes were held in trust for the Diocese of
South Carolina and the national church.

On September 11, 2000, portions of the canons of the diocese and the national church were recorded in the deed books of the office of the clerk of court for Georgetown County. The AMiA group sent a letter to the major Episcopal churches that had existed in South Carolina under the colonial government (1721–1776), suggesting that they join All Saints Parish in a protest against the action of Bishop Salmon by joining in lawsuit against the diocese. The reasoning behind the AMiA's letter was that the former colonial churches were considered different from other churches in the diocese, since they had existed before 1795, the year the Diocese of South Carolina joined the Protestant Episcopal Church in the United States. It argued that these churches were not subject to the canons of the diocese and the national church so far as the ownership of property was concerned. There are approximately eleven of these colonial churches still active in the diocese, and their departure from the diocese would devastate the viability of the diocese as a religious organization. No other parish joined All Saints Parish in the lawsuit.

The gravamen, or essence, of All Saints Parish's complaint was that because the parish had claimed title under a deed of trust in 1745, it owned the property free and clear of any claims of the diocese and the national church, and it asked the court to order the removal of the recorded canons from the office of the clerk of court. I would probably be a witness in the legal proceedings, and therefore, under the South Carolina rules, I was not entitled to appear as counsel for the diocese. The firm of Buist, Moore, Smythe, and McGee filed an answer on behalf of the diocese that counter-claimed that title to the property was vested in All Saints Parish but subject to the canons of the diocese and the national church.

A trust deed became the centerpiece of the controversy. The land was given in 1745 by Percival Pawley and his wife to George Pawley and William Poole "in Trust For the Inhabitants on Waccamaw Neck for the use of a Chapple or Church for divine worship of the Church of England established by law." In the suit, All Saints Parish asked that a guardian *ad litem* be appointed to represent the heirs of George Pawley. When one was appointed, he filed an answer in which it was alleged that the heirs of George Pawley, who died in 1774, as representatives of the last surviving trustee owned the parish property. The guardian *ad litem* asserted that these unknown heirs of George Pawley (there may be over five hundred of them) are the owners of the title to the property under the trust deed of 1745.

Depositions were taken and interrogatories were answered in the lawsuit. It was asked whether All Saints Parish, Waccamaw, considered itself bound by the constitutions and canons of the Diocese of South Carolina.

The answer of the AMiA group was equivocal. It stated that only those canons it deemed to be in accord with its own mission were regarded as binding on that parish. This was not acceptable. In 2001 the diocesan convention voted that All Saints Parish was not in union with the Diocese of South Carolina.

The guardian *ad litem* in the lawsuit filed a motion for summary judgment in which it was alleged that All Saints Parish, Waccamaw, did not own the land on which the church was built but that the land was still held in trust under the 1745 deed. All Saints Parish abandoned its initial position that it owned the property and joined with the guardian *ad litem*'s claim that the real property was owned by the heirs of George Pawley. On October 15, 2001, Judge John L. Breeden Jr. issued an order granting the motion for summary judgment. The diocese and national church appealed the decision.

While the appeal was pending, the vestry of All Saints passed a resolution in October 2003 stating, "All Saints Church will no longer remain part of the Episcopal Church, USA." The vestry had been using "All Saints Church" rather than "All Saints Parish, Waccamaw," as its name. In December 2003 the vestry voted to petition the secretary of state to have its 1902 charter amended to eliminate any reference to the Episcopal Church or the Episcopal Diocese of South Carolina. When Bishop Salmon learned this, he declared the vestry not to be communicants of the Episcopal Church; then he declared the offices vacant and reduced All Saints Parish, Waccamaw, to mission status on December 17, 2003. On January 8, 2004, the congregation of All Saints Church voted to leave the diocese. A minority of the congregation decided not to withdraw; they organized themselves into a loyal congregation. The bishop appointed a vicar for the loyal group, and it was recognized as being in unity with the diocese.

On March 8, 2004, the South Carolina Court of Appeals in a unanimous opinion reversed Judge Breeden's order granting summary judgment to the All Saints Church and ordered the case remanded for trial. All Saints Church petitioned the Supreme Court for a writ of certiorari. That petition was denied on July 8, 2005. The cases are still being litigated, and the irony is that the Diocese of South Carolina is as strongly opposed as the AMiA is to the national church's insistence on the authorizing and blessing same sex-marriages.

I have felt the strong urge openly to defy "815" to the extent of "going to the barricades" with Bishop Allison, even if those barricades are as far away as Rwanda, Africa. It is Bishop Salmon's strategy and the diocesan policy, however, to confront the national church as a united diocese rather than separately as individual parishes.

The consecration of Bishop Gene Robinson, a clergyman living in a homosexual relationship, caused Bishop Salmon to call a special convention of the diocese in 2004 to protest that action. A strong protest was passed overwhelmingly by both the clerical and lay orders.

The question of the diocese's staying in ECUSA, the national church, is placed further in question by the failure of ECUSA to adopt or accede to the Windsor Report, which urged restraint in condoning same-sex relationships by the clergy, at the general convention in June 2006. The election as presiding bishop of a woman who has publicly expressed views favoring the ordination of people living in same-sex unions has exacerbated the conflict between conservatives and liberals in the Episcopal Church.

The archbishop of Canterbury, Rowan Williams, has suggested that the discord within the Anglican Communion might be settled by having constituent churches be in covenant with the Anglican Communion and other churches in association with the communion. Constituent churches would be bound by the structure and rulings of the other constituent churches, while those in association would not and they would not have the right to vote on what policy the constituents adopted. Essentially it would be a matter of churches "opting in" and would offer the Anglican Communion a chance to move forward with a minimum amount of discord.

At a chancellor's conference in 2004, I stated that most Episcopalians in South Carolina did not want to leave the Episcopal Church, but "the *Star of the West* is getting very close to Fort Sumter."

32

Family, Travel, Writing, Libraries, and Gardens

Security is a comfortable dragon. It has been my good fortune, or perhaps bad fortune, never to feel completely secure in my adult life. Maintaining equilibrium between obligations to my wife and family—earning enough money to support a family and give them the unique advantages of our American society—and the imperative to become what I am capable of becoming has been a balancing act I have performed as an adult. As a student at Sewanee, I read Robert Bridges's long poem *The Testament of Beauty.* Several lines of the poem have stayed with me over the years:

> Our stability is but balance
> And conduct lies in masterful
> Administration of the unforeseen.

I have sought that balance in my family life. It was my good fortune to marry a wonderful woman who has stood by me in good times and bad. We are temperamentally and intellectually different, but the pairing of different people and personalities is at the heart of marriage, which requires making concessions and compromises to maintain a loving relationship.

Anne majored in physics at the University of North Carolina at Chapel Hill, where she received a Phi Beta Kappa key. After graduation she worked at the Naval Research Laboratory in Washington, D.C. She taught mathematics to a whole generation at the Florence-Darlington Technical College. While in college I shunned every math course I could and majored in English. Besides practicing law, I have dabbled with the art of writing and history.

Despite our differences our close bond of affection has strengthened over the years. Some of those years were bad years. At times we found it difficult to pay bills, but both of us worked, Anne teaching while I practiced law. Our marriage was strengthened by the fact that we had four wonderful children together who have brought into our family circle four wonderful spouses and eleven grandchildren.

Anne's two sisters, Margaret Stanback and Florence Snider, and their husbands have enriched our lives by their affection and intellectual stimulation. Tom Stanback, Margaret's husband, taught economics at Chapel Hill, and City College of New York. Bill Snider, Flo's husband, was for many years editor of the *Greensboro Daily News*. We think alike, are interested in many of the same things, read a lot, and are Democrats.

By the middle of the 1980s my law practice was established on a reasonably profitable basis. Our older children had finished their education; my two daughters and my older son were married, all within a fourteen-month period. My mother died in 1976, Anne's father in 1979, and her mother in 1980. My aunt Leah Townsend lived with us after my mother died, but she slowly drifted into amiable senility. We arranged for her to live with a nurse who had only one charge. She died in 1981. My younger son, Ben, began his college career at Sewanee in 1988, fifty years after I did.

A real turning point in our financial security came when my cousin Nina McClenaghan Inman, daughter of my great-uncle John McClenaghan, died

The older Zeigler children. Left to right: Belton Townsend Zeigler, Helen Townsend Zeigler Ellerbe, and Nina McClenaghan Zeigler Knowlton, 1999. Courtesy of Jeff Amberg

in 1987, leaving half of her estate to me. It was not a fortune, but it enabled me to contemplate travel abroad. I thus was able to stop being complacent about our nation's position in the world and to investigate it myself. Other than my experience in World War II and my Naval Reserve duty, I had not traveled much. Anne and I had been to the Caribbean, the Bahamas, Bermuda, and Mexico, but I yearned to go to the United Kingdom, Europe, and the Mediterranean, and a little financial security made that yearning a reality.

Nina Inman was my mother's first cousin. She was married when she was young, and that marriage ended in a divorce; she then married Samuel Walker Inman. Nina was a perfectionist, and she had a strong influence on me as a young boy. In fact I developed a deep affection for her when I was a young boy, and I called her "Aunt Nina" until I graduated from high school and she instructed me to drop the "aunt" since her mother, not she, was my great-aunt. She represented in my mind the grande dame of Victorian or Edwardian society. She and her second husband had only moderate means during the Depression, but they moved to Raleigh, and Sam established a chain of small stores that enabled them to accumulate a comfortable nest egg. They had no children. Sam died just at the beginning of World War II, and Nina moved back to Florence. She was more to Anne and me than a cousin; we were almost like her foster children, particularly after Anne's and my parents died. She explained to one of her friends that she was leaving part of her estate to me because I had shown affection for her when she had nothing.

Financial security gave us the opportunity to expand our horizon to England and Europe. We met an English couple through our friend Bertram Cooper, and they became part of our extended travels. Bertram was an unusual and fascinating character. He was a senior when I was a freshman at Sewanee and took a sort of fraternal interest in me because we both sang in the choir. When he graduated, he went to Virginia Theological School, became an Episcopal priest, served as a navy chaplain in World War II, left the ministry, and worked for the State Department. Bertram quipped that a call to the ministry had been issued but it was delivered to the wrong person. I do not know what sort of work he did for the State Department, but he was once stationed in India, where he became a friend of Sir Richard Duckworth and his wife, Alison. Sir Richard was a hereditary baronet; his grandfather had been personal physician to King Edward VII, who rewarded him with a baronetcy. They lived at a place named Shootash near Romsey.

In the 1980s Bertram reestablished contact with Anne and me. He had an outrageously funny sense of humor, and his visits always livened up our circle of friends. It was through Bertram that we became friends with Sir

Richard and Alison Duckworth, who, from time to time, visited us in Florence. We traveled with them to France, Scotland, and Cornwall.

Our other travels, without the Duckworths, included a tour of England in 1988, a trip to Greece and a cruise through the Cyclades in 1996, a cruise around the coast of Turkey in 1998, and two trips to Italy.

When I graduated from Florence High School in 1938, the school annual featured photographs of the senior class with comments the staff considered appropriate under each picture. In my case the comment was, "Of all the arts in which the wise excel, Nature's chief masterpiece is writing well." It has haunted me since that time because I have never felt that I lived up to that prophecy. The reason I give for this failure is an unwillingness to discipline myself by trying to write professionally.

There was a time, however, when Anne and I ventured into the great world of academic literary scholarship. It came about in a circuitous fashion. In the 1960s and 1970s two other couples in Florence, Dorothy and John Hunter and Lucta and Jimmy Allen, joined us to form a supper club. The plan was that we would alternate hosting the monthly dinners, and the host couple would be allowed to invite at least four other people as guests. The hosts would prepare the main course, and the other two members would alternate bringing salad and dessert.

Jimmy Allen had come to admire modern poetry late in life, but whenever he cultivated an interest, he went into it head over heels. During my 1972 U.S. Senate campaign two volunteers in my headquarters in Columbia were Maxine Dickey, wife of the poet James Dickey, and Ellen Greiner, wife of Don Greiner. These charming women were a great asset to the campaign. Their husbands were prominent in the English department at the University of South Carolina, and Don Greiner is a native of Florence, South Carolina. After the campaign Don Greiner invited Anne and me to come to various university functions, and we got to know James Dickey.

It occurred to me that Don and Ellen Greiner might persuade James and Maxine Dickey to come to a supper club dinner at our house in Florence. The invitation was extended and accepted. The Dickeys were to spend the night at our house, and Don and Ellen would stay with his parents. Jimmy Allen was so enthusiastic about our having "the great poet" for dinner that he bought several volumes of Dickey's poetry and read them with intense interest.

Anne decided that a special main course should be prepared for the dinner and that beef Wellington would be appropriate. She even contrived to put the initials JD in the pastry surrounding the tenderloin. Knowing Dickey's egocentric personality, I suggested that perhaps she should have had a baked ham instead of beef. John and Dorothy Hunter prepared bananas Foster for desert. This was no small undertaking since John Hunter insisted on using a half dozen liqueurs in addition to brandy in preparing the special desert.

The Dickeys arrived at our house at about six o'clock in the evening. Dickey was wearing a white hunter's hat with a leopard-skin band, and I was certain he had been drinking before he arrived. Anne showed the Dickeys back to the guest room. The other guests arrived for cocktails and dinner, and a lively conversation commenced. Jimmy was enthralled by Dickey and flattered him by discussing several of his poems.

We went in for dinner. Wine was served throughout the meal, and conversation flowed easily. As a final course John Hunter began his operation on the bananas. I was seated at one end of our dinner table, Anne at the other, with James Dickey on her right. We seated Jimmy Allen next to Dickey since he was our Dickey expert. At some lull in the conversation I heard Dickey say, "All a woman wants is to have big strong man make love to her."

Dorothy Hunter challenged Dickey's statement and said, "I don't agree with that, Mr. Dickey." Dickey made a sound like an animal's growl, and Jimmy Allen said, "I think you have forgotten what you wrote in your poem 'The Death of an American Aviator.'"

"Shut up!" Dickey shouted at Jimmy, "I've had enough out of you!"

Jimmy Allen froze with suppressed anger, and Dickey rose from the table saying, "I didn't know this was going to be a prolonged visit." By that time the bananas Foster were being flambéed in their bath of brandy and liqueurs, adding greatly to the drama of the situation. Dickey lunged from the table, and Lucta Allen said, "Don't you want some bananas Foster, Mr. Dickey?" "Hell no!" Dickey replied, making his way out of the dining room.

Anne followed Dickey back to the guest room and asked if she could do anything for him. "What I want is not on the menu, honey. Why don't you stay back here with me?" Anne replied, "I'm sorry, I have other commitments," and left him. Meanwhile, in the dining room Maxine said to me, "I've thought about divorcing him every day of the year but never have gotten around to doing it."

Jimmy Allen had brought several volumes of Dickey's poems, hoping that he could get them autographed. He was leaving without them, and I said, "You have forgotten your books." Jimmy replied, "Burn them."

The Allens had invited us to their house for lunch. Jimmy was still in a rage and said he had been called out on an emergency and did not appear for lunch. I was struck by the fact that by morning James Dickey had completely changed. During the luncheon he talked about poetry and recited some of Tennyson's verse and was affable and charming. Afterward someone told me that the trouble with Dickey was that he was not "bourgeois broken." So much for professionalism in writing. I could not have stood the strain.

While my reading of fiction has been limited, there are two heroes in my pantheon of fiction writers. My admiration for the novels of Anthony Trollope is enormous, and I now own some forty of his fifty or more novels. Henry James once said that Trollope has an instinct for recording accurately the commonplace. I admire his straightforward presentation of the story and his fairness in assessing character.

I am also an incurable Savoyard. William S. Gilbert had the intelligence and whimsical skill to satirize without slipping into burlesque. The combination of Arthur Sullivan's gifts for tune writing, which musicologists say owe much to Felix Mendelssohn, and of Gilbert's wit and understanding of the cadences of the English language produced the magic of Gilbert and Sullivan. With regard to poetry, I am more comfortable with William Wordsworth. I constantly find myself remembering lines from the *Prelude* and other poems I studied at Sewanee.

My first attempt to write a book goes back to 1966 when, at the request of the rector of St. John's Episcopal Church, Florence, I agreed to write a history of the church. I began writing it but stopped because of many distractions. The history did not get completed until 2002. It was a fortunate delay because by that time I had a clearer grasp of municipal and church history.

The chief reason I knew more about the history of the city of Florence was that from 1988 to 1991 the county and city of Florence celebrated their hundredth anniversaries. I undertook to organize a joint centennial celebration of the formation of Florence County by an act of the South Carolina General Assembly on December 22, 1888, and of the incorporation of the city of Florence on December 21, 1891. As chair of the centennial celebration committee, I realized that not much had been written about the period from 1857, when what eventually would be Florence was the junction of three railroads, and 1888. In order to build interest, I undertook to have a short article published weekly in the *Florence Morning News* chronicling the town's history during that thirty-one-year period. I persuaded several people to help, but I wrote approximately eighty articles. It was good discipline because I was under pressure to produce. Some of my articles were written in such haste that they lacked any literary merit. What they lacked in literary merit however was compensated for by the education the writing of them provided me. One very important feature of the articles was that for the first time the contribution made by black leaders to the development of Florence was brought out.

It was probably as a result of the articles in the *Florence Morning News* that I received an invitation in October 1995 to write an account of the city of Florence that the chamber of commerce was sponsoring. It was promotional in content and a coffee-table book in format. The first half would be a history of the city, and the second half, "Partners in Progress," profiled industries and businesses presently located in Florence.

The publisher, Community Communications located in Montgomery, Alabama, specialized in this type publication and had done several for cities in the Carolinas. With some misgivings I accepted the job of writing both the narrative history and the business profiles.

I had something more ambitious in mind than did the publisher. It was my feeling that the city and county had now reached a turning point in their development. The period up until World War II had been dominated by railroads. Florence was known as a "railroad town" because railroads had brought the town into being and its railroad shops sustained its economic growth for seventy-five years. That changed drastically after World War II. The shops closed, and the railroads went into a decline so that in the 1990s, instead of having over one thousand employees in Florence, the Atlantic Coast Line Railroad now had only five. DuPont, General Electric, ESAB, Hoffman–LaRoche, and two major hospitals were now the chief employers in the city of Florence. It was time for the city of Florence to reinvent itself. *Florence: A Renaissance Spirit* told that story.

The next book I wrote I published myself. I was told that I should incorporate before publishing, so I established Clio Press, Inc., with Anne and me as the only stockholders. I chose "Clio" because she was the muse of history in Greek mythology.

Barnwell Blarney, or Colonel Frank Remembered celebrated my friendship with Hugh Willcox Sr. The chamber of commerce told me that since *Florence: A Renaissance Spirit* was intended to be promotional, things like "runaway industry" and "red light district" should not be included. Since the city of Florence was famous for its red light district for many years and the chamber had encouraged runaway industrial development, I felt it was a part of the city's history that needed to be told.

The third book I wrote, *Refugees and Remnants*, was the most ambitious of all my writing efforts. Its complete title is *Refugees and Remnants: The Story of the Protestant Episcopal Church in the Pee Dee and Saint John's Episcopal Church, Florence, South Carolina*. I published it privately with the Reprint Company, in Spartanburg, South Carolina. It was a deeply emotional experience for me to write about St. John's Church, for I am a third generation member; it is the place where I got my initial spiritual instruction and where my church-going habits developed.

An interest in books, of necessity, is part and parcel of an interest in libraries. My grandfather started the first library in the town of Florence in 1878. It failed, and after his death in 1891 a second library was started; it also failed. It was not until 1925 that a library was built and put under the control of the Florence School District.

The building of the new library symbolized Florence's turning a cultural corner, and the Florence County Library has become a focus of my civic interest. The city of Florence has outgrown its reputation of being just a railroad town. With the construction of the Doctors Bruce and Lee Foundation Library, a truly magnificent structure, a standard has been set for the development and support of other civic and cultural activities in the city. It provides a new definition of who we are and an inspiration for us to be better.

My interest in history, writing, and libraries have come together in two organizations in which I have taken an active interest: the Saint David's Society and the Florence County Historical Society. In 1977 it occurred to me that it would be a gross ingratitude if the upper Pee Dee area (Chesterfield, Darlington, Marlboro, and the upper portion of Florence counties) did not commemorate the two-hundredth anniversary of the formation of the Saint David's Society, the venerable institution that our predecessors had the foresight to establish, primarily for the operation of a school, Saint David's Academy.

The academy operated from the end of the eighteenth century to the 1890s and educated many leaders of the Pee Dee region. Bringing it back to life, primarily as a historical and social organization, also was a means of bringing together the modern generation in the area. The organization has an annual banquet with a distinguished speaker and an annual picnic, and it has printed three books that deal with the history of the Saint David's Academy and the region: *Reminiscences of Early Life in South Carolina* (David Gregg McIntosh), *The Minutes of the Saint David's Society 1777–1835,* and *The Diaries of Evan Pugh.* I wrote a preface for each of these publications.

The Florence County Historical Society, founded in 1949, languished to the point of near extinction. Florence County, despite its progress, has suffered from what almost amounts to historical amnesia. Only Henry Jeffers and I, the surviving treasurer and president, had custody of the society's records. We made a determined effort to revive the organization. We gathered a small group and adopted a plan by which the society would augment the South Carolina Room of the Florence County Library with historical books and material and aid the Florence Museum by helping collect objects of historical interest. The new library building has a large room devoted to

South Carolina history, and the society is adding to its collections. With the help of a bequest from Betsy Lake Pollard, the society has begun a program of installing historical markers in the Florence area and financing the publication of historical books and papers.

Despite the mediocre quality of my efforts at painting, I still get pleasure from time to time from putting my visual impressions down in color on a canvas. The war, the U.S. Navy, and law school did not allow me time to pursue painting, but after I married I began to do some dabbling. I tried to limit my efforts to painting during holidays and on trips to Key West while on Naval Reserve duty during the summer. The difficulty I have with painting as a hobby is that it requires an intense concentration and makes me become antisocial when I attempt to do it on family outings.

One of my perennial interests, from my early youth to the present, is gardening. The setting for the fall of Adam and Eve is a garden, and I like to think that one of the first manifestations of the Deity to mankind was as a gardener. Watching seeds germinate and grow into blooming plants gives a sense of being part of the larger natural world. It is fortunate that most of my life has been spent in a part of the world with a temperate climate friendly to multitudes of shrubs, trees, perennials, annuals, and even to a few subtropical plants. Kenneth Clark in his book *Civilisation* says that all living things are our brothers and sisters. I strongly agree, even at the risk of being thought of as a tree-hugging liberal.

Camellias surrounded the house we lived in on the Darlington Highway, and we moved many to our home on Greenway Drive. The tea olive plants, boxwoods (some of which I had rooted when a high school student), and azaleas also were moved. Many plants on our property had been planted there when the grounds were part of a nursery.

If I had to choose the plant that has provided the most constant pleasure to me as a gardener it would be the *Camellia japonica*, a sturdy, hardy shrub that blooms from September to March in our climate. It blooms profusely when practically all other plants are dormant. Freezes in the winter months kill blooms on the camellias, but a week of temperate weather brings out a new crop of buds.

My connection with camellias goes back to my youth, when I lived on Dargan Street in Florence. There was a large 'Alba Plena' camellia bush my great-aunt had bought from Fruitland Nursery in Augusta, Georgia, early in the 1900s. Camellias were fairly rare in Florence gardens at that time, and even until after World War II. In the 1930s my aunt Margaret McEachin would drive to Augusta, Georgia, with a trailer attached to her car and buy plants from Fruitland Nursery. I went with her on several of these excursions. Fruitland Nursery no longer exists as a nursery. It became the Augusta National Golf Club in 1932.

Over the past twenty years Anne and I have grown fond of orchids. Our interest grew when we built a small greenhouse in our backyard and discovered the large orchid nursery, Carter and Holmes, in Newberry, South Carolina. The amazing fact about orchids is that they have more varieties than most other plants and can live in very high, cold altitudes as well as in the tropics.

From time to time snakes have appeared in our garden. Once, in 1986, a copperhead snake in our front yard bit Anne, and she has at other times called me at my office to come home and dispatch a snake or two. Except for the copperhead, most were nonvenomous and escaped execution. To the best of my knowledge and belief, the tree of knowledge is not in our collection of plants. If, however, we should ever be tempted to taste its fruit, with or without the urging of a serpentine agent, I hope that our punishment will not be banishment from our garden and its pleasures.

33
Understanding Each Other

No one who has lived in the South is isolated from African Americans. The relations of blacks and whites are ingrained in our shared culture and give it a particular character and flavor both enriching and humiliating, with elements of joy and humor mingling with sorrow and shame.

There is no question that black people were treated shamefully for centuries in the South. Chattel slavery was a deviate form of feudalism, naked exploitation, and a perversion of Christianity. The Jim Crow formula of "separate but equal" was merely a fiction. It translated into "separate and unequal," and it is sad that so many have suffered the consequences of such pernicious notions.

The only possible explanation for its acceptance by people of good social and moral sensibilities is that the majority of white southerners in the period from the end of the Civil War to the end of World War II were poor and powerless except in their domination of blacks. Black and white were poor together, and they fell into acceptance of a relationship that was morally wrong and self-defeating. Booker T. Washington was right when he observed that the white man can keep the black man in a ditch, but he's got to stay down in it with him to keep him there.

I began the account of my birth by telling the story of a visit to the hospital by a former black slave, Moloch Smalls, to pay his respects to my mother. I have only a dim recollection of Moloch and vaguely recall being taken to see him when I was a small boy. Most of what I know about him is based on stories that my mother and Aunt Deda told during my youth. From them I have a vivid picture in my mind of who he was and why my mother and aunt were so attached to him. The surviving photographs show him in a rocking chair with my sister, Leah, in his lap. In one she has her arms around his neck hugging him.

Moloch was a seventeen-year-old boy when he and a thousand other slaves worked on the Florence Stockade, where prisoners from Andersonville,

Georgia, were transferred in 1864. He took pride in the fact that as a slave he had belonged to the Williams family in Society Hill. Modern-day social critics would undoubtedly characterize him as an Uncle Tom because of his affectionate recollection of his youth as a slave. He had been taught by the women in the Williams family to read, even though it was against the law to teach a slave to read before the Civil War.

Moloch Smalls and Leah Zeigler, 1919. Collection of the author

Moloch became a Methodist minister after the Civil War and supplemented his meager preacher's earnings by working for various families doing chores and yard work. My family was his favorite because he had known and admired my grandfather Belton O'Neall Townsend, and he took pride in my mother and aunt almost as if he were part of our family. His connection with my grandfather, who died before his two daughters could remember him, ingratiated Moloch to my mother and aunt, creating a bond of true affection. When Aunt Deda was studying for her doctorate in history, she went to the University of Wisconsin for a year. Moloch thought she was brilliant and asked my mother about where she was staying: "Where is that morning star?" Mother told him that she was in Wisconsin. Moloch replied, "Well tell those people she is a morning star mounted in the highest cherubim."

Moloch told the story of a meeting of the black leadership in Florence, headed by William F. Holmes and James R. Levy, two prominent physicians. At the meeting, Moloch said Holmes and Levy urged him to get up and say something. Moloch finally consented and said that he "mounted the stage" and began by saying, "Behold, a lion of the tribe of Judah has been prevailed upon to open the book." He then preached a sermon, the text of which came from Saint Paul's Epistle to the Ephesians, "Servants be obedient to them that are your masters!" It was not what the crowd expected or wanted to hear. Moloch finished his sermon and told my mother, "I bet I made those belching champions [Holmes and Levy] crumble."

My sister, Leah, was only three years old when the United States entered World War I. She was a beautiful child with curly golden hair. Someone decided that she and Moloch would be an irresistible team to solicit money for the Red Cross. They went out together, and when they returned, Moloch said to my mother, "Miss Helen, what ails Leah?" My mother said she had no idea there was anything wrong with her daughter and asked Moloch why he thought there was. "I'll tell you," Moloch said in his most avuncular manner. "When she's playing round the house, she is bold as a lion, but when she gets out in company, hosannas languish on her tongue."

Moloch died in February 1926. My mother and Aunt Deda wanted to place a tombstone to mark his grave, but the Great Depression came in 1929, and the project had to be abandoned. After World War II the project was revived, and with a determination typical of them, they ordered the tombstone made before they learned where Moloch was buried. In fact they never could with any certainty find his grave. Both my mother and aunt died, and Claude Brown, who had made the tombstone, died. In the 1990s I got a call from Billy Brown, who took his father's place in the stone-cutting business, asking what I wanted done with the tombstone my mother and aunt had paid for but that still remained in the shop. I of course had no idea where Moloch's grave was located. I had a line cut at the top of the stone that read, "Born a slave," and at the bottom, "Became a valued citizen." In between were dates of birth and death and my mother and aunt's deep feeling for Moloch. It read, "Beloved of the Lord." A new park was being built in a predominately black neighborhood, so I bought a tree for the park and had the tombstone put at its base.

Black laborers received pitiful wages. In my youth our cook made five dollars for six days' work, but there were also "tot'n privileges." This meant that at the end of the day servants could take food home. White labor was also paid little. When the civil court of Florence was created in 1929, the first judge was paid a yearly salary of four thousand dollars, and that was considered a very good position.

One alternative for blacks was to emigrate from the South. My mother had a black house worker named Josephine Cheezeboro in the 1920s, who left Florence to seek employment in New York City. She stayed "up north" for a year and returned to Florence and worked off and on for my mother in the 1930s.

Josephine's account of her experiences in New York were highly entertaining, but anyone who lived with black people at that time knew that they only told white folks what they thought would please them. It was a way of coping with the inequity of Jim Crow segregation.

When she got to New York, Josephine was employed as a nurse and cook for a Syrian pharmacist who owned a drugstore. He had several small children, and he asked Josephine to bring them to the drugstore for ice cream. When they arrived, her employer greeted her—and here Josephine endeavored to imitate his voice with its foreign intonation— "Come in Josh-uf-ine," he said at the door of the drugstore in an effort to overcome her reluctance to enter a white person's establishment. "Sit down, Josh-uf-ine," he said pulling back a chair for her to sit in at the table where the ice cream was to be served. "There is no difference here." Josephine said she thought as she took her seat, *Jesus, has I got to sit here and look in this white man's face?*

Her names for the Middle Eastern dishes she learned to cook there confused me for years. She said they ate "kilbe" and "boot-a-lie." It took me years to relate these two dishes with kibbeh and tabouleh. She was totally confused by stuffing squash for her employer. "Miss Helen," she told my mother, "they guts they squash. I ain't never heard tell of gutting a squash." Josephine's description of life in a high-rise apartment building was graphic. "Miss Helen," she said to my mother, "they don't does go outside to hang they clothes out to dry on a line. They stands in a window and pins they clothes on a line, then wheeez, they clothes flies out the window. They feets never touch the ground." Josephine may never have heard of the mythical fight between Hercules and Antaeus, but she had the same basic belief that the ancient Greeks had: that you lose strength when your feet don't touch the ground. She said she was glad to be back in the South with all its unjust ways, but one could never be sure those were her true sentiments.

Caroline Jackson was a cook, maid, and nurse who differed from both Moloch and Josephine. She worked for many years in my mother-in-law's house and later helped us from time to time when we had young children. Family members' attitude toward Caroline was ambivalent. Some thought she was a self-sacrificing model of a black nanny, while I heard members of Anne's family refer to her as "a she witch." Caroline was no Uncle Tom; in fact, she was a public advocate for civil rights and an early member of the NAACP who had meetings in the garage apartment behind the Lides' house on Coit Street. William L. Abernathy (father of Ralph Abernathy Jr., the friend and adviser of Martin Luther King Jr.) is supposed to have visited her there. She went to Cumberland Methodist Church in Florence, but she was a card-carrying root doctor. She periodically frightened other servants in Mrs. Lide's household with whom she quarreled by leaving voodoo symbols where they would be found.

I first heard of Caroline Jackson when I came back to practice law in 1949. Aunt Deda told me she was representing a black woman in her fifties who was accused of having pushed her uncle in a well to collect on a life insurance policy she had bought on him. She told me this woman said, "Miss Townsend, they wouldn't treat me this way if I wasn't a motherless child." It was Caroline Jackson.

To understand Caroline Jackson, it is necessary to go back to the Civil War. She was a descendant of Paul Whipple, who was born in New Boston, New Hampshire, in 1840. He enlisted in the First Regiment of the New Hampshire Volunteers at the beginning of the Civil War and rose to the rank of captain in the Seventh New Hampshire Regiment. He was wounded in the assault on Fort Wagner, near Charleston, in July 1863 and at Darby-town Road, Virginia, in October 1864. He is believed to have been in the federal occupying force sent to Darlington District, and he liked the area so much that he bought a large tract of land, built a mansion, and settled in Darlington County. It is gone now, the victim of arson, but I remember going to Captain Whipple's house with Caroline when it stood vacant. It was a fine-looking, spacious structure built in high Victorian style. There was a kitchen structure appended to the rear of the house, and Caroline showed us the cellar under the kitchen that had barred windows. These cellar rooms must have been storerooms, but Caroline insisted they were jail cells in which Whipple confined his children and grandchildren when they misbehaved. He must have had a vast farming operation because Caroline said he had a "composary" from which the tenants and progeny drew supplies.

Caroline told us that Whipple lived with a black woman whom he never married and had children by her. When the female mulatto children of this union reached maturity, he had children by his children, compounding fornication with incest. He would invite his Yankee friends to visit from time to time, and on these occasions he would make his concubines and children leave the mansion and live in cabins until his guests departed. After the visitors left, the family returned to the mansion.

Whipple died in 1915 and was buried in New Boston, New Hampshire. His obituary, published in the Darlington newspaper, stated that he was unmarried, but in his will he left his plantation to "his cook," Kate Raines, for life and after her death to her descendants. It is a safe assumption that her descendants were his also.

Caroline Jackson was a granddaughter of Captain Whipple and worked for the Lide family for over twenty-five years. She was both feared and respected in the black community, and she found it difficult to get along with either whites or blacks. My children tell me that she used to keep them indoors by telling them there was "a bob-tail dog" outside that would attack them if they went out.

She could be both intensely loyal and severely rebellious. Once when Anne was a small girl, she jumped from a bridge into Black Creek, where she saw her father fishing. Caroline, who probably could not swim, jumped in after Anne, and held her until both were rescued.

After she quarreled with Anne's mother, she came to my office to pour out her grievances. At one point she declared that she had not been treated justly even though, as she put it, "I been working for them long-legged Lides for over twenty-five years." I stopped her and told I could not listen to such talk.

Anne continued to help Caroline by getting her admitted to a federal housing complex, where she had a very comfortable apartment. Anne also saw to it that she got to doctor's appointments when they were scheduled. On one occasion she had a conflict, and she asked me to get Caroline and take her to a doctor's office. I had a meeting with a white businessman whom I was representing in a case coming up for trial, and when the time came to get Caroline, I asked if he would mind going with me on this errand. We could continue our discussion in my car. On the way I tried to give my client some idea of who she was and her connection with my family. In order to put a good light on Caroline's character, I said that she was a Christian woman.

When we got to Caroline's apartment, I got out to get Caroline down the steps, and my client got out of the car to be introduced to Caroline. When I had introduced her, my client said, "I hear you are a good Christian lady." Caroline responded enigmatically, "If you're gonna live the life, you've got to die the death."

Suddenly my client threw both arms upward and shouted, "Praise the Lord!" Caroline immediately followed suit by raising both hands and shouting "Praise the Lord!" I found myself in the middle of a charismatic religious explosion in the parking lot of a housing complex.

Caroline lived to be 106. We did not see much of her in her last years because she took up with another family with whom she had a longstanding relationship. She attended both of my daughters' weddings and told someone, "They still comes and gets me when they needs me."

Rosa McCoy Cooper was the opposite of Caroline Jackson, and they saw each other frequently. In fact they served as a conduit for information when Anne and I were dating. Caroline would tell Rosa about Anne's travel plans and Rosa would tell Caroline about my plans. Caroline and Rosa had something in common. My mother said that she was talking with an old resident of Florence who knew Rosa's background, and she remarked that Rosa was a pretty woman. "Huh," the man replied, "she's got some of the finest blood in South Carolina flowing in her veins." We never found out the source of the fine blood, but Rosa was a fine person in her own right. Rosa was a posthumous child and was given the first name "Neverseen." For most of her youth she was called "Seen" as a nickname, but she decided she did not like her name and, on her own, changed it to Rosa. It suited her much better.

Rosa first came to know my family because her brother was in trouble and she went to my uncle Peter and aunt Deda for legal advice. She became so devoted to my aunt that when my grandmother Leah McEachin became old and feeble, Rosa took the job of taking care of her until her death. After my grandmother died in 1945, Rosa worked for my mother and aunt until my mother died in 1976. My children loved her, and she loved them. When my daughter Helen got married in 1980, Rosa came to the wedding and to the reception at the Florence Country Club. One of my cousins went to the table where she was seated at the reception and said she was surprised to see her there. Rosa responded, "Ain't I been raised them chillen?"

When my sister's husband, Frank Johnson, was injured in an airplane accident in 1946, I got emergency leave to help my sister, who had just moved to Burbank, California. Her younger daughter, Jane, was only six months old, and I wasn't much good helping with a baby. My mother persuaded Rosa to go to California to help my sister, and Rosa traveled by train to Los Angeles. I recall seeing Rosa get off the train, and the only thing I could think of was Johnny Mercer's song "(You Smile) And the Angels Sing." When Rosa saw me, she smiled, and I heard the angels sing.

After my mother's death, Aunt Deda lived with Anne and me until her condition required nursing care and we placed her in the home of a retired nurse who cared for her until her death. On one of my visits with Rosa before my aunt died, Rosa said that my mother had visited with her, and she was happy to report that my mother was more satisfied now that we had made these arrangements for my aunt. Her matter-of-fact report of these ghostly visits from my mother made goose pimples rise on me, but if my mother came back to anyone, it would probably have been to Rosa.

After my family moved to the Darlington Highway house, my father farmed on a more extended scale than when we were living in the city. This required help, and two black men, Vander Brown and Henry Commander, were provided a cabin at the back of the property and continued to live there until their deaths. Aunt Deda also needed more help with her flower gardens, and my father had an extensive vegetable garden, a barn with a lot where he kept a cow, a mule, and a riding horse for me.

Vander Brown began working for my father before we moved from the city. He was then a man in his forties and had ingratiating manners and played a guitar he called his "box." It seemed to me that his marital status was always in doubt, or perhaps in flux, because from time to time various women would identify themselves to my father as Vander's wife. At one point Vander declared that he wanted to go through a formal marriage service, and to save money Aunt Deda, as a notary pubic, agreed to marry him to the woman he claimed to be his fiancée.

The marriage ceremony was performed in our dining room, and Henry Commander and I served as witnesses. My aunt read the service from the Book of Common Prayer, and Commander gave vocal approval of various passages by declaring, "Dat all right!" When the formal exchange of vows were to be said, Vander had difficulty with pledging his "troth" to his bride and instead pledged her his "trough," which probably came closer to a description of his financial status.

Vander always referred to my father as "Capt'n Zeigler" and was devoted to him. My three older children would gather around Vander and listen to him play his box in the afternoons. He was constantly killing and eating possums and wild rabbits. Once we gave our children a small live bunny for

Easter. Unfortunately it grew, and a pen had to be built for it, and it had to be fed and given water. One day after my children had lost interest in the adult rabbit, I told Vander he could kill the rabbit and eat it. Vander remained silent, so I asked if he did not want the rabbit to eat. "Naw, sur," he said, "I don't eat nothin' that don't run from me." I approved of his sensitivity but still had to find someone less sensitive to take the rabbit.

Henry Commander was a gentle spirit who always impressed me as being what Wordsworth would call a "creature moving about in worlds unrealized." He also had the blank misgivings of such a lost spirit. Henry came to work for my family after we moved to the Darlington Highway house. Again, his connection with us was that my aunt represented his family in the settlement of an estate. After the legal proceedings were concluded, Henry told my aunt that he had no home to go to and wanted to move out to our house. Since there was a cabin that he and Vander could share, she agreed, and he lived with us until he was struck by a car and had to go to a nursing home.

Henry had nice manners, but he spoke with euphemistic simplicity. He knew nothing of animal husbandry, and when he raked up fallen pears under the trees on the place he took them to the barn lot and dumped them inside, thinking they would be a good bovine feast. As a result the cow died during the night; it couldn't digest pears. Early the next morning Henry reported to my mother and me, "I went to the lot. The cow lie down. I touch her. She ain't move." He added in a high falsetto, "She might be dead." I ran to the lot and found the unfortunate cow on her back, four legs rigidly pointing skyward because rigor mortis had set in, the most obviously dead animal I have ever seen.

On another occasion our cow was about to give birth to a calf, and my father and Vander and Henry were up most of the night serving as midwives. My mother strongly disapproved of my father's having domestic animals, but the birth of a heifer was better than the birth of bull calf. When my mother was eating breakfast, Henry came in the kitchen and announced the birth of a calf. My mother asked whether it was a heifer or a bull. Henry replied, "Us ain't notice." My mother was indignant and ordered him to "go back out there and 'notice' and let me know."

Henry's fear of spirits became a problem. He said that there were "dough faces" he would see in the night from time to time. It got so bad that Henry would not sleep in the cabin, but would bring his bedroll into the house and sleep on the kitchen floor. When my sister, Leah, visited, she would inquire whether "the body" was in the kitchen and would refuse to go in there while Henry was taking his nightly rest. Once when Henry was helping me on one of my archaeological expeditions in a remote area near a swamp, I became so engrossed that I did not realize it was getting dark. Finally Henry looked apprehensively toward the swamp where it was already dark and said, "Dey be comin' out soon." I did not know what it was that Henry thought might be coming out, but I decided it was time for both of us to get out of there.

When my mother and Aunt Deda moved to a house in Florence, Rosa went with them, and Anne and I took over the Darlington Highway house. We found a new maid whose husband worked for the Pee Dee Experiment Station near our house. Lena Dargan worked for our family from 1956 until 1994. Lena was a sturdy, down-to-earth, caring person, and my children adored her. When the family would go to the beach in the summer, Lena went with us and went on crabbing and fishing expeditions with great enthusiasm.

She guarded our children from every type of danger. Once she learned that our daughter Nina had been allowed by Vander to taste some of the possum that he had cooked, and she abused him roundly. She did not like some of the dogs we had for pets. She would chase Whiskey, who was part blue healer, out of the house with a broom because, as she put it, "he's so God almighty mean and stank."

All of these retainers are dead now. We do not have a cook now, but we were fortunate to have help, from time to time, with yard work. Rudolph Burgess is a year younger than I am, served in the navy, and is still able to ride a bicycle around town. He had bad teeth when he started working for us, and I told him I would pay to have them extracted and have false teeth made. I did this, and when I asked him afterward how his false teeth were he said, "I'm not yet tame to 'um." He wore his false teeth for a short time and told another person for whom he worked that he only wore his false teeth when he worked at the Zeiglers.

Once, when Anne and I were preparing to go on a trip to Italy, I decided to learn enough Italian to communicate and to that end bought language tapes to play in my car. One morning I went to pick Rudolph up to work and I had the tape player on. I explained to him that I was trying to learn to speak some Italian. He thought for a minute and said, "I'm glad we don't talk like that, 'cause we can at least understand each other." Understanding each other has been the chief lesson that I learned from all the African American retainers with whom I have been associated. We were friends.

I represented a white farmer of considerable substance in the 1950s. After we discussed his legal problem, he told me that he was having trouble in his church. I made the mistake of asking what sort of trouble. He said that they had called a new preacher, a young man who pleased the congregation for the first several Sundays. But then "he preached a sermon in which he said that niggers were going to be in heaven along with white people. We can't put up with that kind of talk." I said nothing, but I thought that wherever I am in the next world, if some of my African American friends are not there, I will know that I am in hell.

34

The Law and Lawyers

Many professions lured me, but it was probably inevitable that I became a lawyer. I come from a family of lawyers. Three of my children are lawyers, and two are married to lawyers. None of my grandchildren, however, show any interest in the legal professions. This is perhaps illustrative of the generally low opinion in which the legal profession is held today. Not only does the public have a low opinion of lawyers, but lawyers themselves suffer from depression more than any other professional group. Why is that? What are the causes for the decline and what remedies can I suggest?

First, I do not believe that anyone who is not interested in human beings and their problems should become a lawyer. The type of practice in which I engaged allowed me to become involved with many people and a vast array of human problems. While this was satisfying from the point of view of legal practice, relationships with clients can be vexing and exasperating.

Edmund Wilson in his book *Patriotic Gore* quotes George Fitzhugh, an antebellum Virginia author and lawyer, who did not have a good relationship with his clients: "Listening to clients . . . if persevered in, would make a man idiotic. No possible amount of fees can compensate a lawyer for the agonies he suffers from needless repetition of useless details by clients. This horror at the approach of clients is as natural and universal as the dread of snakes." Fitzhugh was probably not a good lawyer, for as Justice Felix Frankfurter asserted, lawyers have to be "masters of relevance."

Second, lawyers themselves have, by their conduct and misconduct, created a bad public image. The public image of the legal profession has always depended fundamentally on the personal character and integrity of its members. The late Judge L. D. Lide summed it up by saying that the legal profession was built on the three *I*s: integrity, intelligence, and industry. Lawyers have to accept the bad effects of their own conduct. I read with dismay in the advance sheets of the South Carolina Supreme Court regular reports of disciplinary action against lawyers, including disbarment. What was regarded previously as a rare and disgraceful end to a lawyer's career, comparable to a court-martial in the military, has become more of a matter of housekeeping and pruning in the legal profession.

It is encouraging that the bench and bar have become increasingly concerned about the lack of ethical behavior in the practice of law, but I do not see this concern as addressing the core problem. I assume that four years of college should assist in developing the philosophy, breadth of social interest, and human concern a person needs to bring to the practice of law. That includes some notion of what right conduct toward one another requires. The president of one of the Ivy League colleges used to make a speech to the entering freshman class. He said, "Young men you are here primarily to develop some philosophy of life. If you have not accomplished that in four years, I doubt you will be much of a success. But what is worse, you will be a menace to the rest of us." A person entering law school should at least understand the fundamental difference between right and wrong. If that lesson has not been learned before entering law school, then the faculty, in three years, will have the daunting if not impossible task of teaching ethics.

Third, there have been articles written about disillusioned, unhappy lawyers who increasingly wish that they had chosen another profession. A Johns Hopkins survey of 104 occupations found that lawyers suffered the most from depression. The September-October 1998 issue of the *South Carolina Lawyer* published an article written by a University of South Carolina Law School graduate, the Honorable Carl Horn, chief U.S. magistrate for the Western District of North Carolina, in which he observes that not only is the general public disillusioned with the legal profession, but "lawyers themselves are also increasingly unhappy. According to survey after survey, finding personal fulfillment in the practice [of law] is ever more elusive."

Lawyers are increasingly disillusioned, and they are unsatisfied and unhappy in the practice of law to the extent that they wish they had chosen another career. One of the principal reasons, if not the principal reason, for this development is a dislike of dealing with people and their problems. Like George Fitzhugh, their dread of the approach of clients is like the dread of snakes. If a person feels this way about human beings then he or she should choose another profession. Professor Austin W. Scott of Harvard said that he had enjoyed being a lawyer because it had given him the opportunity to philosophize about the ordinary affairs of mankind. No matter how obscured by corporate organization or governmental regulation, the main concern of a lawyer should be human beings.

Fourth, increasingly there is concern that lawyers are not civil to one another. Again this is not a new problem. When I was sworn in as a lawyer in 1949, I was required to swear that I would not be the principal or second in a duel. Too many lawyers in the nineteenth century had been eliminated by adherence to the *code duello* as a method of settling personal differences, and the state's constitution required this oath of lawyers. In 2008 it is clear that some progress in intramural relations had been achieved, for the new oath that lawyers swear only requires that they be civil to one another.

Fifth, the increased use of media advertising by lawyers has heightened the public's view of us as a greedy and tactless lot. Although it may not reflect upon the fundamental integrity and character of the lawyer, I find the practice of advertising on radio, newspapers, television, and billboards demeaning to the legal profession. Some of the advertisements list the specific parts of the human anatomy the lawyer claims he can heal with the green balm of money damages. The listing of these parts reminds me of an advertisement for Kentucky Fried Chicken: legs, thighs, backs, necks, and so on. Our present rules only prohibit advertising that is false or misleading. Being tacky, however disgusting or professionally demeaning, does not constitute prohibited impropriety and is protected as freedom of speech. If there must be, out of due regard for freedom of speech, a class of lawyers who engage in advertising, then I think the profession should consider creating another category that is forbidden to do so, if not de jure then de facto.

How do we begin to remedy some of these problems? The late chief justice Warren Burger, in a speech that he made in 1973 at the Fordham University Law School, advocated creating a class of lawyers similar to British barristers. He suggested the creation of a skilled group of advocates who would serve in the trial of cases and would make the judicial system more efficient. Barristers would be required to have an additional year at law school for concentrated study of the law of evidence and court procedure. In addition barristers would have to fulfill an apprenticeship of several years, similar to the internship required of medical doctors.

Chief Justice Burger also saw many side benefits. He argued that creation of a collegiate group called barristers would encourage a sense of camaraderie that is rapidly fading in the legal profession. Citing as an example the friendly and mannerly association in large law firms between the litigators of the firm, he suggested that such a spirit should prevail among barristers. Litigators who are members of a large law firm owe an allegiance to the firm as part of their professional standing and are not independent of the demands of the firm's necessity to generate business. Independence from that necessity would encourage a more friendly, competitive feeling among barristers and strengthen their pursuit of the high ideals of the legal profession.

This independence means that barristers would not be members of law firms, governmental agencies, or in-house counsel for corporations. Their primary allegiance would be to the judicial system. Such an allegiance would encourage a philosophic insight that seems to be waning among lawyers, particularly among in-house counsel of large corporations.

Chief Justice Burger justified his advocacy of the British system of separating the legal profession into barristers and solicitors, saying, "Our traditional assumption, that every lawyer, like the legendary Renaissance man, is equipped to deal effectively with every legal problem probably had some validity in the day of Jefferson, Hamilton, John Adams and John Marshall, but that assumption has been diluted by the vast changes in the complexity of our social, economic, and political structure." While I agree with the accuracy of these observations, they give me the feeling that general practitioners of the future will be like dinosaurs facing extinction in an ice age. However, as the law has become more complicated, so has the need increased for recognizing special areas of practice. General practitioners of the future might be more comfortable and inculcate a sense of greater fulfillment if they were solicitors.

There would be another important beneficial effect of creating a barrister classification in this country. Barristers would not need to advertise since they could only receive briefs from the other class of lawyers, solicitors. Solicitors would deal initially with clients, work up cases, interview witnesses, serve as intermediaries between clients, and evaluate a client's legal affairs. They would be permitted to advertise to their heart's content. Barristers would not.

The modern view of creating greater efficiency in the courts is to require mediation before a case goes to trial. The theory is that if the parties have an opinion from an impartial lawyer acting as a mediator, then the plaintiff will be willing to take less and the defendant will be inclined to give more. If there were a division between solicitors and barristers, then barristers would have to make an evaluation of a case before they accepted it for trial—in effect they would be giving a somewhat independent second opinion and fulfilling the role of a mediator.

The criticism has been made that the British system of dividing solicitors from barristers encourages a sense of clubiness and elitism. This fear of elitism has plagued our profession and our democratic society. But perfect egalitarianism can be counterproductive. Some lines from W. S. Gilbert's *Gondoliers* come to mind. One of the songs recounts the failed attempt of a king to create a classless society by promoting everyone to the top of the tree. In the end the disillusioned king concludes:

In short, whoever you may be,
To this conclusion you'll agree,
When every body is somebodee.
Then no one's anybody!

We want a barrister to be somebody. To put the matter in biblical terms, barristers would be the saving remnant of the legal profession. They would be in fact what all lawyers are supposed to be: officers of the court. It would be part of a barrister's duty to raise a standard to which the wise and the just in their profession might repair. It would be hoped, with this good example before them, that the rest of the legal profession would be irresistibly drawn to emulate their example.

In my earlier days as a lawyer I tried cases everywhere, from the magistrates' court to the South Carolina Supreme Court. My waning days as a lawyer have been made easy by becoming counsel in the large firm of Haynsworth Sinkler Boyd. It is the firm in which one of my two sons is a shareholder as is my son-in-law Bob Knowlton. I am grateful for having been the beneficiary of a relationship with the fine lawyers in that firm at the close of my career.

One of the sure signs of growing old is the belief that the present generation has got it all wrong and that things will never be as right as they were when we were young. I don't believe that. The average practicing lawyer today has more challenges, is required to be better educated, engages in continuing education, and has more stamina than the lawyers I knew when I was first called to the bar. However, professional competence has not produced personal happiness. That comes from a sense of fulfillment and a firm conviction that solving human problems will help preserve the liberal democratic society we have produced. The legal profession has always stood between anarchy and tyranny and an orderly, just society. To be part of that effort should satisfy the most demanding person. In the words Sir Edward Coke attributed to Henry de Bracton, *Non sub homine sed sub Deo et lege* (Not under man but under God and the law).

35

Afterglow

A Postlude

I have known many colorful people in my life. In retrospect I think of some as being like the red of angry conflict, some as being a soothing pink, some as an intellectual yellow, some as a protective lavender, and some as light shades of green, promising growth. They now blend into an afterglow, a prelude to twilight and approaching darkness. In my mind's eye the vision reminds me of those early youthful trips in our Franklin automobile when sunset followed by an afterglow induced a sense of security and well being. This final afterglow now induces a sense of gratitude for my time on earth as a human being.

In old age I do not feel the sense of security and protection I felt in my childhood. We live in a dangerous world, but I continue to believe that despite all of the dangers, injustices, and cruelty in our present society there is a tremendous untapped reservoir of good will in all human beings. All that is wanted is patience, understanding, and skill to reach it. If "altar, sword and pen" have not completely forfeited "their ancient dower" of inward peace and happiness, perhaps security will grow in the years to come. It is my conviction that it will.

I am indebted to Sewanee for planting in my mind a sense of the wholeness of life. When I graduated from Sewanee, I took with me a quotation of John Milton's that I had framed and put in my law library both to inspire me and to make me humble: "I call therefore a complete and generous education that which fits a man to perform justly, skillfully, and magnanimously all the offices both private and public of peace and war."

I know that I have never been able to achieve that wholeness, but if nothing else, it was a reminder of the impossible dream and the continuing struggle to achieve it. At the end of my life I don't know that I deserve the happiness that has been mine, but I am grateful for the portion I have received.

In my struggle to become what I was capable of becoming I endeavored to plant seeds of social justice that would grow and bear fruit. Some of these efforts have been like seed that fell on stony ground; some fell among weeds and thorns; birds got their share; and a few have grown to bear fruit.

I do not deceive myself into believing that we can ever construct a perfect society on earth, but I am convinced that mankind is capable of creating a better society in which justice, kindness, and peace flourish. The peace we invoke in the Nunc Dimittis is best described in a poem by a minor English poet, William Watson, who, reflecting on the special gift that Wordsworth's poetry brought to mankind, wrote that it created a sense of "peace on earth." Watson then defines that peace:

> Nor peace that grows by Lethe, scentless flower,
> There in white languors to decline and cease;
> But peace whose names are also rapture, power,
> Clear sight and love: for these are parts of peace.

Appendix A

Statement of My Candidacy in the 1972 U.S. Senate Race

He [Thurmond] has voted against Medicare and expanded social security benefits which would aid elderly people struggling against costs they cannot afford.

He has voted against tax reforms which would plug up tax loopholes for big business and give relief to the overtaxed medium income earners.

He has brought into this State, Secretary of Agriculture Butz, and sat beside him when he stated that he opposed controls on food prices although every house-wife knows that rising food costs are unbearable.

He supports the policies of Secretary of Agriculture Butz in which the middlemen grow richer while the farmers grow poorer.

He has voted no on a limitation of $55,000 per crop on farm subsidies (that is money which is paid for not planting crops) yet he supports the Secretary of Agriculture who states that family farming will be phased out.

He has voted against equal opportunity legislation which would aid workers, both men and women, seeking to advance themselves.

He has consistently voted against housing programs and urban renewal legislation although poor housing exists in almost every community and slums blight the cities of our State.

He has voted no on increased funds for water and sewer assistance programs, although he rushes forward to announce these grants at every opportunity.

He has opposed the extension of the elementary and secondary education act which helps the vocational education of young people in this State.

He has opposed Federal aid to education and has voted against the Economic Opportunity Act and its related programs which make possible such things as daycare grants for children.

He consistently opposed all civil rights legislation at a time when men of good will were fighting to bring our people together.

He has not successfully sponsored any major legislation dealing constructively with these social problems on which he has taken a negative stand.

Appendix B

My Platform in the 1972 U.S. Senate Race

Tax Reform

Senator Nick Zeigler has called the tax system unfair and full of loopholes for the big corporations. In the state Senate, Zeigler supported the Homestead Tax Exemption Act which has benefited over 49,000 citizens; he also led the fight to change the state-wide system of property tax assessment. Zeigler has said that one of the most urgent measures needed in the U.S. Congress is reform of the tax laws to equalize the burden and diminish the loopholes.

Busing

Busing, Nick Zeigler has stated, should be a temporary measure until quality education is assured for every child. Busing is not the answer to solving the problems facing the school system today. The answer for improving our educational system is equal funding to achieve quality education in every school.

Health Care

Sen. Zeigler proposes a system of national health care insurance for every American from birth throughout their lifetime. Statistics from the State Health Department show that South Carolinians have the shortest life expectancy in the nation, and the third highest rate of infant mortality. Nationally, hospital bills have risen 125% in ten years, and doctor bills have risen 150% in ten years. Zeigler believes that health care is a necessity and should be a right. Three major problems found in a three-week health care tour taken by the Senator are: costs, accessibility of proper medical treatment, and the failure of the government to respond properly. Zeigler contends that a system of national health insurance could and should meet these needs.

Housing

Sen. Zeigler supported the creation of the South Carolina Housing Authority by legislation in the State Senate. Although South Carolina has a higher poverty level than North Carolina, North Carolina received last year over five times the amount of federal funds for low-income housing than South Carolina did.

Gun Control Legislation

Sen. Zeigler has urged the U.S. Congress to pass legislation banning the sale of the "Saturday Night Specials," a small caliber handgun widely used in crimes of violence, but which has no sporting value.

Crime

Crime in South Carolina and the nation is on the upsurge.

In South Carolina, every 26 hours a murder is committed; a robbery takes place every 6 hours; and burglary occurs at the rate of one every 30 minutes. Violent crimes increased by 9% in our nation last year.

Proposals:

Increase funding for law enforcement personnel salaries, for building new facilities, such as replacing out-dated and crowded prisons.

Increase staff, especially in the correctional and rehabilitation fields.

More pre-release centers and half-way houses for inmates due to be released.

More vocational and academic instruction for inmates.

Stricter gun control laws.

More community involvement in programs for inmates and juvenile offenders.

Vietnam War

Sen. Zeigler recently applauded U.S. Senate action to stop funding for further U. S. military activities in Vietnam within four months, provided Hanoi releases American Prisoners of War. Zeigler said the war has divided Americans for too long, and caused serious damage to the moral fiber of this nation. Zeigler called it "the worst run war in history," and said money poured into Vietnam is needed here at home. He also deplores the killing and wounding of thousands of people and the vast destruction of property.

Amnesty

Sen. Zeigler is opposed to complete amnesty for draft evaders or deserters. He believe, however, that draft evaders should be given the opportunity to serve in some capacity such as the Peace Corps or medical corps. Or some similar public service in place of military service. The deserters, the Senator believes, should have to face a military court since he has made a previous commitment to the military before his desertion.

Welfare

Zeigler believes that the welfare system should be re-oriented with a greater emphasis on job training and other educational benefits, and toward finding jobs for needy people. He recognizes that tragedies beyond control exist with many welfare recipients rendering them unable to work. However, he opposes government giveaways for those who are able to work, and feels that one of the keys to improving our welfare system is more jobs and job training.

Social Security

Sen. Zeigler has always been a proponent of Social Security. He has proposed an increase in the amount a person on Social Security may earn per year without losing Social Security payments. He advocates raising the $1,689 per year ceiling on income to $3,000 per year. He would introduce this legislation in the U.S. Senate.

Government Spending

Sen. Zeigler believes that each government—local, state, and national, could provide some funds for needed programs by eliminating wasteful spending practices. He advocates external examination of spending practices on a periodic basis in order to find and eliminate financial waste.

18-Year-Old-Vote

Zeigler was one of four state Senators who co-authored in the 1970 General Assembly, a bill to amend the S. C. Constitution to allow the right to vote at age 18. He has urged that the age 18 be designated as the legal age of majority.

Voting Rights

Zeigler was co-author and floor leader of a bill to provide absentee stations at colleges and technical educational centers across the state. Students would have been able to apply for, and receive, home county ballots from the center at their institution. However, after passage in the Senate, the House of Representatives killed the measure.

State Colleges

Nick Zeigler was floor leader in the Senate in establishing Francis Marion College as a state-supported institution and has been a professor of government at the school. The Senator was also a leader in the establishment of Lander College as a state school, and he was a supporter of Winthrop College co-education.

Index

Wilson, Edmund, Patriotic Gore, 347

Wilson County, N.C., 131–32

Wilson High School (Florence, S.C.), 164

Winslow Boy, The (Rattigan), 108

Winthrop College, 237, 241

Winthrop Hall (Cambridge, Mass.), 77, 82

Woods Bay, S.C., 243

Wordsworth, William: "London, 1802," 352; *The Prelude,* 36, 39, 162; "The Solitary Reaper," 12

Workman, William D., 230

World War II, Republican position on, 298

Wyzenski, Judge Charles E., Jr., 286–87

Yaghjian, Edmund, 118

Yarborough, June, 204–5

Yazoo City, Miss., 87–89

Yazoo River, Miss., 101, 103

yellow dog Democrat, 301

York County fund-raiser, 257

Young, Edward, 158, 159

Young, Dr. Foster, 156

Young, Givens, 20

Young-Dusenbury revolt, 158–59

Young People's Service League, 123

Z (Vassilikos), 254

Zeigler, Anne Lide (Mrs. Eugene N. Zeigler Jr.; wife of ENZ), 94–99, 120, 127, 156–57, 161–62, 172, 197, 209–210, 220–21, 253, 267, 326–27, 329–31, 332, 335

Zeigler, Belton Townsend (son of ENZ), 216, 277, 327

Zeigler, Benjamin Turner (son of ENZ): birth, 221; introduction to the Senate, 234; interview with Strom Thurmond, 270–71

Zeigler, Eugene Noel "Nick," Jr. (ENZ):
—chairs Human Affairs Commission, 272–82
—childhood, 4–12
—education: primary, 8–21; high school, 22–25; college, 31–42; law school, 76–85
—family background, 3–4
—family life, 326–28
—illnesses, 20, 27, 104, 225
—interest in Big Brothers, 122–28
—interest in museums, 112–21
—interest in theater, 103–11
—marriage, 94–99
—member, S.C. Board of Corrections, 289–96
—military service: CMTC, 19–20; U.S. Navy, 36–64; Naval Reserve, 100–103
—political career: 1958 candidate for S.C. House, 153–54; 1960 election to S.C. House, 159–61; 1960–62 service in the S.C. House, 162–67, 168–69; 1962 candidate for S.C. Senate, 169–74; 1966 election to the S.C. Senate, 188–91; 1966–72 service in S.C. Senate, 170–71, 173, 188–89, 246; 1968 election to the S.C. Senate, 212, 214; 1972 candidate for U.S. Senate, 248, 251–59; 1974 candidate for S.C. governor, 270–82; and Democratic Party, 297–301
—service to the Episcopal Church, 305–25
—work as a lawyer, 90–99, 129–44, 178–87, 283–89
—as a writer, 30, 37, 38–40, 104, 105, 106, 107, 329–32

Zeigler, Eugene Noel, Sr. (father of ENZ), 3–5, 7, 13, 32, 46, 95–96 122